THE COMIC HERO

THE COMIC HERO

Robert M. Torrance

Harvard University Press
Cambridge, Massachusetts
London, England

*Publication of this volume has been aided by a grant from the Andrew
W. Mellon Foundation*

Library of Congress Cataloging in Publication Data

Torrance, Robert.
  The comic hero.

  Includes bibliographical references and index.
  1. Characters and characteristics in literature.
2. Comic, The. I. Title.
PN56.5.C65T6   809'.933'52   77-16316
ISBN 0-674-14431-7

To
Harry Levin
and the memory of
Reuben Brower

PREFACE

—— ✂ ——

M Y BOOK originated in a series of lectures first given at Harvard University in 1972 for a Comparative Literature course entitled "Configurations of the Comic Hero." In the course of my work since then my main intention has been to explore, in some of its major instances, the apparent paradox that a *comic* character—whom critics since Aristotle have repeatedly considered beneath us—could be simultaneously portrayed as a *hero* no less authentic than his long more honored (but now widely discredited) counterpart of high character and tragic demeanor.

Much attention has been given in recent years to the festive origins and heroic dimensions of comedy, and both the title and the substance of my book owe a particular debt to Cedric H. Whitman's *Aristophanes and the Comic Hero.* But up till now investigations of comic heroism have been confined, with few exceptions, to studies of single authors such as Aristophanes, Rabelais, and Shakespeare, while comic theory in general has tended to ignore the heroic potential of defiant festivity in a hostile world. Whitman aptly characterizes the Aristophanic comic hero as "a low character who sweeps the world before him, who dominates all society, and sometimes the gods themselves" (*Aristophanes,* p. 51). Yet for Northrop Frye, perhaps our most influential theorist of literature, comedy remains suspended between satire and romance — which resemble each other in depreciating if not excluding heroic choice — and its protagonist is typically an ironical figure whom "the dramatist tends to play . . . down and make . . . rather neutral and unformed in character" (*Anatomy of Criticism*, p. 173). I hope to show that the comic hero has enacted too assertive a part in our literature to be played down or neutralized in any just consideration of the nature of comedy.

But what do I mean by "comic hero"? A fair question not easily answered unless — and then only in part — by my book as a whole. He is too protean a character to be delimited by any prior definition, since he is forever extemporizing his essence. He does not conform to a single character type at all, be it fool or knave, *eirôn* or *alazôn*, but evades fixed categories of every kind by adopting whatever posture suits his imperious ends. What is constant is the potential or actual antagonism between his ways and those of his world. He is comic (in the root sense of *kômos*, the "revels") primarily by virtue of the festive values that he celebrates and embodies: values of biological life and imaginative freedom, of dogged humanity and belligerent selfhood. Because society almost invariably looks askance at his subversive unconstraint, however (festivity being an inveterate stranger to boundaries), he will also normally appear comic in a more negative sense, through the derision that his dissent elicits from those who uphold the social order. In the resulting conflict, or *agôn*, he proves himself a hero by courageous perseverance, resourceful intelligence, and a more or less conscious acceptance of the inevitable risks that he chooses to run in his willfully comic challenge to the deadly seriousness of his world.

The extreme diversity of the comic hero's roles from one age to another is due in large part, therefore, to the changing nature of the world that always confronts him and can never — except in fantasy — be wished away. The character (and the strength) of his adversary necessarily conditions his tactics and even his aims. I shall be concerned in my book with discussing individual comic heroes from Homeric Greece to contemporary America and with suggesting some of the continuities and affinities that underlie their manifold variations. It is surely no idle coincidence that in our own century, despite immeasurable differences in their circumstances, Leopold Bloom and Felix Krull reincarnate, in their own fashion, the primordial tricksters Ulysses and Hermes. Only because it incessantly changes can comic heroism remain, in some essential sense, the same thing. With this in mind I have selected representative comic heroes from different times and places and from a cross section of literary genres, devoting three chapters to classical antiquity, three to the Middle Ages and Renaissance, and three to the last three centuries. Some of my choices were almost inevitable, others (especially recent ones) might easily have been different. But choice was necessary among a profusion of riches, and the interested reader, as I know from experience already, will supply my omissions with numerous candidates of his own; for my subject happily lends itself to almost indefinite extension.

One category of omission calls for especial comment: few of my examples, and none of my central ones, are women. To be perceived as somehow heroic the dissenter against society's values must in the end command admiration, however grudging, for his dissent; and until very recently, in Western society, transgressions condoned (in so far as successful) in men were severely condemned in women. Only in desperate renunciation or bittersweet retrospect could a rare Lysistrata or Wife of Bath flout the standards of conduct prescribed for her sex with some degree of impunity; most comic heroines were constrained, like those of Shakespeare, to adopt gentler forms of remonstrance within clearly acceptable limits. This artificial restriction on female energies seems very unlikely to prevail in the future, and the terrain of comic heroism can only be enlarged by its fortunate lapse.

Since few of my readers are likely to have the comic literature of three millennia at their fingertips—some of it, like the *Roman de Renart,* will be unfamiliar to all but a handful—I have intermittently provided brief recapitulations of the books or episodes under discussion, with the rueful foreknowledge that what is helpful to Paul will exasperate Peter as either too much or too little. In the same spirit, and at still greater risk, I have sometimes hazarded a few general remarks concerning the historical background of a work in order to place it in a coherent context and provide some orientation for its discussion. My aim, it need hardly be said, has not been to write a comprehensive "history" of comic heroism (a labor of Tantalus), but rather to stress its adept responsiveness to widely divergent and often extremely adverse conditions. The truly pertinent and wholly sufficient evidence of a given society's attitudes toward its comic dissidents will of course be contained within each book, however much this fictional portrait may differ from the impartial social historian's. Nor are the continuities and contrasts that I have been concerned with by any means dependent on the direct influence of literary traditions, even though the stimulus given by the *Odyssey* in ancient times and by both the *Odyssey* and *Don Quixote* since the Renaissance has been too immense to ignore. My goal, amid these shoals and eddies, has been to demonstrate that a stubborn impulse to "comic heroism," rooted in the individual's resistance to the demands of an alien order, has been a persistent phenomenon in our literature that transcends customary divisions of time, place, and genre, and has proved to be irrepressible, up till now, against heavy odds.

In this overall demonstration, and in the changed perspective that it continually introduces, rather than in my interpretations of particular works, lies the originality of my enterprise, although the discriminating reader will find something new, I trust, in my discussion of each major book. As for what is borrowed, I have indicated in a note to each chapter the scholarly and critical works pertaining to my subject to which I am consciously indebted; a full bibliography, in a book of this nature, would be cumbersome and superfluous, and much that is of great intrinsic value but marginal to my main concerns has therefore been omitted. In many cases I have made use of standard modern translations of the works I discuss; translations not acknowledged in the notes are my own. Despite painstaking efforts (and several hairbreadth escapes) the possibility of occasional error in a work of such scope is formidable, and I can only hope that readers more expert than myself in a particular area will correct my mistakes in the true (if rare) scholarly spirit of cooperation, and view my endeavor as heroic even when it most strikes them as comic.

It has been, after all, a festival more than an agony, and a task richer in rewards than in pitfalls. Wherefore, as Lucius enjoined in Apuleius' novel, promising profit from the spectacle even of his most asinine labors, *lector intende: laetaberis:* read attentively, and enjoy.

ACKNOWLEDGMENTS

Extracts from the following books are reprinted by permission: Aristophanes, *The Knights,* trans. R. H. Webb, © The University Press of Virginia; James Joyce, *Ulysses,* published by The Bodley Head, Ltd., and Random House, Inc.; and Thomas Mann, *Confessions of Felix Krull, Confidence Man,* trans. Denver Lindley, published by Alfred A. Knopf, Inc., and Martin Secker & Warburg, Ltd. I am sincerely grateful to these publishers for granting permission free of charge or (in the case of The Bodley Head) at only a nominal fee; their enlightened practice, I have discovered, is far from universal. Printed discourse, especially of a scholarly nature, would be severely crippled if permissions came to be regarded as an occasion for rapacity more than benevolence; fortunately, pockets of civilization remain.

I should like to express my deep gratitude to the Society of Fellows at Harvard University for the three years of industrious leisure and unrestricted research that eventually made this book possible, even though I conceived of it several years afterward. Time (not to say money) for reading and thinking is such a rarity in a world where the size of scholarly grants is often proportionate to the triviality of their object that this debt will not be exhausted even by so wide-ranging a book as this one.

Foremost among the teachers and colleagues to whom I am deeply indebted are Cedric Whitman and Harry Levin of Harvard University. Professor Whitman's book on Aristophanes was one of my principal sources of inspiration, and it was Professor Levin who made the fertile suggestion, after my work had begun, that I consider a chapter on the Reynard saga; in addition, both made helpful comments after reading an early draft of part of my manuscript. I am also extremely grateful to Walter Kaiser of Harvard and to Ruby Cohn of the University of California, Davis, for their generous and timely encouragement.

I have discussed aspects of the book with a number of people whose interests partially overlapped with mine, including Terrence Des Pres, Donald Fanger, Janet Biller, and Douglas Butturff. Among many who have given me valuable assistance in various ways are Roland and Barbara Hoermann, Richard Grimm, David Traill, Manfred Kusch, and Marie Ingraham.

There are others to whom my debt, if less immediate, is still greater. Above all, my father and mother, who read me numberless stories, and my aunt, who made me treasured scrapbooks, when I was considerably younger.

And Millie, my hero.

R. M. T.

Davis, California

CONTENTS

———————— ⚬⚭⚬ ————————

De comoedia loquor, quae, si haec flagitia
non probaremus, nulla esset omnino.

Introduction:
Comic Butt
and Comic Hero

———————— ❧ ————————

THE COMIC hero is a contradiction in terms, or at least in perspectives. He is comic because he differs from others and heroic because he is always himself. What others mock is the grounds for his celebration, and in the end he commands our assent by willful adherence to the truth of his own invention.

The fact that we normally do not link the words "comic" and "heroic" tells us something important about our accustomed perception of comedy. From Plato's time until nearly the present critics and theoreticians of literature have been by and large a respectable group disinclined by profession to thumb their noses at social conventions or public morals; not surprisingly, recognition of the comic hero has lagged considerably behind the fact. The prevalent conception of comedy in the classical European tradition, from Aristotle down to Bergson, in effect postulated normal patterns of human behavior from which the comic was a deviation worthy of ridicule and contempt. It remained a socially oriented conception in which the consensus of civilized men presided as arbiter and the comic character was viewed as butt or scapegoat, not hero. The subject was one that dignified critics, following the supposed example of Aristotle, could neglect with impunity or deprecate as unworthy of extended attention. For all its rich diversity and irrepressible popularity, comedy, especially in its more robust forms, long remained almost beneath the threshold of cultured awareness. It was not only laughed at, but laughed off.

Aristotle's indelible contribution, in observations incidental to his penetrating analysis of tragedy in the *Poetics,* was to associate the comic with the trivial.[1] Not only does comedy represent men as worse than they are, while tragedy represents them as better, the writers of the invectives in which comedy had its origin were themselves of the cheaper or more vulgar sort. The subject of tragedy is serious, solemn, good (*spoudaios*); that of comedy is *phaulos,* mean or paltry. The terminology reflects an empirical observation, no doubt. The tragic stage (even that of Euripides) portrayed primarily kings and aristocrats, whereas comedy made do with commoners. But a frank prejudice underlies the assertion and largely explains its persistence, for there is no doubt which subject is more exalted and more suited to the philosophic mind. A value judgment is implicit in the social distinction, and the judgment directly reflects the values of aristocratic society: the comic character, quite simply and by his very nature, is inferior.[2] Other remarks in the *Poetics* are consistent with this assumption. Seeing the roots of comedy in invective and its function as ridicule, Aristotle disputes the derivation of the name itself from the festive *kômos,* or revels; despite his passing reference to phallic ritual, any intrinsic connection between comedy and festivity is far from his thoughts.[3] He appropriates both the *Iliad* and the *Odyssey* as antecedents of tragedy, while reserving the apocryphal (and now lost) *Margites,* a poem about an archetypal blunderer who "could do all things and did all of them badly," as Homer's one contribution — clearly less substantial — in the comic vein.[4] Thus if the origins of comedy remain obscure, as Aristotle comments, principally because it was not at first given serious attention, he himself greatly compounded and ratified that original misapprehension. Succeeding generations had the Stagirite's weighty authority for treating the comic as distinctly second-rate, if they treated it at all.

The value judgment implicit in Aristotle becomes obtrusive

in the theorists of the Renaissance and neoclassical periods, who constructed an openly moralistic and didactic conception of comedy on Aristotle's scant foundations. The underlying postulate of the whole school (as stated, for example, by the sixteenth-century Italian critic Giovanni Trissino) is that comedy "teaches through scorn and censure of the bad and the ugly."[5] The comic writer not only mocks but turns his mockery to a correctional end. By extrapolation from Aristotle's theory of tragedy, laughter is seen as a sort of catharsis purging the spectator of those vices exposed to ridicule on the comic stage.[6] Nor is this moralistic conception the exclusive property of pedants and critics; it finds voice in several of the leading comic dramatists of the seventeenth century. In the Induction to *Every Man Out of His Humour* (1599), Ben Jonson's indignant mouthpiece, Asper, admonishes his audience:

> If any here chance to behold himself,
> Let him not dare to challenge me of wrong;
> For, if he shame to have his follies known,
> First he should shame to act 'em. My strict hand
> Was made to seize on vice, and with a gripe,
> Squeeze out the humour of such spongy natures
> As lick up every idle vanity.

Through such didactic *furor poeticus* Jonson aspires, as he writes in the Dedicatory Epistle to *Volpone* (1607), to raise comic poetry from her sunken condition and "restore her to her primitive habit, feature, and majesty, and render her worthy to be embraced and kissed of all the great and master spirits of our world."[7] More than half a century later Molière, in the long and heated controversy that swirled about the performance of *Tartuffe, or the Impostor,* defended his play as an attack on hypocrisy which fulfilled the aim of comedy "to correct men by amusing them."[8] The "Letter on *The Impostor*" of 1667, possibly written by Molière himself, provides perhaps the most comprehensive single statement of the didactic conception of comedy. The ridiculous, the letter asserts, conflicts with the accepted laws of reasonable conduct; by perceiving this discrepancy we may learn to amend our ways "because, of course, we believe that Reason should govern everything."[9] In such apologies as these Jonson and Molière, like others in their age, endeavored to ascribe to comedy a higher and more respectable function than any that is evident from the scattered remarks in Aristotle's *Poetics.* Yet the fervor of their apologies (which very nearly treat comedy as a branch of the pulpit) testifies to the virulence of the accusations against their disreputable art by English Puritans and French *dévots.* And in its fundamentals their conception is little changed from Aristotle's. Comedy partakes of invective; its function is ridicule; and its characters, being objects of ridicule, are perforce of the meaner sort (morally if not always by birth). Nothing resembling heroism has any place here.

Clearly implicit in this understanding of comedy, as in Aristotle's initial discrimination between characters "better" and "worse" than in everyday life, are some pronounced social presuppositions. The butt of ridicule is essentially one who departs from norms of behavior which have been accepted as standards of civilized society, sanctioned by both usage and reason. Sometimes, as in the case of Volpone or Tartuffe, his violation of those norms gravely transgresses the moral code, and the indignity of derision must be reinforced by stiff penal servitude. More often, as with Sir Epicure Mammon and his deluded brethren in Jonson's *The Alchemist* or Monsieur Jourdain in Molière's *The Bourgeois Gentleman,* derision is a penalty sufficient in itself. Monsieur Jourdain's hilarious efforts to transform himself from sow's ear to silk purse point the moral with unusual clarity: the failure to know one's place in a hierarchic society, and the misguided endeavor to change one's station, are the very fountainheads of ridicule. Ridicule is one of society's most effective instruments for policing its values; and in the conception which we have been considering comedy and ridicule have been inseparable if not synonymous. In this regard, at least, Henri Bergson's influential essay *Laughter* (1900) merely corroborates and refines upon traditional assumption. In Bergson's view laughter is "a sort of *social gesture*" which "pursues a utilitarian aim of general improvement."[10] The didactic function of comedy and its enshrinement of social conventions as the ultimate criteria of human behavior have seldom been more explicitly maintained. "Any individual is comic," Bergson writes, "who automatically goes his own way without troubling himself about getting into touch with the rest of his fellow-beings. It is the part of laughter to reprove his absent-mindedness and wake him out of his dream . . . In laughter we always find an unavowed intention to humiliate, and consequently to correct our neighbour, if not in his will, at least in his deed." Bergson's identification of the fundamental source of laughter as "something mechanical encrusted on the living" simply pinpoints, from a vitalistic perspective, one source of the comic individual's essential inferiority. Again the stress is on the negative, with comedy acting as a sort of Roman Censor sternly recalling men to the roles for which society has destined them. In the light of such theories we may comprehend the comic character as fool or knave (that is, as our intellectual or moral inferior); we cannot yet glimpse the possibility of his being a hero.

The Aristotelian view of comedy, as the examples of Ben Jonson and Molière suggest, may have influenced the practice as well as the theory of later times. (Jonson's restoration of comedy to her primitive habit required a deliberate break with native English traditions.) Yet there is far more to the comic genius of these writers than their own rather narrowly moralistic theories embrace, for even comedy of a satirical kind is not the same as satire. The derision of satire tends toward the relentless diminution of its object to the lowest common denominator, the reduction of the human to the inhuman, of a personal enemy to a curd of ass's milk; but comedy, to succeed at all, must create a world of living people irreducible to inanimate things or mechanical processes. As a result, in a comedy of any distinction the character mocked for his insufficiencies, vices, and foibles is never delimited by them. He persistently eludes one-sided judgments and quite frequently engages reluctant admiration. Jonson's Volpone is a case in point. Lecherous, avaricious, unprincipled, and a fraud, he outrageously violates the moral and ethical standards of any civilized society: but in the Venice of Jonson's play a society fitting that description is ostentatiously lacking. This is a world of knaves, gulls, pimps, and whores in which the foxy Volpone and his wily sidekick Mosca at least succeed (until they outfox themselves at the end) in being bigger and better scoundrels than the others. The spectator may not share, and may deplore, Volpone's morality, but will find it difficult not to be drawn by his dynamism and by his energetic—indeed rhapsodic—faith in his own powers. Though no hero, Volpone is surely a very superior knave.

At the other extreme Molière's gullible Monsieur Jourdain likewise transcends mere derision by his irrepressible if misdirected refusal to acknowledge the futility of his ludicrous efforts to overstep the given limitations of his birth and education. The play's hilarious finale, in which the would-be nobleman is metamorphosed into a Turkish *Mamamouchi*, is both spoof and wish-fulfillment, celebrating even as it mocks. So fatuous a creature is far from heroic stature, yet in his simplicity he exerts an artless appeal lacking in his level-headed detractors; in a less buffoonish play we might ardently applaud his indefatigable enterprise. More complex and interesting is the case of Alceste in Molière's *The Misanthrope*—a figure of ridicule in his own age who could become a hero for another. The hypersensitive, nearly fanatical melancholy of Alceste, and his rigid incapacity to adapt to a social order whose foibles he always sees with a jaundiced eye—these qualities, which Molière and his contemporaries in the age of the Sun King appear to have found altogether derisible, could be portrayed by later generations as the virtues of a champion of nonconformity and rebellion.[11]

This posthumous rehabilitation of Alceste, by Rousseau who condemned Molière's ridicule of an honest man and by the Romantics who wished it away, suggests both the inadequacy of a purely satirical conception of comedy and the extent to which a great comic writer could transcend that conception while not apparently questioning its premises. Nowhere is the supremacy of society as the judge of conduct more firmly entrenched than in the comedies of Molière, and in none more than in *The Mis-*

anthrope. Yet the protagonist of this play, far from being a passive butt of ridicule, attains such stature by tenacious refusal to accept the verdict of others that he surmounts the derision of society and of his ambivalent creator. Alceste thus undermines the entire conception of comedy as mere ridicule. He will not submit to being inferior, and that is its indispensable condition. Tartuffe, however cunning, is undeniably a scoundrel and Monsieur Jourdain, however amiable, a fool; these we may consider worse than ourselves with some degree of complacency. But Alceste disarms satire by the intensity of his scorn for those who would scorn him. His articulate and deeply felt values acquire a weight more than equal to theirs; his last word, as he recoils from an abyss of triumphant vices to seek a more congenial world of his own, is "liberty." An audience sympathetic to his aversions could easily perceive Alceste as a hero — even if, as a consequence, it largely ceased to see him as comic.

The admiration that we often experience for characters exposed to scathing derision is a reminder that more than one response is possible to such comic types, be they knaves or fools. The cardinal limitation of the satirical theory of comedy descending from Aristotle is that it largely adopted the attitudes of the cultured upper classes as unquestioned standards of virtue, decorum, and good sense, thereby slighting if not altogether ignoring the different — and often diametrically opposite — values of the "lower" social classes. In popular tradition the perspective is somewhat different: both the dexterous rogue and the seeming buffoon (who often turn out to be one and the same) have regularly been the objects of unabashed delight and approbation.[12] Through laughter the potential gravity of their transgressions against the social order is effectively defused; ridiculousness is less a penalty than a sanction (like the court fool's cap and bells) affording protection for audacities that might otherwise be hazardous if not capital. The bumbling arch-prankster of German popular tradition, Till Eulenspiegel, successfully plays one outrageously antisocial trick after another, to the relish of his audience; Punch clobbers Judy to his heart's content and hurls his offspring through the nearest window;[13] and (in more fabulous vein) a host of humanoid little animals from ancient beast-tales to Uncle Remus and *Tom and Jerry* repeatedly evoke laughter and applause as they outwit their larger, more predatory, and stupider enemies. The outlook reflected in such perennial entertainments is that of the invincible underdog for whom a sharp wit, a clever tongue, or, in lieu of these, a loud mouth can serve as a weapon (when no other is at hand) *against* a social order that would deny his individuality by confining him to a permanently inferior or even inhuman status. If he is unable to alter or subvert that hostile order he will at least circumvent it, baffle it, and—almost invariably—come out on top. The dubious moral ending of *Volpone* or *Tartuffe,* in which rascality is discomfited and morality shakily reaffirmed, is conspicuous by its absence.

Of course, the worlds of Till Eulenspiegel, Punch and Judy, and Tom and Jerry are not in any way to be confounded with what we call the "real world," the world of mousetraps and gallows where endings are not so dependably happy. There is an enormous element of wish-fulfillment in these popular fantasies, where the little guy always triumphs, the mouse consistently gets away, and Punch can beat up wife and policeman one day and reappear no worse for wear on the morrow. But from this altered vantage point of the lower classes, looking on society from the bottom up, a radically different if largely inarticulate conception of comedy begins to emerge. The comic opponent of established authority, however knavish or buffoonish his character, however ludicrous or indecorous his activities, is no longer primarily a butt of mockery but a vessel of sympathetic identification. Once society with its oppressive inhibitions is seen as the Other, his cause becomes ours and we share in his most preposterous triumphs. And when the invincible underdog of fantasy and fable enters a world we recognize as our own and engages in a struggle with its complexities and dangers, he assumes the dimensions of the comic hero—an underdog no longer invincible, no longer immune to the possibility of defeat, and one whose victories, when he wins them at all, are provisional, precarious, and never final.

The twentieth century, with its cataclysmic breakup of age-old social orders, has been pre-eminently an era when the comic hero (along with his more obstreperous cousin the revolutionist) has been almost the only authentic hero of any kind to emerge from the rubble. The mass slaughter of World War I produced no godlike Achilles and no chivalric Roland, and the disillusioned writers who went through its horrors scathingly exposed the discredited catchwords of valor and glory as hypocrisy and sham. But the literature of the War did spawn at least one true hero of a very different stamp in the person of Jaroslav Hašek's good soldier Schweik who, though always deferring with meek obedience to his superior officers, repeatedly manages to foul up the works and stay safely away from the battle. In a world dedicated to mechanical slaughter he contrives — what accomplishment could be more heroic? — to remain not only alive but fully human and even miraculously sane. For Schweik the only refuge from the insanity of a society hell-bent on self-destruction is the madhouse, where (he blissfully recalls) "You can bawl, or yelp, or sing, or blub, or moo, or boo, or jump, say your prayers or turn somersaults, or walk on all fours, or hop about on one foot, or run around in a circle, or dance, or skip, or squat on your haunches all day long, and climb up the walls. Nobody comes up to you and says, 'You mustn't do this, you mustn't do that, you ought to be ashamed of yourself, call yourself civilized?' I liked being in the asylum, I can tell you, and while I was there I had the time of my life."[14] Clearly the standard of civilized conduct that prevailed, at least as an ideal, in classical comedy has no place whatsoever in Schweik's world. Unlike poor foolish Monsieur Jourdain in a more stable and complacent age, the certified imbecile Schweik becomes *himself* the embodiment of any such sanity or "Reason" as survives; no higher standard exists by which he could be judged deficient. Thus there is no trace of derision directed toward the protagonist of Hašek's comedy. He is a great man, the author writes in his preface, "and in presenting an account of his adventures during the World War, I am convinced that you will all sympathize with this modest, unrecognized hero." His very modesty, his cheerful capacity to shrug off indignity and partake of the common lot of man in the fullness of its inexplicable absurdity, is one thing that makes him so sympathetic — and so essential — a hero.

If work no less than war has been stripped of any residual glamor in our mechanized age, here too a comic hero has appeared in the person of Charlie Chaplin in *Modern Times*. However preposterous his situation may be at any given moment, Chaplin not only wins his audience's affection by his obstinate resilience and gets the girl in the end, but manages to throw a monkey-wrench (even if the monkey-wrench must be himself) into the well-oiled machinery of his would-be masters. As we witness his ordeals and triumphs the little man in the baggy trousers becomes our torch-bearer and paladin; on his destinies ours depend. For the bewildering misadventures of daily life that beleaguer him on every side mark the point where the socially ridiculous passes over into the existentially absurd: we can now no longer pretend to be laughing at a situation that is not ours. Against the lifeless ogres of a depersonalizing civilization this lowly but dauntless champion of irreducible humanity becomes our Lancelot. Rising out of the popular tradition of the invincible underdog into a world too numbed for tragedy and too disillusioned for glory, the Schweiks and the Chaplins are the legitimate and indispensable heroes of our time.

But the comic hero, however contemporary his impact, has a lineage extending back to an earlier day than Aristotle's, when civilization and its coercive demands were less securely entrenched. Greek comedy apparently grew out of primitive rituals celebrating rebirth and fertility;[15] and the hero of Aristophanic Old Comedy, however low a character in the eyes of later moralists and philosophers, normally transcended all obstacles in his path and came out king of the mountain. He was the artisan of his own triumphant vindication, far closer in spirit to Schweik or Chaplin than to Volpone or Tartuffe. Such considerations suggest an alternative conception of comedy as more essentially celebration than satire — celebration, above all, of vital impulse over social constraint — and of the comic protagonist not merely as a butt of derision but as an authentic hero. Comedy, as Susanne Langer describes it, "expresses the elementary strains and resolutions of animate nature, the animal drives that persist even in human nature, the delight man takes in his special mental gifts that make him the lord of creation; it is an image of human vitality holding its own in the world amid the surprises of unplanned coincidence . . . The feeling of comedy is a feeling of heightened vitality, challenged wit and will, engaged in the great game with Chance. The real antagonist is the World."[16] In this perpetually renewed and always lopsided contest between individual and world is the inexhaustible source of a comic heroism that repeatedly consents to encounter anew the unpredictable challenges and bewildering reversals of being alive.

At the same time the two conceptions of comedy, as satire and as celebration, though opposite, are by no means exclusive: reviling and reveling have always been closely akin. In his contest with a relentlessly hostile world the comic hero's affirmation of a subversive (and even anarchical) sense of life necessarily makes him ridiculous and contemptible in the eyes of much of that world. Satire and celebration can be, and normally are, interwoven, and no small part of the comic hero's valor is revealed in his spirited capacity to surmount the derision that continually befalls him. Nor does celebration of the comic hero's values imply that their victory is in any way assured. On the contrary, amid the vicissitudes of the real world (as Falstaff and Don Quixote will painfully discover) the comic hero is no less subject to humiliation and defeat than any other mortal, even though his willingness to risk—and indeed to invite—that defeat may prove to be his most enduring and irrevocable triumph.

I

BEGGAR MAN, KING

⸺⸻ ⟡ ⸻⸺

ARISTOTLE SAW both the *Iliad* and the *Odyssey* as
models of tragedy; in his view a serious work of art could
not, by definition, be comic. But the serious and the comic are
not necessarily exclusive, since only in a serious world can the
comic hero prove his mettle against a worthy antagonist. It will
be more illuminating, as others since Aristotle have done, to see
the *Iliad* as a model of tragedy and the *Odyssey* of comedy.[1]

Achilles is a tragic hero—the archetypal tragic hero—not
merely by fate but by choice: his choice, welling up from within
him, *is* his fate. Tragedy is not something that happens to him
but something he must elect and achieve. The fundamental
terms of his choice are those which he recalls in rejecting the
overtures of Odysseus in a famous passage from Book IX of the
Iliad. His mother, Thetis of the silver feet, has told him, he says,
that he bears a twofold destiny: either to remain at Troy where
he will sacrifice his homecoming (*nostos*) but win immortal
glory (*kleos*), or to return to his fatherland where he will lead a
long life without glory (Il. IX. 410-416). The choice is between
continued life, which is unheroic by nature, and heroic death;
a willed acceptance of violent death is both the token and the
price of glory. At this point Achilles declares for the first alternative. He will leave Troy and return to his father, who will

find him a bride. Not all the wealth of Ilium, he asserts, can be worth as much to him as life. But choice is never unconditioned, and we know — as he himself knows — that this choice is not really viable for him, since it runs counter to everything he is. He is a man, before all else, who will not compromise, and life is nothing if not a series of compromises. Only after Patroclus lies dead by Hector's hand does Achilles understand his destiny and affirm its necessity; from now on his choice is clear. He will kill Hector, he tells his grieving mother, even though he knows that his own death must inevitably follow; once this long-deferred decision has been made he never wavers. To his horse Xanthus, who miraculously speaks to prophesy that his end is near, Achilles answers: "Xanthus, why do you prophesy my death? You need not do so. I myself well know that it is my destiny to perish here far from my dear father and mother; but nonetheless I will not cease until I have given the Trojans their fill of war" (Il. XIX. 420-423). And on the field of battle, Achilles slays with the impersonality of one who has nothing more in common with life. When Hector's half-brother Lycaon beseeches him for mercy, Achilles remorselessly replies that no longer can any Trojan whom the gods put in his hands escape death. "You too, friend, must die: why do you make such lament?" he asks. "Patroclus too died, who was far better than you. Do you not see how fair and tall a man am I? I am the son of a noble father, and the mother who bore me is a goddess; but for me also death and stern destiny are in store" (Il. XXI. 106-110). No appeal to humanity can be binding on one who has already left life behind, and Lycaon's prayers are unheard.

And when, in the final book of the poem, the broken Priam comes to claim the body of Hector and kisses the hand that slew his son, and the two men weep together — Achilles for his father, Peleus, whom he will never see again and Priam for his son Hector, already dead — it is as though both men, in their unquestioning acceptance of the finality of death, have passed beyond the uncertainties of human life and beyond the dividing walls of individuality. As though Priam were weeping not only for his own son but for the son of Peleus who had killed him and for all the other young men who had died and must die in battle, and Achilles were weeping not only for his own father but for Hector's, whose sons he himself had slain, and for all the old men who would lose brave sons in war; as though both these men, the young Achaean warrior and the old Trojan king, were one man and all men weeping from beyond the grave for the sorrow of life on earth. The choice of death which had made Achilles so implacable to the pleas of Priam's sons now unites him for one timeless moment with another mortal no less remote from the exigencies of life than himself. Through the purifying intensity of grief he and his enemy are one; their humanity, indissolubly joining them in contrast to the carefree divinity of the gods, lies not in any shared experience of life's diversities but in the overflowing fullness of their apprehension of death. Here alone the divisions and conflicts of living are irrefutably overcome.

The tragic hero then, as we see him in the *Iliad,* makes a choice. It is not an arbitrary choice but one determined by (and determining) his whole being: his choice becomes destiny. In choosing glory at Troy over return to Phthia Achilles is consciously electing death, not out of morbid longing but from clear-sighted recognition that death is absolute and life is relative. Death is uncompromising and true where life is riddled with compromise and illusion; death is changeless and eternal but life is constantly shifting and soon ended; death has the unblemished dignity of fate and necessity while life is a mixed bag forever subject to the uncertainties of fortune and chance. The tragic hero's choice, for all the sorrow it entails, is essentially a choice to free himself from the vicissitudes of chance that tyrannize over other men. It is, paradoxically, by a voluntary identification with necessity that he attains this definitive freedom, thereby transcending the limitations of merely personal or merely human existence and becoming (like Achilles in the final book of the *Iliad* or the blind Oedipus at Colonus in Sophocles' last play) more an impersonal force or a numinous presence than a living man. The willful assimilation of death is a nullification of death's sovereign power, and thus a momentary immortality.

In Odysseus we have a hero who in almost every respect is

Achilles' opposite. If Achilles is the incarnation of singleness and unbending integrity, Odysseus is the paragon of multiplicity and craft. Achilles cleaves fixedly to truth; Odysseus is one of the world's great liars. "Hateful to me as the gates of Hades," Achilles dourly replies to Odysseus' eloquent plea in *Iliad* IX (312-13), "is he who hides one thing in his heart and speaks another": the art of doing just that is Odysseus' forte. In the stern fellowship of the *Iliad* Odysseus is a stalwart and dependable soldier, but no match for such dazzling spearmen as Achilles or Hector, Ajax or Diomedes. His physique is several times described as short and stocky (not at all the type of Aryan manhood), nor does he convey, like Agamemnon or Menelaus, the prestige of ruling a rich and extensive realm. Standing next to Ajax, who overtowered him by two heads, Odysseus must have looked like a dwarf; and even on the Greek scale of things his barren homeland of Ithaca (two-thirds the size of Staten Island) was not very much of a kingdom. Within a world composed of eminent warriors and godlike heroes — an aristocratic world in which only kings and princes count — Odysseus is something of an outsider and a distinct underdog. In order to stand out among such peers he must be more than he seems.

And here we have one of the cardinal distinctions between the tragic and the comic hero. Achilles is the man for whom there can be no discrepancy between appearance and reality: his godlike form reveals a godlike man. Not only his words but his very looks express, with no trace of disjuncture, his innermost self. Like Hamlet, the tragic hero of a more divided age, Achilles knows not "seems." But Odysseus, the comic hero, is far less single and far more equivocal; he is the man who knows every nook and cranny of "seems." In fact, if the difference between what he says and what he hides in his heart is one characteristic by which wily Odysseus is known to friend and enemy alike, the difference between what he appears at first sight and what he later shows himself to be is no less striking to all. When Helen identifies him to Priam from the walls of Troy in Book III of the *Iliad* (200-202) she says simply: "This is Laertes' son Odysseus of many counsels, who was reared in the land of Ithaca, rocky though it be, knowing all sorts of tricks and crafty schemes." At which Priam's counselor Antenor relates how Menelaus and Odysseus had once before come to Troy to request Helen's return. Menelaus had spoken rapidly, with few words: "But when Odysseus of many counsels uprose, he stood looking down with eyes fixed on the ground, and moved his staff neither backward nor forward, but held it motionless like one who knows nothing. You would have thought him a sullen man, and a fool to boot. But when he sent forth the great voice from his chest, and words that fell thick as the snows of winter, then no other mortal could contend with Odysseus. No longer," Antenor concludes, "were we so surprised at beholding Odysseus' appearance" (Il. III. 216-224). Achilles was the hero for whom appearance, thought, word, and deed were one and indivisible; Odysseus is a different sort of hero who can say one thing while thinking another—and can look like a fool while being the shrewdest of men.

It is this penchant for contradiction in the comic hero—his frequently blatant failure to *seem* appropriately heroic—that logicians and moralists, intent on consistency and decorum, have found hard to condone. In denigrating the comic character as inferior to the mean they have quite possibly been hoodwinked by his appearance. Homer's subtle Odysseus himself was often travestied in later days as a mere deceiver or hypocrite, a smooth operator and accomplished confidence man.[2] He does have talents in that line, beyond doubt. But his notorious guile arises not from any intrinsic dishonesty or shiftiness but rather from a complex awareness that within the kaleidoscopic world of human life truth is never one and unchanging but always multiple and elusive. Only a man who not merely perceives but accepts (as Achilles could not) the inherent discrepancy between appearance and reality in the world could dissemble as Odysseus dissembles. His endless deceptions and ingenious fabrications in the *Odyssey* are both creative acts of an inexhaustibly fertile imagination responding with exuberant vitality to the unforeseeable challenges of life and hard-headed stratagems for survival in an insidious world where the superhuman strength and courage of Achilles or Ajax no longer suffice. The eloquence that spellbound Antenor (if not Achilles) at Troy becomes, in the *Odyssey,* no mere ornament but a potent weapon in the struggle to stay alive. Among the heroes of ancient Greece Odysseus is the unrivaled master of words, and this mastery stands him in good stead long after stronger but less flexible heroes have fallen.

Odysseus' famed virtuosity with words is of course a reflection of his resourcefulness of mind: in a contest in which he is nearly always outgunned, the comic hero's secret weapons are versatility and intelligence. The epithets that distinguish Odysseus in the Greek original of the poem lay simultaneous stress on his multiplicity and his mental powers; he is not called "wide-ruling" like Agamemnon or "swift-footed" like Achilles, but *polymêtis* ("of many counsels"), *polyphrôn* ("much-thinking"), *polymêkhanos* ("of many devices"). The tricks and schemes by which Helen characterized him to Priam are proud hallmarks of his pre-eminent quickness of wit, and in identifying himself to King Alcinous of the Phaeacians he roundly declares: "I am Laertes' son Odysseus who vex all men with my tricks, and my glory reaches heaven" (Od. IX. 19-20). The word for "glory" (*kleos*) is the same that Achilles had linked with death at Troy, but the significance of that word (as Humpty Dumpty would later remark) is subject to alteration. Perhaps the single adjective that most fully characterizes Odysseus is that which appears in the first line of the poem and once thereafter (X. 330): *polytropos,* meaning "versatile, of many twists and turns."[3] (The word appears nowhere else in the Homeric corpus except in the "Hymn to Hermes," where it designates the crafty god of thieves who marked the day of his birth by inventing the lyre and filching the kine of Apollo.)[4] The heroes of the war at Troy, with Achilles at their head, were monolithic and unswerving men. But Odysseus is beyond all others the man who is capable, through mental agility and a nimble tongue, of shifting and veering as need requires in order to thread his way through the intricate and perilous obstacle-course of human life. At the same time, for all the deviousness and diversity of his tactics he is equally renowned for steadfast tenacity of purpose; for he is also *polytlas* ("much-enduring") Odysseus, forever ready to parry the blows of life when he can but able to bear them unflinchingly as often as he must. His countless twists and turns, his incessant tricks and disguises are never — except for the few occasions when he forgets himself — ends in themselves but rather means toward a goal which this man of multiplicity pursues with an almost unwavering singleness of intent.

The choice of destinies offered to Achilles in the *Iliad* was between *kleos* and *nostos,* glory and homecoming; he chose the first to the necessary exclusion of the second. The *Odyssey* is, of course, the story of a homecoming and of all the enormous effort and discipline it involves. As Odysseus reminds Alcinous in announcing his name, for him the second alternative is not without a glory of its own. There is a heroism in the acceptance of life no less than of death; the comic hero, like the tragic, must make a choice, and his choice is scarcely less hard. He chooses — not once and for all, since this choice can never be final, but over and over — to live his life within an imperfect and provisional world, such as it is and such as he is able to make it; he chooses the relative over the absolute with full awareness of its limitations no less than its possibilities. This choice, a conscious and deliberate one, is nowhere clearer than in Odysseus' decisive repudiation of the immortality offered him by the alluring nymph Calypso on the timeless isle of Ogygia. To Calypso, even as she reluctantly frees him from her silken bonds at Zeus's behest, Odysseus' stubborn longing to leave her voluptuous realm for a life of hardship and the aging charms of a mortal wife is beyond divine comprehension. "Zeus-born son of Laertes, Odysseus of many devices," she wistfully chides him,

> "do you now wish, without delay, to go
> home to the country that you hold so dear?
> Well, then, farewell. But if you knew how many
> sorrows remain before you reach your home,
> you would stay here with me, and guard this house,
> and be immortal, however much you yearned
> to see the wife you pine for day by day.
> Surely I cannot be inferior

in bodily form to her! It cannot be
that mortals rival goddesses in beauty."

Odysseus of many counsels answered:

"My lady, do not be angry. I myself
know well how much my thoughtful Penelope
falls short of you in form and height and stature,
for she is mortal, you will never age.
Yet even so I hunger day by day
to see my home as soon as I may return.
If on the wine-dark sea some god should crush me,
I shall endure what comes with stalwart heart.
Countless the trials I have already suffered
at sea, in combat! Let another come."

(Od. V. 203-224)

So Odysseus' eyes are open to whatever may lie beyond the
protective shores of Ogygia. He knows from bitter experience
what he must undergo because he has undergone so much already, yet still he will take it on; his resolution is as firm and
sure as that of Achilles had been. The comic hero thus says yes
to life—to its toils and sufferings and its very brevity as well as
its hard-won joys and pleasures—no less resolutely, no less
clear-sightedly, and no less courageously than the tragic hero
said yes to death. And if the tragic hero's choice was a choice of
freedom through total *acceptance* of *destiny*—of the inescapable necessity of death which is alike for all men—the comic
hero's is likewise a choice of freedom through unwearying *defiance* of *chance* in his confrontation with the unpredictable
fortunes of life which are never the same for any two men on
earth. Time and again the comic hero engages in a contest
where there can be no final victory, but in which he will never,
so long as he breathes, admit defeat.

The "affirmation of life" is doubtless an easy phrase; but the
thing itself can be easy only for one who has experienced little
of life and little or nothing of death. For Odysseus, whose very
name may stem from the word for "pain" or "trouble,"[5] and
who more than once in his long years of suffering momentarily

succumbs to the yearning to die, the affirmation comes hard.
Surely one of the most astonishing assertions of the supreme
value of human life in all literature occurs in the eleventh book
of the *Odyssey:* astonishing because it is spoken in the world of
the dead by none other than Achilles. Forced against his will to
make the fearful descent to the underworld in order to consult
the shade of Tiresias, Odysseus stands in awe before the mighty
spirit of Achilles and addresses him with undisguised envy.

> "I have not yet approached Achaea, not
> skirted my country, but suffer only hardships.
> But no man has ever been more fortunate
> than you, Achilles. Before, when you were living,
> we Argives placed you on a par with gods,
> and now that you are here, you rule the dead
> splendidly. Do not grieve at death, Achilles."

> Such were my words, and thus he swiftly answered:

> "Do not speak soothingly of death to me,
> renowned Odysseus. I would rather be
> a farmhand toiling for an impoverished master
> who barely scraped a livelihood together,
> than reign as king of all the wasted dead."

>   (Od. XI. 481-491)

The figure who makes this statement that *any* human life,
even the most abject and servile, is preferable to death is a de-
pleted shadow of the tragic Achilles of the *Iliad,* who even
while living had attained the inviolate condition of mind for
which life is without temptations and death has no terrors. But
that, of course, is the point: this is not the Achilles of the *Iliad*
but the Achilles of the *Odyssey,* where the values of life are
supreme even in the kingdom of the dead. Achilles maintains
his stately demeanor, but even so he is nothing now but a cast-
off shadow like everyone else in this shadowy place. Here the
hero is not Achilles; nor the silently disdainful Ajax, still sulk-
ing over the wrongs Odysseus had done him in life; nor the
sniveling Agamemnon, stupefied by the fact that *he,* the king

of men, had been butchered by his wife and her lover like an ox at the trough. No, the hero here, for all his wavering reluctance at this nadir of his voyage, is the man who has chosen return and is able to make the most hazardous and difficult return of all: the ascent from the dead to the living.

Even before this surprising affirmation of life by Achilles, who had chosen death, the shade of Odysseus' mother Anticleia movingly exhorts her son to turn his back on the world of shadows. His futile attempt to embrace her impalpable image only embitters his pain, and she tells him:

> "Whoever dies abides by this same law.
> No sinews fasten flesh and bone together,
> but the strong might of blazing fire subdues them
> as soon as spirit leaves the whitening bones
> and life soars fluttering, like a dream, away.
> Long for the light immediately. Remember
> these things, to tell your wife in later days."
>
> (Od. XI. 218-224)

When Odysseus returns from darkness to sunlight, then, it is with the sure knowledge that death is nothingness; with a heightened appreciation of the precious gift of life; and with a resurrected awareness of the guiding purpose nearly forgotten in the sensual oblivion of Circe's island. Only after this most perilous journey will he eagerly welcome any trial that life can send. The alternative is now clear beyond the shadow of a doubt.

So the choice of life is no simple matter for Odysseus. It involves the surmounting of death, the repudiation of the languorous death-in-life of immortality, and the difficult rejection of those enticing compromises with all that is less complete and full than life, such as the loveless pleasures of the enchantress Circe. It also involves, as we have seen, the willing acceptance of uncertainty and change and the unremitting contest with fortune and misfortune. It is this fundamental choice that defines the character and shapes the destiny of the comic hero. If death and communion with death bring even such opposite men as Achilles and Priam to a unity almost beyond the mortal, the repeated encounter with life calls forth instead the rich multiplicity of personality. The tragic hero transcends his individuality through identification with the common destiny of man; the comic hero, through the inexhaustible particularity of experience, develops his to the full. The universality of the tragic hero lies in *exclusion* from himself of everything superfluous, everything but the nakedness of man in the face of death; that of the comic hero stems from *assimilation* to himself of the greatest wealth and widest diversity of the joys and sorrows known to men in this infinitely varied world. Such is the universality, above all, of Homer's multiple Odysseus that he seems to encompass in his single person the actual and possible experiences of all men. As son and father, husband and lover, warrior and diplomat, voyager and homebody, beggar and king, he is perhaps (as James Joyce declared while writing his *Ulysses*) the most nearly "complete all-round character" portrayed by any poet or writer.[6] As such he will serve as a flexible prototype of what the comic hero, in the innumerable twists and turns of his confrontation with life, is capable of becoming.

The nature of the hero's response will be conditioned by that of the world he encounters, and the world of the *Odyssey,* especially in the first half of the poem, is an elemental and primitive one fraught with immediate physical dangers. The grinding Trojan war and the brutal Achaean sack of the vanquished city throw an ominous shadow over Odysseus' protracted homecoming, while savage tribal assaults, cannibalism and witchcraft, shipwreck, and the fury of natural forces unleashed by outraged divinities menace the harried voyager at every turn. In such a world the first and most pressing challenge faced by Odysseus (as the opening lines of the poem announce) is "to save his life" from the many perils, human and extrahuman, that threaten to submerge him — a task in which he succeeds even if he fails, through no fault of his own, "to rescue his companions" (Od. I. 5-6). The tragic hero may find vindication in death; the comic hero's first (though not necessarily his highest) priority is to live to see another day.

It is mainly through his superb attributes of physical strength and courage — and of obstinate endurance — that Odysseus is able to outface and overcome the physical dangers that continually beset him, but his sturdy prowess would be of little avail without the guidance of his agile intelligence. Not even this smoothest orator, to be sure, can talk himself out of a hurricane, but quickwittedness more than once tips the balance between life and death. In the fifth book of the poem, as Odysseus is piloting his raft away from Calypso's island paradise, a storm churned up by the sea-god Poseidon reintroduces him to reality with a vengeance. His first reaction when the tempest hits is an all-too-human feeling of terror. The hero who had just resolved to take on the hardships of mortality now finds himself envying the fortunate Danaans who had died a more dignified death on the plains of Troy. But this untypical faint-heartedness lasts only a moment. When a colossal wave flings him overboard and nearly drowns him, Odysseus' presence of mind returns in a flash; even while spewing brine from his mouth he remembers to lunge for the vanishing raft, thus warding off imminent death. The sea-nymph Ino Leucothea who appears at this critical juncture to counsel Odysseus and offer the protection of her immortal veil is not (any more than the other divinities of the poem) to be understood as a deus ex machina but rather as an externalized dramatization of the hero's inner resources; for the gods of the *Odyssey* give nothing that men have not won for themselves. "Do what I say; you seem to be in your senses," she orders (Od. V. 342); and if Odysseus were not in command of his senses, even amid pounding breakers and screaming winds, no heavenly aid could preserve him.

Even so, Odysseus suspiciously shrinks from the nymph's suggestion that he abandon his raft and swim for shore (a man so adept at deceiving others is wary of being deceived even by himself) and methodically ponders both sides of the question. Just as he is deciding against the divine proposal a wave abruptly alters his intention by splintering the raft beneath him, and he swims for dear life. The welcome sight of land after two nights and days alone in the deep — as welcome to Odysseus as a father's recovery from long illness to his children — spurs him to

new effort, and not only his physical stamina and mental resourcefulness but his passion for life sustain him. Although he
once again despairs when he sees the rocky shoreline and contemplates the bleak alternatives before him, his tenacious intelligence remains unimpaired.

> All his skin would have torn away, his bones
> been crushed, had not grey-eyed Athena minded.
> He quickly seized a rock with both his hands
> and held on, groaning, till a great wave broke,
> and thus escaped; but surging back again
> it struck him hard and hurled him far asea.
> Just as an octopus dragged from his lair
> grips with his tentacles a thousand pebbles,
> so from Odysseus' strong hands the rocks
> tore shreds off as the breaker pulled him under.
> Wretched Odysseus would have met his end there,
> had not grey-eyed Athena given shrewdness.
>   (Od. V. 426-437)

Not an alien goddess but the divine gift of shrewdness (*epi-
phrosynê*) guides him to the safest landing place, where he is
washed ashore, almost unconscious, and kisses the fruitful
earth. Yet again he meditates his course of action and again
finds a way, taking shelter in a dense undergrowth of inter-
tangled wild and domestic olive bushes. His heart laughs as he
rakes together a bed of leaves and covers himself, preserving
the tenuous life within him as a farmer hides a glowing brand
in a bed of embers. The precious flame still smolders un-
quenched despite the worst that wind and waters could do.

The opening four books of the *Odyssey*, narrating Telemachus' quest for his father, were remarkably bare of the extended similes characteristic of Greek heroic poetry, yet in the
passage recounting Odysseus' struggle with the sea occur three
of the most striking comparisons in Homer. The image of the
children rejoicing in their father's recovery from illness underlines the rudimentary will to live that has survived Odysseus'
numbing agony in the waves; that of the octopus clinging to the
rock from which it is being torn highlights his tenacity in the

face of mortal danger; and now this culminating simile of the spark of fire kept alive overnight in the embers reminds us of both the frailty and the priceless value of the life that he has managed to preserve with such toil. It was indeed a difficult choice — and one of inestimable moment — that Odysseus made when he refused Calypso's eternal embraces and elected to take on the burdens of the human condition.

In the high heroic world of the *Iliad* the similes are not only more frequent than those of the *Odyssey* but typically more grand and elaborate. When Achilles engages in combat he can be likened, in his otherwise incomparable ferocity and prowess, to nothing less than the king of beasts:

> On the other side arose the son of Peleus against him like a ravenous lion whom men struggle to kill, the whole people assembled; at first he goes on disregarding them, but when some young man swift in battle strikes him with a spear he whirls open-mouthed, foaming round his teeth, and in his breast the heart groans; with his tail he lashes ribs and flanks on both sides, and urges himself to do battle, and with eyes ablaze rushes impetuously forward hoping to kill one of the men or die himself in the first onslaught. Even so his strength and manly courage urged on Achilles.
>
> (Il. XX. 164-174)

But in the less exalted world of the *Odyssey* the terms of comparison are drawn far more frequently from the humbler aspects of life: the sick father, the octopus under a stone (an everyday sight in Greece), or the farmer laboring in his fields.

And just as the effect of the similes differs from one poem to the other, so might the entire episode of Odysseus' contest with the sea be contrasted with the episode in the *Iliad* where Achilles is pitted against the elements in the shape of the river Scamander. Here the river is personified as a god who rises in fury because his streams have been choked with Trojan blood and pursues Achilles in frenzy over the broad plains of Troy, until the fire-god Hephaestus, fighting on the Achaean side, ignites the corpses strewn on the battlefield into a wall of flame and drives the shrinking river back into his channel. Everything in this stupendous account accentuates the extraordinary, the marvelous, the superhuman dimension of the struggle taking place around Ilium's walls — a struggle in which the gods are no less directly and personally engaged than men. But in Odysseus' battle to survive his ordeal at sea there is nothing — notwithstanding the references to Poseidon's anger, Ino Leucothea's counsel, and Athena's gift — that is not naturally comprehensible and humanly real. What we witness here is a solitary human being relying on no other powers in his life-and-death contest than his own tough body, quick mind, and resilient will. Through his own efforts alone he emerges from the waves, less than dignified, no doubt, in contrast to the storied warriors who fell by his side at Troy, but alive.

Toughness and versatility are resources on which much-suffering Odysseus of the many counsels must repeatedly draw, especially during the four books of fabulous adventures which he relates (with more than a touch, perhaps, of poetic elaboration) during his sojourn among the Phaeacians. His celebrated escape from the Cyclops' den, in particular, is a paradigm of the comic hero's wily art of mastering a stronger but duller adversary. Odysseus has only himself to blame for his peril — in these early escapades the virtue of prudence is notably absent — and conversely only himself to rely on in extricating himself from it. Physical strength, which assists him so often, is bootless here, and he is thrown back entirely on mother wit. Trapped by his own curiosity and the savage's overwhelmingly superior might he has the presence of mind to conceal the whereabouts of his ship by extemporizing a plausible story, and he quickly perceives that he cannot slay Polyphemus without entombing himself and his uneaten men in the cave. Before he inebriates the thick-skulled monster and bores out his single eye, he anticipates his call for assistance by craftily announcing that his name is Nobody. The blinded Cyclops' forlorn complaint that Nobody is tricking him to death is the acme of Odysseus' ingenuity — the triumph of wit and words over mere brawn — just as his getaway beneath a woolly mutton's belly is its fit conclusion, inglorious but thoroughly efficacious. No one can imagine the Achilles of the *Iliad* in such a demeaning posture;

but one secret of the comic hero's success is his willingness to stoop (when need be) to conquer. And conquer Odysseus does by his brilliant devices even if he then recklessly throws everything in jeopardy by his brashness in taunting his vanquished antagonist. Self-discipline will follow but resourcefulness and animal spirits come first. At this point in his saga Odysseus is little more than a Greek Till Eulenspiegel or Brer Rabbit, but such is the stuff that comic heroes are made on.

Physical dangers such as death by water or ingestion by monocular anthropophagi are not of course the only kinds of challenge, formidable though they are, that Odysseus must meet; other, more insidious perils call for far different resources. We have briefly dealt with his refusals of divinity and animality on Ogygia and Aeaea and with his still harder rejection of the enticement of death; we might also recall the oblivious Lotus-eaters and above all the Sirens, whose seductive song offers knowledge only about the tribulations of others. "For we know everything the Argives and Trojans suffered by the will of the gods in broad Troy," they sing to Odysseus (who after all has learned of these things at first hand); "we know everything that happens on the fruitful earth" (Od. XII. 189-191). All these simplistic evasions of life's complexities Odysseus can reject because he himself is too many-sided to be taken in by their reductive allure. But he can meaningfully reject them only after he has experienced them all by exposing himself with open eyes and unstopped ears to their full temptation—only after he has made them a part of himself and assimilated the knowledge of them, so that every encounter and every difficult rejection enlarges rather than diminishes his humanity.

Perhaps the subtlest and certainly the most enchanting challenge faced by Odysseus occurs immediately after his bruising combat with the sea, when he encounters Nausicaa in the childlike kingdom of the Phaeacians. This ingenuous princess, whose virginal thoughts have only begun to turn vaguely toward marriage, exudes a charm still more potent than Calypso's or Circe's as she asks her papa for the family mule-cart and drives off with her frolicsome maidservants to wash the laundry in the stream. They spread the wash out to dry, savor a picnic lunch, and begin to play ball on the beach — by now we have left the blood-spattered battleground of the *Iliad* far behind — when Nausicaa accidentally hurls the ball into the water and a chorus of girlish screams startles Odysseus from his slumber beneath the shrubs. No scene in the *Odyssey* is more delectably comic. With unfailing self-possession the long-sufferer remembers to pluck an olive branch (whether wild or domestic Homer neglects to specify) in order to shield his privates as he leaps out from the underbrush. Like Achilles he is likened to a ravenous beast:

> He came forth like a mighty mountain lion
> rain-soaked and buffeted by winds; with eyes
> aflame, he prowls the countryside for cattle,
> sheep, or wild deer, and, prodded by his belly,
> attacks the folds of densely settled homesteads.
> Just so need drove Odysseus to mingle,
> though naked, with the lovely-braided girls.
>
> (Od. VI. 130-136)

But whereas the lion of the *Iliad* was a defiant symbol of animal strength, this lion (though fierce enough to panic a gaggle of girls in pigtails) is remarkable principally for manginess and an empty stomach. All the maidens except Nausicaa run screaming in every direction as the bedraggled Odysseus — who luckily neglects the custom of extending his olive branch — cogitates even on the run. Once again he judiciously weighs two alternative courses of action and again displays his legendary sagacity in choosing between them:

> She stood and held her ground. Odysseus pondered
> whether to grasp her knees and supplicate
> the lovely maid, or stay apart and ask her
> with honeyed words for bearings — and some clothes.
> Sagely deliberating, he decided
> to keep away and utter honeyed words;
> grasping her knees, he thought, might rile the girl.
> The words he spoke were honeycombed with cunning.
>
> (Od. VI. 141-148)

Now, it was time-honored usage in ancient Greece for a suppliant to embrace one's knees when making his plea; but the thought that a naked man hurtling out of the bushes with matted hair and unkempt beard might think it politic to seize hold of a nubile princess's flanks on a deserted seashore is enough to make us grateful that Odysseus was endowed with a discerning mind. He makes the wiser decision, and addresses Nausicaa from a respectful distance with all the mellifluous eloquence at his command. His gracious words are persuasive as always, and after he has bathed and been anointed by Athena, Nausicaa's indeterminate longings for a husband instantly take definite shape: "I wish so fine a husband as he were mine," she artlessly exclaims, "and dwelt here and were satisfied to stay" (Od. VI. 244-45).

In the scenes that follow, Odysseus is faced with a temptation unlike any he has surmounted before, and he meets the occasion with unsuspected reserves of sympathetic understanding and tactful diplomacy. The enduring appeal of the island of the Phaeacians is not far to seek. Here is the earthly paradise of unfading childhood for which men have so often nostalgically yearned in later, more complicated times: a magic kingdom where time stands still, where evil and war and inclement skies have no place, and the trees yield abundant fruit all year round. It is the promised land, forever eluding recapture, of perennial daydream and legend, glimpsed in scraps of tantalizing memories, or beckoning from just over the rainbow. But like Calypso's Ogygia and Circe's Aeaea—those other paradises he has put behind him—Nausicaa's Scheria is no place for much-suffering Odysseus. He must take leave of this serpentless Eden not merely out of faithfulness to Penelope and Ithaca but because he has already tasted of the tree of knowledge and outgrown childish things, because his guileful multiplicity could never find a home in this realm of guileless simplicity. The Isles of the Blest are for those content to drink the nepenthe of godlike Helen, but the comic hero cannot be at home in a world without troubles. For there is no return from Experience to Innocence, and the fruit of knowledge can be fully savored only when Paradise, once having been lost, is beyond regaining. One island alone can be home for Odysseus, and during his dreamlike passage to Ithaca this man of countless troubles re-poses at last. Concerning the life of Princess Nausicaa after Odysseus has departed we learn nothing more, perhaps because there is nothing to learn.

These are only a few of the many challenges that Odysseus meets in his wanderings; his principal test, of course, still awaits him when he awakens on the coast of an Ithaca he no longer knows. But the peregrinations of the first half of the poem have not been random adventures. Only after coming to grips with such demanding trials and temptations can the piratical plunderer become the disciplined master able to abide, while he must, the taunts of the suitors in his own halls. His ordeals have not been for nothing; now at last he is ready for whatever card Fortune may play.

His new self-mastery is perfectly symbolized by the encounter with Athena that initiates the second half of the poem.[7] Throughout the first twelve books Athena, as Odysseus' guardian spirit or "better self," had never been far from her favorite's side, yet not once since leaving the ashes of Troy had he been aware of her presence. His recognition of the goddess now, at the moment of his homecoming, is thus his first true recognition of the self which he has long been in the process of becoming. And since Athena now beholds her protégé for the first time in the full development of his powers, their reciprocal recognition becomes a confrontation of two kindred spirits reveling in a rare communion of perfect cunning. Athena appears in the guise of a shepherd boy — ever since her debut in Book I she has proved an even defter master of transformation than Odysseus himself — and scoffs at his ignorance when he asks where he is. Unaware that he has met more than his match in the art of dissembling, Odysseus, laughing in his heart when the shepherd names Ithaca, proceeds to spin out a plausible yarn about his flight from Crete on a Phoenician ship after killing a certain Orsilochus . . . and so on: a pack of lies. But far from being offended as she listens to this impudent mortal's outrageous mendacities, Athena unabashedly exults, choosing this moment to reveal herself and to voice her admiration for talents so like her own.

The grey-eyed goddess Athena, smiling,
gently caressed him. Now she seemed a woman,
beautiful, tall, and skilled in graceful crafts.
Her words came flying forth like winged arrows:

"How cunning, how rascally one would need to be
to top your tricks and endless machinations,
even if your antagonist were a god!
Oh, headstrong man of particolored guile,
tireless deceiver, could you not stop cheating
and lying, when you found yourself at home?
Were fraud and fibs indigenous to you?
Come now, enough of this! We are both well versed
in guile. You are by far the foremost mortal
in schemes and yarns, while I, of all the gods,
am famed for crafty plans. Did you not know
Pallas Athena, child of Zeus, who always
stand at your side in troubles, and protect you?"

(Od. XIII. 287-301)

Yet crafty Odysseus, even at this moment of truth when the shepherd boy has changed to a goddess before his eyes, remains suspicious as ever and doubts whether he is truly at home. And again Athena delights in his skeptical wariness and takes no umbrage at his unconcealed distrust. "Always so fixed a purpose in your heart," she affectionately exclaims:

"I can't forsake you in your worst misfortune,
voluble, shrewd, coolheaded as you are!"

(Od. XIII. 330-332)

No higher eulogy could be lavished on mortal man by this canniest of divinities, who goes on to praise the long-lost wanderer's caution in not rushing home to his wife before carefully testing the waters. In pointed contrast to the traditional martial virtues of swift-footed, blunt-spoken, hot-tempered Achilles, the qualities of quickwittedness, ready speech,[8] and cool self-possession singled out for praise by Athena are the quintessence of Odysseus' unconventional comic heroism: a sober and flexible heroism that looks before it leaps and considers discretion the sine qua non of intelligent valor.

This critical meeting of minds on the threshold of home, in which the celestial incarnation of cunning gleefully ratifies the qualities refined by Odysseus during the trials and errors of the first half of the poem, initiates the pattern of recognition that prevails in the second. Throughout the last twelve books Odysseus appears, at Athena's instigation, in the guise of a beggar who makes himself known to each of the other principal characters in turn: to his son Telemachus; to the old maidservant Eurycleia, who recognizes a childhood scar on his leg; to the loyal swineherd Eumaeus and the cowherd Philoetius; to the insolent suitors and faithless servants, whom he methodically butchers; and finally to his wife Penelope and father Laertes. Each of these clearly differentiated recognitions divulges a great deal about both parties involved, but the last two are particularly revealing. When cagey Penelope, who has proved herself worthy of her husband's proverbial guile in baffling the importunate suitors' demands, nonchalantly instructs Eurycleia to move the wedding bed that her husband had long before attached to a living tree, she provokes the normally self-controlled Odysseus to a startled cry of dismay, outwitting the master at his own game; and husband and wife are triumphantly reunited in a marriage of true minds. And when, in the final book, Odysseus comes upon his father, Laertes, in the orchard and starts to embellish still another of his sailor's tales, and the old man breaks down in tears, his son drops his long-habituated mask and impulsively throws his arms around him. The cycle of recognitions is complete and the time for wariness and deception past.

If this succession of recognitions determines the resolution of the poem, however, the persistence of disguise has been no less essential to its development; nor are the two categories exclusive. On the contrary, Athena's shrewd appraisal suggests, and each recognition confirms, that disguise is not extrinsic to Odysseus' character but inseparable from it. Recognition does not annul disguise, since to recognize Odysseus is to know him not only as father, master, avenger, husband, or son, but above all as the man of multiple roles that he has been from the first and cannot cease to be without ceasing to be himself. In consequence, the most comprehensive recognitions of so indefinable a man are by those most similar to himself in versatility and intelligence — Athena and Penelope. Like Proteus, Odysseus is the sum of countless transformations, and it is these — not anything "behind" them — that most nearly define what he is. Without his ingenious fabrications and perpetually shifting (yet always appropriate) roles Odysseus is nearly unthinkable; for in metamorphosis is the comic hero's most stable identity and in make-believe is his truth to himself. An Odysseus content with a single part could only, like Prospero, bury his staff — or rather, his oar — and quietly wait for death to drift in from the sea.

Of Odysseus' many revealing disguises by far the most significant is that of beggar, which he wears for nearly half the poem. From Sacker of Cities he had sunk to Nobody, now he must rise from Beggar to King; and again the roles are closely intertwined. In the Ithaca of the Suitors Odysseus finds himself, before his triumph, in an alien kingdom, and his garb reflects his estrangement. The perils he encounters in this second half of the *Odyssey* come not from raging tempests and cannibalistic ogres, lascivious witches or virginal princesses, but from the everyday brutality and greed of ordinary men in a human society hopelessly out of joint. On the battlefield of the *Iliad* the Achaean warriors, for all their violent dissensions, shared an aristocratic code of conduct and a fierce determination to excel. Only Thersites stood wholly apart and was pommeled for his presumption by Odysseus himself. But in the kingdom of Ithaca, as Odysseus finds it on his return, its lawful rulers are outcasts no less than the lowly swineherd. Odysseus' memory is flouted; Telemachus driven from home and nearly assassinated on his return; Penelope confined to her rooms; Laertes exiled in the fields. The only evident norm of conduct is the acquisitive self-interest of the feudal nobles who rule the island in Odysseus' absence.

In contrast to the ostentatious arrogance of the suitors, which merely masks inward poverty, Odysseus need not scruple to wrap his tested nobility in the outer garb of a beggar. For them the discrepancy between external appearance and their actual condition is a dangerous delusion, for him a purposeful choice. Throughout the poem Odysseus has shown a capacity to adopt the most undignified and (by the standards of others) contemptible postures whenever the urgent caprices of fortune commanded. His deliberate rejection of immortality implied the acceptance of a humbler, indeed a more ludicrous, condition; and he never thereafter more than momentarily shrinks from the uttermost consequences of that choice. On the contrary, he readily identifies himself with the lowliest functions and most fundamental needs of human life—those universal constants that cut across all the artificial barriers erected by man against man. When King Alcinous of the Phaeacians wondered whether his guest might be a god Odysseus answered with an emphatic disclaimer:

> "Perish the thought, Alcinous! Not in the slightest
> do *I* resemble gods who dwell in heaven,
> in body or breed, but mortal men instead.
> Whatever human beings of your acquaintance
> have suffered most, my grief resembles theirs.
> Why, I could tell you hardships past all number
> inflicted on me by the gods' design.
> But let me eat my dinner, despite my anguish.
> Nothing's more doglike than a snarling belly
> that never lets its presence be forgotten,
> even when one is weary and grieved at heart,
> like me, but always bids us eat and drink,
> obliterates the memory of sorrow,
> and clamors to be filled."
>
> (Od. VII. 208-221)

This is an attitude such as Achilles, unmindful of human nourishment in his consuming sorrow for Patroclus, could only have scorned. Yet it is because of this forthright avowal of his biological humanity, with its common needs and limitations, that Odysseus can so easily don the rags of a beggar and establish with swineherd and servant woman a deeper rapport than with any other, apart from his own flesh and blood, in his native land. Even in an aristocratic world the comic hero affirms his lifetime membership in the great democracy of bodily hunger and pain.

Thus the disguise of beggar is no mere deceit. Indeed, since the role that Odysseus is playing (though few perceive it) is again himself, his disguise is the token of his authenticity. The contemptuous mockery of the suitors, on the other hand, lays bare their incapacity to penetrate beyond the empty forms of social distinctions, and its raucous climax presages their end. Moments before the test of the bow—in which Odysseus fully manifests who he is—the suitors are suddenly convulsed by uncontrollable hilarity, and the seer Theoclymenus ominously cries:

> "Ah, wretches, what evil now afflicts you? Night
> covers you from your faces to your knees,
> wailing has broken loose, cheeks stream with tears,
> the walls and lovely beams are daubed with blood,
> the court, the entry way are full of specters
> thirsting for Stygian darkness, and the sun
> fades from the sky, and hideous mist surrounds us."
> (Od. XX. 351-357)

"So he spoke; but all of them," Homer goes on to relate, "laughed merrily at him." Their derision is the symptom of impenetrable blindness and the portent of onrushing doom.

In the *Odyssey* it is not, of course, the suitors but Odysseus who laughs last; the comic hero's triumph, however sanguinary its execution, is unambiguous and complete. There will still be an oar to bury, as Tiresias had foretold, and a gentle death from the sea; but the poem concludes with the restoration of concord that follows the reunion of Odysseus with wife and father and the defeat of the slain suitors' kinsmen. In the opening lines of the epic Zeus had complained to Athena of mankind's perversity in blaming all woes on the gods; now, at the end, he gives celestial sanction to the victory Odysseus has won by his own hands. "With solemn oaths, let him be king forever," Zeus decrees,

> "and we shall wipe away the memory
> of sons and brothers slain. Let all be friends
> as once before, and peace and plenty flourish."
>
> (Od. XXIV. 483-486)

Through superior cunning and endurance the contemptible beggar succeeds in establishing an order on his own terms in place of the one that he remorselessly sweeps away. Athena enjoins an end to strife in the closing lines of the poem, and Odysseus' heart rejoices (as well it might) to obey. Rarely if ever again will the comic hero achieve so sweeping a triumph; more often his lot will be compromise if not defeat, or victory in imagination alone. The antagonist with whom he grapples will increasingly be a world too complex, too highly organized, or simply too big for any single human being to overcome except in fantasy or desire; he will therefore be forced to create an alternative realm of his own. But in the smaller and simpler world of Homer's Ithaca, society has not yet cornered a monopoly of the weapons, and the resourceful individual pitted against it still has a fighting chance. For once the underdog confronts the opposing forces of his world in a roughly equal contest, and decisively prevails. The opportunity will not soon come again; the impulse will remain undiminished.

II

JACKANAPES IN THE
HIGHEST

⸎

EVEN IN rags Odysseus was robed in the dignity of royal
birth and Homeric decorum. At the opposite pole from
any semblance of dignity, we encounter, in Aristophanes'
audacious burlesques, the comic hero in his lowliest and most
irreverent manifestation: the man at the very foot of the ladder
who will settle for nothing less than all. Squared off against a
social order far more immovable than that dislodged by Odysseus, and possessing no such attributes of physical strength,
kingly authority, or divine favor, he is thrown back on wit and
words alone; but with those tools he is able, at his most triumphant, to fabricate a kingdom subject to his own laws in
which the gods in heaven must acknowledge his sway.

So unique is the Attic Old Comedy of Aristophanes that it
has always posed a conundrum for posterity. Its riotous license,
ranging from excremental buffoonery to ethereal lyric, failed
in fact to survive Aristophanes' own lifetime. In his last two extant comedies the brio and chutzpah of his earlier plays have
accommodated themselves to the straitened pretensions of his
defeated city, and the domesticated wit of New Comedy already looms in the offing. Although Aristophanes' elegant
language was admired by the Roman rhetorician Quintilian —
and apparently by the Byzantine librarians who preserved

eleven of his plays—his unbridled excess was clearly a puzzle if not a scandal to the latter-day ancients. Aristotle passed him by and Horace noted only that the liberty of Old Comedy, however praiseworthy, soon became a vice deserving to be curbed by law.[1] And the moralist Plutarch, catholic though he was in his sympathies and interests, delivered the definitive condemnation of a cultivated Greek gentleman writing under the Roman imperium. In an essay comparing Aristophanes and Menander he accuses the former of a coarseness, vulgarity, and ribaldry wholly absent from his polished successor, and sternly declares: "Now Aristophanes is neither pleasing to the many nor endurable to the thoughtful, but his poetry is like a harlot who has passed her prime and then takes up the rôle of a wife, whose presumption the many cannot endure and whose licentiousness and malice the dignified abominate."[2] Once the value-judgments of "dignified" society were accepted as final Aristophanes could only be seen as a boorish anomaly, unquestionably laughable but quite unworthy of serious attention. In Ben Jonson's eyes Old Comedy was an "insolent and obscene" perversion guilty of "reducing all witt to the Originall Dungcart";[3] and for Voltaire (whose satire never took aim at society itself) Aristophanes was an upstart who had even presumed to burlesque a *philosophe* on the stage. "Among us," he indignantly writes, "this comic poet, who is neither comic nor poet, would not have been allowed to present farces at the Saint-Laurent fair; he seems to me much lower and more contemptible than Plutarch depicts him . . . An entire people whose bad government authorized such infamous licenses well deserved what befell it, to become the slave of the Romans and to be the slave of the Turks today."[4]

Only since the Romantic period, when A. W. Schlegel, reacting against the ossified refinement of the French neoclassical stage, praised Old Comedy as "the genuine *poetic* species" of comic drama, a species extending no less than tragedy "beyond the limits of reality into the domain of free creative fancy," has Aristophanes been widely acclaimed as one of the world's great poets. In Schlegel's conception

Comedy . . . is the democracy of poetry, and is more inclined
even to the confusion of anarchy than to any circumscription
of the general liberty of its mental powers and purposes, and
even of its separate thoughts, sallies, and allusions . . . As
Tragedy delights in harmonious unity, Comedy flourishes in
a chaotic exuberance; it seeks out the most motley contrasts,
and the unceasing play of cross purposes . . . The comic
poet, as well as the tragic, transports his characters into an
ideal element: not, however, into a world subjected to necessity, but one where the caprice of inventive wit rules without
check or restraint, and where all the laws of reality are suspended. He is at liberty, therefore, to invent an action as
arbitrary and fantastic as possible.[5]

Even Schlegel, however, for all his discerning praise, expressed
reservations concerning Aristophanes' "vulgar and even corrupt . . . personal propensities" and the offensiveness of his
jokes "to good manners and good taste." The fact of blatant
indecorum remained a stumbling block which proper classical
scholars endeavored to remove by portraying Aristophanes as
essentially a satirist, even a moralist, whose most shocking
indecencies were in reality aimed at *reforming* manners. For
Werner Jaeger, "Attic comedy, the successor of the iambic, was
the first critical poetry in the true and higher sense . . . Comedy
was the censorship of Athens."[6] And to Bruno Snell, Aristophanes was a "romantic reactionary" somewhat implausibly
responsible for the "moralization of poetry" in ancient Greece.[7]
Plutarch's disreputable harlot has been transmogrified into a
thoroughly respectable (if insufferably dowdy) middle-aged
matron.

This Aristophanes *moralisé*—village schoolmaster or university don—is surely a far greater distortion than Plutarch's: an
Aristophanes who has lost the power to shock or outrage! Onto
his name has been grafted the alien theory of comedy as ridicule aimed at laughing its characters (and its audience) into a
more acceptable pattern of conduct. Yet the invective in
Aristophanes' plays is far too scandalously personal to lend itself to reform—it rather invites retaliation—and there is little

evidence to suggest a moral intent. Any criterion of civilized behavior (such as Molière's *Raison*) by which transgressors might be found derisively wanting is utterly absent, and it is this embarrassing lack that has made Old Comedy difficult to treat in the terminology of cultured discourse. In these comedies we are constantly aware, on the contrary—not only in their riotous obscenities and irreverent travesties but in the carnival spirit that percolates through the most scathing abuse—of primordial values and elemental needs that continually threaten to smash the prevailing social order to smithereens. Such a festival of exuberant excess has rarely been tolerated in broad daylight, and certainly not in public religious observances. The miracle is not that Old Comedy died young but that it emerged from the cradle.

The investigations of Francis Cornford and other scholars have linked this festive spirit to rites of fertility celebrating the annual rebirth of the vegetable kingdom. However tentative these speculations must remain, it seems almost certain (on the authority of Aristotle himself) that the *kômos,* or revels, in which comedy had its origin was somehow associated with the phallic worship then actively practiced in the countryside of Greece.[8] Comedy was quite overtly a celebration of biological life; therefore its natural enemy would be whatever restraints impeded the development of the vital impulse. Not only law and order but institutional religion might be challenged by the ungovernable upstart, since comedy (as Nietzsche failed to observe) is far more limitless and "Dionysian" in its impulse than tragedy. "The reign of Zeus stood in the Greek mind for the existing moral and social order," Cornford writes; "its overthrow, which is the theme of so many of the comedies, might be taken to symbolise, as in the *Clouds,* the breaking up of all ordinary restraints, or again, as in the *Birds* and the *Plutus,* the restoration of the Golden Age."[9] If Aristophanes was in any sense a "romantic reactionary," then, it was not to some simpler Athens that he looked back but to the reign of Saturn; and this has its true existence in the potential present, not in the vanished past. His heroes are those who refuse to accept the inevitability of the world as they find it and set out to make it over, come hell or high water. There is ultimately nothing to stand in their way, since "the Gods in Aristophanes," as Cornford rightly observes, ". . . are always inferior to the human protagonist."[10]

The first critic to deal extensively with the implications of the Aristophanic protagonist's confrontation with an antagonistic world was Cedric H. Whitman in his seminal study *Aristophanes and the Comic Hero* (1964). For Whitman, the "primary mode" of Aristophanes' comedy is fantasy, not satire or criticism, and its "poetic core" is the individual. The moral imperatives on which the social order depends are not binding on this individual, for "Morality implies limit, and Aristophanes' affinities are all with the limitless . . . Boundlessness itself, one might say, is the essence of the Aristophanean comic impulse."[11] In his contest with the world this anarchic being makes constant use of the quality which Whitman denotes by the modern Greek word *poneria:* "the ability to get the advantage of somebody or some situation by virtue of an unscrupulous, but thoroughly enjoyable exercise of craft."[12] Whitman thus proceeds to describe the essential comic hero of Aristophanes' plays:

A desperate small fellow, inexcusably declaring himself for a social savior; an utterly self-centered rogue of *poneria,* representing a universal gesture of thumb-to-nose unto all the high and mighty; a coward who runs away from his enemies for the moment, and then dances on their graves with godless cheer; a fast talker, a hoper-for-the-best and a believer-in-the-worst; a creature of infinite ambition, infinite responsiveness, and infinite appetite—the comic hero, as represented in Aristophanes, somehow makes up a figure of salvation, survival against odds; he is the self militant, and devil-take-the-means . . . The world as it is perhaps cannot be transcended, but the comic hero is not stopped by that. He invents his own world and then subdues it.[13]

Through consummate cunning and sheer bravado the comic hero may even succeed where all others fail, in the ultimate labor of scaling the inaccessible heavens.

Responses to the comic hero, as this epitome suggests, have ranged from contemptuous revulsion to spirited approbation. Only when the values of biological life are immediate or urgent enough to challenge the supremacy of moral and social sanctions can so offensive an upstart be perceived as a *hero*; the uniqueness of Aristophanes lies in his bold conjunction of the primitive and the civilized. He exalts the most elemental human impulses in the most artful poetic forms. He takes the roguish trickster of popular fable and catapults him to the skies (trailing clouds of ordure as he goes) in lavish fantasies presented at public expense in the religious festivities of imperial Athens. He beards the idols of a city at war with insolent aplomb and modulates a Bronx cheer with the artistry of Mozart. There has never again been anything remotely like it.

The unrelenting contest of elastic individual with refractory world is the inexhaustible source of comic heroism; and it is therefore no accident that the contest, or *agôn,* lies at the heart of Attic Old Comedy. This contest may well have originated, as Cornford hypothesizes, in a ritual combat between the partisans of Summer and Winter in the rites of autumn or spring. In Aristophanes it frequently remains a life-and-death struggle between the joyous fertility of peace and the barren dearth of war. Nowhere is this antagonism more explicit than in the young dramatist's first surviving play, the *Acharnians,* whose militant protagonist Dicaeopolis ("Justcity") is a full-blown paradigm of comic heroism under the banner of life. The play provides an excellent example of the intricate structure of Aristophanic comedy. In the prologue—the section preceding the entrance of the chorus—we discover the crusty old countryman Dicaeopolis waiting alone for the assembly to convene and grumbling to himself about the paucity of his pleasures since leaving his village for Athens. Today he is fully determined to shout down any proposal except for peace. When the assembly at last begins, a minigod commissioned by heaven to make peace between Athens and Sparta is silenced when he tries to address the citizens, who then applaud a patently phony ambassador from the Persian king. By now good citizen Dicaeopolis has had a bellyful of civic spirit and sends the spurned divinity trundling off to Sparta to bring back a private peace for himself and his family. His heavenly messengerboy promptly rushes back with three bottles of peace which Dicaeopolis sniffs, ecstatically choosing the largest. But the old charcoal-burners of outlying Acharnia, dyspeptic veterans for whom peace is a fighting word, have gotten wind of the godling's treasonous mission and are hard on his heels. Dicaeopolis withdraws into his house as the Acharnians enter (in the brief choral section called the *parodos*) fulminating against the unknown offender who has disrupted their war.

Now the battle lines are drawn and the engagement between the comic hero and an aroused social order begins in good earnest. Dicaeopolis returns from his house with his wife and daughter, carrying a ritual phallus—a graphic exhortation to "make love not war"—and sacrifices to Dionysus in a lovely ceremony of thanksgiving terminated by a shower of stones from the indignant charcoal-burners. He fends them off by threatening to slay a scuttleful of their precious charcoal, and they reluctantly consent to hear his defense. The formal debate, or agôn, follows. The opponents are Dicaeopolis, who scrounges the filthiest rags he can find from the tragic poet Euripides and makes his plea as a lowly beggar, a social pariah; and the blustering general Lamachus—a prominent Athenian commander of the day—who puffs himself up with martial glory and struts forth in full panoply, crowned by a monstrously oversized plume towering toward the heavens. The chorus of hostile old men had already divided in half upon hearing Dicaeopolis' plea for peace; now the spectacle of Lamachus' menacing crest is enough to determine the wavering remnant, and they unanimously reverse themselves and pronounce in favor of the man in rags.

Only halfway through the play, then, the contest has been essentially decided (in other plays it continues until the end), and decided, as in virtually every case, in behalf of the upstart and underdog, the improbable comic hero. The intricate song and dance known as the *parabasis* divides the play in two, like the half-time festivities of a football game. Whatever its ritual origins may have been, for Aristophanes it is a kind of poetic saturnalia in which the dramatist himself exults in the freedoms his hero has won — including the freedom to blow full blast on his own horn. The scenes that follow the parabasis in the *Acharnians* (as in some of the other plays) display the hero enjoying the fruits of his victory and fending off various pests who know a good thing when they see it and hope to share in the spoils. Dicaeopolis, the only man blessed with peace and plenty in all Greece, sets up his own little marketplace and trades on scandalous terms with the wretched starvelings who have continued at war. (A destitute Megarian farmer, for example, sells his daughters as pigs for a ration of garlic and salt, and wishes he could throw his wife and mother into the bargain.) To underscore the contrast even more sharply, Lamachus reappears on one side of the stage and calls for helmet and spear in preparation for a battle while Dicaeopolis, on the other, is calling for soup and wine in preparation for a bash. When they return from their respective engagements moments later, Lamachus limps onto the stage groaning and swathed in bandages, bruised and battered from head to toe; Dicaeopolis, for his part, reels drunkenly into view supported on either arm by a winsome young whore. The moral needs no belaboring, the victory is crushing and total; Lamachus slinks ignominiously away and abandons the stage to Dicaeopolis and his jubilant supporters. The brief finale, often called the *kômos* from the revels that gave comedy its name, is here as elsewhere a festive tribute to the conquering comic hero.

It is worth considering the outline of this earliest extant comedy of western literature, since its dominant pattern is so clearly one of celebration rather than ridicule. The progression from agôn to kômos is an upward movement from dissension and turmoil to definitive liberation from social and moral restraints; and once the pompous upholders of things as they are have been exposed as humbugs and dethroned from their sham elevations there is no one left to pass censorious judgment on the victor. Dicaeopolis is the little man who by his impertinent refusal to defer to authority turns the world topsy-turvy and ends up at its apex. Like Odysseus in a more aristocratic age he submits to derision as the necessary consequence of his choice of life while letting no opportunity slip to turn the tables and impose his own terms. He too adheres with tenacious flexibility to his purpose and exhibits a mastery of verbal legerdemain, and his triumph over Lamachus is no less decisive — though certainly less homicidal — than that of Odysseus over the hapless suitors. Passing through a series of transmutations from disgruntled citizen to Bacchic celebrant and abject beggar, the splenetic old man who had counted (like some character of Samuel Beckett's) no more than four paltry pleasures in a lifetime of tribulations steps forth in the plenitude of comic glory, his zest for life, like his organs of procreation, conspicuously resurrected. His buxom trophies signalize the climactic rejuvenation of a hero who succeeds by gall and imagination in making the hazardous passage from the ridiculous to the sublime.

This pattern of bodily and spiritual regeneration following release from disfiguring social constraint will remain the leading Aristophanic motif throughout the bewildering diversity of the plays that follow. Not until the *Birds,* produced eleven years later, will a comic hero more impressive than Dicaeopolis in converting wish to fulfillment take the boards, but in the intervening plays the full complexity of the contest becomes apparent. Aristophanes is among the few supreme fantasists in all literature, but his wildest fantasy retains immediacy through its close dialectical relationship with the real. Flights of hyperbolic imagination are always held in hand by an ironclad grasp on the present. The comic attitude toward the confinements of existing reality is satire, just as revelry is the comic response to release from those bonds — a release attained, in Aristophanes' poetry, through transfiguring fantasy. Thus satire and celebration are the poles of a single vision; and even the most audacious comic hero will necessarily appear as an object of ridicule to the extent that his very struggle still links him, while unregenerate, with the real.

This intertwining of contrary attitudes is particularly evident in the three plays — *Knights, Clouds,* and *Wasps* — that followed the *Acharnians* in as many years. None of Aristophanes' other comedies is so immediately anchored to his moment as the *Knights,* a timber-shivering broadside against his enemy

Cleon (who had already hauled him to court for *lèse-majesté*) fired off at the very moment of the demagogue's greatest military achievement; for the young playwright was no more deterred by unfavorable odds than his heroes. Against a foe both more odious and far more formidable than the windbag Lamachus, Aristophanes pits a comic challenger of a different stamp, an upstart Sausageseller who triumphs not (like Dicaeopolis) by opposing a positive vision to his antagonist's chicanery but by brazenly one-upping the rascal at his own disreputable game. The play is one protracted agôn nearly from start to finish—a spirited contest in vulgar effrontery and shameless deceit in which the Sausageseller consistently tops every card his desperate adversary can play until he usurps his office, casting out the erstwhile darling of Athens to peddle dog-and-donkeymeat sausages at the city gates. In the course of their long confrontation the Sausageseller exposes the Paphlagonian Cleon not so much for a scoundrel as for a scoundrel manqué, an upstart like himself who lacks the stuff to carry his impudent pretensions to their destined fulfillment.

Because he shares in so many of Cleon's detestable attributes the Sausageseller is, of course, far from invulnerable to the abuse with which the play seethes; but by carrying these qualities to their outrageous extreme he neutralizes their loathesomeness by hilarity and commands applause for his indisputable virtuosity. The chorus, who abominate Cleon, gleefully hail the Sausageseller's superiority in the employment of shifty tricks and wily words, the comic hero's stock in trade. "From heaven thou art come to us As Man's consummate blessing," they exult in R. H. Webb's free rendition, as they exhort their glib-tongued champion on:

> Go wield the trident, rouse the wind,
>   The mighty seas awaken,
> Stirring the whole of humankind . . .
>   And bringing home the bacon![14]

To label such panegyric merely ironical would be to overlook entirely the heroic dimension of Aristophanic burlesque, whose characteristic mode is not deflation but hyperbole. (Aristophanes' affinity with the grandiose Aeschylus was more than sentimental.) Nor is the Sausageseller *only* a more unscrupulous Cleon. He consistently denounces his rival's warmongering and graft—in those departments he will not deign to compete—and the fruit of his victory is not his own advancement alone but the rejuvenation of the Athenian people as embodied in the gruff old gentleman Demos. When Demos emerges resplendent with glory at the end of the play, boiled down to pristine health and vigor in his steambath of youth, and is awarded two nubile young damsels as a token of restoration, the Sausageseller's personal triumph merges, like that of Dicaeopolis before him, with the triumph of life.

Even in this most abusive of Aristophanes' plays the pattern is therefore unmistakably one of festive exultation. Yet the Sausageseller's comic heroism is less complete and convincing than Dicaeopolis' had been. His association with Cleon in the course of their duel has been too intimate to allow him to free himself altogether from the stigma attached to his defeated opponent. For all his panache in the fray his imagination is irredeemably pedestrian, and he undertakes his allotted role only at the prodding of others. In consequence, the qualities that bring him his well-deserved victory in the agôn have disturbingly little to do with those celebrated in the kômos. By an artfully contrived sleight-of-hand the playwright transfers the regeneration of the comic ending from its malodorous agent to a more prepossessing if essentially passive bystander, old Demos. The seams in this patchwork of comedy and abuse are distinctly visible, since for all the play's energetic verve the surplus weight of invective in the *Knights* is almost too much for the comic pattern to sustain.

The swing toward the satirical pole of the comic vision—toward preoccupation with the real over the possible—is evident in very different ways in the *Clouds* and the *Wasps* as well. The *Clouds* has always been Aristophanes' problem play. Like the *Knights* of the previous year it pillories a prominent living figure, Socrates; and for this it has been the object of much retrospective opprobrium, as if the twenty-two-year-old dramatist's spoof were responsible for the philosopher's condemnation almost a quarter-century later. The legitimate problem is one of structure and intent. The play which Aristophanes confidently regarded as his finest to date fell flat in performance, receiving only third prize in the competition, and the disappointed author thoroughly revamped it for publication. The version we have is this subsequent revision, in which the ending in particular seems to have been completely overhauled.

The extant *Clouds* is a play self-consciously written against the grain of the comic pattern: a comedy without a hero in which every principal character is riddled with derision and the climactic element of triumphant regeneration is lacking. It is thus even more thoroughgoingly abusive than the *Knights,* but with a fundamental innovation that completely alters its tonality. Here the poetic fantasy which is normally associated by Aristophanes with the vision of liberation from present constraint (and which had been largely absent from the earthbound *Knights*) is boldly injected into the satirical portrait itself, so that satire becomes fantastic and fantasy satirical. The chorus of Old Comedy, which presumably began as phallic celebrants, continued to wear the badge of their original office ostentatiously girded to their loins; yet here — in what must have been a daring break with tradition — they appear as ethereal cloud-maidens disencumbered not only of the red leather phallus but of any contact with things of this earth.

Yet if the chorus give the play a dimension of lyrical grace in striking contrast to the coarse-grained slapstick of the *Knights,* its characters lamentably fail to raise themselves to any such level of vision. Fantasy enters satire only through the totally spurious association of Socrates' philosophical speculations with the airy regions of the clouds. But the Socrates of this play, who makes his entry in a basket dangling between heaven and earth, is about as ethereal as the Sausageseller, and far less candid: a pure unadulterated humbug, a gross unprincipled charlatan. Old Strepsiades, who goes to school with the shyster, gloatingly anticipates that he will henceforth be held "a bold smooth-tongued audacious reckless patcher of lies" and so on in a rapturous inventory of unsavory rascalities.[15] These, of course, are the qualities which the comic hero is renowned for turning to his advantage (and it is easy to imagine a triumphant Socrates as the comic hero of another play or even of the original *Clouds*); but here they remain sterile and negative attributes because their connection with any liberating vision is so patently a fraud. On the other hand Strepsiades, who turns violently against his adoptive master, is both too gullible and too moralistic to fill the comic hero's role; and his son Pheidippides is an empty-headed fop.

With such a cast of characters the traditional comic structure could hardly make do, and Aristophanes ingeniously improvised both its central elements, the agôn and the kômos. The formal agôn of the play does not engage the principal characters at all; it is instead a debate between the Just and the Unjust Logic in which the wise and upright arguments of the former are resoundingly worsted by the ad hominem obscenity of the latter. The victory of the unjust Socratic Logic, through a hedonistic appeal to promiscuous license, is not, however, a cause for rejoicing as the victories of Dicaeopolis and the Sausageseller had been, since the overturning of law and order that he advocates offers nothing better in their place. Once Pheidippides has graduated from Socrates' thinkery he pictures an alternative order not in the glowing colors of Dicaeopolis' vision of plenty, but only as an unhampered opportunity, through subversion of ancient restraints, to do unto others as they have done unto him — a philosophical justification for beating his father. In opposition to such an alternative the Just Logic's straitlaced advocacy of conventional wisdom is the only positive vision set forth in the play, and Aristophanes' claim in the revised parabasis that his comedy is eminently moral (*sôphrôn*) is hard to dispute. Even the flighty Clouds turn schoolmistress at the end and lecture Strepsiades on his moral culpability as a lover of knavery for his son's corruption: now that they have lured him astray they will teach him to fear the gods!

As if he were seeking respectability in reaffirmation of communal values after his dangerous indiscretions, Aristophanes does appear for once, in the *Clouds,* in the incongruous guise of apologist for things as they are. Under these circumstances the revelry of the traditional kômos would hardly be fitting, and in its stead we behold an orgy of frenzied destruction as Strepsiades burns the hated school to the ground. There is release of a sort but little jubilation in this vengeful climax, since the demolition of Socrates' phony world leaves nothing behind but the world as it was before. Whatever reasons the Athenian audience may have had for finding the original *Clouds* defective, it is hard not to feel somewhat cheated by this second version as we vainly anticipate a regeneration that never comes. By binding itself too closely to a given morality (instead of fabricating its own) the most innovative of Aristophanes' early comedies fails to satisfy the impulse to renewal which is the heart and soul of the comic.

In the *Wasps* the satirical purpose that dominates and to a degree distorts the *Knights* and the *Clouds* is more harmoniously integrated with the comic structure. The protagonist Philocleon is a befuddling bundle of contradictions. As a partisan of Cleon hopelessly addicted to the Athenian mania for litigation he is a conspicuous target of satire, yet he engages our sympathies as no character since Dicaeopolis has done. If Socrates in the *Clouds* seemed a perversion of the comic hero, employing his repertory of arts to no higher end than immediate flimflam, Philocleon is a comic hero in reverse. He achieves the fruits of regeneration by carrying conventionality to its ludicrous extreme in a play best understood as a burlesque of comedy itself.

Having found himself in hot water for open assaults on the social order in his scandalous first plays (difficulties to which he again alludes in this one), and having humiliatingly failed to win over the opposition by his travesty of philosophical novelties in the *Clouds,* Aristophanes now presents his spectators with a bizarre comic hero molded in their own image. By being, in Douglass Parker's phrase, "a calculated insult to the audience's intelligence,"[16] the play is far closer to the anarchic spirit of primitive comedy than the civilized *Clouds.* The element of burlesque is prominent from the beginning when Philocleon (confined to his house to curb his irrepressible urge to sit on juries) imitates the arch-comic hero Odysseus by contriving to escape under a donkey's belly — and is caught. His captor is his son and antagonist Bdelycleon ("Cleon-loather"), and the tangled relationship between these two is at the heart of the play. Bdelycleon, in an amusing reversal of the father-son role, is the advocate of level-headed moderation and common sense in his running battle with his father's obsession, which knows no limit; and since the arguments are all on his side as he methodically exposes Philocleon's self-deceptions, he wins the agôn hands down and easily converts the wasplike old men of the chorus, his father's fervent supporters, to his cause.

Just because Philocleon's idée fixe does indeed know no limit, however, it exerts a wacky attraction absent from his son's sober logic. Both the resourcefulness of his stratagems (even if all are abortive) and the grandiosity of his schemes proclaim Philocleon's imagination the most fertile of any Aristophanic protagonist since the *Acharnians*. This legalistic fanatic soars in unbridled fantasy beyond all law and all order, and dares to proclaim his authority on the jury bench equal to that of Zeus in the heavens. Instead of surrendering his cherished vocation after defeat in the agôn, Philocleon proceeds, at his son's instigation, to set up a private courtroom at home and to create (as Dicaeopolis had done in his private market) a world subject to his own laws. The hilarious trial of a dog arraigned for eating a Sicilian cheese is definitive proof of how far Philocleon's jurisimprudence has gone toward the liberation of absolute lunacy. It is therefore poetically just that the kômos should celebrate the regeneration not — as expected — of the victor in the agôn, the prim Bdelycleon, but of his reprobate father who returns from a banquet roaring drunk, a torch in one hand and a flute-girl by the other, after breaking every pate in his path and every law on the books. This ending is not so much a volte-face for Philocleon as his unmasking: a revelation to himself and others of the paragon of lawlessness and disorder that he had always been. Having transferred his congenital excess from litigation to a more suitable domain, he celebrates his emancipation with an explosion of dance that leaves his demoralized son and the outclassed chorus panting breathlessly in his wake. This most foolish and accidental of Aristophanes' comic heroes exploits the opportunities of the revels, at least, with unsurpassable savoir-faire.

After the intricate convolutions of the comic pattern explored in the three preceding plays, the *Peace* — Aristophanes' fifth extant comedy in five years — strikes a note of purposeful simplicity. It is the closest of all the plays to pure festivity. The heavenward flight of Trygaeus on a dung-beetle's back symbolizes the comic hero's inglorious acquisition of glory, and his rescue of Peace from the pit in which she has been impounded by War reaffirms his deepest impulse, obscured in the *Knights, Clouds,* and *Wasps*: devotion to life. The satirical element is strictly muted in a play where lyrical celebration predominates long before the culminating union of Trygaeus (whose name is redolent of *trygê,* the vintage) with Opôra, or Harvest, in the matrimonial kômos. (Opôra is attended by Theôria, a personification of the theater audience, so that the play might be seen as a myth of the birth of comedy — sometimes called *trygôdia* — from the spirit of peace.) But if the comic pattern is delineated with unusual clarity, the play's limitation lies in the absence of meaningful conflict: there is no developed agôn, and the formulaic intruders are brushed aside without effort. As a result Trygaeus is very nearly Aristophanes' least memorable protagonist. He triumphs, and through his triumph regenerates a thankful land; but there have been no major obstacles to thwart or test him. Acting "on behalf of all the Hellenes"[17] in a play that smacks of allegory he seems little more than a symbol. And no comic hero can be an abstraction except by abdicating the individuality that declares him authentic.

The *Birds,* produced seven years later, has been acclaimed as Aristophanes' masterpiece, but there has been scant consensus concerning its meaning, if any. Some have viewed the play as a satire on its hero's ambitions;[18] others have categorized it as "pure" fantasy and escapist flight. To A. W. Schlegel it seemed "a harmless display of merry pranks, which hit alike at gods and men without any particular object in view";[19] to Gilbert Murray, "an 'escape' from worry and the sordidness of life, away into the land of sky and clouds and poetry."[20] But from our perspective the *Birds* illuminates the limits and potentialities of the Aristophanic comic hero in his contest with the world by unraveling the hitherto tangled skein of satirical and festive motifs. In this play satire is unequivocally directed against existing society — *all* existing society — and fantasy lavished on the limitless possibilities of a world elsewhere. The "meaning" of the comedy lies in its hero's bold transcendence through imagination and language of a reality which he can otherwise neither escape nor change, and in the burgeoning of his latent powers that results from his transformation.

In the prologue we meet two disillusioned elderly Athenians, Euelpides ("Hopeful") and Peisthetaerus[21] ("Persuasive" or "Trusty"), who have fled their native city in quest of a better lot among the birds. Repelled by the legal bickering of the Athenians (Philocleon's passion in the *Wasps*), they are seeking mellifluous song and perpetual leisure. One insuperable limitation to the comic hero's desires is clear from the outset: these men no longer aspire, like Odysseus in an earlier age, to supplant the offending regime by main force. Instead they must discover — or, if need be, invent — an alternative world for themselves. At first their only purpose is flight, but a turning point soon occurs when Peisthetaerus, in a moment of inspiration, proposes that the birds reclaim their lost supremacy by founding a city in the sky. With this he alters at a stroke the terms of his enterprise. Instead of fleeing from urban congestion to celestial freedom (an escapist daydream of ancient vintage!) he will combine these seemingly irreconcilable spheres — *polis,* "city," and *polos,* "sky"; *nomos,* "law," and *nomos,* "birdsong" — into a new creation shaped and governed by his own fecund intelligence.

For the heavenly city will be the work of man; Peisthetaerus will lead and the birds will follow. First he must win them over, and this is his task in the agôn. His go-between is the once-human Hoopoe, who summons the variegated chorus of birds to "learn of a revolution"[22] and acts as Peisthetaerus' advocate in the contest that follows. The instinctively hostile birds threaten to tear the cowering human intruders limb from limb,

but the Hoopoe persuades them to hear the strangers' pro-
posals. They are enemies by nature, he concedes, but friends by
mind; and this comedy will be the triumph of mind over nature. The birds remain understandably wary of so deceitful a
creature as man, but consent to give ear; and in his stirring
appeal for the restoration of their former dominion — the fabled
reign of freedom before the ascendancy of Zeus — Peisthetaerus
exhibits a mental dexterity and a verbal command such as wily
Odysseus himself might have envied. The agôn is his without a
squawk of dissent as the awestruck birds proclaim him their
savior and endorse his grand design of wresting away the scepter of empire from the usurping Olympians. They will provide
the muscle, they promise, and leave the thinking to him.

So the stage is set for the comic hero's most audacious and
most definitive undertaking — his assault on the seat of everything inimical to his boundless desires, the throne of Zeus. In
the dazzling parabasis (the first and more elaborate of two in
this play) the birds trace their genesis to the primeval union of
Chaos and Love, and assert their primacy over the gods both in
birth and in usefulness to men. The grave and nonsensical
merge in this festival of imagination unshackled by terrestrial
logic. The two refugees then reappear, transformed into birds,
and Peisthetaerus hits on a high-sounding name for their ethereal city: Cloudcuckooland, where in days of yore (he declares)
the young Olympian gods had bested the earthborn giants in
the bruising battle of braggadocio. While Euelpides departs to
oversee the building of their circumcelestial wall, Peisthetaerus
bids a priest make sacrifice "to the new gods"[23] — a grave religious offense in the Athens which he has fled and in which this
play was being performed. Before his showdown with the old
gods, however, there are human challengers to be overcome.
One by one and with mounting repulsiveness — from rhapsodic
poetaster to oraclemonger, surveyor, government inspector,
and peddler of proclamations — the representatives of the old
order crowd onstage, eager to enjoy benefits of the new; and
one by one they are driven off with curses and blows. These
charlatans and bureaucrats incarnate everything that Peisthetaerus has put behind him, and his repudiation of their claims

gives surety that his brave new world will not be tainted by the corrosive vices of Athens.

Having repulsed this first onslaught of mortal invaders he re-emerges to learn that a god has penetrated Cloudcuckooland's new defenses. The birds mobilize for war; but the interloper is only the harmless Olympian messenger Iris, whose bluster instantly dissipates when Peisthetaerus threatens to incinerate Zeus's palace and thrust his visible battering-ram between the goddess' thighs. With breathtaking impudence the comic hero perpetrates the most blasphemous *hybris* (Iris' own word)[24] and makes it stick. The gods who had won supremacy by outblustering the giants are defeated on their own turf by a brazen upstart who reasserts the prerogatives of the earthborn in the skies.

A herald from the world of men presents Peisthetaerus with a golden crown in recognition of his unparalleled gifts, and another drove of intruders enters clamoring after wings. Each of these johnny-come-latelies embodies a misapprehension of the comic virtues that have elevated Peisthetaerus. To the brash young parricide (as to Pheidippides in the *Clouds*), transcendence of human law means only the license to beat his father: not liberation but inversion. Plus ça change, plus c'est la même chose. For the dithyrambic poet Cinesias, floating effortlessly on a cushion of bombast, words are not a means of transformation but the be-all and end-all. He aspires not to the empyrean but only as high as the vaporous clouds. His more sinister counterpart, the stool pigeon, views wings as nothing more than an instrument of his degrading profession. Peisthetaerus' explanation of their true meaning—

> By words alone the mind is raised on high
> and man exalted[25]—

goes over his head, and only the whip can send him flying.

Once these pretenders to unmerited wings have been disposed of Peisthetaerus is set to face down the omnipotent gods. But by now there is no real contest; these Olympians prove to be a sorry lot. They may once have toppled the Titans down to

Tartarean night and hurtled the hundred-handed giants from
their mountaintop, but they are clearly no match for a comic
hero in his prime. It is appropriately the tragic liberator of
man, Prometheus, who divulges to his comic successor that the
gods have been cut off from the nourishing fumes of sacrifice
by the rebellious birds' blockade, and are slowly starving.
Armed with Promethean foresight Peisthetaerus outmaneuvers
the divine ambassadors, Poseidon, Heracles, and the inarticulate Triballus, with a dexterity equal to that employed by Odysseus against the subhuman Polyphemus. Having given incontestable proof of man's capacity to raise himself to the heavens
he now draws the gods down to earth and pits his overflowing
wits against their shrunken bellies. The outcome is never in
doubt. By talking circles around a baffled and famished Heracles—the deified paragon of traditional valor—Peisthetaerus
not only wins Zeus's scepter for the birds but takes Divine Sovereignty (Basileia) as his own bride, thereby demonstrating
once and for all the decisive superiority of the human to the
divine.

Thus if the Aristophanic comic hero begins by recognizing
his impotence to alter the physical world, this limitation gives
rise to his transmutation of reality through the potency of the
word. The hymeneal sung in honor of Peisthetaerus as he
emerges wielding the thunderbolt of Zeus and leading his newly
won bride, though of course a spoof, is at the same time a joyous tribute to the awakening of prolific faculties long dormant.
To perceive such a kômos, with its festive song and dance, as
primarily satirical would be to misconstrue the regenerative
spirit of comedy *toto caelo*. To be sure it is all a joke, but what
of that? The comic hero shows his prowess above all in this, that
he finds the world a deplorably bad joke (a joke on *him*) and
makes it over into a smashing good one. To be sure it is "only"
fantasy, "only" nonsense, signifying nothing in the sober quo-
tidian world; but the exultant capacity to forge transcendence
of human limit out of sheer nothing may well be, as Cedric
Whitman suggests, the supreme achievement of comic heroism
at its acme of glory. "Meaning is a word," Whitman notes,
"and it requires a hero to give the word meaning."[26] To Aris-

tophanes, as to Shakespeare, reality would be a poor affair without the shimmering superstructure of fantasies that we build upon its immutable yet insubstantial foundations; and in this exalted craft Peisthetaerus is a master-builder worthy of the intrepid poet who gave him birth.

Produced in 414 B.C., the year of the fateful Athenian expedition against Syracuse, the *Birds* both reacts against the aggressive spirit of that enterprise and partakes of the heady self-confidence that inspired it. The dispatch of this vast armada to crush a maritime rival on distant shores brought to a climax the arrogant militarism that Aristophanes had lampooned in Lamachus eleven years earlier. The irrevocable commitment of Athenian energies to imperial conquest may indeed have contributed to the crystallization of Aristophanes' comic outlook in the *Birds*. No longer would comedy couple with satire in quest of reform; that chimerical hope, if Aristophanes had ever truly held it, was of the past. Instead of competing with the enemy on his own terms (like the Sausageseller of the *Knights*) or reconciling himself to the social order by cauterization of its gangrenous tissue (like Strepsiades in the *Clouds*), the comic hero now resolutely determines to fabricate a celestial empire at the opposite pole from everything that imperial Athens has come to embody. The result is his most unqualified and stupendous triumph. At the same time Peisthetaerus shares in the energetic spirit that propelled the would-be conquerors of Sicily. Giving short shrift to Euelpides' vision of indolent luxury he torpedoes every obstacle in his path by refusing to recognize its existence. In this he is more successful, in a world where fantasy rules without serious opposition, than the Athenian commanders who engineered a debacle from which their city never fully recovered.

During the years of impending defeat that followed the Sicilian calamity the heroes of Aristophanes' plays, like the Athenian populace, learned to satisfy themselves with diminished dreams. The three surviving comedies produced before the capitulation of Athens in 404 are among the dramatist's most accomplished, but all three reflect an atmosphere of sobered illusion and muted aspiration in which no heroic visionaries challenge the powers that be or reshape the universe in their own image. Lysistrata is the equal of any Aristophanic hero in the resourcefulness and determination with which she pursues her sexual boycott of the Athenian soldiery, but for the first time in the "peace plays" cessation of war has become a sufficient end. Nothing remains of Dicaeopolis' subversive exposé of the war-mongers, nor of the ebullient hope that followed Trygaeus' rescue of the demure goddess Peace. The terrible dilemma of the play is that Lysistrata is compelled to deny—if only for the nonce—the impulse to fertility whose celebration is comedy's deepest meaning and primal source. The *Thesmophoriazusae* of the same year (411) is a brilliantly executed "pure" comedy—portentous of the genre's future—in which the great comic theme of metamorphosis is reduced to transvestitism, and the protagonist displays heroic resources only in saving his skin. The searing ridicule and soaring fancy of the earlier plays are easily reconciled to the less demanding ends of stylistic parody now that the will to imaginative transformation has lamentably passed from citizens and sausagesellers to poets alone.

In the predominance of its literary motifs the *Frogs* of 405 resembles the *Thesmophoriazusae*, but this last of Aristophanes' masterpieces, performed when surrender and possible annihilation were at the gates of Athens, portrays the grand poetry of the city's past as a force undefeated even by death. In the restoration of Aeschylus from the underworld, the comic theme of regeneration finds one of its noblest expressions. Yet regeneration does not derive from the comic protagonist Dionysus (who is merely a referee in the belated agôn between Aeschylus and Euripides) but from a power outside and finally above him. The tragic Aeschylus, for all the hilarity of his half-incomprehensible rant, is the victor in the agôn and the hero hailed in the solemn kômos; while the comic Dionysus, who has undergone the most humiliating mishaps in his quest for vanished honors, is content to follow behind in hope of some reflected radiance from the resurrected poet's splendor.

It is often said that comedy is a recurrent and tragedy an infrequent phenomenon; but comic heroism, at its Aristophanic apogee, is a growth at least as rare and precarious as its tragic counterpart. The comic hero holds in suspension the normally incompatible conditions of human indignity and human glory. He seizes godhead in the frailty of his flesh, outsoaring Icarus astride his dung-beetle and returning to tell the tale. In the *Birds* this hodgepodge of contradictions wangles apotheosis; by the time of the *Frogs* a fatal dissociation of the comic from the heroic has already begun. Yet the cringing and much belabored Dionysus, though sadly fallen and only a god after all — a god interchangeable with his own slave — is nevertheless a comic hero who surmounts ignominious ridicule and wins his object, even if another must show the way. He prefigures a comic heroism dependent on shrewd tenacity rather than daring imagination, and able to feast on crumbs when ambrosia is not in its grasp. Having briefly attained the forbidden heavens, the comic hero must don his mendicant rags and come down to earth, where he began.

III

BONDSERVANT AND BEAST OF BURDEN

⁓❦⁓

IN GREECE the versatile role of comic hero could fall to Homeric king or citizen of imperial Athens; in a pinch, even to a god. In Rome, where stern *pietas* dictated that heroism lay in the sacrifice of individual impulse to the collective will, such a part was worthy only of a slave or an ass. And of a Greek slave or Greek ass, at that.

The world of Attic New Comedy, as it developed in the fourth century B.C. several generations after the brief hegemony of the Old, was not a world of heroes comic or otherwise. The plays of Menander, whose wit and grace Plutarch so emphatically preferred to Aristophanes' ribaldry, are civilized to the core. Far from posing a challenge to the social order they constitute a humane affirmation of its final sufficiency and essential wisdom. The scheme suggested by Menander's one complete surviving comedy, *The Grouch* (*Dyskolos*),[1] and corroborated both by numerous fragments and by Roman adaptations, is one of initial dissidence and separation resolving themselves in the course of nature toward harmony and reunion. It is a durable pattern of romance that descends from the tragicomedies of Euripides and looks forward, by way of Greek and Italian prose romances, to Shakespeare's comedies and many an early novel. The New Comic universe tends to polarize into old

60

curmudgeons and young profligates, dour spoilsports and affable pleasure-seekers, with the latter almost invariably triumphant. In Menander's play the solitary outcast, Cnemon, is no comic hero (as Aristophanes' testy Dicaeopolis had been) but an ill-tempered misanthrope determined to isolate his charming daughter from any human contact unless he can find her a husband as disagreeable as himself. A young Athenian gentleman, Sostratus, has fallen in love with the daughter at first sight but his hope of persuading her father seems destined to failure—until the old grouch falls into a well and obligingly repents his unmannerly ways. In the end even he is reconciled to life as he grumblingly consents to take part in the festivities celebrating his daughter's betrothal. The vice of antisocial seclusion, that cardinal sin of socially oriented comedy, has been miraculously if imperfectly cured, and the amiable virtues of good sense and good will, embodied by Cnemon's sympathetic stepson Gorgias, prevail in a kômos not of uncontained revelry but of temperate merrymaking.

Throughout this slight piece there is a subtle suggestion, as in its Euripidean prototypes, that divine providence solicitously guides events toward a happy end. The action significantly takes place near the grotto of Pan, who delivers the prologue and presumably watches over the outcome. But the true divinity of New Comedy is *Tychê*: Luck or Chance. In many known plays by Menander and his contemporaries this goddess (whom we might irreverently secularize as pure coincidence) works her mysterious way through intricately contrived discoveries culminating in the happy reunion of long-lost siblings or lovers, or of fathers with children. Plautus' romantic comedy *The Rope* (*Rudens*), modeled on a lost Greek original by Diphilus, is a fine example. Again a deity speaks the prologue and makes his unseen presence felt; and by the end of the play not only has a father identified his daughter (like Shakespeare's Pericles centuries later) by tokens fished up from the sea, and restored her from the danger of prostitution to her lover, but the sinister pimp—archetypal killjoy of the New Comic world—is himself integrated into the joyous conclusion.

One result of domination by Chance, whether conceived as

providence or accident, is a lack of opportunity for meaningful heroism. The characters do not grapple with the unforeseeable, like Odysseus, in order to shape their own destiny, but are blindly carried on the tide of the plot toward Act V, where all will be well. By and large the happy lovers are scarcely agents at all, since their ineluctable reunion usually comes about through no doing of theirs. "For the righteous-minded," Menander writes, "Fortune is ally,"[2] and she stands by her friends. Of course Chance can be given a nudge, and the lovers sometimes play a less passive role, affecting the course of things either by their own devices or (more characteristically) through the offices of a clever slave or parasite. The comedy of intrigue is a variation on the comedy of coincidence; but even in a play dominated by intrigue Chance is frequently paramount. In Terence's *Phormio* (based on an original by Apollodorus) the young Antipho, who has married in his father's absence, resorts to the arts of the parasite Phormio and of the slave Geta in order to dissuade his father from forcing him to divorce his bride and marry his cousin. But the intrigues prove to be subsidiary if not superfluous, since the happy ending is brought about by the chance discovery that his bride *is* his cousin. It is not Phormio whose name Geta invokes in his astonishment at the unexpected fulfillment of their hopes, but that of a far more astute and cunning intriguer: "O Fortuna, o Fors Fortuna!"[3] When so potent and awesome a deity effectively rules the affairs of men the significance of merely human initiative might well appear marginal.

In several of Plautus' comedies, however, the active role of the human agent, and in particular of the clever slave, is greatly enhanced, and a new comic hero arises to challenge the benevolent despotism of providential coincidence over man. It is difficult, in the absence of Plautus' Greek originals, to determine how much of this important shift in emphasis was his own. The striking contrast, however, between his plays and those of Terence, whose polished adaptations were surely closer to Greek New Comedy, suggests that Plautus' modulations in tone and style were of a fundamental kind.[4] Though the differences between them are far less radical, Terence was long held up as a model of decorum against the purported crudities of Plautus, much as Menander was contrasted with Aristophanes. In this, Montaigne and Ben Jonson merely varied Horace's stricture that Plautus lacked urbanity.[5] He does; but the lack is not necessarily a failing—it may be a sign of vigor—and his "inurbanity" has deep roots in his time and circumstances. In the aftermath of the devastating Punic wars Plautus' world was far less benign and complacent than Menander's had been. Behind the elegant façade of New Comic artifice, with its gentlemen of leisure piloted by the natural order of things to an erotically satisfying and socially acceptable conclusion, we frequently glimpse an unmannerly milieu of each for his own in a rough-and-tumble game of catch-as-catch-can. Plautus' much deplored coarseness is not the product of bad taste, primitive Latinity, or inability to mimic Attic grace, but his response to wholly different conditions and the token of his originality. He was writing not parlor comedies like Terence's but festive entertainments for the uncultured Roman populace, and he clearly altered his Greek models to suit their taste and his own artistic needs.

Thus Plautus is certainly no mere Latinizer of Greek but a comic poet of creative genius. On the other hand, Erich Segal's attempt to represent him as the "most 'saturnalian' comic playwright of them all," in whose plays "the very foundation of Roman morality is attacked in word and deed,"[6] though a valuable corrective to earlier distortions, is equally one-sided. There is not the remotest equivalent in Plautus to Cloudcuckooland or the Boar's Head Tavern, nothing to suggest the possibility of *imaginative* liberation that pervades Aristophanes and Shakespeare. The world of Plautine comedy was not one of which Cato the Elder would have approved, to be sure. But this hardly implies a subversion of everything Roman, since that severe gentleman found abundant cause for censure in the misdemeanors of his own time and place. Both in satire and in celebration Plautus oversteps the niceties of Menander and Terence, yet contains himself within generally circumspect limits, as far from the personal vituperation of the *Knights* as from the cosmic epithalamium of the *Birds*. His tonalities are harsher and his conflicts more bitter than in Menandrine comedy, but the underlying structure of his plays remains for the most part unchanged. The social outcast is again not the hero (as a "saturnalian" pattern would demand) but the villain; and since the villain is always defeated if not always redeemed, the social order is vindicated rather than overturned. The covetous pimp and pompous blowhard are beyond the pale, disdained by young and old alike; nor would a highly class-conscious society view such riffraff as surrogates for patrician dignitaries. On the other hand, the slaves that beat the rascals at their own game, though often outrageously insolent, always steer clear of any real collision with their masters and are well rewarded for their pains, while the insubordinate lovers are careful to triumph within acceptable limits. This morality may appear more "Greek" than "Roman" in its ready indulgence of love and pleasure. But to the Roman plebeians and veterans who applauded his plays the Plautine morality was surely more accessible — and even more edifying — than the Catonian, for it is finally a morality that reaffirms the equilibrium of society not as it should be, if censors were kings, but more or less as it is.

Far from throwing down the gauntlet to contemporary mores, then, Plautus normally operates within the convenient New Comic fiction that everything will somehow work out for the best. No convention could be less subversive. But because in his less refined world the enemies of happiness are frequently more sinister and effective than in Menander's well-made plays Plautus sometimes strikes a harsh note that makes him the most moralistic rather than the most festive of ancient dramatists. At the end of *The Braggart Soldier* (*Miles gloriosus*) an intemperate outburst of castigation displaces the kômos, as the swaggering lecher Pyrgopolynices, having been covered with blows, is threatened with the gelding knife. Among earlier surviving comedies only Aristophanes' revised *Clouds* had anticipated such a vindictive finale. Once poetic justice has been accomplished the bruised offender can acknowledge the error of his ways — "I judge this justly done,"[7] he ruefully declares — and warn other malefactors by his ill-starred example. In the moral censure to which it gives vent Plautus' *Braggart Soldier* is far less close to the genial plays of Menander than to such later masterpieces of satirical comedy as *Volpone* or *Tartuffe,* where the transgressor against accepted patterns of conduct must likewise incur a stiffer penalty than laughter alone. It is now the butt and not the hero, the loser and not the winner, Lamachus and not Dicaeopolis, who occupies center stage and will long continue to hold it.

If the offender is more obnoxious and more virulently derided in several of Plautus' plays than in other post-Aristophanic ancient comedies, his opponents are correspondingly more astute in their efforts to cope with the aggravated peril. Fortune is not so dependably mechanical now in her workings, nor so inevitably beneficent in her effects, and there arises in consequence an expanded opportunity for a dexterous comic hero. Not that this world is susceptible to radical transformation either through deeds as by Odysseus or through words as by Peisthetaerus, but much leeway remains for significant and even decisive intervention in the operations of Chance. The Plautine comic hero is a swift-footed artful dodger who has inherited the craft and virtuosity (if not the high imagination and bold ambition) of his Homeric and Aristophanic forebears. His hallmarks are trickery and deceit, *dolus* and *mendacium,* flanked by an auxiliary squadron of kindred virtues—*fallacia* and *perfidia, sycophantia* and *malitia, industria* and *astutia, fraus, facetia, audacia,* and the like. His goal is not to overturn an inimical order but to get out from under; he can sympathize with others in evil plight, but makes it his principal business to look out for himself.

Not all of Plautus' lovers have the patience to wait (like Menander's Sostratus) for their adversary to fall into a well; some precipitate events by going on the initiative. In *The Braggart Soldier* it is not omnipotent Chance that defeats the blustering Pyrogopolynices and resolves the action by a miraculous discovery but the clever courtesan Philocomasium who contrives (in collaboration with others) to pull the wool over her captor's eyes and engineer her escape with her lover. Her versatile skills are a theme of rapt admiration: "What a face and tongue she has," the slave Palaestrio marvels, "what unscrupu-

lousness, rascality, effrontery, poise, firmness, deceitfulness!
Accuse her, and she'll outswear you on oath. She's completely
at home with false talk, false deeds, false witness, with tricks
and coaxing ways and deceptions."[8] With such qualifications
Philocomasium can even pass herself off as her own twin sister,
and nothing is likely to stand in her way.

In *The Braggart Soldier,* however, the starring role belongs
to the titular *gloriosus,* whose graphic humiliation completely
upstages the victory of his crafty opponents. It is in the *Pseudolus,* a mature production for which no single Greek source is
known to have existed, that the Plautine comic hero comes incontestably into his own. Here the dramatic action is decisively
dominated neither by imperiled lovers nor vainglorious gulls
but by the quick-witted, fast-talking, self-possessed, and
masterful slave of the title. A character-type who had apparently remained subsidiary to Fortune's whimsical dictates in
Greek New Comedy here takes matters in hand and appropriates the role of destiny as his own. From the opening lines he is
in command as he listens with ironical compassion to the
plaints of his lovestruck master Calidorus. It is to Pseudolus
that Calidorus naturally looks for salvation when he learns that
the sale of his darling Phoenicium to a Macedonian soldier may
soon bring an end to their paradise of bitten lips, squeezed
breasts, and tight-pressed bodies. Pseudolus views the whining
lover with dry-eyed contempt—"Why weep, cuckoo? You'll
live"[9]—yet promises to devise a way to save him; no one, he solemnly warns, must believe a word he says on this day. Even in
the service of another the comic hero's arts will be unmistakably
his own.

His antagonist is the pimp Ballio, Phoenicium's whip-crack-
ing owner, who boasts that he would break off a sacrifice to
Jupiter if a chance for profit arose. Not surprisingly this trader
in flesh is deaf to pleas for pity and demands cold cash; he is
equally immune to vilification, since every conceivable insult
tickles his vanity. After this monster's departure Pseudolus
ponders his course of action alone. He has no plan to liberate
Phoenicium but puts his trust in the tested resources of brashness, tenacity, shrewdness, and an imagination almost uniquely

fertile among the slaves and parasites of Greco-Roman comedy. In his monologue Pseudolus momentarily transcends the upstart cunning of his breed and reincarnates the inventive genius of comic heroes past. "Just as a poet, when he takes his tablets in hand, seeks what is nowhere on earth," he rhapsodizes, "yet finds it, and makes what is a lie seem like truth, now I shall become a poet."[10] A poet who must employ his gifts, it is true, not in regaining a kingdom or founding a heavenly city but in scrounging a harlot's ransom—yet a poet all the same, and one proudly aware of his talents. He will not wait for Fortune's favors but seize every occasion to coerce and secure them, and his talent for improvisation never fails him. Through a happy conjunction of luck and skill he waylays the Macedonian's messenger and tricks him out of the letter intended for Ballio, then with the aid of another slave as glib as himself he deludes the wary guardian into surrendering the girl. Not merely deceit, nor unassisted coincidence, but agility in exploiting Occasion has brought Pseudolus victory, and his assessment of Fortune is correspondingly different from that of the awestruck slave in Terence. Although she often vanquishes the schemes of the wisest, Pseudolus affirms, "each man's excellence lies in the use he makes of Fortune, and it is in this that everyone proclaims him wise."[11] The theme of the play is not Fortune's supremacy over man but man's capacity to turn opportunity to advantage, and Pseudolus proves himself an incontestable past master of this difficult art.

Although Plautus' shameless slave outwits one master (Calidorus' father Simo) in the interest of another and triumphantly sweeps all before him, he never poses a serious challenge, in the manner of Aristophanes' heroes, to the social order, but helps to restore its balance. The spokesman for good sense in the play, Callipho—a forerunner, like Menander's Gorgias, of Molière's *raisonneurs*—chides Simo for his severity toward foibles of which he himself had been guilty when young. In these humane sentiments the eavesdropping Pseudolus concurs. Callipho seconds the slave's proposal that Simo pay the girl's ransom if Pseudolus succeeds in setting her free, and even promises to make good if Simo defaults. Thus the sensible

Callipho's endorsement places Pseudolus' frankly avowed chicaneries within the bounds of propriety, and Simo himself will concede his claims—and pay his price—in the end.[12]

If Plautus' play is far from challenging existing society, it is nevertheless much closer in spirit to Aristophanic comedy than anything we know of in Menander or Terence. The familiar figure of the clever slave steps out of the wings and into the limelight, where, by supplanting Fortune as the play's prime mover, he ceases to be an amusing sidekick and emerges, for perhaps the first time, as a hero. And although he by no means confronts or subverts the social order (except in the form of its most despised perversion) in either word or act, he does show himself supremely adept in the slippery art of evasion that will typify many a comic hero to come. Caught between two masters and threatened with the mills (the dreaded *pistrinum*) by each for loyalty to the other, Pseudolus somehow survives without injury, and in acknowledgment of this feat the boisterous kômos is reserved for him in preference to the insignificant lovers. He himself exultantly exclaims "victor sum" when Ballio delivers Phoenicium, and exhorts his fellows "to the tankard of triumph";[13] he himself collects his reward (under safe-conduct of inebriation) from his rueful but resigned elder master with an impudent "vae victis!"[14] If he has not turned society upside down he has given proof that the lowest man on the social ladder can use his god-given wits to clamber into a temporary place in the sun. In a far from heroic world this is an achievement of mythical dimension, and Pseudolus' stature is repeatedly magnified during the play by association with legendary names from a grander past. Simo likens him to Socrates in persuasiveness of speech and declares that if he accomplishes his goals he will have outshone King Agathocles (who rose from a potter to royal dominion in Sicily). And after Pseudolus has done all that he promised Simo can find only one comparison worthy of his consummately cunning and versatile slave. "Pseudolus," he admiringly proclaims, "has surpassed the stratagem of Troy, and Ulysses himself": *superavit dolum Troianum atque Ulixem Pseudolus.*[15]

Through Simo's frustrated tribute the patron saint of quick-witted underdogs, Odysseus himself, imparts the legitimacy of his regal name to a servile descendant. And like other comic victors before him Pseudolus too is permitted to celebrate his triumph as he tipsily exults in emancipation from the mills and from the dreary constraints of his daily condition. A triumph and emancipation, however, whose provisional nature and brief duration are painfully evident. This kômos may provide a release but can promise no lasting renewal, no hope of regeneration. Neither the joy of reunion with wife and father nor the jubilation of apotheosis but only a temporary immersion in the sensual indulgence that constitutes his masters' holiday routine can fall to Pseudolus' lot as the spoils of his victory, since this is the only alternative envisaged within the narrow horizons of this comedy's world. To Pseudolus' clouded eyes, to be sure, these succulent delights are sufficient to place him "next to the gods."[16] But intoxication and debauchery are notoriously fragile experiences of the divine, and the drunken slave's revels hold little prospect of outlasting the morning after.

In the wily arts of survival Pseudolus has proved himself, within the confines of this workaday world, not unworthy of comparison with the archetypal comic hero Odysseus; yet in his moment of triumph he more nearly resembles one of the nameless shipmates spellbound by Circe's transfiguring wand. The failing, of course, is not peculiar to Pseudolus. On the contrary, a fundamental limitation of perspective seems implicit in a form of comedy that never calls into question — even in its bolder Plautine variation — the adequacy of existing society as the framework for any possible human self-realization. The saturnalia in Plautus, such as it is, can be nothing more than a momentary respite offering the starved imagination, like the sated body, no sustenance for the morrow once the brief holiday is over and done.

Heroism of any description demands a rare confidence in the possibility of significant human action, and the comic hero will perform his most audacious exploits when this sense of heroic possibility is at its peak or just beginning to decline. To the Greeks of Homeric and early classical times the comic hero was the worthy counterpart of the tragic, asserting his defiant in-dividuality with equal bravura in opposite yet analogous fash-ion. Odysseus fittingly complements Achilles, and Peisthetaerus Antigone; the comic hero's breathtaking presumptions (as Aris-tophanes saw in the *Frogs*) could not long survive the collapse of that tragic greatness in the face of insuperable odds on which he likewise had thrived. By this token Aristophanes is more nearly akin to tragic Aeschylus than to comic Menander. For Menander's worldly-wise urbanity postulates the amusing futil-ity of all heroic pretensions, if not all human endeavors; and in comedy Menander was the wave of the future. Never again will a culture, whether Greek or barbarian, enshrine a rogue like Odysseus in a national epic or celebrate scamps of Aristophanic feather in its sacred festivities. The comic hero of less rash and exalted days will be constrained to adopt a more unassuming posture and learn the circumspect virtue of lying low.

The Romans too had their heroes, of course, in abundance; and Plautus' elevation of the Menandrine slave to modestly heroic stature coincides with the first flowering of Roman epic in the years that followed the crushing victory over Hannibal. Pseudolus' conviction that a man excels by the uses he makes of fortune echoes Ennius' dictum: "To brave men is fortune given."[17] Yet few civilizations have been more hostile to the ir-reverent spirit of comedy than the Roman. The tragic heroism, or *aretê*, of Achilles presupposed the supremacy of the autono-mous individual capable (within the limits of mortality) of shaping his destiny by his own decisions and with his own strong hands. For that reason it could engender, as its mirror image, a comic heroism no less resolutely determined to forge a different destiny by equivalent means. The comic hero too could lay claim to *aretê*. But Roman *virtus* requires the strict subordina-tion of individual impulse to the demands of family, clan, and commonwealth—requires in effect the selfless extinction of personality. To such spartan austerity no comic counterpart is conceivable unless by denial of its very foundations.

The culture-heroes of Augustan literature, Horace's Regulus and Virgil's pious Aeneas, learn to sacrifice the last vestiges of self in their dutiful devotion to a transcendent cause. In such a setting the comic hero, whose transcendent cause *is* self, has no place at all. The counterpart to public heroism for Horace and Virgil — a counterpart that carries far deeper conviction for their personal lives — is bucolic rather than comic; withdrawal rather than defiance; the unperturbed cultivation of one's own garden, beehive, or Sabine farm. The erotic poets too have their private plot to till; for them the public world is no more than a meddlesome intrusion on their serious pastimes. Except for satire, with its outraged assaults on the increasingly glaring lapses from Republican virtue, there is no comic literature worth mentioning in the Golden and Silver Ages of Roman letters. For comedy, in contrast to eclogue or elegy, implies a deliberate (if sometimes unwanted) engagement with intractable realities beyond the sheepcote gate or bedroom door. Unlike satire, that most desolate of ancient genres, it can field a combatant capable of holding his own. In classical Rome, where public heroism could only exist in a cause that obliterated the individual — and where even private victims of oppression acted with Stoic self-denial, opening their veins *pro bono publico* — a conception of heroism *pro bono suo* was an incomprehensible and subversive oxymoron. To the grave Roman the comic was a contemptible perversion characterized, in Ciceronian phrase, by turpitude and deformity.[18]

The inurbane Plautus, in making a hero of a mendacious Greek slave, had briefly exposed his rigid compatriots to foreign and popular outlooks alien to their native bent; but for centuries to come the dispossessed underdog, though he no doubt flourished in the farcical mimes of the age, was to have no place in the literature of a people destined to rule. Not until the second century A.D., in the peaceful reign of the Antonine emperors, did attitudes subordinated since the premature death of Roman comedy again find voice in the loosely articulated new medium of prose fiction. The first known Roman novel, Petronius' fragmentary *Satyricon* of the previous century, was a sardonic epicure's portrayal of universal decadence in an aristocracy vulgarized by freedmen and parvenus. Once Caesar stood unmasked as Nero caustic mockery inherited the offices of heroic praise. But the *Metamorphoses,* or *Golden*

Ass, of the North African Apuleius, composed in the mid-second century, is a horse of another color: a variegated medley of incongruities strung together around the preposterous misadventures of the last and most sorely tried comic hero of the ancient world. Its inquisitive author typifies the syncretism of a restless and polycentric age. He was born in Madaura; traveled to Carthage and Alexandria; immersed himself in Greek literature and philosophy at Athens; and took up the practice of law in Rome after mastering the Latin language. His rhetorical skills are attested by florid excerpts from orations aglitter with learned allusions and lilting alliterations. Besides his juridical and forensic pursuits, he composed philosophical treatises in the Platonic vein; purportedly dabbled in the magical and alchemical arts; and, "moved by my religious fervour and my desire to know the truth" (as he relates in his *Apologia*), was initiated into solemn "mysteries of many a kind, rites in great number, and diverse ceremonies."[19]

In a time when inherited certainties of parochial national cultures lay pulverized under the millstone of Empire, Apuleius was eager to leave no pebble unturned in his ingenuous effort to fabricate a mosaic of ecumenical truth from the bits and scraps of local ritual. His literary aspirations were equally eclectic and scarcely less grandiose. "Empedocles," he declares in a pompous "Panegyric on His Own Talents," "composed verse, Plato dialogues, Socrates hymns, Epicharmus music, Xenophon histories, and Xenocrates satire. But your friend Apuleius cultivates all these branches of art together and worships all nine Muses with equal zeal. His enthusiasm is, I admit, in advance of his capacity, but that perhaps makes him all the more praiseworthy, inasmuch as in all high enterprises it is the effort that merits praise, success is after all a matter of chance."[20] By this canon, at least, there can be little question that Apuleius richly deserves the fervid praise that he lavishes unstintingly on himself.

The *Golden Ass,* in its diversity of inspiration and range of experience, is the comic epic in prose of the cosmopolitan Antonine world. The central plot of a young man's transformation into an ass Apuleius took from a tale called *Lucius the Ass,* attributed to the Greek satirist Lucian, or from a common ancestor. He elaborated this leading thread with a colorful patchwork of entertainments: ribald "Milesian tales" of deception and adultery; hair-raising yarns of witches and ghosts; brutal sketches of banditry and murder; romantic love stories and entrancing fairy tales. Nor does the diversity of these narratives merely vary the literary fare; together they constitute a compendium of the heterogeneous society of Apuleius' day. Though set in one small corner of Greece the *Golden Ass* embraces virtually every stratum of the vast imperial scene. In its pages we witness, in their bizarre multiplicity, the sexual practices and superstitious fears, along with the flagrant injustices and pitiless cruelties of the time. We enter patrician houses and bandits' caves, baths and amphitheaters, mills, bakeries, and tombs; we consort with goddesses and tenant farmers, magistrates, soldiers, and slaves. This hugger-mugger of chaotic impressions acquires a kind of cohesion through the pilgrimage of its woebegone protagonist, Lucius, who profits both by his own misfortunes and by the grim example of others, and is humanized in the upshot.

To many readers the solemn initiation of Lucius into the mysteries of Isis in the closing book of the *Golden Ass* has seemed out of keeping with the ribald exuberance of earlier episodes. Yet solemnity and exuberance are not necessarily incompatible, and Apuleius' greatest originality lies in their bold conjunction. Powerless to shape his own destiny within a world whose irremediable degradation he learns through painful (if often hilarious) mishap, Lucius regains his human aspect only by transcending the animality that surrounds him and devoting himself to an altogether higher sphere of existence. Yet Apuleius' spiritual hero is none the less essentially comic. Unlike the Christian ascetic, to whom the mere temptation to carnal sin is an abomination against the spirit, Apuleius' pilgrim never repudiates the experiences that he passes through and beyond. In the overall scheme of the *Golden Ass,* Lucius' early bout of fornication with the servant girl Fotis is an error that he will rue and outgrow, but with such evident gusto does he remember the girl's nectared breath and plunging spine that the reader

relishes his trespass in all its undeniable titillation. Only by
running the gamut of human experience—notably including
its "lowest," least dignified, most animal forms—and assimilating it all, not by evading its pitfalls or gainsaying its charms,
can the comic hero enlarge his own experience and turn it to
spiritual profit.

In this regard there is little distinction, after nearly a thousand years, between Apuleius' plodding ass and Homer's quick-
witted king. Lucius, in recounting his bondage at the mill, recalls that Homer's "man of highest prudence" had attained the
summit of virtue by his knowledge of many countries and
peoples, and he gratefully acknowledges that his own asinine
incarnation has multiplied his knowledge, if not his prudence.[21]
This is the comic hero's abiding credo, that every experience of
life retains its intrinsic worth even after it has been left behind
for a higher and more enriching fulfillment. Fotis is not a
demon to be exorcized from the memory but a diversion on the
journey to Isis, much as Circe and Calypso were detours on
Odysseus' return to Penelope; their ultimate insufficiency need
not consign them to a cheerless oblivion. The *Golden Ass* is a
parable no less divine because comic. Not the straight and
narrow path, it suggests, but the broad public highway may be
the road to enlightenment and salvation. The fuller one's
personal knowledge of this world in all its perversity the more
certain his final transcendence; during his apprenticeship in
the arena, therefore, the hero is comic not accidentally but in
essence. This is the paradoxical insight that informs Apuleius'
novel and unifies its seemingly disconnected components. The
Golden Ass reserves its greatest pleasures for the attentive
reader: "*lector intende,*" the author admonishes; "*laetaberis.*"[22]
Only to the negligent will the seriousness of the final book seem
discordant with the comedy of the whole.

The brisk immediacy of the opening is typical of Apuleius'
narrative art. His individual periods may tend toward orotund
prodigality, but his tales are paced with the veteran storyteller's
economy. Lucius comes upon a traveler, Aristomenes, who relates a chilling tale of black magic that sets the tone for the
early books of the novel. In a public bath Aristomenes had en-

countered his former companion Socrates, reduced to misery and rags. At a nearby inn to which they went, Socrates explained that he had fallen prey to the sexual charms of the witch Meroe, whose transformations of men into animals he recounts in grisly detail to his increasingly disquieted comrade. After the two fall asleep the tale takes on the eeriness of nightmare as their door bursts suddenly off its hinges and Aristomenes' bed flips over on top of him. Two gruesome hags (the voluptuous Meroe and her sister) enter, and at the sound of their bloodcurdling incantations Aristomenes' fatuous nonchalance dissolves in spasms of terror that make the bed rattle and dance on his quivering back. For a moment of ineffable horror he watches Meroe plunge a sword into Socrates' neck and tear out his heart with the solemnity of a sacrificial rite, stopping up the wound in his throat with a sponge which she prohibits from crossing a stream. The mood turns macabre as Aristomenes picks himself up from a pool of witches' urine (they had emptied their bladders on him in departing) and attempts to hang himself from the rafters, tumbling ludicrously down just as the porter bursts in and Socrates rises cursing from the mattress. An uncanny calm descends on the final pages as the two travelers pause for lunch by the wayside, having resumed their journey as though nothing had happened, and Socrates begins to turn pale. When he bends down to drink from a stream his throat ejects a blood-drenched sponge; he is, of course, dead.

Now, a story of such intensity is a masterpiece in itself, but it will also focus the diligent reader's attention on several principal themes of the novel. From the beginning, when Socrates describes the bestial shapes into which Meroe has turned her fascinated lovers, the motifs of curiosity and magic, sexuality and transformation are closely intertwined; and these will be fundamental to the adventure of Lucius. Each is an expression of incomplete humanity. Curiosity, forever insatiable and forever unsatisfying, is the thirst for stimulus rather than understanding; magic, the perversion of religion, is spiritual power turned to corporeal ends; sexuality is desire without love; and transformation into animal form is the consequence of all three. It is no accident, then, that this wayfarer's yarn is followed immediately by Lucius' sojourn in the house of Milo, from which he emerges a braying jackass. His frenzied obsession with magic causes him to question the reality of everything he sees and thus prevents him from truly discerning the nature of the world around him. When he learns from his wealthy friend Byrrhaena that Milo's wife Pamphile is a witch able to transform her lovers to beasts his curiosity is exacerbated to the point of madness, and it is with open eyes if demented judgment that he plunges headlong into the pit. This frantic passion to master Pamphile's arts is the motivation behind his orgiastic courtship of her servant girl, too; and once curiosity, magic, and sex combine, his humiliating but apt metamorphosis is accomplished in all but appearance. In still another respect Aristomenes' story presages his listener's future. After burying Socrates by the stream Aristomenes had abandoned home and family to wander through pathless solitudes, as if himself guilty of murder — demonstrating (as Socrates had forewarned) that subjection to Fortune's vicissitudes is the most tyrannical of all fates. This lesson, that Fortune enslaves the unwary, is one that Lucius will soon be taught to his sorrow.

Lucius remains unaware of any connection between Aristomenes' cautionary narration (which he calls a "charming tale")[23] and himself, and his unawareness is part of its meaning. Throughout the early books of the *Golden Ass* Lucius, like nearly everyone else, is guided in thought and action by self-delusion. He lacks the first defense of earlier comic heroes, wariness or cunning; indeed, his gullibility makes him the laughingstock of a world of fools, a butt of derision among the brotherhood of the blind. In the luxurious surroundings of Byrrhaena's banquet party he hears gales of wild laughter from the dinner guests in response to a certain Thelyphron's gruesome account of how ghouls had devoured his nose and ears during a deathwatch in a murdered man's tomb. Again Lucius sees no pertinence to himself beyond another incitement to witchcraft, but this time the parallel is thrust upon him. Returning from Byrrhaena's he slays three robbers; next morning (on the festival of the god Laughter) he is dragged in terror,

like an expiatory offering, through mobs of guffawing spectators to his public trial in the theater of Hypata. Lucius pleads
his cause with desperate ingenuity, but when he tearfully
stretches out his hands to implore their mercy he beholds his
audience dissolved in hilarity. Denounced by the mother and
widow of one of the slain, and confronted with the instruments
of torture, he is forced to uncover the bodies, only to discover,
amid howls of mirth, that his nocturnal victims were wineskins,
not men. This brilliant episode—the climax of the early
books—exhibits with mock-ritual solemnity both the cruelty of
a world dedicated to sham and the blindness of a protagonist
incapable, in his willful derangement, of distinguishing phan-
tasm from fact or of knowing either his world or himself. In
comparison with the heartless onlookers, possessed (like the
doomed suitors of the *Odyssey*) by paroxysms of self-mocking
hysteria, Lucius attains through conscious anguish the status of
sacrificial victim, and is heaped with honors once his ordeal is
past. In his first heroic trial he has struggled like Hercules with
monsters of the nether world, and his safe return from Proserpina's doorstep foreshadows his spiritual resurrection at the end
of the novel. But these are no more than premonitions; for the
moment, his manic delusion exposes him to the well-deserved
mockery of those whom he has acknowledged as judges and
sweeps him heedlessly on to his transformation.

When a mistaken unguent applied by Fotis to her avid lover
turns him into an ass, his eagerly sought metamorphosis (in
contrast to those of Odysseus or Peisthetaerus) bears witness to
the stupefaction of his mental faculties. Throughout long
wanderings and perilous scrapes as a beast of burden he will
have to make his way without the intellectual and verbal resources of his more adroit predecessors, and nothing but his
obstinate will to live and tenacious endurance of injury will
sustain him. Not until his transformation does Lucius begin to
perceive reality at all, both through the compulsory schooling
of his own hard lot and through deepened attentiveness to the
miseries of the human condition around him. Only when he
finds himself reviled as the lowest of beasts and forced to relinquish his delusions of magical grandeur does he begin to distin-

guish animality from humanity and to grope toward justification of his life. His loss of the dubious boon of misdirected intellect thus proves a necessary step toward the development of self-awareness. The stories he hears during his asinine incarnation again have a bearing (however oblique) on his personal destiny. The enchanting fable of Cupid and Psyche narrated by an old woman in the bandits' cave is wholly unlike the grotesque tales of sorcery that he had imbibed in the past; it suggests the possibility of a spiritual ascent such as Lucius is now unwittingly in the act of commencing. Like Psyche he has suffered the consequences of foolish curiosity and is atoning for his error through many wanderings and trials (even if the object of his search is unknown), and like her he will be reborn and transfigured at the conclusion of his ordeal. Both finally attain to a higher purity through patient submission to abasement. But in its subtle alternation of playfulness and tender sentiment this delicate fable could hardly afford a sharper contrast to the gross realism of Lucius' narrative; for he is no fairy-tale princess but a creature of flesh and blood who must re-enact the soul's migration, in the less than ethereal guise of a donkey, amid haphazard comic vicissitudes in this world of bruises and thumps.

The parable of the soul's difficult ascent to reunion with divine love thus adumbrates the pattern of the second half of the *Golden Ass* and prefigures its ending, but Lucius will have to discover that pattern for himself through perilous trials and ridiculous errors. He will be trampled and bitten by rutting stallions, pricked and scorched by a sadistic farm boy, threatened with the gelding knife and butcher's cleaver, flogged by homosexual priests, harnessed to the mill, and trained to copulate in the arena. Kickings and beatings will attend him every step of the way. In the course of these bruising misadventures he at last develops the wariness that he lacked in his human incarnation, as time and again, with a well-placed kick, a timely squirt, or a prudent lunge he sidesteps the perils into which he had fatuously rushed shortly before. His impertinent curiosity still occasionally betrays him (he is, after all, an ass), but he slowly accumulates a precious modicum of understanding, even of wisdom. Before, he had rashly aspired to supernatural power through necromantic arts; now (like Socrates in Aristomenes' story) he acknowledges subjection to the wayward despotism of Fortune. The beneficent deity of New Comedy has revealed herself to be a capricious tyrant, *Fortuna saeva;* and though Lucius cannot withstand her on an equal footing or outmaneuver her like a latter-day Odysseus he does comprehend that deliverance will not come from blind submission to her whims. He has taken the first long step toward freedom, which is to know himself a slave, and from now on his desire to regain human form becomes an increasingly purposeful (if still inarticulate) struggle to liberate himself from bondage.

The debaucheries and cruelties crowded into the latter half of the novel expose to Lucius' wakening consciousness a universe abandoned to homicidal greed and lust. A landlord butchers a farmer's three sons for opposing his seizure of a neighbor's plot; a legionary highhandedly robs a poor gardener of his ass; disfigured slaves and mangy horses waste away in smoky mills; a mother poisons her stepson for declining her advances—such are the everyday occurrences (along with many more venial peccadilloes) of a world ruled in contempt of justice by the dictates of Fortune. The animality of the human world highlights the unextinguished humanity of the lowly ass who observes and finally judges. In the midst of rampant depravity Lucius' artless innocence (which formerly made him a laughingstock and led him blindly into error) becomes his source of strength, for by now it is a seasoned innocence increasingly conscious of its own resources and of its incompatibility with the pursuits and aims of a brutalized world. Thus the foolhardy ass proves himself heroic by stalwart endurance and a mounting resolve to seek emancipation from Fortune's tyranny. He is not averse to taking his pleasure when a matron of insatiable libido thrusts herself upon him—*he* is not the ass here—but he shrinks with revulsion from the bestiality of public fornication with a woman condemned for murdering, among others, her husband and daughter. To such contagion he prefers even death; with this determination his career as an ass is near its end.

In the amphitheater of Corinth, on the day of his scheduled performance, Lucius watches an elaborate re-enactment of the Judgment of Paris and bursts into denunciation of universal corruption when Venus is awarded the prize. He is in fact what he ironically dubs himself: a philosophizing ass. For the suffering beast has gradually become the sole representative of moral integrity in the novel, so that his verdict on the Judgment of Paris and subsequent travesties of justice irreprievably condemns the venal society that he has witnessed from top to bottom. In the theater of Hypata during the festival of Laughter Lucius had been the accused and the victim; here he is the judge, and he votes with his feet. By his flight to the sea and his moving prayer to the Queen of Heaven for restoration of his human form he makes a deliberate (if belated) choice of his destiny, and firmly repudiates the delusions that he had embraced while outwardly man. His august dream-vision of the goddess Isis entails a self-recognition no less than Odysseus' encounter with Athena on another coastline, but what Lucius discerns is not divine confirmation of his native resourcefulness but his absolute need for help from above. His own endurance and adaptability had preserved him from mortal danger, and his own renunciation of a world unfit for man or beast has brought him to purifying waters; but by his supplication and dream he acknowledges the inadequacy of all such heroic attributes and entrusts his redemption to a higher power.

His second transformation, unlike the first, is freely chosen, since it depends not on the vagaries of chance but on the changeless divinity worshiped throughout the world in multiple shapes and by various names. In the Egyptian myth related by Plutarch (from whom Lucius proudly claims descent) the god Osiris is periodically dismembered by the obstructive Typhon, whose animal shape is the ass, and reassembled by his wife and sister Isis, who wanders over the earth, much like Psyche, in search of her immortal lover's scattered remains. Osiris is "uncontaminated and unpolluted and pure from all matter that is subject to destruction and death," Plutarch writes; and with his inutterable beauty, "Isis, as the ancient story declares, is for ever enamoured and pursues it and consorts with it and fills our

earth here with all things fair and good that partake of generation."[24] From frenzied subjection to sexuality and stupid obsession with magic Lucius has ascended, through his humiliating
pilgrimage as an ass, to this majestic vision of divine love, and
thereby his metamorphosis into truly human form is accomplished. The options of Odysseus and Peisthetaerus have been
exhausted; the one alternative to a world depraved beyond
remedy lies not in its physical or imaginative transmutation but
in selfless devotion to a higher reality than this world can
afford. In this is Lucius' triumph and liberation; by partaking
of the all-seeing goddess' vision he wins acquittal at last from
the persecution of blind Fortune. In the exultant procession of
Isis, where Lucius regains his manhood, the priest declares that
since he has made his way from tempestuous seas to this haven
malicious Fortune is impotent against him. Suffering was
necessary to bliss, and heroic endurance to self-abnegation;
fortune was providence imperfectly understood. In the service
of Isis is freedom, and by solemn initiation into her rites Lucius
submits to a voluntary death and returns from Proserpina's
dark realm to a resurrected spiritual life. Curiosity, magic, and
sexuality have been resolved, on a higher plane of cognition, in
wisdom, devotion, and love; these too entail transformation.
By consciously living out the role of ass, to which most men are
unknowingly condemned, and by aspiring beyond it to a more
meaningful condition, Lucius has uniquely embodied the
authentic vocation of man.

To the Greeks in the heady confidence of their prime the sovereign individual was capable of triumphing on his own,
through the artful tricks of the comic hero, over the marshaled
opposition of a slow-witted world. But to the civic-minded
Romans individual man was strictly subordinate to Public
Thing, and under their stern gaze and heavy hand no impertinent upstart ventured to turn society on its head or rout the
gods from their stately abodes. The comic hero makes his unassuming appearance, under protection of Hellenic garb, only
near the beginning and near the end of classical Roman literature; his role is not central and assertive, as in Homeric epic or
Aristophanic comedy, but marginal and prudently aware of its

limits. The wily Plautine slave employs the tools of the militant comic hero to more pedestrian ends in the service of others, envisaging no higher freedom for himself than that of his masters in their crapulous interludes; he operates, however saucily, "within the system." The ass of Apuleius' novel, at the opposite extreme, elects a more radical alternative than that of his Greek prototypes by renouncing this uncertain world altogether in his evident powerlessness to alter its dehumanizing conditions. Unlike Odysseus' reunion with Penelope or Peisthetaerus' wedding of Basileia, Lucius' submission to the superpersonal Isis demands the sacrifice of the comic hero's primal source and final cause — his sine qua non and raison d'être, the belligerent self. His victory is won by strategic capitulation. This different end accords with a no less fundamental difference of character and means. In a world teeming with scoundrels the beleaguered underdog takes refuge in the armor of a fool. His weapons, in a struggle that can only be won when abandoned, are not versatility and cunning but dogged pertinacity and thickskinned immunity to contagion. Not active defiance but passive resistance is his part. Experience is the proving ground of innocence, and worldly folly the nonage of transcendental illumination. The Apuleian comic hero might fittingly be designated a comic saint, since the derision of a profligate world is his only spur to self-knowledge and the surest index of his ultimate salvation.

IV

RENEGADE VASSAL

&

T O SOCIETY'S eternal "Thou shalt not" the comic hero insistently answers "I will"; not surprisingly there is often bad blood between them. Even in the exceptional case of ancient Greece, where unabashed approbation for the wily trickster of folk tradition survived well into classical times, his status was hardly secure. Resourceful Odysseus himself fell into bad odor, despite Homer's monumental prestige, as the balance shifted in favor of more social virtues. "May such a character never be mine, father Zeus," Pindar fervently prays, "but may I cleave to life's straightforward paths!"[1] Amid the convolutions of politics and war the straight and narrow path of integrity found much to recommend it—Homer's versatile hero becomes a conniving opportunist in Sophocles and Euripides—and with the defeat of democratic Athens the brash heyday of Aristophanic license gave way to an aftermath of Spartan self-discipline. In the reformed republic expounded by Plato through the mouth of Socrates every citizen must devote himself to a single calling and no falsehood is to be tolerated except by the rulers "for the public good." The uniformity of communal virtue annuls all personal multiplicity. "Neither ought our guardians to be given to laughter," the Platonic Socrates declares; for "persons of worth, even if only mortal men, must not be represented as overcome by laughter, and still less must such a representation of the gods be allowed,"[2] as in Homer. In the name of an inflexible higher truth the educator of Greece was summoned to account for his fictional deviations and only the subterfuge of allegory eventually secured his acquittal. And if the comic hero found himself persona non grata even on Hellenic soil, in more rigid cultures he was given short shrift indeed. Neither Roman gravity nor Hebraic righteousness could accommodate the self-serving trickster. To Virgil the guile of Ulysses and Sinon is the source of unspeakable sorrow; to the Prophets Jacob's deception of Esau is among the transgressions expiated by his faithless descendants.[3] The God of Israel, like the Roman State, demanded upright conduct and wholehearted allegiance — and brooked no dissent. To bear false witness was to sin against the Lord.

To all these traditions medieval Christendom fell heir, and few climes would appear to provide more meager sustenance for the growth of comic heroism. The early Christian might indeed be a vilified underdog, but his kingdom was ultimately not of this earth, and the comic hero knows no other. Unlike Apuleius' pilgrim the Christian strove for enlightenment and salvation not through apprenticeship to the world but through repudiation of it; St. Augustine recounts the illicit loves of *his* youth with salutary revulsion, "passing again in the bitterness of remembrance over my most evil ways that Thou mayest thereby grow ever lovelier to me, O Loveliness that dost not deceive."[4] The Christian's most sacred duty was to bear witness to truth, and his word for "witness" was martyr. To dissemble, as St. Peter thrice dissembled, was tantamount to denying the Lord. If Christians seemed impostors it was because they dared to speak a truth which the Jews found a stumbling block and the Greeks a folly. "We have renounced disgraceful, underhanded ways," St. Paul instructs the Corinthians; "we refuse to practice cunning or to tamper with God's word, but by the open statement of the truth we would commend ourselves to every man's conscience in the sight of God."[5] Such a singular truth was clearly uncongenial to the comic hero's more circuitous apprehension of things, nor was a religion that viewed the world as a dismal exile easily reconciled with the joyful affirmation of life that remained his essential creed. Worst of all, the outlook of self-denial came to permeate secular as well as sacred ideals; the medieval knight, no less than the saint, was deemed to be in the service of God. On the field of Ronces-valles, in the *Chanson de Roland,* the heroic ideal of death for one's king is exalted to Christian martyrdom by the archbishop who fights and dies at Roland's side.

> Pur nostre rei devum nus ben murir.
> Chrestientet aidez a sustenir! . . .
> Se vos murez, esterez seinz martirs.[6]

The victory of Christendom over Pagany was the single object worthy of the noble warrior. With the Crusades preached by Urban II and St. Bernard, the amalgamation of secular and sacred purposes seemed complete; the saint was militant and the soldier sainted. What dissent could there be, in a homogeneous and hierarchical world, from ideals of Christian conduct shared by prince and prelate alike? In his literary manifestation, at least, the ancient Adam appeared to have undergone total eclipse.

Yet the comic hero was only dead, and not buried; signs of imminent resurrection were already at hand. The age of *chansons de geste* and Crusades was also the age of the courtly troubadours who celebrated not the sacrifice but the joyous fulfillment of self in this present life. The first known poet in a modern vernacular, Count William IX of Poitiers, writes uninhibitedly "of love and joy and youth," and in one ribald poem recounts his sexual exploits in the guise of a deaf-mute.[7] His successors in the Provençal tongue were normally more restrained. But the love which their decorous songs extolled was emphatically not of the Virgin; the altar of the courtliest adoration remained the bed. The tendency of this aristocratic poetry—inherited by the *trouvères* of northern France—was to assimilate the passions of the heart to the code of chivalric honor, which it thereby completely transformed. Although the troubadours may vie with one another to promote the holy

Crusade, in most of their poetry allegiance to Crown and Church is superseded by devotion to a high-born lady, and the proof of nobility is not so much martial prowess as fidelity in the service of *fin'amor*. The Arthurian romances of Chrétien de Troyes and his contemporaries in the late twelfth century picture this service as an arduous ordeal whose accomplishment is the touchstone of the true knight.

Such a radically revised conception of chivalry was bound to conflict with earlier feudal and religious ideals, not only because of its compromised goal, but because of the equivocal tactics it demanded. In the *Chanson de Roland,* as Erich Auerbach notes, "nothing of fundamental significance is problematic. All the categories of this life and the next are unambiguous, immutable, fixed in rigid formulations."[8] But in the romances everything is problematic. In part this is owing, no doubt, to the "romantic" atmosphere presumably transplanted, with fascination but incomplete understanding, from oral Breton lays to courtly French epics. More fundamentally, it arises from the always inherent (and often explicit) contradiction between the new values and accepted Christian morality. The contradiction is readily apparent in the frequent palinodes of amatory writers like Andreas Capellanus, who caps the first two books of his influential manual of "courtly" love with a third book affirming that "for many reasons any wise man is bound to avoid all the deeds of love and to oppose all its mandates."[9] It is apparent, too, in the thirteenth-century recasting of certain Arthurian tales as moral exempla or religious apologues; Lancelot, the nonpareil of courtly lovers, becomes a figure of tragic dimensions as he struggles, in the monumental "vulgate" cycle, to resist a love which he cannot overcome.

The conflict was of course unavoidable, since the exaltation of illicit love involved a violation of the seventh commandment, if not the first. It also involved a systematic practice of deception that ran counter to every canon of Christian conduct. In the *Chanson de Roland* it is the villain Ganelon and the infidel Saracens who engage in subterfuge and deceit; in the romances the hero himself is constrained to obliquity by the need to con-

ceal his love. Chrétien avoided adulterous subjects by preference and composed his romance of Lancelot, *The Knight of
the Cart,* at the express wish of his patroness, Marie of Cham-
pagne; but in other writers dissimulation plays a more central
role. The troubadours pride themselves on their skill in the arts
of concealment no less than in the art of song. But it is in the
romance of Tristan and Iseult, above all, that trickery in the
pursuit of erotic gratification is endowed with a long-forgotten
prestige. Few comic heroes have been so versatile as Tristan in
his repeated hoodwinking of King Mark, or so adept at equivocation as Iseult when she swears, in Béroul's romance, that no
man has ever come between her thighs except the King and the
scurvy leper who carried her piggyback over the ford (and who
is in fact Tristan). Those who yielded to the allure of such
romances could only do so, like Dante's Francesca, at the peril
of their immortal soul.

The world of courtly love and chivalric romance thus reflects
a fundamental reordering of values in which the grueling self-
sacrifice of martial epics and saintly legends gives way, as the
goal of the happy few, to refined self-indulgence of the gentle
heart. It is a strictly aristocratic world from which not only the
commoner is excluded, as in the chansons de geste, but even
the rude-mannered noble. All men are divided by breeding
between *cortois* and *vilains,* gentlemen and churls; and "a dead
gentleman," Chrétien frankly states, "is worth far more than a
living churl."[10] Tristan's disguises as leper or minstrel, unlike
Odysseus' beggarly rags, betray no sympathetic identification
with the lower orders, for the social outcast finds no place
within the charmed circle of romance except as an object of
scorn.

If this courtly literature nevertheless exerted an enormous influence—far greater than that of the epics—outside the exclusive milieu for which it was intended, this is principally owing
to its implict reaffirmation of the world and (in Marc Bloch's
phrase) "rehabilitation of the individual,"[11] which cut across
the rigid distinctions of class. A similar revaluation found
humbler expression in the literature of the unprivileged many.
The footloose clerics crisscrossing Europe were of lowly origins

and knew begging at first hand; their fraternity, unlike the closed guild of the troubadours, was open to one and all, whether righteous or sinful, halt or hale, burdened with frigid age or aflame with youthful desire.

> Secta nostra recipit   iustos et iniustos,
> claudos atque debiles,   fortes et robustos,
> florentes etatibus,   senio onustos,
> frigidos et Veneris   ignibus combustos.[12]

The "wandering scholars" held holy orders, but their dominant themes—the delights of spring, love, and drink, *Ver, Venus,* and *Vinum*—were more frankly secular and sensual than any openly celebrated in Latin verse for many hundreds of years. The language in which these poems are composed is racier than any vernacular then written, and their style often has a directness altogether alien to the courtly poets. "Iam, dulcis amica, venito," one of the eleventh-century "Cambridge songs" begins, ". . . intra in cubiculum meum"[13] ("Come now, sweet mistress . . . enter my bed"); it is the message of the troubadours stripped of evasions and trimmings.

The masterpiece of goliardic poetry, the confession of the anonymous Archpoet of Cologne, is an open challenge to age-old moral imperatives in conflict with experience. The Archpoet makes no endeavor to drape his appetites in spiritual garb or exalt them as genteel yearnings; it is a most arduous thing, he affirms, to conquer nature and maintain a chaste mind in a virgin's presence. He rejects the burdens of earnestness for the delights of play, which is sweeter than honey—

> Mihi cordis gravitas   res videtur gravis,
> iocus est amabilis   dulciorque favis—

and with an impudent inversion of hallowed priorities he declares himself more eager for pleasure than salvation. "Since I'm dead in my soul," he writes, "I take care of my skin":

> voluptatis avidus   magis quam salutis,
> mortuus in anima   curam gero cutis.[14]

No formulaic palinode can annul the defiant individualism of these lines. The man who avowedly cares more for his skin than for his soul in the century of the first Crusades is self-consciously pitting himself, like the comic heroes of ancient times, against the most venerated values of the established social order.

A similarly irreverent spirit infects the vernacular literature of the so-called "bourgeois" tradition that came into being toward the end of the twelfth century in northern France and Flanders, where the resurgent city life of the Middle Ages had taken deepest root north of the Alps. Next to nothing is known about the poets or their audience, although some of the former must have overlapped with the hand-to-mouth clerics who composed ribald Latin verses for their own amusement. Among the prototypes of the *fabliaux* is one of the Latin "Cambridge songs," which tells a story of marital infidelity and retribution with the moral that "fraud outdid fraud."[15] But when such scurrilous tales began to be widely circulated in the vernacular, their auditors no doubt included the disreputable burghers of the new towns. The fabliaux came to prominence, as Joseph Bédier remarks, simultaneously with the bourgeois class;[16] they constitute that class's charter of emancipation from the exclusive dominion of aristocratic taste. The meter of these brief tales is normally the octosyllabic couplet of the romances, but in nearly every other respect the two genres are diametrically opposed. Swift of pace and spare of adornment, the fabliaux tell a bawdy tale in the most unceremonious manner, leaving little to nuance. Among the townsmen, priests, and peasants who make up their recurrent dramatis personae, adultery is sardonically stripped of all romantic trappings and woman rudely brought down from her pedestal of courtly adulation. Lechery and deceit are unredeemed by the elevating devotion of a Lancelot or Tristan.

The disparity in tone and manner between the worlds of romance and fabliau testifies, in itself, to the depth of class division between noble and commoner in feudal society. Not that these two literatures existed in watertight compartments. On the contrary, there seems to have been, in Bédier's phrase, a "confusion of genres and promiscuity of publics."[17] The merchant or artisan of the commune could no doubt be spellbound by a fabulous legend of the Round Table just as the lord of the manor might be amused by a rowdy tale of plebeian vulgarity. A versatile minstrel could handle a varied repertory, and goliard, jongleur, and trouvère may sometimes have been a single entertainer in sundry guises.

Even if the two literatures continually overlapped, the division between them nevertheless remained profound. The romances give expression to the ideals of an aristocratic élite whose field of action was passing from the battlefield to the court. Despite their inherent contradictions, they openly break with neither the feudal ethic nor the Christian faith, and pay lip service to both. "I have forgotten chivalry and the life of a knight at court," Béroul's Tristan laments. ". . . I ought to go to another land where I could fight battles to win rewards . . . I swear to God that, if I could, I should willingly arrange for Yseut to be reconciled with King Mark, to whom she was wedded as the Law of Rome prescribes."[18] The Church might with reason suspect the romances of heretical worldliness, but their elevated tone and suggestive symbolism made them susceptible of orthodox reinterpretation, and in the Cistercian *Quest of the Holy Grail* the adulterous Lancelot's virgin son Galahad can even appear as an earthly figuration of Christ. But few fabliaux could be reconciled, despite an occasional moral tag, to any spiritual purpose. They remained, when not beneath notice, beyond redemption: the resolute negation of any ideal at all. The tellers of fabliaux, Bédier observes, "do not elevate themselves to satire" but content themselves with caricature.[19] The jongleur, as Brunetto Latini pictured him in the thirteenth century, "mocks at himself, at his wife, at his children, at everybody."[20] To the courtly ideal of the feudal noble the barely emancipated citizen, who had not yet commissioned ideals of his own, had nothing to oppose, in these coarse tales, but an outpouring of unbridled burlesque whose function lay not in affirming new values but in leveling the old.

It was not in the fabliaux, where heroism of any kind was unknown, that the lower orders found an imaginative champion, however, but in the exploits of an irrepressible fox whose fame took medieval Europe by storm and soon rivaled that of Charlemagne's and King Arthur's boldest knights. The origins of Reynard's international saga are the subject of controversy, but the extant literary sources are few. Among these is the Aesopian fable, which enjoyed great popularity with the monks of the early Middle Ages, mainly in Latin prose versions of ancient fabulists such as Phaedrus and Avianus; the most widespread of these collections was known as *Romulus*. Most of these fables were later adapted to French verse by Marie de France and others anonymous in the twelfth and thirteenth centuries; they called their books *Isopets,* after Aesop.[21] Tales of rivalry between fox and wolf (or fox and bear) were especially current from an early date, and several Latin poems on the subject survive. In the late eighth century a Carolingian poet, possibly Paul the Deacon, versified an Aesopian fable (not preserved in earlier Latin versions) in which the fox cures the sick lion and avenges himself on his enemy by prescribing a bearskin as the lion's medicine. This tale, however disseminated, seems to have formed a nucleus for the saga of Reynard. It reappears in a much expanded version (with the wolf as the victim) more than a century later as the central episode in a poem of 1200 lines, the *Ecbasis cuiusdam captivi*.[22]

Then, in the mid-twelfth century, a full-blown epic in seven books, now known as the *Ysengrimus* and attributed by scholars to a certain Nivardus of Ghent, narrates the checkered adventures of the wolf Ysengrimus in his running battle with the crafty fox Reinardus.[23] Not only are the names of the two antagonists, and of the bear Bruno, first introduced in Nivardus' poem; many of their most renowned exploits here make their appearance, some elaborated from familiar fables, others recorded for the first time. A generation later, around 1170, the earliest known vernacular versions were composed in northern France, and these proliferated until about 1250, with later imitations continuing into the fourteenth century. The so-called *Roman de Renart* is not a single work but a haphazard collection of more or less brief poems (called "branches") by different and mainly anonymous hands; the most inventive and influential branches date from before 1200. These French tales proved immensely popular and were soon adapted in High German (by the Alsatian Heinrich der Glichezâre) and in Flemish. The Flemish poet Willem's *Reinaert de Vos,* dating from about 1250, gathered the various stories into a continuous narrative, which an anonymous follower greatly expanded a century later. A prose rendition of this Flemish poem became the main source, directly or indirectly, for most of the subsequent adaptations in English and German. Chaucer's *Nun's Priest's Tale,* like the anonymous Middle English story of the fox and wolf in the well, probably derives from French sources, but virtually all later versions, from Caxton's *History of Reynard the Fox* in 1481 to Goethe's *Reineke Fuchs* in 1794, hark back to the Flemish. In France the tales were all but forgotten once classicism gained the ascendant; La Fontaine completely ignored them. In fact, they were never printed until Méon's edition of 1826.

It was only after Goethe's poem and Méon's edition, and after the revival of interest in the Middle Ages, that a German scholar, Jacob Grimm, published in 1834 the first major study of the early Reynard poems. In accordance with his own Romantic conception of folk poetry, Grimm argued that the various medieval versions were in effect fragmentary survivals of a lost Germanic beast-saga orally transmitted from immemorial times.[24] Grimm's theories, though disputed in both France and Germany, prevailed throughout the nineteenth century, and in 1892 the French scholar Léopold Sudre undertook to demonstrate, through collation of folklore motifs from many countries, that "the epic of the fox and the wolf arose from the crowd and not from books."[25] This view has since been effectively rebutted by Lucien Foulet in his authoritative study *Le Roman de Renard* (1914). Rightly charging his predecessors with neglecting the texts we have through preoccupation with versions we lack, Foulet sets out to examine the *Roman de Renart* as a work of twelfth-century France. He convincingly demonstrates the direct influence of the Latin *Romulus* and *Ysengrimus* on the French poems; places these in the literary context of their age; and denies to an amorphous "people" any significant part in their formation.

There can be little doubt of Foulet's principal conclusions. The vernacular poems are not bits and pieces of a primeval folk-epic but creations of inventive and skillful craftsmen thoroughly versed in contemporary French and Latin poetry. At their best they are masterpieces of a very high order, and Foulet is fully justified in his astonishment that "one of the most finished and most original productions of old France" was long passed off as "an incoherent jumble of refurbished and patched up texts."[26] Yet this correct judgment does not preclude the possibility — however difficult of proof — that tales of the fox and wolf may have circulated orally among the peoples of northern Europe and provided important raw materials for Nivardus and his vernacular followers. There is no need, as Foulet proposes, to choose between folklore and literature as if they were incompatible;[27] the example of recent poets such as Yeats and Lorca, who have made use of both, refutes the assumption. The extensive parallels with European and oriental folktales unearthed by Sudre and others strongly support the conjecture that the Reynard poets drew on popular fables current among the peasants and burghers of France and Flanders as well as on learned sources.

The contemporary phenomenon of Arthurian legend suggests an analogy. Stories of King Arthur and his knights must have survived and ramified for centuries among the Celtic-speaking peoples of Wales and Brittany without attaining literary form. It was only after Geoffrey of Monmouth made use of some of these tales in his Latin *History of the Kings of Britain* — soon adapted in Anglo-Norman French verse by Wace — that the Arthurian legends came to the attention of Europe. Yet Chrétien de Troyes and his fellow romancers drew only peripherally on these written sources. Quite apart from individual inventiveness there must have been, as R. S. Loomis has persuasively demonstrated in his discussion of the Grail legend,[28] a widespread oral diffusion of Breton tales which the French poets exploited for their own ends as soon as Geoffrey's pretended history, by making the matter of Britain respectable, had revealed the fabulous trove of native folktales long lying at hand. Nivardus and his French successors very possibly followed a similar procedure with their more humble material, fleshing out the skeleton of Aesopian fable with colorful exploits from current popular lore.

The *Ysengrimus,* with its convoluted rhetoric, ponderous wit, and tendentious satire, could not be less popular in style; yet beneath its crust of monastic classicism the poem betrays unmistakable affinities with folk tradition. This is especially evident in its author's marked sympathy for the poor and oppressed, who find an articulate spokesman in the crafty fox. "The man who can do most acts worst," Reinardus tells his avaricious uncle, the wolf, "and the poor man makes up for it all . . . what the rich man and poor man have all belongs to the rich."[29] Honor, he bluntly asserts (in anticipation of Falstaff), is too dearly bought at the price of death, and nobility is worthless if it cannot alleviate hunger.[30] Fortunately, however, "the great are often dull-witted, and the small often clever."[31] Such attitudes were not derived from a perusal of Latin manuscripts.

Nor do the Latin sources give any hint either of the diversity of tales in Nivardus or of the names by which he calls the fox and wolf. Now we happen to know, from a single reference in the chronicler Guibert of Nogent some forty years earlier, that the name Isengrin (to give its French form) was not Nivardus' invention. During an uprising at Laon in 1112 the unfortunate Bishop Gaudry was discovered hiding in a barrel by one of the rebels and dragged to his death. "Now, as a joke," Guibert writes, "the bishop used to call this man Isengrin, because he had the look of a wolf and that is what some people commonly call wolves [*sic enim aliqui solent appellare lupos*]."[32] Foulet, who virtually denies the existence of any popular lore, regards the bishop's sobriquet as a recondite allusion to some lost Latin precursor of the *Ysengrimus.* But both Guibert and an anonymous commentator of the time portray Gaudry as a notably coarse and uneducated prelate, "worth nothing at all in letters, [and] holding the literate in scorn."[33] In this context, the passage suggests instead that Isengrin was a name given to the wolf by the common people in northern France, just as *renard* is still the name by which they call the fox, formerly known as *goupil.* These names could only have become current through widely circulated and extraordinarily popular tales that antedated the literary versions we possess. Guibert's explanation of the name implies not that it was an erudite allusion, as Foulet contends, but that it required clarification, in Guibert's judgment, for readers of Latin outside his native region.

It seems safe to postulate, then, that the Flemish monk who composed the *Ysengrimus* had the happy inspiration of enriching well known fables of learned provenance with a hitherto untapped mine of popular legends concerning the escapades of a fox, a wolf, and a bear whose names — all Germanic in origin — significantly remain constant, though others vary, in every subsequent continental version. (In Norman England, which lay in another cultural sphere, the name Reynard is first recorded in "The Fox and Wolf in the Well" toward the end of the thirteenth century, and Chaucer, a century later, called his fox Russell; the Flemish forms Isegrim and Bruin were introduced by Caxton's *History* in 1481.) Once Nivardus had revealed the literary resources of fable and folktale it was not long — perhaps twenty years — before others began to exploit the same material in French verse. By composing racy couplets in their native tongue they brought the tales of the fox and the wolf, enhanced by their own art and learning, back within the reach of the people from whom they had sprung — and of their newly enfranchised city cousins. By minimizing ecclesiastical satire and heightening chivalric parody they both burlesqued the high and mighty nobility and elevated beasts of ignoble descent to far-famed paladins of forest and field. And by casting not Isegrim (as in the *Ysengrimus*) but his crafty foe Reynard as their protagonist they exalted this archetypal self-server, this unscrupulous champion of the main chance, to the epic stature of full-blown comic hero.

The *Roman de Renart* remains untranslated in English, but even a partial summary of a few of its branches will give some idea of its character. Two branches in particular are of exceptional scope and importance. The earliest of all, according to the researches of Foulet, was probably the poem which the manuscripts divide into two parts, numbered II and Va in the edition of Ernest Martin. A certain Pierre de Saint-Cloud is several times mentioned in later branches, and to him Foulet ascribes the composition of this remarkable and original poem. The author is well aware of its novelty. "Seigneurs," he begins—for the listeners of these mighty deeds, like the animals who perform them, are invariably ennobled—"many a story have you heard, for many a storyteller tells how Paris ravished Helen, and the pain and suffering he had from it; and of Tristan, as recounted by La Chièvre, who spoke so finely about him; and fabliaux and chansons de geste. Many another tells romances of Yvain and his beast throughout the land." But there is one story that they have never yet heard, he continues, for no storyteller has sung it till now: the long and desperate war between Reynard and Isegrim.

> Mais onques n'oïstes la guerre,
> Qui tant fu dure de grant fin,
> Entre Renart et Ysengrin,
> Qui moult dura et moult fu dure.[34]

To begin with, the fox's deeds are by no means glorious; he appears as a barnyard predator re-enacting Aesopian fables. His first exploit is the encounter, later immortalized in English by Chaucer, with the cock Chantecler, whom he disarms with flattery and snatches between cockadoodle and doo, only to lose his prey when he opens his mouth, at Chantecler's prompting, to taunt his pursuers. He fares no better with a titmouse who shrewdly evades his kiss or with Tibert the cat, who pushes Reynard into the trap set for him. His only success, echoing the best-known fable of all, is in enticing the crow Tiécelin to let fall a hunk of cheese; a meager recompense for his strenuous efforts. But everything changes when Reynard stumbles into Isegrim's hidden grotto and finds his enemy's wife, Hersent, alone with her cubs; he not only wins the lady's compliance in love but adds insult to injury by bepissing and thrashing the cubs before he departs. Isegrim is not unnaturally incensed, and war begins in earnest. Reynard wins the first skirmish when he lodges the pursuing she-wolf headfirst in a foxhole and assaults her repeatedly from behind. Hersent and Isegrim bring charges before the court of King Noble the lion (in Branch Va), and Reynard is summoned to judgment. But he balks at the invitation to swear to his innocence on the tooth of the mastiff "Saint" Roonel, who is playing dead in a ditch, and reaches the safety of his impregnable refuge, Maupertuis, just ahead of a pack of pursuers. In consequence of his illicit amours the bungling prowler of the opening episodes has become a formidable outlaw defiantly pitted against the rest of the animal kingdom.

The episodes of the *Ysengrimus* show little interconnection beyond a common cast of characters and satirical intent; the fox's rape of the she-wolf, for example, is almost as devoid of consequence as in the isolated fable told by Marie de France.[35] Pierre de Saint-Cloud, by focusing on Reynard and the genesis of his feud with Isegrim, gives his poem an impressive protagonist and a purposeful unity of action. Even so, his episodes betray their origin as separate fables, and the implications of Reynard's momentous conflict with King Noble's court are no more than suggested. It remained for the anonymous author of Branch I to complete the process of exalting the lowly trickster of popular tradition to an authentic comic hero. "Pierrot, who put his skill and his art into making verses about Reynard and his dear companion Isegrim," he begins, "left out the best part of his matter, since he forgot the plea and the judgment that was made in the court of King Noble the lion."[36] The trial of Reynard by his assembled peers is the grand theme of the tale which stands first in every manuscript of the *Roman de Renart,* and which captured the imagination of northern Europe. The Flemish and German versions from Willem to Goethe are mainly elaborations on this great poem.

Winter was past and Ascension at hand, the poet relates, and the rose and hawthorn in flower when Sire Noble the lion convoked all the beasts of his realm to hold court at his palace. None was so bold that he failed to attend, excepting only "the rascal, the wicked thief,"[37] Reynard, and on his head the others eagerly heap accusations. His dalliance with Dame Hersent seems a paltry cause, as his cousin Grimbert the badger pleads in Reynard's behalf, for so much clamor. Only Bernart the ass is convinced by her oath that she has done nothing a nun would not do, but King Noble is reluctant to shatter the peace of his realm for a peccadillo. At this critical juncture a mournful procession, led by Chantecler and his wife, Pinte, arrives with the bier of Pinte's sister Copée, whom Reynard has slain; and the outraged king vows to bring the felon to justice. Hunger has violated a deeper taboo than lust, and amid the universal outcry no one pauses to ask how lions, wolves, and bears fill their stomachs. The culprit's arraignment, however, is no easy task. One by one the King's emissaries, first Bruin the bear, then Tibert the cat, experience the ravenous hunger for which the fox was indicted, and once they yield to his artful temptations they barely escape with their lives. They differ from Reynard not in their appetites but in their ability to sate them. Only after the third envoy, Grimbert, tremblingly delivers a royal summons commanding Reynard to appear at court with a noose around his neck does the renegade vassal at last obey his lord.

Before his assembled accusers Reynard elevates himself to the heroism that instinctive defiance has thrust upon him. He disdains to show a coward's face and defends himself with head high. The verdict is swiftly delivered and a gallows as swiftly erected, but in extremity he changes tack and cheats death by feigning submission. With ostentatious avowals of repentance he dons the pilgrim's wallet and shoulders the cross, saluting only King Noble and his haughty queen, Dame Fière, who gives him her ring and asks for his prayers. But no sooner is the court behind him than he snatches up his chief tormentor, Coart the hare, and from a lofty precipice profanely defies the assemblage below. The stunned barons give pursuit, with Tardif the snail in the lead, but Reynard again gains the ramparts of Maupertuis. Two appendages, Branches Ia and Ib, continue the tale. In the first, Reynard thwarts a protracted siege of his fortress and brazenly adds the drowsing Queen Fière to his conquests, escaping execution by the skin of his teeth. In the second, he reverts to guerrilla tactics, disguising himself as an itinerant jongleur after falling into a dyer's vat. He befuddles Isegrim with a polyglot dialect of his own invention and entices him into a trap, where a dog unmans him (to Hersent's loud distress); then returns home in time to intercept his wife Hermeline's remarriage and roundly disabuse her of the untenable notion that he is dead.

These two poems form the nucleus of the *Roman de Renart,* much of which consists of repetitive variation on their major themes. Several other early branches, however, are equally accomplished on a more modest scale. Branch III, for example, relates how Reynard, in his unremitting search for food, plays dead by the roadside when he sees a cartload of fish and eels approaching. The passing merchants obligingly throw their unexpected booty onto the cart, where Reynard rises up with a laugh at their premature plans to dispose of his hide; with a bellyful of herring and a necklace of eels he jumps down from the cart and bids the astonished merchants a cheery farewell. At home he enjoys another laugh when he initiates the drooling Isegrim, who has been drawn by the tempting fumes of his catch, into the order of fish-eating monks, and tonsures him with boiling water. He then teaches the credulous novice to fish through a hole in the ice with a bucket tied to his tail, and abandons him to a troop of hunters when the water predictably freezes; Brother Isegrim is fortunate to escape with the loss of his tail. Branch IV narrates the no less famous story of the fox and the wolf in the well. After raiding the chicken coop of an abbey Reynard mistakes his own reflection at the bottom of a well for his wife Hermeline and, when she fails to answer, lowers himself to the bottom, where he discovers his error. Isegrim opportunely arrives, and Reynard's native resourcefulness quickly makes amends for its earlier lapse. He solemnly apprises the wolf that he is "the late Reynard" whom "you loved more than your brother";[38] now he is in paradise, he avows, savoring the delights of inexhaustible victuals. The gullible wolf implores permission to join him and after brief penitence and unseemly prayer draws Reynard up in one bucket as he descends in the other. Reynard makes good his escape but Isegrim is hauled out by irate monks and beaten within an inch of his life.

Though told with the art of practiced minstrels, these sprightly anecdotes exemplify the popular outlook characteristic of the *Roman de Renart.* Their point of view could not be more different from that of Aesopian fable, especially in its medieval form. In one well-known fable of "Aesop," for example—recorded in Greek and in Phaedrus, though not in medieval Latin—a fox escapes from a cistern when he lures a goat after him, then climbs out on his back and leaves the goat in the lurch. Not the fox's cunning but the goat's folly is the point of the fable: "A sensible man," Aesop's moral makes plain, "never embarks on an enterprise until he can see his way clear to the end of it."[39] Such counsels of prudence are the stock in trade of medieval fable, and for one monastic fabulist of the early thirteenth century, Odo of Cheriton, the story of Isegrim and Reynard in the well contains an even more solemn warning. The fox, Odo writes, "signifies the Devil, who says to man, 'Descend to me in the well of sin and you will find delights and many good things.' The fool acquiesces and descends into the well of guilt, and there finds no refreshment."[40]

The stories told in the *Roman de Renart* differ from such sententious fables in zest of inventiveness and wealth of detail and in the antithetical values that inform them. The prudential admonishment still prominent in the initial episodes of Pierre de Saint-Cloud's seminal poem soon surrenders the field to ill-concealed admiration as the trickster out-tricked blossoms into the trickster triumphant. In his running war with the dim-witted wolf and with the leagued forces of the animal kingdom, Reynard becomes an archetype of the immemorial underdog employing the weapons of the weak and the little against the big and the strong. His true affinities are not with the animated exempla of moral Aesop and his monastic epigoni but with sly mischief-makers like Hermes in early Greek legend, or with Aristophanes' irrepressible scamps. His ends are as elemental as his means are ingenious; with a mental and verbal agility reminiscent of Odysseus in the Cyclops' den, and with total disregard for the self-serving morality of his betters, he unabashedly pursues the age-old morality whose first and most urgent commandments are filling his belly and saving his skin.

The prevalence of such primordial motifs in the stories of Reynard clearly indicates a substratum of popular lore which the poets could not have derived from their learned sources alone. In some ways, these tales reflect a still more primitive stage of folk memory than the wanderings of Odysseus. The comic hero of antiquity was on intimate terms, as we have seen, with the animal kingdom; he chose not to follow virtue and knowledge, as imposed from above, by the sacrifice of what he shared with the beasts. His humanity was an outgrowth, not a denial, of his animal nature. But that humanity was none the less paramount. Odysseus insists that Belly be fed but shuns Circe's trough; Peisthetaerus dons feathers only after remodeling the birds in his image; Lucius learns through laborious asininity to be more wholly a man. For the ancients the animal story was either lighthearted parody, like the mock-Homeric *Battle of Frogs and Mice,* or illustrative apologue, like the fables of Aesop; heroes, whether comic or tragic, were men. If primeval bear-legends underlie the tales of Odysseus, they had been forgotten long before Homer. But Reynard the fox, like the Coyote of native American myth and the Afro-American Brer Rabbit, belongs to a no doubt older tradition of the animal trickster, in all probability handed down by oral transmission from paleolithic times.

The *Roman de Renart* thus gives sophisticated comic expression to pagan folktales that must have survived for millennia in the imperfectly christianized countryside of northern Europe. The conflict with Christian morality is everywhere in these tales, and one of Reynard's frequent epithets identifies him with the most ill-famed of deceivers, the devil himself. The epithet is a humorous tribute more than a warning, for the comic Reynard retains a trace of the awesome faculty, ascribed by Jung to the trickster-figure of primitive myth, of being "both subhuman and superhuman, a bestial and divine being."[41] He drags divinity down from the heavens and redeems the durable animality that Christianity had disparaged for ages.

Perhaps the comic hero of the Middle Ages could only have been an animal, since the qualities he embodies were deemed unworthy of admiration in a man. The polarization of class ideals in medieval society is nowhere more evident than here. Achilles and Odysseus could be comrades in arms, but Galahad and Reynard cannot share the same species; there is no common ground between them. The models of Christian virtue propagated through saints' lives and chivalric epics were scarcely pertinent to the commons, who had no alternative paradigms to follow, since the alternative to the saint was the sinner. Whatever exemplary virtues the lower orders might later evolve, apart from submission to their betters, were not evident in the twelfth century even to themselves. There was no recognized theoretical basis in feudal society on which to challenge John of Salisbury's dictum that the feet of the commonwealth owed obedience to the head and soul.[42] But if Church and nobles could lay down the law for human society, the animal world lay beyond their jurisdiction; here fantasy was given rein to defy the existing order with unwonted impunity. The wily fox who repeatedly perpetrates outrages punishable among men by death and damnation, and escapes with no more than a loss of fur, was a hero with whom the disgruntled could identify at last. It is not surprising that poems which so vividly articulated long quiescent impulses of this nature should have enjoyed such instantaneous and widespread acclaim.

If the raw material of these animal legends is primitive and universal, the poems are at the same time, however, intensely contemporary and local. The hero of the *Roman de Renart,* whatever his genesis, is not the undifferentiated Trickster of folklore but a rebel within and against the society of his own place and time who gives birth to a new awareness by reincarnating age-old traditions. The old stories could only have been preserved among the conservative peasants of the countryside, but the auditors who gave occasion to the new literature were almost certainly the very burghers who took delight in the scandalous fabliaux and who represented the element of change and potential insurrection in medieval life. For the burghers of twelfth-century Europe, despite the phenomenal prosperity of their more industrious representatives, were still (in Henri Pirenne's words) "a class of *déracinés,*"[43] despised by baron and bishop alike. The merchant in particular was a displaced person in a settled world, an alien in outlook no less than in appearance and speech. "This rover, this vagabond of trade," Pirenne writes in *Medieval Cities,* by the strangeness of his manner of life must have, from the very first, astonished the agricultural society to all of the customs of which he went counter and in which no place was set aside for him. He brought mobility to the midst of people attached to the soil; he revealed, to a world faithful to tradition and respectful of a hierarchy which fixed the rôle and rank of each class, a shrewd and rationalist activity in which fortune, instead of being measured by social status, depended only on intelligence and energy. And so it is not surprising that he gave offense. The nobility never had anything but disdain for these upstarts come from no one knew where, and whose insolent good fortune they could not bear.[44]

Such disreputable misfits were tolerated (and strenuously encouraged) only because the traffic they carried on profited the local lord as much as themselves.

Far from being a respectable profession, commerce was barely distinguished, especially by the ecclesiastical authorities, from fraud and pillage. Abbot Guibert of Nogent, whom we have already encountered, gives an indignant account of bourgeois practices in twelfth-century Laon, comparing the unscrupulous tradesmen to "barbarians or Scythians, people who have no laws." An unwary buyer might find himself locked in a bin until he ransomed himself: "These things and others like them," Guibert affirms, "were done in the city."[45] Even apart from such banditry, which Guibert considers business as usual, the frank quest for profit was deplored as the sin of avarice, and usury forbidden to all but unbelievers. Condemned by a Church and despised by an aristocracy whose spiritual and temporal hegemony he nonetheless continued to acknowledge, the burgher found himself morally on the defensive even as his economic influence was immeasurably expanding. His demand for municipal self-government frequently resulted in open violence, like the uprising at Laon that followed Bishop Gaudry's ill-advised attempt to revoke a recently granted charter. Once established, a commune became a privileged sanctuary governed by laws of its own, where a runaway serf could win his freedom by living within the walls for a year and a day. The burghers, having purchased or seized the right to manage their own affairs, were by and large content to accept with suitable deference the social and cultural pre-eminence of feudal prince and feudal prelate. They knew their place yet continually chafed against it; they were no revolutionaries, yet it was in the commune, as Marc Bloch observes, "that the really revolutionary ferment was to be seen, with its violent hostility to a stratified society."[46] The newly enfranchised burghers of the twelfth century had not lost the memory of recent serfdom, nor had differences of wealth and occupation within the walls yet hardened into the rigid class divisions destined to plague the urban life of the later Middle Ages. Despite a social structure whose strict "subordination of the individual to the whole" Pirenne likens to that of ants and bees,[47] by the medieval world at large the townsman was scorned as a lawlessly insubordinate upstart —and not without reason.

The crafty renegade fox of the *Roman de Renart* might be called the vicarious comic hero of a class without the self-confidence to evolve their own heroes; a class at once defiant and diffident toward *seigneurs* whose authority they alternately acknowledged and flouted. By his audacious refusal of every constraint on his allegiance or constriction of his anarchical will he accomplishes in fable the emancipation which they dared not aspire to in fact. Their own paradoxical attitude is reflected in the pervasive parody of feudal society central to these poems. Parody is not adventitious but essential; it serves not only (and not primarily) to satirize the nobility but, more importantly, to exalt the animal trickster of popular legend, through comic association with knightly prowess, to a hitherto unimagined glory. Without the foil of high chivalric adventure Reynard could have been no more than a common malefactor and his saga merely another fabliau. But through extravagant burlesque of aristocratic traditions as much admired as derided, the poets of the rude new order expropriated the heroic idiom of chanson de geste and Arthurian romance for their own wholly different ends. The underling's challenge to the exclusive dominion of courtly values is clothed in an act of homage.

The uses of parody in the principal branches of the *Roman de Renart* are many and varied, ranging from the honorific epithets and chivalrous phrases of animal converse to elaborate travesties of feudal institutions and practices. The incongruity between palatial trappings and barnyard antics is an unfailing source of entertainment as the poets narrate with mock-epic inflation the mighty contests arising from trivial things. More is involved, however, than amusing effects; for along with the mannerisms of courtly convention an entire society is held up to burlesque, and against that society's exacting prerogatives a single outcast stands obstinately opposed. In the person of Reynard innocuous parody of feudalism passes into subversion of its cardinal assumptions; he deliberately challenges the norms that the other beasts unwittingly caricature. Most fundamentally, he ignores and thereby undermines the hierarchical principle on which the orderly functioning of the animal kingdom depends. It is Reynard's impertinent absence from the assemblage convoked by King Noble in the opening lines of Branch I that unleashes the pent-up swarm of accusations against him. From the beginning he is a renegade in a world of vassals, and this is his unforgivable crime.

Without formally repudiating the bonds of feudal allegiance, Reynard negates their force by evading any obligation that might hamper his will. He laughs without shame at his unemancipated victims and in his defense in Branch I he disdainfully subverts the bestial nobility by dismissing his enemies as "serfs by nature."[48] In the true order of things, Reynard haughtily tells the King, *he* is the head and they the tail. Small wonder that the united barons condemn to death the dissenting marauder who, by following his own "vile law,"[49] has set all established law at naught. By his saucy disregard for their vaunted (if frequently violated) code he spurns the sacrosanct virtues of fealty and respect and arrogates the opprobrious epithets of felon and traitor, thief, caitiff, and lecher as his titles of honor. His very success in fulfilling illicit desires that his fellow brutes patently (though covertly) share is the source of their implacable envy, which leagues them against him. Their self-esteem has become conditional on the destruction of the upstart who declines to esteem them. By now the struggle between them is no casual skirmish or personal feud, as before Reynard's trial and conviction; it is now a fight to the finish, since the anarch's continued existence perpetually calls the legitimacy of their order in question. So long as the outlaw thrives there can be no lasting peace in King Noble's dominions.

Among the hallowed institutions which Reynard profanes, two are paramount: love and religion. The *Roman de Renart* not only divests courtly love of its finery, like the purely cynical fabliaux, but elevates physical love to a new comic eminence in its stead. Pierre de Saint-Cloud's great poem, like the romances of Chrétien de Troyes, is a story of the formative power of love. Through his amatory encounter with Dame Hersent, Reynard's life is transformed as Yvain's had been, or Tristan's or Paris'; from this crisis the woebegone chicken thief of the opening episode, the fox habitually outfoxed, emerges as a brigand and lecher of universal renown. An exploit so crucial to the hero's development is solemnly distinguished from its ignominious precursors by the lofty name of "adventure," which signified, in the parlance of romance, a ritual test of destiny in which the worthy alone might prevail. When Reynard first stumbles upon the secret lair and finds himself in the presence of the Constable's lady he hesitates for a moment, like many another bold knight before the unknown. To Hersent's reproach that he has avoided her company he makes the excuse that Isegrim has wrongly accused him of loving her as his paramour. Up to this point decorum has prevailed, but Hersent now casts aside the punctilious reticence known by courtly poets as "danger" and seizes on the suggestion that her shrinking lover had shunned. "Embrace me, kiss me," she cries,[50] and with truly heroic decision Reynard promptly obeys.

In this delightful travesty courtly love is brought down to its animal underpinnings, as a poem that began by imitating Aesop passes in a trice from fable to fabliau. Yet unlike the isolated encounters of the fabliaux Reynard's adventure marks a turning point in his fortunes. Never again will he be unable to see through a rooster's wiles or match wits with a titmouse; never will he falter in love or tremble before such a name as

Isegrim, now that he has discovered his prowess. Henceforth he will follow his appetites with abandon, cuckolding Constable and King, and will boast of his conquests in open contempt of accepted convention. In the scatological Branch VII Reynard confesses to Brother Hubert the hawk that his limbs quiver and his hair stands on end at the mere memory, not of Hersent's eyes, lips, or skin, but of the part that discreet courtly poets left unnamed:

> Car ce est li plus nobles nons
> Qui soit en cest siecle que cons.[51]

By his brash ennoblement of the female pudendum the libertine fox flouts aristocratic manners and Christian morals and affirms the dignity of tenacious plebeian values. Under shelter of comic vulgarity he dares to exalt a love born not of pure spirit or gentle heart, but of the inveterate and irrepressible flesh.

Religious burlesque was endemic in the religious Middle Ages, and nowhere more than in northern France, where such blasphemous mimicries as the braying Ass's Mass afforded a safety valve for the robust saturnalian instincts of the populace.[52] Much of the parody of things sacred in the *Roman de Renart* is lighthearted spoof, like the solemn funeral and subsequent miracles of the martyred hen Copée in Branch I. In many such instances Reynard employs his acumen to the detriment of his credulous fellow creatures. He easily dupes Isegrim, as we have seen, with his evocations of fish-eating monks and of paradise in a well; and in Branch X he entices the mastiff Roonel—whose sainted tooth he had shunned in Va—into a snare by persuading him that it contains miraculous relics. In each case the fox adroitly manipulates a victim who gullibly mistakes hunger pangs for spiritual cravings—a mistake to which Reynard is altogether immune.

The culmination of his irreverence comes at the point of his greatest peril in Branch I, after sentence of death has been pronounced; and it is here that good-humored parody abruptly gives way to sacrilege of breathtaking temerity. In the face of the gibbet Reynard's exploitation of religious credulity is put to the test. "There is no escaping," the poet warns, "unless his ruse is very great."[53] By professing repentance and supplicating permission to take up the cross and go over the sea, Reynard invokes the supreme conjuncture of secular and spiritual ideals, the Crusade; and when his advocate Grimbert extols his courtesy and prowess even the skeptical King can only relent and commute his sentence. This travesty of penitence and absolution is outrageous enough, but once Reynard has borne his cross out of danger and reached the heights commanding the valley he indulges in an act of gratuitous blasphemy perhaps without precedent in the literature of a Christian country. "Reynard has taken the cross in his hands," the poet relates, "and cries to them at the top of his voice: 'Lord King, take your rag, and may God confound the leper who encumbered me with this tatter and with the staff and satchel!' He wipes his ass with them, in the sight of the beasts, then throws them at their heads and says aloud to the King, 'Sire, listen to me! Nureddin sends you greetings by me, who am a good pilgrim: so greatly do the pagans all fear you that they are almost ready to flee.' "[54] With these words and this gesture Reynard attains his ne plus ultra of audacity and rebellion. By scandalous desecration of the cross and insolent association with the Moslem enemy in the Holy Land, the self-willed outlaw proclaims his contempt for the Christian religion itself, and by so doing apparently cuts the last tie that bound him to feudal society. Henceforth this devil in fox's clothing will be the public enemy of every decent and respectable beast.

Not since Peisthetaerus tonguelashed Iris and commandeered Zeus's bride had a comic hero so recklessly defied everything his society held sacred. Reynard vividly reincarnates, at the very height of the High Middle Ages, the underdog who fights with every weapon at his disposal against domination by a social order inimical to his ungovernable sense of life. Yet unlike the ancient comic heroes he has no hope of transforming the world or creating a new one; his dreams are not so grandiose nor his aspirations so high. He contents himself with guarding his own preserve and making frequent raids on the enemy's turf. Only after he has been lowered into his grave in Branch XVII do the values he has espoused in the teeth of the world's condemnation seem momentarily on the verge of triumphing. The archpriest Bernart the ass eulogizes him from the pulpit as a martyred apostle and decrees universal indulgence for those who propagate his ways:

> Foutre convient, si con moi semble.
> Pour ce vous di a touz ensemble
> Que foutre n'iert ja deffendu.
> Pour foutre fu le con fendu . . .
> Et cil qui mon conmant feront,
> A joie en paradiz seront.[55]

But Reynard can no more remain dead than the world can ever be peopled with Reynards. No sooner does the first spadeful of earth strike bottom than the sanctified corpse springs up and snatches Chantecler in his jaws, and the unending cycle begins anew. Escape is provisional as always and resurrection itself not final, for symbiotic adversity is Reynard's mode of existence and without an antagonist in the struggle he would have no reason for being. No Penelope or Isis will mark an end to his labors, and he envisages no victory beyond tactical advantage. With all his noble trappings he remains, like the commonest fox, more nuisance than threat.

The same might be said of the poems that celebrate him: they are the literature of a class whose self-assertion confined itself to animal fable, relinquishing the terrain of human society to the adversary's all but unchallenged possession. The *Roman de Renart*—in this regard more akin to Punch and Judy or the buffooneries of Till Eulenspiegel than to Aristophanes' libelous dramas—never bids fair to disrupt the complacency of a social order that could laugh off its obloquies as coarse and inconsequential burlesque. *De aliis,* they might safely conclude, *fabula narratur:* with them this fable had nothing to do. For all his impudent defiance of feudal institutions Reynard, like the slaves of Plautus, affirms the necessity of an order that he harasses by repeated outrages but never—in the absence of any considered alternative—calls into serious question. Neither transformation nor transcendence is accessible to him. His refuge of Maupertuis is not an autonomous kingdom like Cloudcuckooland but a walled stronghold surrounded on every side by King Noble's inescapable domain. Reynard has no real option but continuous depredation, and in this he is like his intransigent opponents; they decry the success of his stratagems, not their object, which all fundamentally share.[56] This comic hero's audacity does not extend, in short, to ends; he professes what all would gladly practice and desires not other but more. Perhaps it is for this reason that Isegrim's legendary enemy remains through thick and thin his dearest friend and bosom compeer, and the outcast from the animal kingdom never ceases to acknowledge King Noble as his rightful liege lord. Having defiantly emancipated himself from his world he discovers that he knows no other and lingers on around its fringes, neither wholly belonging nor entirely apart: a pest and, by the same token, parasite.

V

MONARCH OF MAKE-BELIEVE

———————— ❧ ————————

I N REYNARD'S world, as in that of Odysseus, deceit was
among the comic hero's most effective weapons against his
dull-witted opponents, whom he regarded with indisputable
malice. But Shakespeare's Falstaff is "a knave without malice,"
as Maurice Morgann remarked in the eighteenth century, and
"a lyar without deceit":[1] a comic hero wholly lacking in guile
who reigns supreme in his own dominion of revelry but finds
himself defenseless against the cunning of a "serious" world.
Yet by his undauntable exuberance he calls into question—in
defeat no less than in triumph—the sufficiency of a world that
is able to do without him.

Not Jonson or Molière but Shakespeare is the legitimate heir
to Attic New Comedy; his romantic festivities are far closer to
Menander than their classical satires. In *The Comedy of
Errors,* one of his earliest plays, Shakespeare adapted a Plautine farce, the *Menaechmi,* in such a way as to amplify the
mysteries of divine providence. Not only the Antipholus twins
and their identical servants but also their long-separated father
and mother are reunited in the closing scene, and the abbey
where these wonders occur is a christianized counterpart to the
groves and grottoes of Pan or Apollo in the ancient comedies
and romances. The atmosphere of miracle is still more pro-

nounced in Shakespeare's last plays. The reunion of father and
daughter in *Pericles* is reminiscent of Plautus' *Rope* (even
though Gower was a more immediate source); and the resurrection of Hermione in *The Winter's Tale,* with its uncanny
echo of Euripides' *Alcestis,* harks back to the dimly remem-
bered origins of New Comic convention in the matrix of tragedy. Finally, in *The Tempest,* the beneficent presence watching over the destiny of errant mortals finds consummate embodiment in Prospero, and the countless discoveries of New
Comedy culminate in the one that gives meaning to all:

> in one voyage
> Did Claribel her husband find at Tunis,
> And Ferdinand, her brother, found a wife
> Where he himself was lost; Prospero, his dukedom
> In a poor isle; and all of us, ourselves,
> When no man was his own.[2]

Through Shakespeare's potent art the mechanical contrivances
of an age-old convention are once again permeated with the
mysterious suggestion of a higher providence that long ago
attended their birth.

Yet this providence, from the abbess of the first comedy to
the magician of the last, frequently manifests itself through a
human agent who participates with more or less conscious purpose in its unfolding. Sometimes, like Prospero in *The Tempest*
or the Duke in *Measure for Measure,* this agent stands largely
apart from the action which he oversees and guides toward its
end; but more often — like the heroines of the middle comedies,
Portia, Rosalind, Viola, Helena, Beatrice — she is herself
deeply involved in the outcome. Providence takes the form of
nature in these plays, and Shakespeare's heroines, by being
closely attuned to nature's rhythms and keenly aware of her
exigencies, are able to cooperate fruitfully in the evolution of
happiness from sorrow and of order from chaos by which
nature attains to her ripest fulfillment. Yet even though these
spirited heroines far surpass their ancient prototypes in discerning the intricacies of human destiny, their scope for action

remains severely restricted by the sovereignty of that destiny, to which they themselves are knowingly subject. The intelligent Rosalind, for all her ironic self-knowledge, is no less a thrall to the dictates of love than the moonstruck lovers of *A Midsummer Night's Dream*. The most she can do is help guide preordained events toward their poetically apt if logically preposterous finale, when (as the god Hymen sings) "earthly things made even Atone together."[3] In so universal a concord only a sullen outsider like Jaques is quarantined from redemption by being immune to folly.

The essential presupposition of final harmony through the restorative power of love defines these comedies as "romantic" despite the emphatically unromantic attitudes of their most perspicacious characters toward the extravagances performed in love's name. ("Love is merely a madness," Rosalind instructs her pupil Orlando, "and I tell you, deserves as well a dark house and a whip as madmen do; and the reason why they are not so punish'd and cur'd is, that the lunacy is so ordinary that the whippers are in love too.")[4] The scene of Shakespearean comedy is no conventional arcadia. There is rough weather in Arden, sickened appetite in Illyria, and distemperature even in fairyland. Yet the remoteness of these exotic settings from the harsh immediacies of treachery and violence that rend the outside world mitigates and finally annuls disruptions unmasked as much ado about nothing. Indeed, the prevalence of *un*reality is the prime condition for the spectator's willful suspension of disbelief in a comic resolution that no one in his right mind would otherwise believe for an instant. This is a world designed for the lover, the madman, and the poet in everyone; it is not a craven flight from reality but a resolute sublimation of desire. It is a world in which the laws of probability are suspended sine die in favor of the overriding prerogatives of imagination; a world of transfiguring dream and clairvoyant madness. Metamorphosis is its form of identity and dissimulation its means of discovery. Through the artifice of impersonation the disinherited find their roundabout way back to nature, and after everyone has again been transmuted into himself disguise can at last be abjured as extraneous.

Character is never differentiated to the point of irreconcilable distinction in this realm of emergent affinities (except for those unhappy few excluded from its enchantment), since in atonement all are destined to be at one, and every dissonance is modulated with an eye to ultimate concord. In consequence the protagonists of Shakespeare's romantic comedies, however steadfast and inventive, have little need of heroic temper. Their vocation is not to challenge a hostile order but to bring a benevolent one to its latent fruition; the values that they articulate are the natural birthright of all. Only the occasional discomfiture of an unassimilable alien—a Malvolio or a Caliban —suggests the potential gravity of a conflict that has never, in this comic asylum, been joined in earnest. But when such conflict succeeds in breaching the magic circle, comedy itself is imperiled. Since the festive autonomy of the comic world demands the abrogation of the unnatural law that governs society in everyday life, an antagonist intent on enforcing that law inevitably shatters the artifice essential to the illusion of nature. Shylock in *The Merchant of Venice* and Angelo in *Measure for Measure,* with their legalistic mentalities and predilection for death, are too radically opposed to the anarchic order of comedy (and too intensely individualized) to be either convincingly assimilated or readily extruded; they suggest a dimension of irresolvable conflict more appropriate to the world of tragedy. In *The Merchant of Venice* the challenge evokes a fit response from the soberest of Shakespeare's comic heroines, who turns legalism itself to the uses of life and adroitly reestablishes the shaken equilibrium. But in *Measure for Measure,* where a providential stage manager is called upon to impose a formally comic resolution on the havoc wrought by his fanatical deputy, the strain is too great for the fragile convention to bear. The illusion of a possible harmony has been shattered beyond repair by emotions too vehement for comedy to contain.

Strife and suffering, then, are not excluded even from Shakespeare's romantic comedies, but are kept at a proper distance. These are plays of the golden moment when creative nature reigns in abeyance of man-made law, and time is postponed till tomorrow. The world of the history plays is the opposite in every essential. Here the scale is not individual but national, and time overshadows every human endeavor; discord, murder, and war hold center stage; and law is a fragile bulwark against the outbreak of violence and the onset of chaos. Both of Shakespeare's historical cycles span generations of conflict and terminate with a respite of peace as fervently wished for as its permanence is uncertain. Their heroes are monarchs who selflessly discipline themselves to bestow the blessings of ordered rule on their subjects. The unique achievement of the two parts of *Henry IV* in Shakespeare's total work is to bring the contrary (and finally incompatible) perspectives of comedy and history, timelessness and time, together in a single orbit and to give them roughly equal weight in the contest that arises from their collision. Against a backdrop of wars and conspiracies the education of a Christian king in his solemn responsibilities coincides with the reign of a flagrantly irresponsible Lord of Misrule, and the conflict between their rival sovereignties becomes gradually inescapable.

Within the large cyclical pattern the hero of the two parts of *Henry IV* is of course the future King Henry V, who is destined to restore the stability of a kingdom shaken by his father's usurpation of the throne from his weak-willed predecessor, Richard II. Before undertaking the awesome task of reuniting his realm through victory in war the youthful Prince must learn to repudiate the companions whose reprobate ways threaten to turn him aside from his mission. The theme of political regeneration prominent in the Tudor historians thus merges with that of personal redemption central to the Morality plays and interludes popular in the sixteenth century: only by the Prince's self-renewal through renunciation of vice can his afflicted people be restored to unity and peace. The values that Henry comes to personify in his progress from dissolute youth to "mirror of all Christian kings"[5] are among the most sacrosanct of Shakespeare's age. Church and State had been effectively yoked, for the moment, through the national Reformation of Henry VIII, and under the rule of his prudent younger daughter the social classes were united as seldom before in common allegiance to the throne. (The respectable burghers of Queen Elizabeth's day would surely have had scant sympathy for a seditious rebel like Reynard.) Yet the values of exuberant excess that Shakespeare's Prince is obliged to abjure in making himself the pattern of Tudor monarchs are of no insubstantial nature; they too have imperious claims and a spokesman unsurpassed in the annals of comic persuasion to make them.

The inevitable conflict between these irreconcilable values long remains latent only because the Prince appears in disguise, so that the revelers rashly mistake their nemesis for one of themselves. On this crucial point Shakespeare parted company with his sources. Holinshed concedes in his *Chronicles* that the Prince "was youthfully given, grown to audacity, and had chosen him companions agreeable to his age, with whom he spent the time in such recreations, exercises, and delights as he fancied"; but pleads in extenuation of such levity "that his behavior was not offensive or at least tending to the damage of anybody, sith he had a care to avoid doing of wrong and to tender his affections within the tract of virtue."[6] In the anonymous *Famous Victories of King Henry the Fifth* the scapegrace Prince makes a worthy companion to Sir John Oldcastle and his rowdy crew, and only when his grieved father reproaches him with following "this vile and reprobate company"[7] does the future king undergo a sudden change of heart and renounce his mistaken ways. But in Shakespeare the Prince's temporary adherence to Falstaff's world is not an error but a stratagem. He knows from the beginning, as he declares in his first soliloquy, that he will "throw off" his "loose behavior" as soon as the moment is opportune (1.I.ii.). Meanwhile he remains firmly if surreptitiously in command of his regal faculties despite the mistaken estimate of friend and enemy alike.

In this dexterous use of stratagem Prince Hal may appear to resemble the classical comic hero. Like his fellow king Odysseus, he skilfully simulates a posture below his rank, then dramatically abandons it when the day of reckoning comes; his disguise, too, is designed to restore order to a troubled land. But the differences are fundamental. Every part played by Odysseus expressed a facet of his multiple being, and through his disguise as a beggar he discovered his kinship with the most abject of his subjects. His roles were not extrinsic but part and parcel of his changing identity, so that beggar and king were indissolubly one. But Shakespeare's Prince differentiates appearance from reality in the most categorical terms; what he seems and what he is have—by his own estimate—nothing in common. The opening lines of his soliloquy emphatically assert this disjuncture. "I know you all," the Prince begins,

> and will awhile uphold
> The unyok'd humor of your idleness,
> Yet herein will I imitate the sun,
> Who doth permit the base contagious clouds
> To smother up his beauty from the world,
> That when he please again to be himself,
> Being wanted, he may be more wond'red at
> By breaking through the foul and ugly mists
> Of vapors that did seem to strangle him.
>
> (1.I.ii.)

The sun may be momentarily obscured by the clouds but always remains "himself" despite their apparent contagion; in reality he cannot be tainted. Prince Henry's role, as his metaphor suggests, is not a versatile and innovative response, like those of Odysseus, but a carefully calculated decision. It expresses not multiplicity but duplicity. He adopts his disguise by deliberate choice ("Yet herein will I imitate the sun") and will throw it off again at his pleasure; the *self* remains inviolate and unchanged through it all.

The Prince's contemptuous reference to "base contagious clouds" and "foul and ugly mists" displays a haughty disdain for his drinking companions strikingly different from Odysseus' sympathetic rapport with swineherd and serving woman, and this attitude is apparent even in his seemingly casual banter earlier in the scene. In quick-witted repartee he is not inferior to Falstaff himself, but his wit returns with mordant insistency to images of the gallows and sewer, which implicitly underscore his awareness of the distance between them. "Thou hast," Falstaff remarks, "the most unsavory similes"—or perhaps (as the early quartos and the Folio print the line) "unsavory smiles" (1.I.ii.). Prince Hal may not in fact be so unaffected by the company he keeps as his soliloquy avows, but his contempt for the carefree life of the tavern unavoidably subverts his pretension to "know you all." The self-consciously remote outsider is seldom the best judge, in Shakespeare, of the values held by others; in this regard the Prince, despite his mask of participant, resembles Jaques, Malvolio, or Angelo.

In the play-acting skills that he adeptly employs to "falsify men's hopes," on the other hand, he recalls the most versatile and unscrupulous of Shakespeare's kings, Richard III, who lays claim to an illustrious lineage:

> I'll play the orator as well as Nestor,
> Deceive more slily than Ulysses could,
> And like a Sinon, take another Troy.
> I can add colors to the chameleon,
> Change shapes with Proteus for advantages,
> And set the murtherous Machevil to school.[8]

Prince Henry intends, of course, to turn his skills not to murder and self-aggrandizement, like Richard, but to the benefit of his people and the glory of his kingdom. Even so, in his calculated adoption of a largely external role and in his readiness to use others as instruments to his end he resembles Shakespeare's Richard far more than Homer's Odysseus. Deception and falsity are intrinsic to his policy no less than to that of his troubled father, whom the impetuous Hotspur angrily calls "vile politician" and "king of smiles" (1.II.iii.); both father and son have been schooled in Machiavelli before their time. This is not to imply that Shakespeare is blackening the Prince's character or presenting him as a covert villain; on the contrary, Hal's stature continues to grow as he progressively makes known the heroic and kingly stuff that he has artfully concealed. What it does perhaps suggest is that judicious pretense and astute dissimulation may be inherent attributes of effective leadership in a world of treachery and deceit. Not Hotspur or Antony but Henry V or Octavius is cut out to rule. Yet the willful singleness of purpose by which the ruler instills obedience in his subjects can only be purchased through the sacrifice of those ungovernable excesses — Falstaff's or Cleopatra's — that his well-ordered government necessarily precludes.

In the context of English monarchical history, as Shakespeare presents it, Falstaff and his unruly crew are clearly intruders who must be drummed from the scene if a sense of majesty is ever to be restored; they are the clouds that will dim the sun until scattered. At this point, however, the sober values informing the historical plays stand in open conflict with the pattern of comedy. In Shakespeare's comedies, as in Aristophanes', existing social reality is normally an ineffective barrier against the overriding demands of imagination; they are "saturnalian," as C. L. Barber has argued, in celebrating the triumph of festive liberty over everyday restraint. In these comedies the intruders from the serious realm are for the most part peripheral and easily dismissed. Even the more disquieting Shylock can be exorcized, in a patently make-believe world, by a quibble. But the comic intruder in the two parts of *The History of Henry IV* is the very substantial Sir John Falstaff, and for that reason the issue is inescapably joined. "In *Henry IV*," as W. H. Auden writes, "Shakespeare intrudes Falstaff, who by nature belongs to the world of *opera buffa*, into the historical world of political chronicle with which his existence is incompatible, and thereby, consciously or unconsciously, achieves the effect of calling in question the values of military glory and temporal justice as embodied in Henry of Monmouth."[9] With reckless disregard of sobriety and order Falstaff sets up a rival camp in the heart of Henry IV's troubled realm and reigns as uncrowned monarch of a freer and happier world. In Part One, at least, the pattern of comedy predominates, and reality momentarily conforms to the liberating exigencies of festival. Falstaff and the Prince miraculously avoid collision and arrive at parallel triumphs by opposite paths.

Conflict, as the Prince's soliloquy admonishes, is present from the beginning, however, and if this conflict calls forth a comic hero of monumental substantiality it also pits him against an adversary of formidable credentials. In the preponderantly comic world of Part One, where claims of political loyalty are sapped by dissension and revolt, Falstaff establishes so pre-eminent a domain that the temporal perspective of the history cycle is largely eclipsed. As a result, at least on the stage, it is not Falstaff and his men but the representatives of the crown who come to seem the intruders. To quote Auden once more, "When Hal or the Chief Justice or any others indicate that they are not bewitched by Falstaff, reason might tell us that they are in the right, but we ourselves are already bewitched, so that their disenchantment seems out of place, like the presence of teetotalers at a drunken party."[10] Yet *these* spokesmen for the social order are not hapless buffoons like Lamachus nor distorted misfits like Shylock; they cannot be dismissed and will not go away. History may be upstaged but waits in the wings, and Prince Henry is no man's sweet wag but the future king who will embody the most revered values of his people.

At the same time, this prince of the blood is a master, as we have seen, of the art of dissimulation. Against this fusion of power and cunning in a legitimate king Falstaff is left with no other resource than the contagious enchantment of his own example, to which the Prince has declared himself immune. The comic celebrant's injection into the adverse world of history deprives him of his privileged sanctuary and demands new qualities of heroic assurance and belligerent self-assertion, for here the odds are not in his favor. Falstaff rises magnificently to the occasion, yet in his total dependence on the Prince's continued good will he is vulnerable as no comic hero has been before. His merry principality at Eastcheap may succeed for the nonce in outshining the tarnished court at Westminster, but there is never a moment's doubt that if the tension between them should break into open conflict Falstaff and all his old lads of the castle would be swept away like the most insubstantial pageant. The outcome of any head-on encounter in the alien arena of history will inevitably spell defeat for those who can win only by inventing the rules. In so one-sided a contest the fat knight will find himself as defenseless as any christom child, since his kingdom, for all its corporeality, is finally not of *this* world.

The movement of *Henry IV* is determined by continual juxtaposition of opposing visions of life. King Henry opens Part One by expressing a feeble hope of peace through intensely vivid images of war:

> So shaken as we are, so wan with care,
> Find we a time for frighted peace to pant
> And breathe short-winded accents of new broils
> To be commenc'd in stronds afar remote.
> No more the thirsty entrance of this soil
> Shall daub her lips with her own children's blood,
> No more shall trenching war channel her fields,
> Nor bruise her flow'rets with the armed hoofs
> Of hostile paces.
>
> (1.I.i.)

Strife is so integral to the weary king's world that even his vision of concord is infected with the vehemence evident in his impetuous rhetoric. After such a prelude it is no surprise that this opening scene is dominated by ill tidings that compel the King to set aside his hopes for a crusade to the Holy Land. Not the least of the uneasy monarch's weighty cares, amid rumblings of rebellion and war, are the "riot and dishonor" that stain his heir apparent's brow, in contrast to the martial virtues of young Percy Hotspur, whom he ruefully calls "sweet Fortune's minion and her pride." Yet the virtues that ought to incriminate the Prince's reputed failings are under suspicion from the beginning. The realm is plagued by riot more virulent than any tavern's, and the honor that emblazons Hotspur is already tainted by rumors of insubordination and pride.

The sharply delineated Falstaffian counterpart to this troubled world is one whose cups of sack and capons and fair hot wenches in flame-colored taffeta have nothing to do, as Prince Henry shrewdly remarks in the following scene, with the time of day. Its reputed riot appears a welcome refuge from the intestine broils that menace the court. After his father's stilted eloquence the colloquial verve of the Prince's speech reflects the salutary influence of his low companions, even though his sardonic wit has a cutting edge that hints at detachment. His barbs take aim at others, never himself. But Falstaff, though able to give as well as he gets, speaks the wholly different language of rhapsody. "We that take purses go by the moon and the seven stars," he proclaims:

> Marry, then, sweet wag, when thou art king, let not us that are squires of the night's body be call'd thieves of the day's beauty. Let us be Diana's foresters, gentlemen of the shade, minions of the moon, and let men say we be men of good government, being govern'd, as the sea is, by our noble and chaste mistress the moon, under whose countenance we steal.
>
> (1.I.ii.)

This speaker, for all his great girth, is far from "fat-witted with drinking of old sack," as the Prince has called him; his wits are very much about him. It is not, however, his verbal dexterity that impresses us most—here the Prince is his equal—but the buoyant inventiveness that expands the cutpurse's nocturnal preference into a fantasy worthy of *A Midsummer Night's Dream*. Not cups and capons but moonlight and forest shadows are the fabric of his vision, and through the enchantment of his words a band of smalltime thieves is transfigured into a chivalry liberated from "the rusty curb of old father antic the law" and subject only to nature's dominion.

If Hal brings this flight of fancy promptly down to "the ridge of the gallows" (1.I.ii.), no wonder; the good government envisaged by Falstaff is incommensurable with that of England or any state. Falstaff's moon and the Prince's gallows aptly symbolize the conflicting orders at loggerheads in these plays: the emancipating order of nature that prevails in the timeless world of comedy and the restraining order of law that governs society in historical time. These rival orders, as Falstaff fails to perceive, are in fact exclusive; that tragic perception will be forced upon Antony in a later play. Only the prolonged but temporary *dis*order of history permits Falstaff to reign unchallenged in his seemingly autonomous sphere, for in the perspective of history an order that eludes all social constraint is mere anarchy.

If Prince Henry performs his part with rare finesse, masking his kingly majesty from all but the audience, Falstaff is an actor of another kind who zestfully projects himself into whatever role he undertakes. Where all life is play the player's self is the sum of his roles, for without distinction of true from false parts there can be no deceit. At one moment Falstaff mourns the Prince's corruption of his innocence, and at the next moment leaps at the suggestion of snatching a purse. In both he is true to form, since Jack the highwayman is a practiced role no less than John the Evangelist, Sir John Sack and Sugar no less than Monsieur Remorse; Falstaff commodiously embraces them all. His frank inconsistency precludes insincerity; " 'Tis no sin," he argues with disarming logic, "for a man to labor in his vocation" (1.I.ii.). His object is not to deceive but to confound. He mocks the serious world not by railing at its defects ab extra, like Thersites, but by incorporating and magnifying its follies in his own preposterous person; he makes a laughingstock of virtue as well as vice by mimicking both in hyperbolic dimensions and inviting others to laugh at themselves in him. He is consistent in nothing but paradox and constant only in fluctuation; his individuality is the multitudes he contains.

Through this intrinsic multiplicity, this innate resistance to definition, Falstaff inevitably calls into question the exclusive categories and hierarchical distinctions on which the social order is founded. He does not take arms against the established powers or flagellate them, like Peisthetaerus, out of his kingdom, but explodes their pretensions and subverts their prerogatives by placing their world on an equal footing with his own; between sweet wag and sweet wench, Heir Apparent and Hostess of the Tavern, he makes no fundamental discrimination of rank. No man can be alien to him except by denying a part of himself, because all humanity is grist for his transubstantiating mill. Falstaff's inventive mimicry not only assimi-

lates but transforms; from the fragments of partial realities—
saint or sinner, barmaid or king—he fabricates in his own
ample person an image of corporeal plenitude and imaginative
abundance in which reality is given flesh by illusion. He redeems the inadequacies of the world as it is by including it all in
himself, and making it new.

In the Gad's Hill robbery and its sequel Falstaff's powers of
improvisation are put to the test and triumphantly vindicated;
no intractable facts can cramp his invincible fancy. The endeavor of Poins and the Prince to unmask him postulates a discrepancy between action and word that proves untenable, for
the holdup is no less farcical than Falstaff's fantastic account.
We behold the man-mountain toiling uphill as stealthily as a
herd of buffalo, crying out at the top of his lungs against the
stony-hearted villains who have taken his horse. Neither danger
nor booty seems to have much appeal for this *soi-disant* forester
of Diana; " 'Sblood," he vows, "I'll not bear my own flesh so far
afoot again for all the coin in thy father's exchequer" (1.II.ii.).
And when told of the travelers' numbers, " 'Zounds," he
cries, "will they not rob us?" A less likely desperado would be
hard to imagine. Yet Falstaff succeeds against all likelihood in
overwhelming the flabbergasted travelers with sheer bravado
and in making off with their goods, only to lard the earth in
headlong flight when the Prince and Poins set upon him
moments later. Even without designing it, Falstaff lavishly provides "argument for a week, laughter for a month, and a good
jest forever," as the Prince has sought. His hilarious discomfiture can only augment his renown, for by bringing laughter
down on himself Falstaff is laboring willy-nilly in his authentic
vocation.

Falstaff is impervious to mockery because he laughs unre-
strainedly at himself and immune to ignominy because he
makes it his glory. His outraged indignation at Hal and Poins
when he overtakes them at Eastcheap can scarcely be called
dissimulation, since the misadventure at Gad's Hill is only his
latest pretext for zestfully indulging the familiar role of Innocence Wronged. "A plague of all cowards, I say, and a vengeance too! . . . Is there no virtue extant?" (1.II.iv.). Such

hyperbolical protestations are essentially guileless, for Falstaff's blatant incongruities are conspicuous to all, himself included. The sorrow that he laments with earnest fervor, as he guzzles sack and denounces the roguery of villainous man, is the poverty of a world where Falstaffs are so few. But like everything else his own melancholy is fair game for laughter, and he mocks in the very act of mourning. "There lives not three good men unhang'd in England," he morosely avows, "and one of them is fat and grows old, God help the while! a bad world, I say. I would I were a weaver, I could sing psalms, or any thing." By deploring virtue in such lugubrious wise he not only dispels the sanctimonious air of its puritanical adherents, who are too single-minded to detect their own incongruities, but affirms the legitimacy of the virtue that he embodies even in the role of Vice. "When *I* use a word," as Humpty-Dumpty will later tell Alice, "it means just what I choose it to mean — neither more nor less . . . The question is, which is to be master — that's all."[11] At Eastcheap Falstaff is indisputably master, and virtue means what he chooses.

In this world where role and reality are one, truth too is a word at Falstaff's command, so that when he launches into his tale of the men in buckram he will be extremely difficult to refute. For Falstaff the lie is not an instrument, as it was in the main for Odysseus, but an end in itself: a revelry of fancy in which deception is incidental to invention. He cannot be trapped by contradiction when incongruity is his essence nor convicted of falsehood when play-acting is his profession. As the buckram-suited assailants of his tale multiply apace we witness his fervid imagination at work, with sovereign disregard for verisimilitude, transmuting a trifling fiasco into a contest of legendary proportions, a Falstaffian precursor of Agincourt. Seven of the original two attackers have already fallen and victory over the other four seems assured when three knaves in Kendal green come up from behind. How many of these three Falstaff might have slain before yielding to their overpowering numbers we will never know, for the Prince chooses this moment to attempt to confute lies "gross as a mountain" (1.II.iv.) with the calipers of common sense. "Why, how couldst thou know these men in Kendal green when it was so dark thou couldst not see thy hand? Come, tell us your reason." But Falstaff's fantasy is no more assessable by the criteria of reason than Tertullian's God. With the ardent conviction of a martyr for truth he replies, "What, upon compulsion? 'Zounds, and I were at the strappado or all the racks in the world, I would not tell you on compulsion . . . if reasons were as plentiful as blackberries I would give no man a reason upon compulsion, I." The Prince will not be deterred, however, and relentlessly presses toward the dénouement he has so artfully contrived: "Mark now," he sternly proclaims, "how a plain tale shall put you down." Against Falstaff's spirited fictions he marshals sober facts, and is sure of his prey: "What trick, what device, what starting-hole," he demands, "canst thou now find out to hide thee from this open and apparent shame?"

Here at last is the moment of recognition, the inevitable unmasking, toward which the drama of Gad's Hill has been tending since its inception. But without a mask there can be no unmasking. The dénouement that occurs is not the reversal — not the open and apparent shame — anticipated by Hal, but the culmination of Falstaffian ingenuity. "By the Lord," he confides with a laugh, "I knew ye as well as he that made ye. Why, hear you, my masters, was it for me to kill the heir-apparent?" (1.II.iv.). Falstaff's open and palpable lies can no more be confuted than believed; there is no pinning Proteus down. On his own turf he is invincible, since the more he shifts ground the more he remains himself, and no starveling bull's pizzle of a prince will best him with so paltry a weapon as a plain tale. Having dissolved all conflict in laughter he calls for a kômos to celebrate his achievement. "What, shall we be merry," he cries to his baffled accusers, "shall we have a play extempore?"

All life for Falstaff is a play outside time; in making the play overt, however, he seals his triumph by imposing his theatrical terms on the others. Their meager facts have failed to trammel his outrageous fictions, so fiction will now reign unchallenged. By sheer verbal dexterity the butt of Gad's Hill has re-established his unimpeachable title as monarch of Eastcheap, and he proceeds to crown instinct with art. He effortlessly ascends the throne of England for which others had spilled rivers of blood, and in the guise of a Henry IV less wan with care than ruddy with sack he bestows royal approval, among all his son's disreputable companions, on one alone: "there is virtue in that Falstaff" (1.II.iv.). Falstaff is thespian to the fingertips, and in every word and gesture cries *plaudite*: "O Jesu," his tickle-brain queen exults, "this is excellent sport, i' faith!" His opposite, the Prince, is an actor too, but one whose success depends on escaping notice; for him, as for Prince Hamlet, the play serves an ulterior end. When he assumes the crown and reprimands Falstaff, in the role of prince, for his unseemly converse with "a devil . . . in the likeness of an old fat man," excellent sport imperceptibly gives way to a private joke in grim earnest. Comical though his epithets are—"that trunk of humors, that bolting-hutch of beastliness, that swoll'n parcel of dropsies, that huge bombard of sack, that stuff'd cloak-bag of guts, that roasted Manningtree ox with the pudding in his belly, that reverent Vice, that grey Iniquity, that father ruffian, that vanity in years"—his indictment reveals the close association, in the Prince's mind, of vice and corruption with the pleasures of the belly dear to comic heroes since Homeric times. This revelation, however, is cloaked by the spirit of play into which the Prince has only apparently entered. Unknown to the others, he is not so much playing a role as casting one off. He anticipates, in the part of Henry IV, the self he will later be pleased to manifest as Henry V, and his estimation of his companion is therefore ominous: wherein, he asks, is Falstaff worthy, "but in nothing?"

From the beginning Prince Henry has seen "fat-guts" in terms of a gross physicality that he finds amusing but secretly disdains. The imaginative vitality of Falstaff's vision altogether escapes him, since play-acting is synonymous, in his eyes, with dissembling, at which Sir John is notably inept. To the Prince's torrent of hyperbolic derision Falstaff eloquently replies, "If sack and sugar be a fault, God help the wicked! If to be old and merry be a sin, then many an old host that I know is damn'd" (1.II.iv.). Sensing that the terms of his play have been altered, he appeals to the future king for the inclusion of his calumniated virtues in a realm that now knows them only as iniquities. He pleads for a kingdom in which reality may correspond to imagination and fact to fiction; where the court may be commensurate with the tavern: a kingdom, in short, capacious enough to contain Sir John Falstaff body and soul. "No, my good lord," he protests: "banish Peto, banish Bardolph, banish Poins"—*these* may know nothing but cups and capons—"but for sweet Jack Falstaff, kind Jack Falstaff, true Jack Falstaff, valiant Jack Falstaff, and therefore more valiant, being as he is old Jack Falstaff, banish not him thy Harry's company, banish not him thy Harry's company—banish plump Jack, and banish all the world." To all of which the Prince and King-to-be answers only: "I do, I will."

The emancipating laws of comedy can only prevail by universal consent of the governed, so that if there is to be harmony the skeptic must be either expelled or converted. Otherwise a single disbeliever can indeed banish a world. Falstaff's magniloquent claim to encompass *all* the world depends, like every role he plays, on the willing suspension of disbelief which is faith. But Hal remains coolly aloof from his spell, as he had from the first; his allegiance is not to the realm of imagination. Within his own sphere Falstaff is supreme and his peroration is irresistible. But the Prince stands outside his sphere and no more succumbs to Falstaff's reckless abandon than Falstaff perceives his ironic detachment. By means of the play he can speak in dead earnest, and no one is the wiser. Thus the tour de force of Falstaffian make-believe is accompanied by the simultaneous triumph of princely dissimulation. If the farce contrived by Hal and Poins exposed a Falstaff superior to contradiction by fact, the play contrived by Falstaff reveals—though only to the audience beyond the Boar's Head—a prince immune to contagion by fancy. For the moment all is laughter, and not even the arrival of the sheriff, the symbol and embodiment of society's law, can disrupt the carefree self-sufficiency of Falstaff's comic world. "Out, ye rogue, play out the play," he protests, "I have much to say in the behalf of that Falstaff" (1.II.iv.). Yet a fatal rift has been opened, unbeknownst to the revelers, between unreal illusion and disillusioned reality; and if Eastcheap and the present are Falstaff's, England and the future, as the event will show, can only be Hal's.

The dissensions menacing England have encroached on the tavern, as a somber prologue to Falstaff's play, with news of the Percies' rebellion; henceforth they will dominate the scene. Hal's antagonist on the historical stage, Henry Percy (called "Hotspur"), is of a very different kind from the "whoreson round man" who enthrones himself at the Boar's Head. Hotspur is a perfect gentle knight born at the wrong time, a paragon of chivalric honor who shrinks with unconcealed revulsion from the hypocrisy that surrounds him. "Why, look you, I am whipt and scourg'd with rods," he cries to his less excitable father and uncle, Northumberland and Worcester, "Nettled and stung with pismires, when I hear Of this vile politician, Bolingbroke" (1.I.iii.). Nor does he display more patience with the "skimble-skamble stuff" (1.III.i.) of his pompous Welsh ally Glendower. With the brash self-confidence of one who is knowingly sweet Fortune's minion, he not unnaturally thinks it "an easy leap To pluck bright honor from the pale-fac'd moon" (1.I.iii.), and looks forward eagerly to the "sport" — excellent sport, i' faith! — of civil war.

For the "nimble-footed madcap Prince of Wales" (1.IV.i.) whom Shakespeare makes his contemporary Percy feels nothing but scorn, and not even the King can suppress the envious wish that his son and Northumberland's had been exchanged in their cradles. The King (like everyone else) is of course mistaken in his son; Hal will soon prove more than Hotspur's equal in valor. The true contrast between them is of another kind. Hotspur's irascible aversion to sham reflects an unbending temper wholly insusceptible to adaptation or compromise. Through passionate self-assurance he mistakes his intentions for accomplishments and admits no evidence that fails to conform to his will. He confounds fact with fiction no less cavalierly than Falstaff, but without Falstaff's conscious mastery. He is not a king of illusion but its thrall. The Prince (unlike his admiring father) perceives this chink in the shining knight's armor and remarks ironically to Poins, "I am not yet of Percy's mind, the Hotspur of the north, he that kills me some six or seven dozen of Scots at a breakfast, washes his hands, and says to his wife, 'Fie upon this quiet life! I want work' " (1.II.iv.). Make-believe may be victorious in the comic world of the tavern, but on the battle-field it is no substitute for logistics. When the crisis comes, Worcester pleads in vain with his nephew to postpone battle until reinforcements arrive, and hesitates to entrust to "A hare-brain'd Hotspur, govern'd by a spleen" (1.V.ii.) the Prince's theatrical challenge to single combat. Through his own mis-guided conjecture, as Lord Bardolph will tell the Archbishop in Part Two, Hotspur recklessly

> lin'd himself with hope,
> Eating the air, and promise of supply,
> Flatt'ring himself in project of a power
> Much smaller than the smallest of his thoughts,
> And so with great imagination,
> Proper to madmen, led his powers to death,
> And winking, leapt into destruction.
>
> (2.I.iii.)

Thus Hotspur's defeat by the Prince in the dénouement of Part One is the defeat of illusion by realism no less than Boling-broke's victory over Richard II had been; the outcome ratifies not only Hal's personal bravery but the shrewdness of his calcu-lations. "Percy is but my factor, good my lord," he had told the King, "To engross up glorious deeds on my behalf" (1.III.ii.); and so it proves. Yet if the Prince has planned and executed well, the partiality of his shrewd discernment — and the cost of his famous victory — will soon become evident. In Hotspur (as in Falstaff) he detects the fatal illusion without perceiving the larger vision of which it is indivisibly part; he not only defeats an error but kills a dream. Hotspur's death assures the ascen-dancy of a conqueror magnified by usurpation of his rival's glory, but with him there vanishes from England a dimension of impetuous generosity which all the Prince's machinations will never restore.

For the moment, however, the loss of Hotspur is counterbal-anced not only by the Prince's victory but also by the comic heroism of his still undefeated rival, who adapts the stratagems honed in the tavern to the uncongenial theater of war. The master craftsman of make-believe is under no illusions concerning the stubborn realities of armed conflict: "Though I could escape shot-free at London," he quips, "I fear the shot here" (1.V.iii.). He is not one to line himself with hope or flatter himself with a madman's imaginings. Falstaff's presence on the battlefield is in itself a challenge to the exalted pretensions of the contestants, and on this incongruous occasion he articulates his challenge with unprecedented self-awareness. The comic hero's repudiation of values hostile to life has never been more emphatic than in Falstaff's catechism on honor just before the battle. "Can honor set to a leg?" he asks:

No. Or an arm? No. Or take away the grief of a wound? No. Honor hath no skill in surgery then? No. What is honor? A word. What is in that word honor? What is that honor? Air. A trim reckoning! Who hath it? He that died a' Wednesday. Doth he feel it? No. Doth he hear it? No. 'Tis insensible then? Yea, to the dead. But will't not live with the living? No. Why? Detraction will not suffer it. Therefore I'll none of it, honor is a mere scutcheon. And so ends my catechism.

(1.V.i.)

Now, few men have known better than Falstaff the power of words to fabricate reality, and we might expect him to concede that capacity to the word honor. But honor is a word expropriated by the enemy; a word used not to discover but to conceal; a word without any relation to the actions performed in its name; a word, in short, belied by the living and insensible to the dead. The combatants who allegedly vie for honor at Shrewsbury impugn one another in this very scene of "violation of all faith and troth" (1.V.i.), and both the Prince's flamboyant challenge to Hotspur and the King's "fair" offer of peace are immediately discounted for the empty words that they are. ("It will not be accepted, on my life," Hal promises his father.) Only Hotspur, in either army, takes the protestations of honor at face value, and his hare-brained credulity proves to be his

ruin. Precisely because Falstaff is so accomplished a virtuoso of
make-believe he is uniquely able to see through the hollowness
of those who cannot give substance to their illusions; therefore
he'll none of it.

Falstaff's is not the commentary, however, of a self-righteous
calumniator of other men's failings. He claims no exemption
from vice and frankly advertises his own ample imperfections.
"Thou knowest in the state of innocency Adam fell," he replies
to Hal's strictures at Eastcheap, "and what should poor Jack
Falstaff do in the days of villainy? Thou seest I have more flesh
than another man, and therefore more frailty" (1.III.iii.). By
his conscious self-parody of faults as open and palpable as his
lies Falstaff flagrantly exhibits the vices that others labor to
conceal, even from themselves, under names like honor, and it
is thus that he poses his gravest threat to the equilibrium of the
social order. In acknowledging that he is marching his rag-of-
muffins off to their death as "food for powder" (1.IV.ii.), he
punctures the age-old glorification of war, and by his outrageous high jinks in the guise of Turk Gregory he lampoons the
sham valor of a battle fought less by the king than his ward-
robe. He contributes more than his share toward making the
Prince's climactic triumph at Shrewsbury seem nearly as farcical as his own inglorious discomfiture at Gad's Hill. Besides exposing the fraudulence of the martial virtues, moreover, Falstaff puts something substantive in their place. The blatant
buffoonery that can proffer a bottle of sack as a pistol in the
heat of battle raises burlesque to the pitch of sedition. Not the
Prince's honorable foe but his disreputable subject is the true
rebel on Shrewsbury field; for what he repudiates is far more
than allegiance to a Bolingbroke king. "I like not such grinning
honor as Sir Walter hath," Falstaff muses as he contemplates
the corpse and envisages the skull of Blunt. "Give me life,
which if I can save, so; if not, honor comes unlook'd for, and
there's an end" (1.V.iii). These are the words not of a coward
(Falstaff is the opposite of a boastful soldier) but of a comic
hero who will risk any ignominy in defense of life and intrepidly
confront even honor when it can no longer be avoided.

Stalwart adhesion to life even in the teeth of opprobrium is the essence of comic heroism, and at Shrewsbury Falstaff proves himself worthy of his illustrious precursors. In the supreme test of his insuperable instinct for self-preservation Falstaff falls before the onslaught of Douglas at the very moment when the Prince is valorously slaying Hotspur. Standing over the bodies of his formidable rivals Hal delivers a perfunctory — and condescending — valediction to each, and quits the field. His the victory, and he lavishes no tears on foe or friend. But Hal has reckoned without the comic hero's talent for resurrection. No sooner has the Prince left the scene than his triumph is upstaged by one still more astounding: "Falstaff," the stage direction reads, "riseth up" (1.V.iv.). Hal's triumph was to win honor by overcoming his honored foe; Falstaff's is to vanquish honor itself (such grinning honor as Sir Walter hath) by turning death into a sham. His consummate play-acting wins him an even more resplendent victory on the battlefield than in the tavern, and at this apex of comic glory Falstaff explicitly articulates for the first time his governing belief in the superior reality of make-believe. " 'Sblood, 'twas time to counterfeit," he declares, "or that hot termagant Scot had paid me scot and lot too."

> Counterfeit? I lie, I am no counterfeit. To die is to be a counterfeit, for he is but the counterfeit of a man who hath not the life of a man; but to counterfeit dying, when a man thereby liveth, is to be no counterfeit, but the true and perfect image of life indeed. The better part of valor is discretion, in the which better part I have sav'd my life.

Just as Falstaff proved himself no coward by his bold repudiation of honor, so he exonerates himself of falsehood by making life the sole criterion of truth. If death is a counterfeit through denial of life, then to affirm life by counterfeiting death is the essence of truth, and Falstaff's make-believe in extremis is the proof of his authenticity. The audacity of the logic is staggering; here indeed is a thoroughgoing revaluation of values.

Nor does Falstaff spare the sensibilities of his audience by declining to match words with deeds. We are delighted when he calls death a counterfeit, but scandalized when he stabs a dead *man;* we cease laughing when our own taboos are no longer inviolate. But heroes have an uncomfortable way of going whole hog, Falstaff no less than Achilles, and for the present his barefaced effrontery sweeps all before him. The Prince is constrained to share his honors in the hour of his greatest triumph; but his willingness to gild Falstaff's preposterous lie implies no lasting concord between them. On the contrary, Falstaff's arrogation of honor (which he has no reluctance to accept once the danger to life is past) exacerbates the implicit rivalry between them, for Falstaff is now trespassing on society's jealously guarded preserve. One challenger to the peace of the kingdom has been eliminated according to plan, but another has unpredictably rearisen. And the refractory will to life engrossed in the person of Falstaff will not so easily be expropriated on the Prince's behalf as Hotspur's garland of honor.

In Part One of *Henry IV* Falstaff could play king and warrior, and the Prince could pass for a wag; the worlds of pleasure and power were able to interact, to the great enrichment of both. In Part Two these worlds break asunder and each diminishes apart from the other. The disintegration in the political world is primary, if not causal, for the comic imagination battens on heroic reality and shrinks with its diminution. "It is from the prince," as C. L. Barber remarks, that Falstaff "chiefly gets his meaning, as it is from real kings that mock kings always get their meaning."[12] The world of history is characterized in Part Two by the total perversion of whatever honor partially redeemed it in Part One, and treachery is the residue. The loss is brought home through the absence of Hotspur, since without his heroic aspirations reality is stripped of glamor, and illusion of substance. The Prince and Falstaff come face to face only once in Part Two before the end; a long separation precedes their divorce. Hal may continue on occasion to hanker after small beer and fat comrades, but by now he is constantly aware that such "humble considerations" (2.II.ii.) are flagrantly at odds with his greatness. He speaks of Falstaff with disdain—"I do allow this wen to be as familiar with me as my dog"—and no longer debases his majesty by frequent epiphanies in the tavern. Indeed, his one return to the old boar's old frank requires a deliberate act of external disguise: a "low transformation" from prince to prentice which he compares to Jove's from a god to a bull. In his own person he is inexorably drawn into the orbit where he will finally unmask himself, as king, and "mock the expectation of the world" (2.V.ii.).

The sphere of high politics, as we behold it in this play, is unprepossessing in the extreme. The grotesque figure of Rumor, "painted full of tongues," who speaks the induction to the play strikes its dominant note of deceit —

> I speak of peace, while covert enmity
> Under the smile of safety wounds the world —
>
> (2. Induction.)

and from first to last hypocrisy breeds betrayal. Rebel camp and royal court alike are subject to the pestilence of anarchic self-interest, and law and order, society's raisons d'être, are nowhere in evidence among its would-be protectors. "The times are wild," Hotspur's father, Northumberland, declares in the opening scene; contention, like a runaway horse, has madly broken loose "And bears down all before him" (2.I.i.). And in the wildness of his own grief at the news of his son's death he cries,

>   let order die!
> And let this world no longer be a stage
> To feed contention in a ling'ring act;
> But let one spirit of the first-born Cain
> Reign in all bosoms . . .

It is this murderous spirit of every man for himself that prevails on Northumberland to desert the Archbishop of York and his other allies by fleeing to Scotland. The Archbishop, who compares the sickened commonwealth that exchanged Richard for Henry to a dog howling after its own vomit (2.I.iii.), knows there is no trust in these times, but even so will be unprepared for the cynical deceit of his enemies.

On the other side King Henry is more tormented than ever

by the unease which deprives him of the gentle sleep that his
lowliest subjects enjoy. The rank diseases afflicting the body of
his kingdom seem the fulfillment of Richard's prophecy "that
foul sin, gathering head, Shall break into corruption" (2.III.i.).
Any semblance of justification for the violence tearing England
to shreds is now lacking. At Shrewsbury, where Hotspur fell,
there was still sufficient honor to feed Falstaff's splendid parody; at Gaultree Forest, where the rebels meet their end, honor
makes a mockery of itself. The shameless betrayal of their
promises to the rebel leaders by Westmoreland and Prince John
of Lancaster destroys every vestige of legitimacy in their cause;
it is they, far more than the "traitors," who stand convicted of
treason. Shakespeare has followed the more discreditable of
Holinshed's versions of this event, and placed in Prince John's
mouth the most blatantly hypocritical words of the play. "Will
you thus break your faith?" the Archbishop asks before he is
sent to his execution, and Lancaster replies:

> I pawn'd thee none.
> I promis'd you redress of these same grievances
> Whereof you did complain, which, by mine honor,
> I will perform with a most Christian care.
>
> (2.IV.ii.)

"God, and not we," he righteously concludes, "hath safely
fought to-day"; to such a nadir have honor and piety been reduced. Prince Henry, it is true, does not dirty his own hands in
this affair, but he finds no fault with the brother whom he respects (he once declared) "as my soul" (1.V.iv.). And Hal himself, after he takes the crown from his dying father's bedside, is
plausibly accused by the King of intending the most heinous
treason of all:

> Dost thou so hunger for mine empty chair
> That thou wilt needs invest thee with my honors
> Before thy hour be ripe?
>
> (2.IV.v.)

The Prince, after all, had once before invested himself with the honors of a slain rival, and in a world ruled by the spirit of Cain no one is above suspicion.

By contrast with the sickened perfidy of the political world, that reverend vice and gray iniquity Falstaff seems a figure from the state of innocency before Adam fell. Nothing which this "abominable misleader of youth" (1.II.iv.), with his gross and palpable failings, might teach the crown prince could compare in depravity with the cynical lessons taught by his brother John. Falstaff himself is in bodily health (as his water declares) despite the constitutional infirmities of dissipation and old age, and his mind has never been keener. The articulate self-awareness to which he gave expression at Shrewsbury characterizes him from the beginning of Part Two; he is now unmistakably conscious of the role he is playing. "The brain of this foolish-compounded clay, man," he forthrightly asserts, "is not able to invent any thing that intends to laughter more than I invent or is invented on me: I am not only witty in myself, but the cause that wit is in other men" (2.I.ii.).

Like Peisthetaerus among the birds, Falstaff elicits the latent inventiveness of others by giving free play to his own. Whoever falls under his spell, from prince to page, is to that extent transformed. Only by laughter can he hope to maintain his liberating dominion, since by laughter the deadly earnestness of the temporal world is neutralized and held at bay. The decline of Falstaff in Part Two is therefore most strikingly evident in his impaired ability to make others laugh: for the first time he encounters antagonists who are immune to his power. In his stand-off with the Lord Chief Justice a confrontation of polar opposites supplants the rich interplay of his earlier run-ins with Hal. The Chief Justice's power lies in compulsion, not enchantment, and he too asserts it forthrightly: "To punish you by the heels," he tells the ostentatiously heedless Falstaff, "would amend the attention of your ears, and I care not if I do become your physician" (2.I.ii.). Falstaff acquits himself brilliantly by turning the magistrate's censures to his own advantage and mocking that most ridiculous of vices, the inability to laugh at one's virtues. To the Justice's unsparing arraignment of old age — more humorless if not more severe than Hal's in the earlier play — Falstaff impudently replies, "My lord, I was born about three of the clock in the afternoon, with a white head and something a round belly. For my voice, I have lost it with hallowing and singing of anthems . . . The truth is, I am only old in judgment and understanding; and he that will caper with me for a thousand marks, let him lend me the money, and have at him!" Yet the unblunted vigor of Falstaff's wit, which can turn gravity to gravy in the twinkling of an eye, meets a blank wall in a magistrate whose conception of judgment and understanding makes no allowance for capers. Equally impervious to Falstaffian subversion is Prince John, who threatens the reprobate knight with the gallows minutes after sending the Archbishop off to the block. "Good faith," a chastened Falstaff remarks, "this same young sober-blooded boy doth not love me, nor a man cannot make him laugh; but that's no marvel," he adds, "he drinks no wine" (2.IV.iii.).

In comparison with the atrocities soberly performed in the name of God and honor, Falstaff's avowed addiction to sherris-sack is, as he calls it, a most "humane principle" (2.IV.iii.). Under circumstances as unpropitious to comedy as to heroism, his lament for virtue "in these costermongers' times" (2.I.ii.) becomes, more than ever before, a lament for his own increasingly manifest inability to fashion a world in his image. In the world as it is he has no place, and cannot change it: "pregnancy is made a tapster," he mourns, "and his quick wit wasted in giving reckonings; all the other gifts appertinent to man, as the malice of this age shapes them, are not worth a gooseberry." He resolves, as a last resort, to "turn diseases to commodity," but the material is unpromising and the profit can only be meager. For without the power to make men laugh — the only power vouchsafed to fertile invention in such a time — the heroic Falstaff who once presumed to identify his corpulent person with "all the world" now finds himself more and more a superfluous man.

In the world of the tavern, at least, he maintains his supremacy as of yore. Hostess Quickly may indict him before the law as

a honeysuckle villain, but Falstaff quells this domestic rebellion
far less homicidally than Lancaster his. He remains without
peer among the irregular humorists of Eastcheap, easily putting his swaggering challenger Ancient Pistol to flight. "Thou
art as valorous as Hector of Troy, worth five of Agamemnon,
and ten times better than the Nine Worthies" (2.II.iv.), Doll
Tearsheet exultantly cries; and so long as we are assured that
Falstaff has not left "fighting a' days and foining a' nights," we
know that the heart of a comic hero beats in him still. Even so,
his easy rout of Pistol is a far less memorable feat than his fantastic victory over the numberless men in buckram at Gad's
Hill, and in his one encounter with the Prince there is a weary
sense of déjà vu about his triumph, if such it be. Again he is
trapped and again turns all to merriment, as Poins had feared,
by a glib excuse. But we have seen it all before, and in this
repeat performance Falstaff essentially neither invents nor
causes invention in others. He and the Prince come together
again at last, but their deferred reunion is barren; in place of
triumphal play-acting the scene ends with an almost elegiac
parting of ways. "Falstaff, good night," are the Prince's last
words as prince to his sometime companion; and in the Hostess'
farewell to Falstaff there is more depth of human feeling than
any courtier or son will show for the dying king. "Well, fare
thee well," she says. "I have known thee these twenty-nine
years, come peascod-time, but an honester and truer-hearted
man — well, fare thee well."

Henceforward Falstaff will be cut off from court and tavern
alike, with only the starveling Justices Shallow and Silence to
nurture his famished wit. "It is certain," he remarks, "that
either wise bearing or ignorant carriage is caught, as men take
diseases, one of another; therefore let men take heed of their
company" (2.V.i.). In his own isolation from fellow men of
good government his inventive capacities find no employment
except to prey upon others; he himself falls victim to the corrosive self-interest of a costermongers' world and becomes, in
sober reality, little better than one of the wicked. Taking purses
had given scope to heroic imaginings; taking bribes occasions
only cynical reflections. "If the young dace be a bait for the old

pike," Falstaff declares with an eye on Shallow and his beeves, "I see no reason in the law of nature but I may snap at him: let time shape, and there an end" (2.III.ii.).

What time shapes, once the moon's former minion enters his service, can only be Falstaff's end. His glory had been to fashion a comic world of corporeal and imaginative fulfillment beyond the reach of Time's injurious hand, but by now the foundations of that world have eroded beneath him. For the world of comedy is a consciously alternative world and its character will inevitably be modified by its opposite; it is never self-sufficient except as the culmination of Aristophanic fantasy. The comic hero is heroic by virtue of the high values that he appropriates for his own ends: Odysseus' heroism inverts Achilles' as Reynard's parodies the Arthurian knight's. Falstaff's triumphant refutation of honor in the name of life, in Part One, was dependent on the meaningfulness, to some at least, of the discredited illusion. The bright honor that Hotspur strove to pluck from the moon was validated by the manner of his death just as Falstaff's resolute choice of life was legitimized by his resurrection. The values of life and honor, though opposed, drew strength from their stout collision. But now, in a world devoid of honor and incapable of laughter, Falstaff's comic virtues not only fail to offset the vices of the political world, but become nearly indistinguishable from them. He too, on a sadly shrunken scale, is a big fish snapping at smaller fry and justifying his rapacity, if not by his Christian honor, by the law of nature. His grand burlesque becomes a pitiful farce as soon as he ceases to incarnate a feasible alternative to the values which he now unwittingly travesties; his inability to perceive that his changed world has brought about a corresponding change in himself transforms this one-time master of make-believe into the dupe of delusion.

Falstaff's vision, in Part One, of a gallowless England unbridled by the rusty curb of old father Antic the Law was a conscious flight of fancy no less than the fabulous tale of Gad's Hill; he never confused his fantasy with the reality that furnished its matter. His kingdom was Eastcheap, not England; and Eastcheap was world enough. With the news of King

Henry's death in Part Two a stunted Falstaff no longer capable of *inventing* adequate illusions confounds his own fanciful hopes with literal fact—the fatal error of Hotspur. "I am fortune's steward," Falstaff jubilantly cries after Ancient Pistol has proclaimed his tidings of golden times; "the laws of England are at my commandment" (2.V.iii.). They are not, of course, and never will be, for Eastcheap may rival England but scarcely annex her. The rejection of Falstaff by the new king is now all too clearly inevitable. In a world unable to laugh at its follies Falstaff has surrendered whatever dominion he had, and by recklessly laying claim to the laws of England he legitimizes their authority to command *him*. The incompatibility of the two realms was never more apparent than now, when Falstaff cannot see it.

The inevitability of the rejection brings no compensation, however, for the loss it entails. The victory of compulsion—embodied in the Chief Justice and Lancaster, who hold the stage at the end—can only come about through the defeat of enchantment. If Eastcheap cannot annex England, England proves too small to encompass Eastcheap; the unity of the realm can only be achieved by amputation. "I know you all," Hal's first soliloquy began; but his last words to Falstaff make us wonder if he had ever known them at all:

> I know thee not, old man, fall to thy prayers.
> How ill white hairs becomes a fool and jester!
> I have long dreamt of such a kind of man,
> So surfeit-swell'd, so old, and so profane;
> But being awak'd, I do despise my dream.
> Make less thy body hence, and more thy grace,
> Leave gormandizing, know the grave doth gape
> For thee thrice wider than for other men.
>
> (2.V.v.)

Whatever Falstaff has become since his palmy days he is surely much more than this. The contemptuous moralism of the young king's peremptory speech underlines the narrowness of a vision in which reality must exclude illusion, and virtue pleasure. For in despising his dream he is repudiating not one profane old man but the fundamental comic values of emancipated fantasy and exuberant life that his erstwhile companion so prodigally embodied. God knows and the world shall perceive, he affirms, "That I have turn'd away my former self": the disproportionate brutality of his words suggests that through Falstaff he is exorcising a self that he never deigned to acknowledge as his own. By simultaneously magnifying Falstaff's failings and disclaiming any defilement from them—by attributing all vices to his surfeit-swelled scapegoat and only virtue to his newly purified self—the King is able to glitter all the more brightly in his own eyes as well as those of his subjects—with no apparent awareness that in so doing he is "glitt'ring o'er my fault" (1.I.ii.).

For the first time a comic hero has met irrevocable defeat. Death Falstaff could outwit, but from the righteous judgment of a Christian king there is no reprieve; he stands defenseless, as no pagan or heretic comic hero ever stood, against his anointed antagonist's monopoly of moral authority. But when the disruptive comic world must be consigned en masse to the whipping-post and the Fleet, so that order may be restored to England, the defeat is not Falstaff's alone. Not all the world, but an irreplaceable segment of it, is banished with him. The government imposed by King Henry V and his beadles seems a disturbing prefiguration of Angelo's rule of virtue in *Measure for Measure,* except that here there is no wise Duke to right the balance by reforming the reformers. The English must henceforth fall to their prayers or meet the fate of the King's misleaders; on such terms will their shattered unity be at last repaired. The price of any restoration that deposes Falstaff can only be heavy; and it is not reassuring that Prince John of Lancaster, who is expert in such matters, unhesitatingly endorses "this fair proceeding of the King's" (2.V.5).[13]

The dying King Henry IV had counseled his son to "busy giddy minds With foreign quarrels," and thereby "waste the memory of the former days" (2.IV.v.). By incarcerating the principal repository of his own youthful memories the new king takes his first indispensable step toward the brilliant accomplishment of that plan. On the eve of his most glorious victory, in the play that bears his name, King Henry V will walk in disguise among his men at Agincourt and calm their fears by assuring them that war is the king's just beadle, punishing on the battlefield those whose crimes have gone undetected before. "Every subject's duty is the King's, but every subject's soul is his own," he argues; therefore each soldier should "wash every mote out of his conscience; and dying so, death is to him advantage."[14] It is fortunate for the unity of England on that famous Saint Crispin's Eve that the one subject who would surely have challenged this comforting assumption—" 'Tis not due yet, I would be loath to pay him before his day" (1.V.i.)—will by then have been safely gathered to Arthur's bosom. Where self-sacrifice is demanded of all and a spotless conscience is the talisman of salvation if not survival there is no place for Falstaff. The King has acted on that knowledge and thereby, as the Hostess will say, has killed his heart.

VI

ABERRANT HIDALGO

———————— ❧ ————————

N O CHARACTER in the literature of the world was ever more comically heroic than the ingenious hidalgo Don Quixote de la Mancha; yet among comic heroes, as among knights errant, he cuts an incongruous figure. Odysseus and Peisthetaerus, Reynard and Falstaff, all championed the dignity of man's animal nature in defiance of codes of behavior imposed by an alien social order. The gaunt Knight of the Sad Countenance, in contrast, resolutely mortifies his flesh and practices a chastity that would shame an anchorite in his single-minded devotion to an exalted ideal of conduct. His first priority is not the preservation of life and fulfillment of self but the benefit of his fellow man, and he recklessly courts danger and hazards death in pursuit of this selfless end. Unlike his scandalous predecessors the chivalrous Spaniard sets forth not to challenge the dominant values of his age but to defend them. In his eyes there is nothing more sacred than the honor flouted by Falstaff, and he spurns all conscious dissimulation or falsehood. Modeling himself on the famous knights of romance he more nearly resembles Achilles or Galahad in his high aspirations and noble ardor than Odysseus or Reynard, and by his "imagination proper to madmen" he recalls not Falstaff but the impetuous Hotspur, for whom reality was forever smaller than his smallest thought.

To begin with, at least, Don Quixote is heroic on purpose but comic only by accident; his grand enterprise is ridiculous to others because it so flagrantly violates the conditions of the world as they know it. The true comic heroism of an age that had ceased to live in accord with its own beliefs, Cervantes clairvoyantly saw, lay not in defiance of society's values but in the insane endeavor to uphold them in practice. The effort demands, in fact, a defiant spirit, and by his dedication to so audacious an undertaking the Christian knight reveals a surprising resemblance to comic heroes less altruistic in temper. In conjuring up a world of freedom, and in repudiating any reality that falls short of its exalted demands, not even Aristophanes' more fortunate visionaries excel him. Above all, he willingly encounters repeated ridicule and humiliation in the course of his many adventures and rises above them more determined than ever before. In this respect, at least, the deranged Don Quixote is one with his classical opposite, the wily Odysseus. And if Don Quixote, unlike Odysseus, eventually fails, his endeavor has been immeasurably greater: not to return to the home from which he departed — therein *is* his failure — but to revive for all mankind an age that has never existed outside his impossible dreams.

The age of gold, as Don Quixote lyrically depicts it among the goatherds, was a time when truth and sincerity were untainted by fraud, deception, and malice; but the world he discovers in his actual travels is one of conflicting tricks and devices which he is finally impotent to oppose. In his contest with a fraudulent world the comic hero of the modern age, like Apuleius' ass at the end of the ancient, must resist deception by a vulnerable adhesion to truth. To engage in prevarication would be to meet the enemy on his own terms. Except in the popular tradition embodied in Reynard and Eulenspiegel — and in their Spanish equivalent, the folk hero of Cervantes' play *Pedro de Urdemalas*[1] — in Christian times the unscrupulous trickster more often resembles Virgil's sinister Ulysses than Homer's resourceful Odysseus; his wiles serve the interests only of power and greed. The crafty dissemblers of the late Middle Ages and the Renaissance, from Chaucer's Pardoner to Jonson's Volpone, apply their skills to the victimization of others, and no heroic end redeems the villainy of their means. Far from challenging the values of their world they accommodate them to the requirements of their own ambition. "Thou art virtue, fame," Volpone exclaims to his hoarded gold, "Honor, and all things else. Who can get thee, He shall be noble, valiant, honest, wise."[2] In the monomaniacal disregard for every human cost with which they pursue their goal, such pretenders are not unlike Tamburlaine, Richard III, or Iago. The gulf between profession and practice in an increasingly secularized Christian world made hypocrisy the characteristic vice of the age and demanded a comic challenger radically different from the guileful impostors of a less convoluted time.

If Chaucer's mountebank Pardoner, who preaches his venomous sermons "under hewe Of hoolynesse, to semen hooly and trewe,"[3] is an early paradigm of the trickster as hypocrite, exploiting the delusions of others without enhancing his own sense of life, the outspoken Wife of Bath gives bold new voice to the age-old rebellion of nature against authority. She is memorable not for her run-of-the-mill mendacities but for her almost unparalleled frankness. Christ, she bluntly asserts, spoke to those who aspired to live perfectly, and she is not of their number: "I ne loved nevere by no discrecioun," she avows, "But evere folwede myn appetit."[4] The disarming forthrightness with which she proclaims her sensuality constitutes her challenge to a morality founded on the falsehood of denying the body its due. Only a fellowship as truly catholic as that of the Canterbury pilgrims could have indulged her supplication to speak her own mind:

> If that I speke after my fantasye,
> As taketh not agrief of that I seye;
> For myn entente is nat but for to pleye.[5]

By Shakespeare's time the graver implications of unrestrained candor will have become apparent to the guardians of order, and Falstaff and his Ephesians will be banished, John of Lancaster tells the Chief Justice, "till their conversations Appear more wise and modest to the world."[6]

In the heady years of the young Renaissance, however, when confidence in man's unassisted powers reached its zenith and the opposition had not yet fully mustered its forces, the exaltation of long-reviled instincts could attain gargantuan dimensions. In Rabelais' gallimaufry of popular folklore and Humanist erudition, insatiable heroes, giant and human alike, imbibe the manna of learning no less robustly than a hogshead of wine and quote Plutarch as readily as *Pierre Pathelin*. As true Pantagruelists they are no more reticent than Master François himself either in celebrating corporeal and mental exuberance or in demolishing pedants and agelasts. Concealment is so utterly foreign to their nature that even the trickster Panurge perpetrates his gratuitous pranks with guileless zest and distinguishes himself by effrontery rather than cunning. From the utopian Abbey of Thélème all hypocrites and impostors are barred, as the inscription over its gate proclaims, for here the sole commandment is "Do what you will."[7] In Rabelais' fabulous world, tailored to the measure of titanic desire, every constraint may be suspended at will in the limitless good cheer of a new Saturnian age. Its fundamental spirit, as Mikhail Bakhtin writes in his important study *Rabelais and His World,* is one not of satire but carnival, characterized by its emancipating defeat through laughter of "divine and human power, of authoritarian commandments and prohibitions, of death and punishment after death, hell and all that is more terrifying than the earth itself."[8] Those who were great lords in this life must scrape out a paltry livelihood in the underworld while impoverished philosophers become great lords in their stead, so overt is the saturnalian impulse that permeates what Bakhtin not implausibly calls "the most festive work in world literature."[9]

Yet in this disregard of all limit is the book's limitation as well as its glory. Unlike the festive comedies of Aristophanes and Shakespeare, Rabelais' is a kômos without an agôn. The doughty deeds, the "faictz et prouesses espoventables,"[10] of the gigantic protagonists are too horrific to admit of any real contest, and the allegedly human Friar John is hardly less irresistible. When a mishap, like decapitation, befalls one of their band a few timely stitches suffice to repair it. Panurge, it is true, may never succeed in avoiding a cuckold's lot if he marries (for human nature cannot be *wholly* transmuted), but with such friends and protectors his other worries are few. He need not, like Aristophanes' equally undignified heroes, enter the arena alone.

Rabelais himself was familiar, of course, with the intense hostility that his merriment could provoke. He bore the brunt of repeated condemnation by the Catholic Sorbonne as well as Calvin's denunciations of "curs who assume the attitudes of comedy in order to enjoy greater freedom to vomit their blasphemies,"[11] and the odium of theologians may even have culminated — the facts are unknown — in the author's confinement and death. Nor were future generations always charitable to his memory. The libertine boldness of his "inexplicable" and "monstrous" book, as La Bruyère called it,[12] long continued to give offense. "Only a few eccentric persons," Voltaire wrote two centuries after its publication, "pride themselves on understanding and esteeming this work as a whole; the rest of the nation laughs at the jokes of Rabelais and holds his book in contempt."[13]

But however perilous Rabelais' defiance of authority may have been, in his book the menace of the real world is deliberately reduced to a farce. And because society's (and nature's) laws are suspended for the carnival season the merrymakers are never obliged to risk the penalty of challenging their dominion. Their wars are all waged, like the "straw battle" with the Chitterlings in Book Four, against straw men.[14] Their success is therefore never in question from beginning to end, and once they embark on their voyage in search of the Holy Bottle Bacbuc nothing in heaven or earth — not even the author's inopportune death — can prevent their arrival. So festive a world is innately devoid of significant conflict for the celebrants fortunate to inhabit its privileged confines; and despite its unending profusion of "heroical deeds and sayings,"[15] a world without conflict is a world without heroes.

The self-confident partisans of the Renaissance, with Rabelais as their antipope, might momentarily succeed in dismissing their dour antagonists as remnants of a vanquished though lingering past, but with the encroachment of Reform and Counter Reform the existence of a dangerous opposition could no longer be ignored. In Shakespeare the conflict of cakes and ale with a deprecatory virtue casts its shadow on the gayest comedies and culminates, as we have seen, in the ascendancy and demise of a comic hero who can no longer, like Rabelais' invulnerable giants, escape shot-free from the struggle. In Cervantes the contradictions apparent in Shakespearean comedy are still more exacerbated, and the comic hero's response correspondingly more problematic.

Cervantes himself shared both in the noblest dreams and in the most dismal disillusionments of his time. His youth coincided with the apogee of his nation, and the impressions made by his stirring adventures during those years never left him. The hand maimed at the great naval victory of Lepanto appeared not ugly but handsome, he wrote more than forty years later, because he received it "on the most memorable and lofty occasion" of any century past or to come;[16] and throughout his plays and novels he nostalgically reverts to his years of captivity by the Turks in Algiers. But in Spain, where this decade of heroism was followed by half a lifetime of drudgery, Cervantes found little scope for high aspiration. His attempts to live by his pen met recurrent frustration, and in his unglamorous career as a government tax collector he suffered excommunication and imprisonment. It was in prison, he seems to imply in *Don Quixote* (which brought him belated fame at fifty-seven), that the contrast between his narrowed surroundings and spacious longings engendered in his brain the figure of an emaciated gentleman "full of various thoughts never imagined by anyone else" (I.Prologue). This fertile contradiction between physical poverty and imaginative plenty is at the heart of his work.

In both its native and Italianate variations Spanish literature in the sixteenth century continued to reflect the division between "idealizing" and "realistic" tendencies inherited from the Middle Ages.[17] The chivalric novel is as sharply opposed to the picaresque as the pastoral romance to the worldly novella. Cervantes, though strongly drawn in both directions, could be satisfied by neither extreme. More than any other Spaniard of his day he strives in his writings, with very uneven success, to bridge the widening gap between reality and the ideal.

In a world where dreams found scant fulfillment in action the hero could be truly at home only in the sphere of romance. This rarefied world exerted a lifelong appeal for Cervantes, from his first published work, the pastoral *Galatea* (which he never abandoned the hope of continuing), to the posthumous *Labors of Persiles and Sigismunda*. Yet no one was more acutely aware that pastoral fictions, as the canine moralist Berganza discovers in "The Dogs' Colloquy," are "dreams well written to amuse the idle, and not truth at all."[18] A convention that gave so little scope for action violated not only verisimilitude but an essential dimension of the heroic ideal. The action-packed "Byzantine" novel *Persiles*, on the other hand, was no less wildly improbable than the popular novels of chivalry ridiculed in *Don Quixote*. A heroic romance was finally a contradiction in terms, for by safely remaining within a sphere so remote the sheltered protagonist evades the encounter with an alien reality that is his truly heroic task.

Chivalric novels on the model of *Amadis of Gaul*, with their unfailingly valiant knights and lovely ladies, thrilling adventures and fabulous places, appealed to sober men of action as well as to crackpots like Don Quixote. When Cortés's band of soldiers first saw the spires of Montezuma's capital rising from the lagoon of a continent unknown a generation before, "we were amazed," their plain-spoken chronicler Bernal Díaz recounts, "and said that it was like the enchantments they tell of in the legend of Amadis . . . And some of our soldiers even asked whether the things that we saw were not a dream."[19] Only in surroundings so uniquely exotic as those of a newly discovered world, however, could reality plausibly correspond to romance. In the well-trodden Old World, tales of knights and ladies, or of shepherds and shepherdesses, or tempest-tossed lovers, were unmistakably a refuge from an actuality resistant

to dream. The novel of chivalry, as Ortega y Gasset has remarked — and the same might be said of the pastoral or Byzantine romance — lacked one essential characteristic of the epic,
its "belief in the reality of what is told."[20] Only a fool or a madman could possibly confuse its world with his own.

At the opposite pole, however, Cervantes found a still more
fundamental lack: the "realistic" literature of his day gave
scarcely a hint of the aspiration toward the ideal without which
any heroism was inconceivable. The picaresque novel is the
outright negation of the romance, for the ragtag *pícaro* inhabits a world in which he must disencumber himself of illusion if
he hopes to survive. In the anonymous *Lazarillo de Tormes*, the
prototype of the genre, the young protagonist is initiated into
the ways of the world when the blind man whom he is guiding
smashes his head against a stone bull and gleefully instructs his
pupil "that a blind man's boy has got to be sharper than the
devil!"[21] In a ruthless world where no quarter is asked and none
given, the essential skill in life is to shift for oneself; and in his
reliance on native cunning in the struggle for self-preservation
the pícaro resembles the resourceful comic hero of classical
times. He too knows from hard experience that Belly must
somehow be fed; indeed, Lazarillo, who employs the artfulness
of a Penelope in scrabbling crumbs from a stingy master's
locked chest, declares himself "convinced that hunger was my
guiding light in finding these solutions to my troubles. After
all, they say it sharpens the wits, whereas a full belly does the
opposite."[22] But far from being distinguished from his fellow
men for conspicuous wile, as Odysseus was, the pícaro begins
his career as a babe in the woods and learns from painful misfortune to give as well as he gets. His cunning is a defensive art
that enables him to adapt to a world where deceit is the norm;
instead of pitting himself against the mores of his society he
becomes adept in going along. "I did what the others did" (*Hice
lo que los otros*) is the watchword of Guzmán de Alfarache, the
narrator of Mateo Alemán's influential picaresque novel;[23]
whether in crime or repentance he finds his values conveniently
at hand. Lazarillo, too, knows the futility of kicking against the

pricks. "I made up my mind a long time ago," he obligingly tells the Archpriest who is sharing his wife, "to keep in with respectable people."[24]

The comic hero's imperative need to oppose a world of freedom to the reality that confines him is thus utterly foreign to the compliant pícaro; only in the artificial paradises of romance—the Arcadia of pastoral fiction or the Firm Island of *Amadis of Gaul*—does it find a pallid equivalent. The pícaro, like the unprincipled cony-catchers of contemporary Elizabethan England, feels no need to seek an alternative to a social order whose practices are so compatible with his own. "For truth it is," Cuthbert Cony-Catcher affirms in an anonymous "Defence" of the swindler's art, "that this is the Iron Age, wherein iniquity hath the upper hand, and all conditions and estates of men seek to live by their wits, and he is counted wisest that hath the deepest insight into the getting of gains: every thing now that is found profitable is counted honest and lawful: and men are valued by their wealth, not by their virtues. He that cannot dissemble cannot live."[25] Like his English counterpart, the Spanish rogue achieves a modus vivendi with the age of iron, and in this complacent assent to existing reality he is the very antithesis of a hero.

The mode of romance no doubt appealed more directly to Cervantes' temperament than the picaresque, but for that very reason his efforts in the romantic vein are almost wholly derivative. Unlike Shakespeare in *As You Like It* he was never able to include a more critical perspective within so stylized a genre. Because he came to realistic fiction with a consciousness fully awake to its limitations, however, his treatment is far more original and persuasive. In the *Exemplary Novels* he both moralizes the Boccaccian novella of amorous intrigue by shifting its focus from the versatile arts of deceit to its motives and consequences and—in the most interesting tales—infuses the picaresque with the antithetical spirit of romance.

Far from simply adopting the picaresque model, as he had the pastoral, Cervantes fundamentally alters it to accord with his own very different ends, and in so doing completely transforms its tone and spirit. Only Berganza, in his lopsided colloquy with his friend Scipio, follows the picaresque convention of establishing verisimilitude by narrating his observations of everyday life *in propria persona,* and both Berganza and Scipio are dogs: characteristically Cervantes reserves his most unadulterated realism in the *Exemplary Novels* for a flight of fancy, since "for us to speak," as Berganza avows, "seems to me to pass beyond the bounds of Nature."[26] His difference in species guards Berganza against the temptation to conform, like Lazarillo or Guzmán, with the rascalities of the human world that he repeatedly encounters during his checkered career. In Cervantes' other quasi-picaresque tales a protective distance is maintained by the sympathetically ironical author, who shields his youthful protagonists from the perils of unreconstructed reality. The appealing young vagrant Rinconete, in "Rinconete and Cortadillo," is saved by his understanding and his innate good disposition from the depravities of Señor Monipodio of Seville, whose introductory lesson in organized knavery he greets with spontaneous laughter. He is therefore able to savor the adventures of a footloose life, "carried away by his youth and lack of experience,"[27] for a carefree interval without succumbing to the degradations of penury and crime. In contrast to Señor Monipodio's subservient band Rinconete retains his lighthearted detachment and with it his innocence, and this is the source of his charm.

What most deeply appeals to Cervantes in the picaresque mode is a spiritual and imaginative vagabondage more akin to the Arcadian shepherd's existence than to the callous pícaro's. Several of his finest stories are in fact romances in picaresque clothing. Thus in "The Illustrious Kitchen Maid" the "virtuous pícaro" Carriazo is no orphan of ignominious birth but a gentleman's son who takes to the open road when he finds himself "carried away by a picaresque inclination . . . simply for his own whim and pleasure."[28] The picaresque is transmuted beyond recognition by its removal from the sphere of necessity to that of freedom. In so idyllic a story, where all seasons are spring and a hayloft as soft as sheets of holland, it comes as no surprise that the beautiful kitchen maid with whom Carriazo's wayfaring companion falls in love should turn out, in the best tradition of romance, to be Carriazo's lost half-sister by a lady of gentle birth, or that nuptials should bring the holiday to a festive conclusion. In "The Little Gypsy" the ideal freedom of the nomadic life is transferred from tavern to forest. That remorseless observer of human nature, Berganza, was convinced by his brief experience of gypsy rascality that "the only thoughts that enter their minds are how and where they may cheat and steal";[29] but in this story gypsy life is irradiated with the glow of poetic vision. "We are lords of the plains, the crops, the woods, the forests, the fountains, and the rivers," the old Gypsy lyrically declares to the young nobleman Andrés, who has joined his band out of love for the gracious gypsy girl Preciosa (who will of course, like the kitchen maid, prove to be of illustrious birth). "Our gilded roofs and sumptuous palaces are these huts and tents we carry with us; our Flemish pictures and landscapes are those that Nature gives us in those lofty crags and snow-clad cliffs, wide-stretching meadows, and thick woods that meet our eyes at every step." In short—and this is the sum of their felicity —"We have all we want," the old Gypsy says, "for we are content with what we have."[30] In this sylvan life free of worldly care is a realization of the age of gold that lay outside the pedestrian pícaro's ken and beyond his desire—the age, extolled by the captive Aurelio in Cervantes' autobiographical first play, when liberty reigned and the hateful name of servitude was unknown.

> Entonces libertad dulce reinaba
> y el nombre odioso de la servidumbre
> en ningunos oídos resonaba.[31]

Through the incorporation of liberty, reality is transmuted into a tangible embodiment of the ideal, and the iron age of the unregenerate pícaro is revealed to be in potential an age of gold.

Yet the polarization between dream and fact central to Cervantes and his age is transcended, in such stories as "The Illustrious Kitchen Maid" and "The Little Gypsy," only by assimilating reality to romance. An idyll, whatever its setting, presupposes the virtual absence of conflict and therefore of heroism.

During the centuries of the Christian Reconquest of Spain from the Moors, as portrayed in the anonymous ballads of the *Romancero,* a militant ideal had taken up arms in a world recognizably flesh-and-blood. Cervantes, who deeply revered the old ballads, turned for the subject matter of his heroic drama, *The Siege of Numantia,* to an episode from the glorious and even more distant past. Elsewhere in the secular literature of his own time, however, the enterprise of confronting reality with a loftier ideal had been all but abandoned. It was left for the great religious writers to take up the challenge. In quest of a martyrdom denied in their native Ávila St. Teresa and her brother agreed in their childhood, as she recounts in her *Life,* "to go off to the country of the Moors, begging our bread for the love of God, so that they might behead us there,"[32] and only the hindrance of having parents frustrated their courageous intention.

Teresa later diverted her childhood ardor to the foundation of convents and the exploration of inner vistas that no parental obstacle could impede. Her more militant contemporary, St. Ignatius Loyola, set forth on muleback, with no other weapon than his invincible faith, to engage the world in combat as a knight errant of God. While recuperating from a wound as a young man he requested books of chivalry for his amusement — books by which St. Teresa, too, had been inspired and led astray in her youth — and was given lives of Christ and the saints instead. Henceforth he became the ascetic paladin of a Church beleaguered on every side by new and dangerous foes. Nothing before Don Quixote himself could be more quixotic than the vigil over his arms, a traditional ritual of knighthood, by which St. Ignatius inaugurated his service in the militia of Christ. "He went on his way to Montserrat," he recalls in his autobiography,

thinking as always about the deeds he would do for the love of God. As his mind was full of ideas from Amadis of Gaul and such books, some things similar to those came to mind. Thus he decided to watch over his arms all one night, without sitting down or going to bed, but standing a while, before the altar of Our Lady of Montserrat where he had resolved to leave his clothing and dress himself in the armor of Christ . . . He arranged with the confessor to take his mule and to place his sword and his dagger in the church on the altar of Our Lady . . . On the eve of the feast of Our Lady in March in the year 1522, he went at night as secretly as he could to a poor man, and stripping off all his garments he gave them to the poor man and dressed himself in his desired clothing and went to kneel before the altar of Our Lady. At times in this way, at other times standing, with his pilgrim's staff in his hand he spent the whole night. He left at day-break so as not to be recognized.[33]

For Ignatius, founder and commander of the Society of Jesus, the faithful were a disciplined order arrayed to do battle with spiritual weapons against the champions of evil here on earth. For his fellow imitator of Amadis, Don Quixote, the knight is likewise God's minister on earth and the instrument of his justice. "Chivalry is religion," he says to Sancho, "and there are sainted knights in glory" (II. 8). But the difference between himself and the great Christian knights of the spirit, Don Quixote declares near the end of his final journey, "is that they were saints and fought in the divine way, and I am a sinner and fight in the human" (II.58). And in the fallible sinner the saint's faith in the reality of things unseen will seem little more than madness.

It is in *Don Quixote* of course that a colloquy—not to say altercation—is finally opened, as Harry Levin has put it, "between the romance and the picaresque, so to speak, between *Amadís de Gaula* and *Lazarillo de Tormes*";[34] and the world in which it takes place is one where kitchen maids tenaciously resist idealization. For this reason the hero who commits the folly of stepping forth from the sheltered sphere of romance to confront reality with his uncompromising ideal will be intrinsically and unavoidably comic. Don Quixote's reckless madness is comic because it precipitates the commitment to action that Hamlet's contemplative madness impedes. In both the comic and the tragic hero, however, madness (or its facsimile) arises in response to an age "in which the immanence of meaning in life has become a problem," as Georg Lukács writes, "yet which still thinks in terms of totality."[35] "The contingent world and the problematic individual," Lukács observes, "are realities which mutually determine each other . . . The positing of ideas as unrealisable and, in the empirical sense, as unreal, i.e. their transformation into ideals, destroys the immediate problem-free organic nature of the individual."[36] In Don Quixote's case the consequence is an insane endeavor to act (in disregard of all evidence) *as if* the ideal could be real.

In its simplest form the lunacy of the addle-brained hidalgo seems an involuntary obsession, spawned by infatuation with novels of chivalry, that incapacitates him from distinguishing between his native La Mancha and the never-never land of romance. Reality and the ideal are two distinct matters which Don Quixote absurdly confounds. His reflexive identification of every inn as a castle is the perfect illustration of Bergson's theory of the laughable as something mechanical encrusted on the living, and Sancho's bewildered attempts to correct his master's misapprehensions provide a hilarious counterpoint whenever the obdurate knight refuses to call a spade a spade or a windmill a windmill. Only in retrospect, if at all, will we pause to ask whether Sancho's automatic identification of every inn as an inn may not be a reflex no less conditioned than his master's: for the moment we laugh without reservation at the knight's inability to discern what Sancho and we ourselves see so clearly.

Yet the gentleman of La Mancha is not simply the helpless victim of delusion. From the beginning he *resolves* to be mad, and by fidelity to his deranged resolution he soon transforms himself into an incontrovertible comic hero. The mania for chivalric romance is by no means peculiar to Don Quixote within the world of the novel. Even the inquisitorial priest and barber express delight in the handful of books that they exempt from the flames, and the credulous host, in whom "little is lacking," Dorotea tells Cardenio, "to make him the second part of Don Quixote" (I.32), vehemently upholds the veracity of the genre. But the difference between the host and his lunatic guest is enormous. Others may more or less share the yearnings to which the romances give expression, but Don Quixote, and

Don Quixote alone, hastens (as we read in the opening chapter) "to put into effect what he desired" (I.1); and this impetuous determination "to wait no longer to put his thought into effect" (I.2) already distinguishes the nascent knight errant from those who contentedly separate the ideals from the conduct of life. Instead of merely misapprehending things as they are, he deliberately challenges their being so and audaciously strives to amend the disparity between belief and practice to which others are blind or indifferent. For this, as much as his visionary hallucinations, the world is unanimous in calling him mad. Even his supposed hallucinations, for that matter, suggest defiant resolve, for by their means a hand-to-mouth hidalgo of mediocre attainments transfigures himself, within the span of the opening chapter, into a fictional knight destined to eclipse the renown of the most illustrious paladins of romance.

His capacity for transformation allies him with the fellowship of comic heroes long past, for in fertility of invention his madness yields nothing to Odysseus' cunning, and in the sweep of his fantasy only Peisthetaerus is his peer. Like Aristophanes' disgruntled Athenian refugee, Cervantes' aging Manchegan landowner envisages a reality corresponding to his thwarted desire and brings it to pass by magically endowing it with a name. To see his scrawny nag (*rocín*) as surpassing Alexander's Bucephalus and the Cid's Babieca may testify to no more than warped judgment, but to immortalize the beast by an appellation as sonorous as theirs requires a tour de force of imagination to which the hidalgo rises triumphant when, "after many names that he formed, erased, and threw aside, added, scratched out, and remade in his memory and imagination, it finally came upon him to call him *Rocinante*" (I.1). He transmutes his own undistinguished name (whatever it was) into the grandiose title Don Quixote de la Mancha and fashions out of whole cloth, and the memory of a handsome farm lass, a peerless lady whom he determines to call Dulcinea del Toboso: "a name, in his opinion, as musical, outlandish, and significant as all the rest that he had attached to himself and his belongings." From a singularly drab actuality this petty nobleman of an indeterminate village somewhere in the wastes of La Mancha has summoned into existence, within a few rapturous pages, three of the most celebrated characters in world fiction, and his achievement inevitably suggests that conscious invention as well as unwitting delusion may henceforth play an appreciable role even in his zaniest fancies.

Nor do the indignities to which his mad decision subjects him as soon as his militant vision collides with stolid realities have power to shake his purpose. On the contrary, the rudest buffets only confirm his resolve. His courageous choice has transformed his own life, if not yet that of others, and he will not betray it for all the world. His first expedition ends in ignominy when he is unhorsed by Rocinante and pummeled by a Toledan muleteer after demanding acknowledgment of Dulcinea's preeminence. A laborer from his village finds him reciting snatches of popular ballads and pastoral romances while hopelessly entangled in his own armor. (For this farcical episode Cervantes made use, as Menéndez-Pidal has shown, of an anonymous dramatic interlude concerning a peasant driven mad by his reading of ballads.)[37] Yet at this nadir of inglorious buffoonery the fallen knight elevates himself to truly heroical heights by a ringing affirmation of faith. "Look, your worship, sir," the puzzled laborer rejoins to his townsman's apparently delirious ravings,

> "as I'm a sinner, I'm not Don Rodrigo de Narváez, nor the Marquis of Mantua, but Pedro Alonso, your neighbor; and your worship is not Baldwin or Abindarráez, but the worthy hidalgo, señor Quixana."
>
> "I know who I am," replied Don Quixote, "and I know that I can be not only those whom I have said, but all the Twelve Peers of France and all the Nine Worthies as well, for my deeds will excel all that they have performed, all together and each by himself."

(I.5)

Defeat has no power over him who defies it; such heroism the gentiles call madness.

Whatever the nature and source of Don Quixote's insanity, it is incontestably valorous. Though illusions lie shattered all about him he will shrug off disillusionment so long as his confidence in himself and his vision remains unshaken. And who can refute his claim? Once he has acted on his momentous initial resolve the worthy señor Quixana is no more (even if the tidings of his demise have not yet reached his village), and Don Quixote is secure — though completely alone — in his knowledge of who he is and what he is capable of becoming. Before long the world will learn of his famous exploits, but few whom he encounters will look upon him far differently than his skeptical neighbor Pedro Alonso, or think his professions worthy of greater credence. The comic hero is seldom taken seriously even when demonstrably sane, and nowhere does Don Quixote, whose madness is apparent to all, show more heroical stature than in withstanding the incredulity of the world while keeping his own faith intact.

Don Quixote's mad heroism thus involves a continual effort of imagination and will. The goal toward which his enterprise (like that of his paradigms in romance) is directed is the righting of the world's wrongs: a supremely heroic goal made comic by the recalcitrance of wrongs to knightly redress in a world where chivalry no longer prevails. The first results of his undertaking are mainly calamitous both for the battered knight himself and for those whom he endeavors to succor. "For the love of God, sir knight errant," the peasant boy Andrés pleads, "if you meet me again, don't help me or assist me, even though you see them cutting me to pieces, but leave me with my misfortune; for it can't be worse than what will come of your worship's help" (I.31). Such fiascos are a consequence of his deluded misapprehension of reality. In his liberation of the galley slaves, on the other hand, and in his defense before the officers of the Inquisition, Don Quixote exhibits a lucid heroism mad only in defying the world to practice what it professes.

The lunatic knight's mistaken judgments were evident to the dullest observer when he insisted on seeing windmills as giants, a flock of sheep as an army, or a barber's basin as Mambrino's helmet. But his perception of the galley slaves as victims of oppression is, to say the least, less clearly demented. The sensory data are not in dispute; Don Quixote assents to Sancho's identification of the men as convicts being led to the galleys. The two differ not in their perception but in their response. What Don Quixote questions is not the fact of involuntary enslavement but the reasons for it, and not even the authority of the king, which Sancho finds sufficient, can allay his misgivings. He determines that "here is a place to practice my occupation: to right wrongs and to assist and care for the wretched" (I.22), and thereby places his own conception of justice above the law.

Far from acting with the reckless impulsiveness that we have come to expect, however, Don Quixote judiciously investigates the cause of each prisoner's misfortune. What he hears is enough to give the sanest listener pause. One has been condemned to a hundred lashes and three years in the galleys for stealing a basket of linen; another broke down on the rack; a third lacked ten ducats to pay a lawyer; a fourth and a fifth face long terms for pimping and fornication; and the explanation of the last of these holds good for all: "I lacked influence; I had no money" (I.22). Even the famous desperado Ginés de Pasamonte (whom the reader will meet again) is a colorful rogue of literary ambitions whose picaresque *Life* promises to surpass that of Lazarillo de Tormes. Don Quixote listens with sympathy to each story, and warmly extols the procurer's profession as "most necessary in a well-ordered republic." It would be hard to fault his considered verdict that "it could be that this man's deficient courage under torture, that one's shortage of money, lack of influence in another, and finally the judge's distorted judgment has been the cause of your destruction and of your failure to attain the justice that was rightly yours."

Sancho shares his master's compassion and gives a gold coin to the stricken procurer. But sentiment is one thing and action another: a fundamental condition of the reality principle that Don Quixote courageously disdains to observe. Roundly declaring that "it seems to me a hard case to make slaves of those whom God and nature made free" (I.22), he displays his madness by "saying and doing" one and the same thing when the startled guards refuse his command to unshackle their charges. Here more clearly than ever his madness (if madness it be) lies in the attempt to put into practice, without equivocation or fine discrimination of circumstances, and without a thought for his personal safety, the exalted principles that a Christian society proclaims and endorses only so long as no one is rash enough to apply them.

By giving to God what is Caesar's Don Quixote violates a basic taboo of the social compact, and only insanity can protect him from sharing the rigorous sentence of those whom he rescues. His lunacy is indeed the one possible sanction, in the Spain of Counter Reformation and Inquisition, for such audacious defiance of things as they are in the name of things as they might be. The episode ends in buffoonery when the galley slaves pelt their liberator with stones for demanding obeisance to Dulcinea, but this reversion to farce cannot obscure the seriousness of Don Quixote's comic challenge to the existing order. "I was born, by heaven's wish, in this iron age of ours," he had said, "to bring the golden age back to life" (I.20); and for Cervantes, as we have seen, the age of gold was a time when liberty reigned and servitude was unknown. Don Quixote thus demonstrates his affinity with earlier comic heroes not only in inventiveness and endurance but in his sympathy with social outcasts and, above all, in his dedication to human freedom.

No values were more important to the author himself. In a perceptive comment on this episode Harry Levin remarks that the key words "liberty" and "unfortunate" (*libertad* and *desdichados*) in the chapter heading, "Of the liberty that Don Quixote gave to many unfortunates who were being taken, against their will, where they did not want to go" (I.22), significantly echo two of the brief references in the novel to the author's own life. One of these occurs in the Captive's tale of imprisonment in Algiers, where "a Spanish soldier named somebody de Saavedra" (that is, Cervantes) is said to have performed deeds "that will remain in the memory of those people for many years, and all to achieve his liberty" (I.40); the other, during the inquisition in Don Quixote's library, when the priest describes his friend Cervantes, the author of *Galatea*, as "more versed in misfortunes [*desdichas*] than in verses" (I.6).

For Cervantes, who knew imprisonment at first hand, there

could be no greater misfortune than deprivation of liberty, but for his brainchild Don Quixote the connection between these conditions only slowly becomes apparent. From the beginning Don Quixote takes the part of the wretched against their oppressors, but not until he has met with repeated failures does the Knight of the Sad Countenance discern that he himself "was born," as he laments to Sancho early in Part Two, "to be an example of the unfortunate" (II.10). Liberty, he passionately affirms, is one of the greatest treasures on earth or in the sea (II.58). Yet in consequence of the chivalric mission to which he has devoted his labors his own liberty presupposes the liberation of others, and until that task — whose impossibility becomes more and more evident — is accomplished he must share the common misfortune of all who live in an age of iron.

Despite his distress, therefore, "to see himself so injured by the very men for whom he had done so much good" (I.22), Don Quixote does not repent his rash emancipation of those whom God and nature made free. To the ecclesiastical troopers who later attempt to arrest him he makes explicit the irreconcilable antagonism of human liberty to the order of church and state. "Do you call it highway robbery," he demands with a scornful laugh, "to liberate the enchained, to set convicts loose, to succor the wretched, to lift up the fallen, to assist those in need? . . . Come here, you troop of thieves — not troopers," he insolently tells them, "but highway robbers under license of the Holy Brotherhood!" (I.45) The mad knight's slaphappy profession of faith to Pedro Alonso has become a deliberate credo that subverts constituted authority by defining as malefactors those who uphold an unjust law in conflict with the God-given freedom of man. The liberation of the galley slaves is an act which Don Quixote cannot repudiate while remaining himself, for by identification with their misfortunes he has made their freedom — and the freedom of all who share their enslavement — the precondition of his own.

It is less the liberty of the golden age, however, than its truth and sincerity that Don Quixote emphasizes in his eulogy among the goatherds (I.11), and he remains confident (as he says to Sancho before they leave their village for the last time) that "if

naked truth reached the ears of princes, without the garments
of flattery, . . . other ages would be considered iron ones rather
than ours" (II.2). But the pursuit of truth in a world of deception is no less comically mad than the quest for liberty in a
world of bondage — and no less certainly destined to frustration
and defeat. Therefore, although his insistent sincerity sets Don
Quixote apart from the great virtuosos of mendacity from
Odysseus to Falstaff, his truth paradoxically resembles their lies
in its challenge to the accepted platitudes and practices of his
age. A madman's truth is by nature inventive; it complicates
reality by multiplying its potential significations in defiance of
single-minded attempts to circumscribe it within conventional
limits. It is a truth that affirms imagination and discloses itself
through masquerade. And in the last resort it may turn out to
be a truth that cannot, after all, dispense with deliberate falsehood.

If truth were simply opposed to fiction Don Quixote would
be its most unlikely proponent. But from the beginning of Cervantes' novel this easy antithesis is called into question and by
the end it has been obliterated beyond recall. In contrast to the
fabulous novels of chivalry *Don Quixote* is firmly placed in the
landscape of contemporary Spain familiar to Cervantes' readers from *Lazarillo de Tormes* and its picaresque successors. But
the multidimensional realism of *Don Quixote* is distinguished
from the verisimilitude of *Lazarillo* in the opening sentences of
the two books. "Well, first of all Your Grace should know,"
Lazarillo matter-of-factly begins, "that my name is Lázaro de
Tormes, son of Tomé Gonzáles and Antona Pérez, who lived in
Tejares, a village near Salamanca."[38] The reader is firmly situ-
ated and his bearings secure. He learns Lazarillo's vital statistics on the best of authority, since narrator and protagonist are
one, and has no reason to doubt the circumstantial accuracy of
the account that follows. The initial paragraphs of *Don
Quixote* could hardly be more strikingly different. "In a place
in La Mancha, whose name I do not wish to remember," the
novel begins, "there lived not long ago an hidalgo . . . They
suggest that his surname was Quixada, or Quesada, for there is
some difference among the authors who write of this matter,

although by very probable conjectures it can be assumed that his name was Quexana. But this matters little to our story; suffice it that its narration not depart by a jot from the truth" (I.1). Here everything is uncertain from the first. The hero's village is better forgotten and his name — until he boldly invents one — remains indeterminate.

More importantly, we are left in the dark concerning the most essential question of all. We receive the most solemn assurances of the narrator's punctilious regard for the truth. But who is this narrator, and on what authority does he make his assertions? Far from resolving our doubts, his strenuous protestations of veracity (and the dubious "probability" of his conjectures) only engender suspicion. Whatever confidence we might have in the narrator's objectivity is further shaken when we learn that his information, far from being firsthand, is derived, through the mediation of a capricious translator, from an Arabic manuscript attributed to a certain Cide Hamete Benengeli and discovered by chance at a silk merchant's shop in Toledo. Since our narrator owns that he knows Don Quixote only as a character in a book, his credence (and ours) in the truth of the story for which he vouches has no better foundation than Don Quixote's belief in the knights and ladies of chivalric romance. His attempt to resolve the incertitude that adheres to his history is perplexing at best. "If any objection can be made concerning its truth," he declares, "it can only be on the grounds that its author was Arabic, since it is characteristic of men of that nation to be liars; although, because they are so much our enemies, it might rather be thought that he made too little of the truth than too much" (I.9). Our Spanish scribe is either the most naive or the most ironical of logicians. In either case, his supposition that an Arab author's probable ill will toward a Christian subject whom he praises argues for his essential accuracy is less than totally reassuring.

When Cide Hamete himself later swears to the truth of one episode (II.27) on his faith as a Catholic Christian (though he is a Moor) and classifies another as apocryphal (II.24) on account of its improbability (what then is *his* source for the story?), the reader finds any remaining ground cut away from beneath him. In Part Two Don Quixote himself sows doubts about the truthfulness of adventures previously recounted (as he learns from the Bachelor Sansón Carrasco) in a book entitled *The Ingenious Hidalgo Don Quixote de la Mancha,* that is, the book we have just read. "No truth could be expected of the Moors," we are told, "because they are all impostors, counterfeiters, and fantasts" (II.3). Henceforward Don Quixote and Sancho appear, both to us and to those whom they meet in their travels, simultaneously as "real" people (within the fiction of Part Two) and as fictional characters (known from the questionable Part One); and by the time they learn—as Cervantes himself learned—that an unauthorized continuation of their adventures is in print, and even encounter a character from its pages who denounces the other Don Quixote and Sancho as frauds, any simple distinction between truth and fiction has become impossible to maintain. The true madmen, perhaps, have been those who most glibly assumed it.

The effect of these bewildering ambiguities is not, however, mere mystification of the reader or gratuitous undermining of his belief. On the contrary, the commingling of truth and fiction strengthens the reader's sense of Don Quixote's and Sancho's reality. He learns not that truth is a fiction—a facile conclusion which author and hero alike refute—but that fiction has an undeniable truth; and this is of course the very perception that Don Quixote persistently affirms in the novel. Don Quixote, Sancho Panza, and even the phantom Dulcinea del Toboso continue to appear "real" to us as the gallant Amadis, faithful Gandalin, and fair Oriana of *Amadis of Gaul* no longer can, not because they are less obviously fictions (none but a madman could believe that they ever traversed the plains of La Mancha) but because they are richer and more imaginatively convincing fictions who incarnate dimensions of human experience unknown to the dreamy chivalric novels.

Perhaps Don Quixote's belief in Amadis was after all, despite his deranged fundamentalism, not wholly dissimilar to our belief in Don Quixote. For this threadbare nobleman of a nameless village the fictional knights errant of romance gave form to potentialities of the human spirit scarcely conceivable within the confines of his humdrum existence. His willful belief in Amadis, or in what Amadis represents, is in any case fundamental to ours in him, for without it he would not be Don Quixote at all but only Master Quexana, Quesada, or whatever his name — the merest wraith of a fiction. The dying hidalgo may at last renounce the fables that once inspired his forlorn endeavor to resuscitate the truth of the golden age, but by then he has won the reader's inalienable allegiance to a fiction impossible to dismiss as untrue. To that extent, at least, his mission has achieved a triumph that no repudiation can cancel.

Don Quixote's mad devotion to truth becomes heroic in proportion to his growing consciousness of the obstacles in its path. In Part One there are scattered hints already that he is more aware than others suppose of the close association of truth and illusion. The historical existence of Amadis of Gaul, he explains to Sancho in the Sierra Morena, is altogether less significant than the perfection he exemplifies. Homer, who pictures prudence in Ulysses, and Virgil, who embodies piety in Aeneas, do not paint or describe them "as they were," Don Quixote observes, "but as they should have been, to serve as examples of their virtues for men of the future. In the same way," he opines, "Amadis was the polestar, the morning star, the sun of brave and enamored knights, and all of us who ride to war under the banner of love and of chivalry ought to imitate him" (I.25). And on the subject of Dulcinea herself the infatuated lover concedes that "not all the poets who eulogize mistresses under a name that they give them according to fancy really have them. Do you think," he asks,

> that the Amaryllises, the Phyllises, the Sylvias, the Dianas, the Galateas, the Alidas, and others that books, ballads, barbershops, and theaters are full of, were truly the flesh-and-blood mistresses of those who extol and extolled them? Of course not; they fabricate most of them to provide a subject for their verses, and in order to be thought lovers, or men who gain credit for being so. Therefore, it is sufficient for me to think and believe that the good Aldonza Lorenzo is

fair and demure; her lineage matters little, for no one needs
to delve into it with the intention of giving her some robe,
and as for me, I account her the most exalted princess in the
world.

Don Quixote clearly discerns, then—at least in his lucid in-
tervals—that the truth which he has sworn to revive is the product of determined invention, believed *because* it is vividly
imagined. When the wind is southerly he knows a hawk from
a handsaw. Within his chosen sphere he is therefore impregnable to the skepticism of others. However the rest of the world
may decide, "in Don Quixote's imagination," we read near the
end of Part One, the packsaddle remained a harness, the basin
a helmet, and the inn a castle until Judgment Day (I.45). But
his faith is under continual siege from without, and because he
is sporadically conscious that truth must be imagined to be convincing, he is not immune from assault. His heroic madness will
face its severest trials, indeed, when his confidence in its self-
sufficiency begins to waver at last.

The celebrated episode of Dulcinea's "enchantment" at the
outset of Don Quixote's last expedition irrevocably alters the
terms of his enterprise by raising, for the first time, a substantive doubt in the adequacy of his own inventive capacities. In a
stunning reversal of expectation it is Don Quixote, when Sancho disingenuously describes Dulcinea and her attendants be-
dizened with gold and gems, who replies in bewilderment, "I
see nothing, Sancho, but three peasant girls on three donkeys"
(II.10). The comedy of the scene, in which Don Quixote sees in
Sancho's Queen and Lady only a flat-nosed country wench, is
more complex than any in Part One. It derives not only from
the immediate incongruity of a bumpkin portrayed as a princess but from the contradiction between the knight and squire
as we see them now and as we have known them before.

What was constant in the world of the novel has been trans-
posed, and the implications for Don Quixote and his valorous
mission are momentous. The reflexive madness that provided a
source of hilarity throughout Part One will not recur except as
a brief and regressive anomaly. Henceforth it will be a contin-

ual exertion on Don Quixote's part to generate the illusions that formerly appeared automatic — and to persuade *himself* of their truth. The unsavory peasant girl becomes a beautiful princess only through his desperate determination to picture her as he cannot see her, now that fantasy no longer obeys his will. In consequence, this unsurpassably comic episode is at the same time more melancholy than its predecessors. "And to think that I did not see all this, Sancho!" Don Quixote laments: "Now I say again, and will say a thousand times, that I am the most unfortunate of men" (II.10). The inability to transform reality by imagination is indeed the misfortune in which this hero surpasses all other men once he partakes of their disinheritance, for misfortune consists, as we have seen, in the loss of liberty, and for Don Quixote no greater liberty can be lost than the transfiguring power of invention.

Conscious pretense plays a newly prominent role in Part Two of Cervantes' novel, from Sancho's benevolent dissimulation to the callous mockery of the Duke and Duchess, and Don Quixote himself acts with increasing deliberation as he reluctantly acknowledges the deceit of the world. Far from being intimidated by the awareness, however, he resolutely seeks out adventures (like those of the lions and the enchanted boat) as if to demonstrate to himself and to others a valor that he, more than they, has begun to doubt. He arbitrarily determines to show his fearful spectators "whether I am a man who is frightened of lions" (II.17), and having demonstrated his courage, acknowledges the temerity of his deed. Bravery is a mean between rashness and cowardice, he tells the level-headed Don Diego de Miranda, who finds his action inexplicable, "but it will be less injurious for one who is brave to rise to the zenith of a rash man than to sink to the nadir of a coward." When such an ordeal fails to vindicate his hope, on the other hand, as in the sad debacle of the enchanted boat, his sense of defeat is far more bitter than in the past. Instead of exhorting his bruised squire to seek out new adventures, as he had done so often before, he now gives voice to an unaccustomed fatigue: "I can do no more" (II.29).

In no adventure does Don Quixote so unsparingly test himself as in his descent to the Cave of Montesinos. What he here puts to the proof is the problematical reality of his most cherished illusions. The elaborate vision that he relates upon his return from the chasm—a vision of marvels "whose impossibility and grandeur," the chapter heading proclaims, "causes this adventure to be considered apocryphal" (II.23)—presents a disquieting contrast to the spontaneous hallucinations of his earliest forays. Its circumstances are derived from a ballad in which the warrior Durandarte, having been mortally wounded on the field of Roncesvalles, commands his cousin Montesinos to cut out his heart and present it to his lady Belerma.[39] It is these majestic figures of song and story—the white-bearded Montesinos, the speaking corpse of Durandarte, and the mournful Belerma, who clutches her lover's mummified heart —that Don Quixote claims to have seen, forever enchanted by Merlin's spell, during his sojourn under the earth. But far from jumbling images from his reading together with carefree abandon as in his pristine delusions, Don Quixote fashions his strange narration with labored contrivance; it is no delirious outpouring but a painstakingly artful tableau. At the same time a new and disruptive incongruity intrudes on his vision. The consistently exalted tone of earlier fantasies is shattered when Durandarte replies to Montesinos' hope that Don Quixote will disenchant them: "if it should not happen, O cousin, I say, patience and shuffle the deck." The earthy proverbialism of Sancho's discourse has somehow made its way into the once inviolate sphere of romance, and before the knight's bizarre tale is over Dulcinea, in the rustic incarnation foisted upon her by Sancho, has reduced sublimity to a shambles by cadging money from her chivalrous lover and cutting a caper two yards in the air.

The meaning of so enigmatic a vision has eluded commentators ever since Cide Hamete Benengeli himself, who wisely leaves it to the reader to judge. The fact, however, that the scrupulous Moor—though refusing to believe that Don Quixote could tell a lie—records his improbable tale "without affirming it as false or true" (II.24) raises the possibility that the honest knight may have shored up his faltering powers of vision by a consciously fictional invention. Once the spontaneity of madness has been lost the dissident truth of imagination to which Don Quixote has devoted life and honor very nearly resembles dissimulation, and it is not inconceivable, in this quandary, that the champion of truth should have summoned falsehood to his aid.[40] "The most ingenious character in a play," he says to Sansón Carrasco at the outset of Part Two, "is the fool's, for one who wants to be thought simple must not be so" (II.3); this self-conscious awareness of playing a role not identical with himself is new and portentous. Sancho soon suspects, with the growing shrewdness that characterizes his perceptions, that his master's vision involves something other than his usual delusion. "For my part, begging your worship's pardon," he bluntly says, "I hold that it was all humbug and falsehood, or at least things that you dreamed" (II.25). The borderline between humbug or falsehood and dream—between premeditated and spontaneous invention—defies precise definition. But Don Quixote does not repudiate Sancho's suggestion, and the ambiguous oracles of Master Pedro's prophesying ape and the Enchanted Head, which he questions concerning the veracity of his vision, do nothing to resolve his troubling incertitude.

Resurrection from the nether regions has brought Don Quixote no sudden illumination, no expansive sense of renewal, then, as it did to comic heroes before him, but only deepened perplexity about the truth that he once set forth to revive. Whatever the nature of his vision may have been, he himself can no longer believe it with the unquestioning faith of earlier days. In this uncertainity—and in the ominous possibility that the paragon of sincerity may have no alternative, in a fraudulent world, but to lie—Don Quixote's heroic enterprise confronts its most dangerous challenge. No longer, after this adventure, will the sad-faced knight have the comfort of seeing every inn as a castle; from now on he must struggle without intermission to uphold the illusion vital to truth and to ward off the disenchantment which could only be its death—and his own. But if his capacity to accomplish greater exploits than the Twelve Peers or Nine Worthies comes into question along with the confidence in his visions that gave his boast substance, his courageous determination to persist in his course remains as firm as before. Dulcinea del Toboso may indeed not exist on this earth: "These are not matters," Don Quixote soberly apprises the Duke and Duchess, "whose verification may be carried through to the end" (II.32). But by his willingness to continue his labors in behalf of this Dulcinea who may be no more than a dream he gives proof that not even insuperable doubt can undermine his heroic devotion to a fiction in which everything that is noble and true in his world resides. Only after he has been compelled by defeat to forswear the action indispensable to his vision does Don Quixote despair of chivalry at last, yet not even his final repudiation can revoke his achievement. For the "real" Alonso Quixano the Good, who renounces illusion and dies, thereby liberates his invincible alter ego, the fictional Don Quixote de la Mancha, from everything that is not fantastic, immortal, and true. In the imagination of readers the woebegone hidalgo will forever remain a valorous knight errant no less surely than the basin remained a helmet in Don Quixote's. Of this nature, surely, is the truth that he strove to revive in an age of iron.

In Part One of Cervantes' novel, where heroism was a product of madness, the stolid Sancho Panza served, with unfailingly comic results, as a levelheaded foil to his reckless master. But despite the manifold contrasts between them, in viewpoint, motivation, and goals, as well as in physical appearance and speech, the crackpot knight and his foolish squire are united by the mockery of a world that sets them apart and by the devotion that binds them together. Though doggedly skeptical of his master's fancies, which he vainly strives to restrain, Sancho believes with quixotic fervor in Don Quixote himself, and his loyalty takes on heroic proportions as the derision of a hostile world becomes increasingly malevolent and acute. From the outset of Part Two, in particular, we are less aware of the outward contrasts than of the secret affinities between master and man, who seem to the priest "to be cast in the same mold" (II.2); and both Don Quixote's colloquial turns of speech and Sancho's imaginative sallies testify to the intimacy of their association.

Salvador de Madariaga has suggested that "Sancho's spirit rises from reality to illusion" in the second part of the novel while "Don Quixote's descends from illusion to reality."[41] The interrelation between the two is far more complex, however, than a turnabout in direction. What they share, as both discover, is not the alienation of madness and folly alone (for in this they are no more than victims) but a purposeful and therefore heroic resistance to the far greater madness and folly of the world that disdains them. The recrimination that punctuated their strained partnership in Part One gradually gives way to a deepening affection as each comes to understand their essential resemblance.

Even the apparent reversal of roles in the episode of Dulcinea's enchantment eventually takes its place in a developing pattern of rapprochement. It is not in his new inventive talent only, as it seems at the moment, but in the *deliberateness* of his inventions that Sancho will later discover an unsuspected similarity between himself and the master whom he here so adroitly bamboozles. His deception is founded on a shrewd assessment of the nature of Don Quixote's mania, as we ourselves have observed it in Part One. "Well, since he's mad, as he is, and with a madness that most often takes one kind of thing for another, and judges white black and black white," he reflects, "as was apparent when he said that the windmills were giants, and the monks' mules dromedaries, and the flocks of sheep enemy armies, and many other things to this tune, it won't be very difficult to make him believe that a peasant girl, the first one who comes my way hereabouts, is the lady Dulcinea" (II.10). Though the stratagem brilliantly succeeds, the estimation which it appears to confirm soon proves to have been inadequate. Sancho acknowledges in this same soliloquy that by attaching himself to such a master he partakes of his madness; what he later begins to suspect is a corresponding affinity not in delusion but in cunning.

For if the possibility exists that Don Quixote has consciously lied about what he saw in the Cave of Montesinos—a supposition which he is inclined to disbelieve but cannot wholly reject —then he may share in Sancho's guileful sanity no less than

Sancho in his visionary madness. Don Quixote himself appears to countenance such an interpretation when he characterizes Sancho's visions during the abortive flight of the wooden horse Clavileño as either lies or dreams and whispers in his squire's ear: "Sancho, since you want me to believe what you have seen in the sky, I want you to believe me about what I saw in the Cave of Montesinos. I say nothing more" (II.41). It is not that Sancho and Don Quixote have exchanged roles but that both have arrived from opposite starting points at a shared understanding, or tacit agreement, that only their united endeavor can sustain the illusion to which each is now dedicated. In order to believe in anything they must first believe in themselves and each other. In a world of mockers it is Sancho Panza who eloquently affirms his master's simplicity and goodness, and Don Quixote who clearly discerns that his garrulous squire is more philosopher than fool. No sooner has Sancho departed from the ducal court to govern his island than Don Quixote becomes aware of his loneliness; and Sancho returns with the knowledge that his master's company "was more agreeable to him than to be governor of all the islands in the world" (II.54). So necessary has each become to the other that neither they nor we can imagine them apart.

Thus the crass and skeptical peasant who set forth from his village in hope of a lucrative island to govern becomes, through heightened consciousness of his folly, a comic hero no less than his magnanimous master. The knight's example transforms his faithful squire, if not an unbelieving world; and this alone would be sufficient to vindicate his heroical undertaking. But if Sancho is infected by Don Quixote's noble ideal—"He can do harm to no one," he proudly asserts, "only good to everyone" (II.13)—Don Quixote is equally captivated by Sancho's wise humility. "When I think he is going to trip himself up like a dolt," he confides to the Duke and Duchess, "he comes up with wise sayings that raise him to the sky" (II.32). During his governorship of the inland isle of Barataria Sancho is able, through his unpretentious sagacity, to transform the Duke and Duchess' idle pastime into a momentary realization of his master's humane ideal of a golden age uncorrupted by favor or interest.

For he had seen the earth as a mustard seed, from his heavenly vantage astride Clavileño, and apprehended how little greatness there was in governing something so small. "I love a single black part of my soul's fingernail more than my whole body," he tells his master, "and I can feed myself, as plain Sancho, just as well on bread and onions as a governor can on partridges and capons" (II.43). It is this circumscription of desire and acceptance of self that makes Sancho worthy, in Don Quixote's admiring words, "to be governor of a thousand islands."

Nor is the one-time dreamer of impossible dreams insusceptibe to the moderating influence of his squire's example. Throughout Part Two Don Quixote's vaulting aspiration is tempered by awareness of insurmountable limit. In setting forth on his last expedition he no longer expects to win eternal renown, as in the bright dawn of his illusion, but only the calumny with which "virtue is persecuted wherever it exists in eminent degree" (II.2). Instead of charging every windmill in his path, he is wont to rein in his steed and give ear to Sancho's healthy advice with a new respect for prudence. He does indeed continue to seek out occasions for valor, but his insane disregard of existing reality is by and large a thing of the past. His imagination, like Sancho's appetite, has accommodated itself to bread and onions.

This reluctant acknowledgment that reality is impervious to imagination implies no diminishment of Don Quixote's heroism but its most severe trial. Even after his visions have been clouded by doubt, and illusions lie shattered around him —including the seminal illusion that desire might find fulfillment in action—he bravely persists in his chastened endeavor to embody in his own person the virtue that he no longer hopes to revive in an irredeemable world. To the madman of Part One heroism was second nature. With the onset of lucidity, however, Don Quixote's defense of his elevated ideal against the perils of disenchantment becomes immeasurably more difficult, for his adversary now stands revealed not as a host of malignant demons but as the immense majority of those whom he once intended to save. This clear-sighted heroism of the mature Don Quixote is no longer intrinsically absurd. The bridal couple at Camacho's wedding gratefully proclaim him "a Cid in arms and a Cicero in eloquence" (II.22), and the waiting woman Doña Rodriguez appeals to him for a justice she can find in none other (II.52). What makes his heroism seem comic now is the determination of this complacent majority to avert through mockery the menace of his dissenting example.

It is above all the hard-won knowledge of his own limitations, which he learns through association with Sancho, that makes Don Quixote's perseverance in his mission not merely mad but heroic, yet despite their profound affinity his awareness must be of a different order than his squire's. Self-knowledge, for Sancho, consists in humble acceptance of a God-given nature freed from false ambitions by devotion to a generous master. "Sancho I was born, and Sancho I expect to die" (II.4), he tells Sansón Carrasco in the opening chapters of Part Two, and by the experience of his ill-starred governorship he confirms "that naked I was born, naked I find myself now; I neither lose nor gain" (II.53). But Don Quixote was born, and will die, not Don Quixote but Alonso Quixano (or Quixada, or Quesada . . .), and in consequence his self-knowledge must be more complex than either Sancho's simple faith or the dying hidalgo's disillusioned repudiation. "I know who I am," he proudly told his astonished neighbor at the outset of his heroic career; and neither the mockery of the world nor his own disquieting doubts prevent him from reaffirming to the Knight of the White Moon at the moment of his defeat: "Dulcinea del Toboso is the most beautiful woman in the world, and I am the most unfortunate knight on earth, nor is it right that my weakness should defraud that truth" (II.64). This simultaneous declaration of ineluctable misfortune and of the unimpaired truth of his radiant invention epitomizes Don Quixote's knowledge of a self created by willful imagination and sustained by courageous defiance of unbelief. To affirm this in a world not of castles and giants but of immutable inns and refractory windmills — and to proclaim it with full consciousness of its desperate folly — is an act of deliberate heroism no more ridiculous than sublime.

VII

MORAL RAKE AND

MASTERFUL LACKEY

꽃

B Y THE time of Cervantes, on the threshold of the seventeenth century, the passionate sense of human possibility
inherited from the High Renaissance had already been over-
clouded by a consciousness of inescapable limit. Between conception and action the interim now seemed a phantasma, so
that heroism itself took on the aspect of madness. Don Quixote,
the heir of Orlando and comic contemporary of Hamlet, died
without legitimate issue, for the classic age of European
comedy that culminated in the plays of Molière had little use
for impossible dreams and audacious adventures. In an era of
royal and literary absolutism uncongenial to upstarts and outcasts of every kidney the comic poet, in his eagerness to rehabilitate a disparaged profession, readily embraced the flattering role of censor of morals.

The satirical comedy propounded by Humanist scholars now
attained retarded fruition in the deliberately classical plays of
Ben Jonson and Molière, for whom the dissident claims of the
"vulgar," given voice in the popular comedies of Shakespeare
and Lope de Vega, are a theme of unfailing derision. Against
"such foul and unwashed bawdry as is now made the food of
the scene" Jonson rails with the moralist's vocational indignation, declaring it his "special aim" in *Volpone,* ". . . to put the

177

snaffle in their mouths that cry out: We never punish vice in our interludes, &c."[1] The monomaniacal characters of Jonsonian comedy, even when they are less severely penalized than the unlucky Fox — and even when they finagle a makeshift triumph, like Face in *The Alchemist* — are exposed to ridicule by the indelible humors that limit their vision and trammel their actions. For all their dynamism and zest they function, as Hazlitt wrote in anticipation of Bergson, "like machines, governed by mere routine, or by the convenience of the poet, whose property they are."[2] Rogue and gull are alike in their blind infatuation, and there is finally little to choose between Volpone and Sir Epicure Mammon.

The misfits of Molière, though more complex, are seldom if ever permitted, like Falstaff or Don Quixote, to rise superior to those who disdain them. In this they are true to the age of Louis XIV, which was pre-eminently, as Paul Bénichou remarks in his excellent study, a time when "the heroic sublime was in general disrepute."[3] Once the rebellion of the Fronde had been quelled the domesticated noblemen of Versailles resigned themselves to play the parlor game of intrigue and love in accord with rules laid down by the king, and any divergence from norms of behavior sanctioned by both reason and breeding was held in general contempt. For the worldly courtier the politic virtue of good sense superseded the hazardous glory to which Corneille's eloquent heroes had lately aspired, and in Molière, as Bénichou observes, *le bon sens* "is often only the sense of conformity to the prevailing customs."[4] Comic characters who deliberately flout the accepted code may compel a perverse admiration, since much can be said for duping Orgon or dumping Célimène; but not even the accomplished impostor or determined misanthrope can safely violate the consensus of a society supremely sure of its values. Only after this aristocratic *bienséance* came to be viewed, much later, as decadence and corruption could Rousseau castigate Molière's theater as "a school of vices and bad morals";[5] only after the captious Alceste had ceased to seem comic could he be acclaimed as a hero.

The plays of Jonson and Molière are comedies without heroes, since their lackluster paragons of decency and decorum are hardly ever a match, either in energy or in wit, for those who incur universal opprobrium by reckless perfidy or bad manners. Often they are mere passive victims rescued from villainy only when the rascals fall out among themselves, as in *Volpone,* or a beneficent monarch opportunely intervenes, as in *Tartuffe.* The judicious *honnête homme* who chides the vices of excess in Molière's comedies is typically, like Philinte in *The Misanthrope,* a well intentioned bystander peripheral if not irrelevant to the outcome; for good sense, when all is said and done, is not the stuff of which heroes are made. The one major play in which the butt of derision finds himself completely outclassed by his antagonist (much to his disbelief) is *The School for Wives.* In Agnès, whose responses are dictated not by calculation but instinct, Molière has sketched a captivating character with the potential for heroic resistance to the artificial constraints placed on nature. "I see nothing wrong," the refractory pupil tells her thwarted preceptor, Arnolphe, when he upbraids her with openly loving another, "in anything I have done".[6] Her ingenuous protest, like Alceste's indignant refusal, portends an insurrection against the dictates of Reason that ridicule will be powerless to put down.

In the comedy of the English Restoration witty talk among the superfluous leisure classes largely usurps the place of action, and sexual love (along with the means to enjoy it) overrides all lesser concerns. Yet within its severely narrowed sphere this notoriously artificial and unheroic comedy celebrates a way of life that demands bold resolve of its embattled and disreputable young protagonists. The Puritan hegemony was an ominously recent memory when Wycherley scored his first success; before Congreve began to write, the Glorious Revolution had firmly reinstated the Protestant middle classes under a monarch not notably merry. In such hostile circumstances the outnumbered rakes and wits of comedy waged continuous partisan warfare against the leagued enemies of love and pleasure.

At first their raids were impudently open. In Wycherley's *The Country Wife,* to take one brazen example, the salacious Horner succeeds outrageously in enjoying his neighbors' wives under cover of impotence, and exults in his triumphs. The response to such challenges was predictably thunderous. After diatribes in the vein of Jeremy Collier's *A Short View of the Immorality and Profaneness of the English Stage* (1698), it is not surprising that Congreve's young blades are more chastened — even resigned — than Wycherley's in their almost melancholy pursuit of enjoyment. Despite their adept command of the social graces Congreve's lovers are inobtrusively at loggerheads with the way of the world. It is the fatuous Witwoud who plumes himself, in the play of that name, that "a wit should no more be sincere, than a woman constant." The hero Mirabell, on the contrary, sadly concludes that "a man may as soon make a friend by his wit, or a fortune by his honesty, as win a woman by plain-dealing and sincerity."[7] The lovers define and discover themselves through opposition both to frivolous dupes like Lady Wishfort and to cynical knaves like Fainall; they excel their unprincipled antagonists at a game they would rather not play. The accomplished Millamant's ostensibly heartless coquetry stands exposed as the fragile self-defense of a vulnerable woman when she confides, in a telling moment of candor, "Well, if Mirabell should not make a good husband, I am a lost thing, — for I find I love him violently."[8] Congreve's heroes are those who never confound their own feelings with the social roles they adopt by necessity and play with reluctant adroitness. "The comedy draws toward an end," Valentine beseeches Angelica in *Love for Love,* "and let us think of leaving acting, and be ourselves"; and although Angelica protests that "the pleasure of a masquerade is done, when we come to show our faces,"[9] she too longs for the unmasking that will confirm her lover's generous passion.

In this respect the comedies of Congreve recall Shakespeare's rather than Jonson's and anticipate those of his French successor Marivaux, in which the surprises of love are likewise the roundabout path to self-revelation. The cunningly contrived "false confidences" by which Dorante gains Araminte's love in Marivaux's final masterpiece culminate in his perilously forthright disavowal — to which no worldly valet prompts him — of any falsity that might compromise the truth of his feelings. "I had rather regret the loss of your love," he declares, "than owe the enjoyment of it to the success of an artifice; I had rather suffer your hate than the remorse for having deceived her whom I adore."[10] Even in the most refined comedies of manners the voice of natural sentiment thus registers its earnest dissent, and from this latent conflict between spontaneity and an artificial civilization a new comic heroism would soon be engendered.

On the whole, however, the classic theater of the seventeenth and early eighteenth centuries remained a bastion of strictly aristocratic values in which the upstart bourgeois was a favorite object of ridicule and servants showed their superior sagacity by knowing their place. It was not in comic drama but in picaresque fiction that representatives of the unprivileged classes began to articulate needs and desires in conflict with the established order. In Grimmelshausen's *Simplicissimus* a simple farm-lad swept into the maelstrom of the Thirty Years' War shrewdly exploits the advantage of being considered a fool as he masters the art of survival and eventually—like Apuleius' ass long before—indicts the false idols of his disordered world. "The glorious deeds of heroes would merit high praise," he tells a secretary who has eulogized the noble conquerors of the past, "if they were not accomplished with the destruction and damage of other human beings. But what kind of praise is it which is soiled with so much innocently shed human blood? And what kind of nobility is it which is achieved and won by the ruin of so many thousands of other human beings?"[11] But although Simplex calls the murderous heroism of his age to account from the vantage point of its untitled victims his alternative to the horrors of war is by no means comic. Instead of elevating the defiant standard of self with Dicaeopolis, Falstaff, or Schweik he devotes himself, in the end, to the otherworldly renunciation of the Christian hermit. When life is no more than a dream, and the dream an unrelieved nightmare, lasting refuge cannot be won by the comic hero's dubious virtues.

Not every adventurer felt obliged, of course, to repudiate a world that sometimes offered amenities proportionate to its hardships. Lesage's easygoing Gil Blas is a truant affably winding his way toward satisfactory accommodation with things as they are: the pícaro as peripatetic bourgeois. In the hedonistic laxity of its decline aristocratic society had left its rear door ajar and the once-despised social climber was suddenly à la mode. Even a peasant, as Marivaux demonstrated, could turn the practiced skills of the parvenu to brilliant advantage. As for the middle classes, their escutcheon was wealth and their doors had never been closed. In Defoe's veracious novels the distinction between felonious arts and entrepreneurial virtues is at best a nuance. Far from posing a challenge to middle-class values by her unsavory life of whoredom, incest, and theft, Moll Flanders "at last grew *Rich,*" the title page of her checkered narrative reassuringly informs us, "liv'd *Honest,* and died a *Penitent.*" In her uphill contest with a hostile and resolutely respectable world this daughter of Newgate must rely on the versatility and quick wit of Odysseus, but despite the severity of her handicaps she never questions the rules of the game by which, after all, she too makes her fortune. If her seamy past sometimes causes her qualms, in the end "all these little Difficulties were made easy,"[12] she complacently concludes, by a repentance that allows her to relish her ill-gotten gains with a quiet conscience, serene in the happy morality of having her cake and eating it too. The transition from hardened cutpurse to pious matron proves to be disconcertingly smooth. From this quarter, at least, would come no challenge to the high professions and sharp practices of the up-and-coming bourgeois world.

For centuries the lower orders of a society still feudal in structure had relegated heroic honors, for what they were worth, to the social superiors whose wealth and power they were sedulously usurping. Their own models of conduct, above all in Protestant England, were patriarchs and apostles. But after the Settlement of 1689 and the installation, a quarter-century later, of a Hanoverian king the confident English middle classes began to cast about for paradigms from their own station in life whose labors might find exemplary recompense in a world at last responsive to virtue. Moll Flanders, who possessed all the bourgeois virtues except bourgeois virtue, presented an image which they preferred not to recognize as their own; but in Samuel Richardson's chaste Pamela they hailed a model of rectitude to which the most humble maidservant might safely aspire. "I will die a thousand deaths rather than be dishonest any way,"[13] Pamela vows before the opening round, and throughout her epic struggle against a lascivious master's advances she never flags in defense of a virtue handsomely rewarded, after numberless tribulations, by her baffled antagonist's hand. Not only crime but morality (which was certainly safer) promised handsome dividends, and in the unprecedented acclaim bestowed on his novel Richardson must have found vindication for his pious trust that Pamela's triumph might bring comfort and hope to others who found themselves in like peril—or held out for a comparable bonanza.

By firmly instituting sexual virtue in place of martial glory as the canon of human merit—male as well as female—for the new bourgeois age, Richardson decisively altered the terms of heroism in fiction; after Pamela's spirited example morality might be flouted but hardly ignored. (Witness even the lubricous Fanny Hill in Cleland's *Memoirs of a Woman of Pleasure,* who thinks it fitting to end her bawdy narrative with a frankly improbable paean to "the infinitely superior joys of innocence" and "the so delicate charms of VIRTUE,"[14] thus surpassing Moll Flanders herself in the art of painless repentance.) The dialectical interplay between comic heroism and its "serious" counterpart is nowhere more clearly attested than in Henry Fielding's complex response to Richardson's unintentional challenge. About his aversion there is no ambiguity: his rival's sanctimonious paragon he promptly and gleefully pilloried, in the pseudonymous *Shamela,* as a conniving "young Politician" virtuous in direct proportion to her anticipated reward. Among "the many notorious FALSHOODS and MISREPRE-SENTATIONS"[15] derided in this scurrilous parody none was more blatant than the smug assumption that morality pays. "There are a Set of Religious, or rather Moral Writers," Fielding later remarked in *Tom Jones,* "who teach that Virtue is the certain Road to Happiness, and Vice to Misery, in this World. A very wholesome and comfortable Doctrine, and to which we have but one Objection, namely, That it is not true" (XV. 1).

The fraudulence of Richardson's novel, as Fielding saw it,

lay not only in its self-evident falsity to experience but in its heroine's prostitution of virtue through calculation of its effects. Fielding was no less intensely concerned than Richardson with morality in his writings. He held the conviction, however, promulgated most influentially by Lord Shaftesbury, that neither fear of punishment nor hope of reward can "consist in reality with virtue or goodness, if it either stands as essential to any moral performance, or as a considerable motive to any act, of which some better affection ought alone to have been a sufficient cause."[16] If true virtue spontaneously arises from natural "affection," as Fielding believed along with the latitudinarian moralists of his age, then a self-consciously scheming virtue *must* be sham. There can be no essential difference between Richardson's prudent heroine and such hypocritical scoundrels as Fielding's Jonathan Wild or Master Blifil, whom the world likewise venerates for greatness and virtue until their perfidy is providentially exposed. The very vehemence of Fielding's uncharacteristically malevolent (and never publicly acknowledged) travesty of Richardson bespeaks the intense importance of moral questions in his own life and work. He vilified Pamela not to impugn but to rehabilitate a virtue severely compromised by her flagrant venality.

To a man of Fielding's robust temper and satirical bent—the latter honed by apprenticeship in the London theater—ridicule of Pamela's spurious virtue was second nature. To flesh out in fictional form the natural goodness of heart in which true virtue consists was a far more rigorous challenge. The most estimable paragons seldom enthrall, and Fielding's exemplary figures are not exempt from the tediousness of the breed. Heart-free, in *Jonathan Wild,* counters Wild's hypocritical "greatness" with absurdly ingenuous goodness, and the gentle Amelia of Fielding's last novel merges into an indistinguishable flock of patient Griseldas consigned to oblivion by being too good for this world. Because their goodness is not acquired but innate these saintly figures are not even susceptible to temptations that might make their long sufferance a meaningful (not to say an interesting) struggle; such unworldliness is a privilege traditionally reserved for infants and idiots. Before the insidious wiles of their craftier adversaries the naturally good are shorn of every defense, and only the happy circumstance that providence exhibits a like benevolence (as in the romances of every age) shelters them from the customary fate of the innocent. Theirs is a virtue less contaminated, no doubt, but also emphatically less heroic than Pamela's strenuous rectitude, and its reward seems to that extent gratuitous and unearned.

Fielding's alternative to the mercantile morality derided in *Shamela* was fortunately not confined to the erection of contrary paragons. Between Pam and Sham, the earnest and the burlesque, lay the intermediate realm of the comic to which the author, in his Preface, explicitly assigns his first novel, *The History of the Adventures of Joseph Andrews, And of his Friend Mr. Abraham Adams,* which he published less than fifteen months after Richardson's provocative prototype. Comedy is intrinsic to goodness as portrayed in this book, since in a world given over to artifice and pretense the spontaneity of true goodness evokes inevitable derision. Only when they passively suffer the wrongs that afflict them can the good be seen as pathetic; Joseph and his Friend are comic because they *act* on the impulse of nature. In his theory of comedy, as outlined in the Preface to *Joseph Andrews,* Fielding hardly goes beyond satire. "The only Source of the true Ridiculous (as it appears to me) is Affectation,"[17] he writes; and his mirthful exposure of Lady Booby, Mrs. Slipslop, Parson Trulliber, and a legion of others richly illustrates the hypothesis. But his true originality lies in the introduction of a comic character distinguished not by affectation but by its conspicuous absence — a character whose estimable virtues prove no less conducive to laughter than the vices of those who are held up to scorn.

Fielding's "comic romance" transcends its burlesque beginnings, in which the illustrious Pamela's brother Joseph defends *his* virginity, by attaching itself to a higher model than Richardson; for it is written, its title page announces, "in Imitation of The Manner of Cervantes, Author of *Don Quixote.*" Like the restless champion of vanished chivalry before him Parson Abraham Adams, patriarchal innocent in a fallen world, gives no thought to so poor an impediment as reality whenever he discerns a wrong to be righted, even though mockery be his only earthly reward. Cervantes' vexed ambivalence toward his hero, however, has vanished. The ingenuous parson, unlike the lunatic knight, engages nearly unqualified sympathy from beginning to end, and even his manifest failings endear him. Our laughter springs not from the sudden glory of scoffing at our inferiors (as philosophical theorists from Aristotle to Hobbes decreed) but from humane fellow feeling for one raised above his tormentors by absence of the vanity and hypocrisy that demean them. By thus reincarnating Don Quixote in a more genial guise Fielding contributed greatly, as Stuart Tave argues in his important study of eighteenth-century wit and humor, toward creating a new comic type, the "amiable humorist," in whom the warm-hearted and good-natured could take indulgent delight in laughing at their own hyperbolic reflection.[18]

In defense of innocence Adams is no less dauntless than his chivalric prototype. "Whilst my Conscience is pure," he un-flinchingly tells Lady Booby, "I shall never fear what Man can do unto me."[19] This militancy gives his good nature a heroic edge lacking in more purely whimsical successors like Sterne's Uncle Toby. But whereas the mad Don Quixote methodically challenged the existing order of things, the benevolent pastor is a menace to none but himself. Opposition is forced upon him against his inclination, and he is far too benignant to dream of questioning the comfortable assumptions about human nature which the author familiarly shares with his like-minded read-ers. Through unwordly selflessness he elicits sympathetic response and becomes the touchstone for every reader's good-ness of heart. In commending him, imperfections and all, we thus give proof of our own benevolent instincts; he is more akin to Pickwick than Falstaff in being altogether too easy to love. This Adam who has never acknowledged the Fall is an anachronistic remnant of Eden, the idyllic Genius of a pastoral world in which the romance of childlike lovers is menaced by no more redoubtable a foe than the ludicrously concupiscent Lady Booby, and a strawberry birthmark may restore a long-lost child to his parents. Under circumstances so singularly propitious the comic hero is happily spared the unpleasant necessity of giving offense to any but the most demonstrable knaves.

The fastidious footman who spurns his mistress's lewd advances in the opening chapters of *Joseph Andrews* leaves the corruption of London quickly behind as he journeys, under the custody of Adams and the star of his winsome Fanny, back toward the redemptive simplicity of his native village. In Fielding's next major novel, *The History of Tom Jones, A Found-ling,* both myth and hero are far more complex. Tom's eventful peregrinations from Somersetshire to London following his rude expulsion from Paradise Hall are a movement away from childish innocence toward the maturity of manhood, and he himself (unlike the unswerving Joseph) by no means ignores the enticements that continually threaten to lure him astray. If the title page of the earlier novel alludes to Cervantes, the epigraph of *Tom Jones—Mores hominum multorum vidit,* "He saw the manners of many men"—refers back to the *Odyssey,* via Horace. In this, at least, Fielding's hero accords with the paradigm of Odysseus, that he zestfully embraces the most diverse and unexpected vicissitudes of human existence. Not abstinence but experience is his school, and he rashly succumbs to the succulent charms of Britannic Calypsos and Circes more tempting than Lady Booby by far. He will of course prove to be no abandoned rake in the end, no Lovelace or Lothario, but a certifiably moral hero such as his scrupulous age demanded. But because his morality springs direct from the heart it is subject, no less than Odysseus' pliable glory, to conspicuous lapses and unpredictable fits and starts. Virtue for Tom Jones is not a preordained code of conduct, as for Pamela Andrews or her equally continent brother; it is not the starting point but the goal of a tortuous exploration whose by-paths and blind alleys are seldom devoid of gratification. This tolerant morality is not prohibitive but affirmatory; it seeks not to extirpate or suppress but to train and moderate the unruly impulses of a generous temper. And because it presupposes the unregulated discord of nature as the seedground of any meaningful virtue it is a morality inherently (if only provisionally) comic.

To the solemn practitioners of more traditional virtue, a morality so indulgent was tantamount to none whatsoever; and from their number Fielding's novel evoked an outcry of nearly unanimous censure. Richardson fastidiously shrank from reading "the truly coarse-titled Tom Jones" (or so he professed in an admonition to two insufficiently loath young ladies). He nonetheless peremptorily reprehended its hero as "the Lowest of all Fellows" and its author as "too prescribing, too impetuous, too immoral, I will venture to say, to take any other Byass than that a perverse and crooked Nature has given him; or Evil Habits, at least, have confirm'd in him."[20] And Dr. Johnson, to Boswell's perturbation, was still more blunt in pronouncing Fielding "a blockhead" and "a barren rascal."[21] Johnson loftily disdained Fielding's demeaning attentiveness to what Horace Walpole called "les moeurs du vulgaire,"[22] and for Boswell's edification he heartily endorsed Richardson's sneer "that had he not known who Fielding was, he should have believed he was an ostler."

The condescension of the high-minded classicist toward the innately trivial comic writer had by no means diminished in the two millennia since Aristotle. Underlying the apparently gratuitous snobbery of these libels, however, is the fundamental stricture forthrightly voiced by Sir John Hawkins in 1787, when the danger of social unrest was becoming acute. Fielding's morality, he sternly warns, "in respect that it resolves virtue into good affections, in contradiction to moral obligation and a sense of duty, is that of Lord Shaftesbury vulgarised, and is a system of excellent use in palliating the vices most injurious to society."[23] Even in his most moral guise the comic hero thus reaffirms his seditious vocation, and by his very goodness of heart — "the virtue," Hawkins sniffs, "of a horse or a dog" — imperils the stability of a social order founded on the systematic suppression of nature.

Fielding wryly anticipates the remonstrances of the virtuous when he confesses himself obliged, in his novel, "to bring our Hero on the Stage in a much more disadvantageous Manner than we could wish; and to declare honestly, even at his first Appearance, that it was the universal Opinion of all Mr. *All-*

worthy's Family, that he was certainly born to be hanged"
(III.2). From the day of his birth the foundling is under a dark
moral cloud which time does little to disperse. "Faugh, how it
stinks! It doth not smell like a Christian" (I.3) is the scandalized
housekeeper Mrs. Wilkins' outspoken verdict, and in the judgment of more erudite censors Tom's behavior, as he progresses
toward manhood, no more corresponds to a Christian's than his
infantile odor. Such heinous delinquencies as the theft of a duck
betray his ingrained depravity at an early age, and his vices
"were, moreover, heightened," the author declares with chagrin, "by the disadvantageous Light in which they appeared,
when opposed to the Virtues of Master *Blifil,* his Companion"
(III.2). Revealed Religion and natural Virtue, as embodied
respectively in the reverend Thwackum and the philosopher
Square, achieve rare unanimity in decrying the scapegrace
bastard's deplorable absence of morals, and despite an occasional murmur in the boy's favor his adoptive father, the irre-
proachable Allworthy, reluctantly accedes to society's harsh
estimate and banishes the miscreant from Paradise Hall.

The reprobation of Square and Thwackum is not altogether
disinterested. Their favored pupil, the politic Blifil, "had
Address enough at sixteen to recommend himself at one and
the same Time to both these Opposites" (III.5), we are told, by
being all Religion with one and all Virtue with the other, and
both are not only cajoled by his unction but prudently mindful
of his prerogatives as heir to Allworthy's estate. But the common antipathy of philosopher and divine to Jones's impulsiveness transcends duplicity; in this sentiment the most inveterate
hypocrite can be sincere. The deep-seated prejudice of the
well-established against the unruly upstart who might challenge their elevated status if not confined to his proper place is
reinforced by their reflexive hostility to any irruption of candor
potentially subversive of the artifice on which so beneficial a social order reposes. Even if Blifil were not an apparent heir his
"sober and prudent Reserve" would be incomparably better
adapted, whatever his other deficiencies, to any stable society
than Jones's "naturally violent animal Spirits" (V.9). It is therefore no accident that the contrary systems of Square and

Thwackum coincide in excluding "all natural Goodness of Heart" (III.4) from their purview. There could be no greater danger, either to rational or dogmatic morality, than to regard the undisciplined impulses which these diligent tutors have castigated in their wayward alumnus not as consummate vices but incipient virtues.

It is by the exuberance of his animal spirits that Tom most obviously aligns himself with the robust comic heroes of old, much to the dismay of polite society in his own and throughout the Victorian age. In his unabashed compliance with the ancient demands of Belly and Body he is the successor not to Abraham Adams or Don Quixote but to Falstaff and Odysseus. Even the most exalted heroes, Fielding affirms, "are liable to the worst Infirmities, and subject to the vilest Offices of human Nature," and it is therefore "no Disparagement to our Heroe to mention the immoderate Ardour" of an appetite unsurpassed even by the voracious Ulysses "in that eating Poem of the Odyssey" (IX.5). Jones's ardor is equally unrestrained in his impulsive amours, for "what can be more innocent," he exultantly asks on discovering Square ignominiously asquat in Molly Seagrim's makeshift boudoir, "than the Indulgence of a natural Appetite? or what more laudable than the Propagation of our Species?" (V.5). With this sentiment not only Square, who is momentarily at a disadvantage, but the impartial author concur: "The wise Man gratifies every Appetite and every Passion, while the Fool sacrifices all the rest to pall and satiate one" (VI.3). Far from being depraved by original sin, as traditional Christianity held, man's biological instincts are good by virtue of nature. Fielding held no brief for unbridled license, and against the scurrilous Aristophanes and Rabelais he sternly objected that "their Design appears to me very plainly to have been to ridicule all Sobriety, Modesty, Decency, Virtue and Religion, out of the World."[24] Such a purpose was far indeed from his own. On the contrary, his fallible hero very soon discovers that indiscriminate gratification of even the most natural appetite may incur afflictions at least proportionate to the pleasures it brings. "Prudence and Circumspection," as the author admonishes (and commentators have never tired of repeating), "are necessary even to the best of Men" (III.7), and Tom must sooner or later acquire a modicum of discretion to supply the imperfections of natural goodness.

Until it manifests virtue, however, prudence can only mask vice, and its temporary abeyance is all to young Jones's moral advantage. His sexual appetites are remarkable not for promiscuity or insistence—his conquests are few and obliging—but for heedless impetuosity. Such cravings arise from nature, and no man is without them. The respectable Square, it transpires, shares not only Jones's lust but its object, and even Blifil, for all his sober reserve, "was far from being destitute of that Appetite which is said to be the common Property of all Animals" and which makes him regard Sophia "with the same Desires which an Ortolan inspires into the Soul of an Epicure" (VII.6). But Square and Blifil, like Bridget Allworthy and many another, are continually mindful that activities "tolerated in some Christian Countries, connived at in others, and practiced in all, are however, as expressly forbidden as Murder, or any other horrid Vice, by that Religion which is universally believed in those Countries" (IX.3), and they conceal their desires and derelictions accordingly. Tom, on the contrary, zestfully indulges his appetites with little or no regard for "outward Ornaments of Decency and Decorum" (III.7). It is this incorrigible openness, rather than any erotic excess, that convicts him of imprudent conduct in the eyes of a social order devoted to subterfuge in deeds no less intently than to virtue in words. As a result of Allworthy's regretful anathema and Sophia's impassioned disdain Jones learns the unhappy consequences of giving way to precipitate impulse, yet the very indiscretions for which he must pay with lavish remorse are indispensable to his final redemption. Only the heartfelt chagrin that his rashness inevitably occasions can teach him to regulate his incontinence by hearkening to the painful admonishments of experience. In such a manner, by however erratic a route, the imprudent at last encompass a virtue which the calculating and circumspect, who venture nothing, can only dissemble.

In responsiveness to the diversity of life, as in vigor of appetite, Tom Jones is a comic hero cast in the antique mold. "A true Knowledge of the World is gained only by Conversation," Fielding observes, "and the Manners of every Rank must be seen in order to be known" (XIV.1); from Somersetshire and Molly to London and Lady Bellaston Tom mingles with the most diverse representatives of his kind and learns from every encounter. The learning process entails conflict, as it did for Odysseus, but the battleground has shifted. Not guile but the ineradicable candor of "one who utterly detested every Species of Falshood or Dishonesty" (XV.9) pits Jones against a society predicated on their unchallenged supremacy. The antagonism between spontaneity and constraint is compounded by being internalized. In opposition to Jones's irrepressible biological drives stands the equally innate *moral* principle that distinguishes the good man as one swayed, in Shaftesbury's words, "by the natural temper or bent of his affections . . . primarily and immediately, and not secondarily and accidentally, to good and against ill."[25] The appetites are not irreconcilable with the moral principle, since true prudence can accommodate their demands, but their thoughtless indulgence gives rise to a conflict that Jones, who "was very strongly under the Guidance of this Principle," cannot evade or deny: "For though he did not always act rightly, yet he never did otherwise without feeling and suffering for it" (IV.6). Even desire for so forward an object as Molly meets with genuine if ineffective resistance in Tom, "For tho' his Constitution urged him greatly" to possess her person, the author informs us, ". . . his Principles no less forcibly restrained him" (IV.6).

If Tom's scruples concerning Molly are soon allayed by her ill-concealed prodigality in granting her favors, the potential antagonism between Constitution and Principles nonetheless remains unresolved. And when the impecunious foundling is suddenly smitten with love for Squire Western's eligible daughter the sporadic clash of contrary impulses bursts forth as "a constant Struggle between Honour and Inclination, which alternately triumphed over each other in his Mind" (V.6). Neither Odysseus nor Peisthetaerus, Reynard nor Falstaff, would have permitted honor (as defined by others) to oppose their imperious inclinations; but in his reverence for the ideals of a social order whose practices his impetuous example impugns, Tom Jones is the spiritual heir of Don Quixote.

As a *comic* hero he exposes and undermines sham affectations of virtue and honor while at the same time, as a *moral* hero, affirming and finally incorporating their substance. His task is to reconcile an Odyssean constitution with a Quixotic adherence to principle. But first he must fully experience and consciously grasp the contradiction between them. The conflict finally comes to a head in Tom's severely compromising liaison with Lady Bellaston, for here the spontaneous gusto that partly redeemed his more casual affairs with Molly and Mrs. Waters dwindles to mechanical intrigue. Only now, when the satisfaction of natural appetite requires systematic deception, does it clearly become an intolerable vice, and prudence an imperative virtue: this wholesome lesson Tom's joyless entanglement belatedly teaches. In the happy if seemingly impossible prospect of marriage with Sophia, by contrast, inclination and honor for the first time coincide, because Tom at last ascertains that "the very best and truest Honour," as he tells the wavering Nightingale (XIV.7), is identical with Goodness, and thus with the deepest and most abiding inclination of his own nature.

With others in the novel, aside from Sophia, Tom's affinities, though significant, are superficial and soon exhausted. In goodness of heart Allworthy resembles his unruly ward, but this sententious gentleman farmer, who has never owned to a single imprudence, altogether lacks the capacity acquired by Tom through painful indiscretions and barely averted calamities to discriminate between goodness and its simulation. Without experience of the manners of men true benignity proves a sitting duck for pretended virtue. The jovial Squire Western, on the other hand, loudly applauds the generous instincts and lusty appetites that scandalize Tom's restrained elders, but his approbation abruptly stops when he finds that the "liquorish Dog" (V.12) has trespassed on his private preserve by falling in love with his daughter. No sympathy with the unfortunate, such as Jones exhibits in his concern for the families of Black George and the highwayman Anderson, or for the wronged Nancy Miller, ever breaches the impenetrable class prejudice of

Squire Western, who "did indeed consider a Parity of Fortune and Circumstances, to be physically as necessary an Ingredient in Marriage, as Difference of Sexes, or any other Essential; and had no more Apprehension of his Daughter's falling in Love with a poor Man, than with any Animal of a different Species" (VI.9). In contrast to these well-to-do gentry Tom's servant and sidekick Partridge sometimes echoes the impertinences of comic heroes of old. "What matters the Cause to me, or who gets the Victory," he asks in Falstaffian vein, "if I am killed?" (XII.3). But the cringing barber is in fact the buffoon that Falstaff artfully played, and to a young master quixotically avid for glory he gladly relinquishes all heroism, comic or other.

Only Sophia can respond to Jones's ardent nature in kind and comprehend the qualities that make her hapless lover somehow heroic. She is to Tom as Penelope was to Odysseus, both counterpart and consummation. Her appetites are more tempered than his, as befits her sex and station, but in contrast to Richardson's provident Pamela she acts, no less than Tom, on pure impulse. Instinct leads her, against the nearly unanimous verdict of society, to honor Tom and scorn Master Blifil "almost as soon as she knew the Meaning of those two Words" (IV.5), and not even her undisciplined suitor's flagrant infidelities can destroy her faith that "he is all heroic Virtue, and angelic Goodness" (VI.13). She vehemently spurns her worldly aunt's conception of marriage as "a Fund in which prudent Women deposite their Fortunes to the best Advantage, in order to receive a larger Interest for them than they could have elsewhere" (VII.3), and in her peremptory but sufficient objection to Blifil she reveals the heroic intransigence of her temper: "I hate him." Her headstrong defiance of her family's wishes and her rash flight to London are acts of monumental imprudence for a well-bred young lady of her century; but in pointed contrast to the funereal consequences of Clarissa's tragic disobedience in Richardson's recently published novel Sophia's impetuous decision is validated by the event. "Simplicity, when set on its Guard," the author comments, "is often a Match for Cunning" (VII.6), and his heroine is living proof of the maxim.

Against her determined innocence (and providential good fortune) the insidious wiles and treacherous snares of Lady Bellaston and Lord Fellamar can do nothing. No less than her rehabilitated lover Sophia is finally seen to embody the very virtues whose counterfeits she had scorned. At the climax of the novel she even reveals herself — on her own terms, to be sure — as the paragon of a dutiful daughter. "All the Spirit of contrary, that's all" (XVIII.12), Squire Western fumes when his fractious offspring disdains the repentant libertine who has suddenly redeemed all his faults by becoming Squire Allworthy's heir: but Sophia adroitly turns aside wrath by a meek (if not wholly artless) reversal. " 'Well, and will you consent to ha un to-morrow Morning?' says *Western*. — 'I will be obedient to you, Sir,' cries she."

Virtue, then, is rewarded in *Tom Jones* no less unstintingly than in *Pamela,* as both Tom and Sophia are welcomed back to a fold that has purged itself of pretenders and learned from its prodigal children the meaning of goodness. Nothing impedes reconciliation because the comic hero of so moral an age has never repudiated society's cherished values but only their counterfeits; when the masks are torn off the improvident rake is revealed to be virtuous and even, miraculously, prudent. He does not, like Odysseus or Don Quixote, his antithetical prototypes, push dissent to its truly heroic conclusion in victory or defeat, but achieves a reasonable compromise between impulsiveness and restraint through his chastening love for Sophia. *Tom Jones* is a comic fable not without a serious moral, and union with the fair damsel whose name signifies Wisdom is a fitting prerequisite to the hero's restoration to Paradise Hall. The happy discovery that Jones is in fact Squire Allworthy's nephew aptly betokens the outcast's reclamation, and to demur at so satisfying an ending on the grounds of improbability would be to emulate the acumen of Partridge as critic of *Hamlet.* The author has not been bashful in manifesting his dexterous presence, and we may take delight in his skillful contrivance no less than in Tom's good fortune.

Yet the patent artifice of the ending does raise a legitimate question concerning the meager role of this comic hero in an outcome that he himself (more like Menander's lovers than Richardson's) does little or nothing to effect. The confrontation of values in *Tom Jones* is a real one, as the outraged revulsion of readers like Richardson and Johnson attests; for even a comic hero as moral as Tom strews his primrose path to acceptability with broken taboos and neglected commandments. The dénouement, on the other hand, in which the foundling is discovered to be his rich benefactor's relation and enabled to wed his equally rich neighbor's beautiful daughter, provides a transparently fictional resolution to a conflict stubbornly actual. The hero's triumph, unlike his troubles, is sheer romance. The kindhearted reader will surely begrudge Tom neither his victory nor the rewards that lavishly crown it, but these are bestowed upon him, as on Cinderella, or Job, by an agency above and beyond him. In the last analysis it is only the benevolent author's vaunted capacity to manipulate events within the province where he exerts sovereign power "to make what Laws I please" (II.1) that preserves his favorite from the pitfalls that surround and very nearly undo him. Without such deft intervention *ab extra* Tom Jones would be at least as defenseless against the superior wiles of a hostile world as Falstaff or Don Quixote before him.

Jones is a hero not of the head but the heart, and this cogitative deficiency greatly redounds to his final advantage. Because he feels no need to define or articulate his instinctive antipathy to a social order conducive to Blifils, or to question its ideological underpinnings like Falstaff at Shrewsbury, he easily complies with its expectations as soon as he finds himself restored to its graces. His triumph is a compromise in the British tradition of benignly obscuring the issue. In contemporary France, where intellectual dispute tended toward acerbic polarity, the lines were more sharply drawn, and against existing society a determined militia of dissenters pledged a war of rhetoric to the bitter end. Yet amongst these thoroughly social individualists of the French Enlightenment ironical acceptance continually vies with polemical resistance. Society is irreparably flawed, but the critical philosopher possesses nothing actual to put in its place and must therefore content himself with the usages of this world while impatiently plotting its demolition. Voltaire alternates between righteous outrage and amused detachment as he contemplates Calas or Candide; despite his own withering denunciations of persecution and infamy the much-bandied protagonists of his satirical fictions typically resign themselves, like Babouc in "The World As It Is," to the knowledge that "if all is not well, all is passable,"[26] and provide for impending deluge by cultivating their gardens.

Between these poles of repudiation and compliance oscillates, with baffling disregard for consistency, the most elusive of French *philosophes,* Denis Diderot. The penchant, nay genius, of this celebrated Encyclopedist and beacon of the Enlightenment is not for clarity and logic but for paradox and self-contradiction—hence not for irony alone, in the style of Voltaire and his fractious philosophical brethren, but (almost uniquely among them) for comedy as well. Along with his comrades-in-arms against a senescent regime Diderot more or less obliquely deplored the intolerable discrepancy between the ramshackle society of his time and the laws of reason or nature, but he was far more tentative and ambiguous than most about the dilemma of living as a resident alien in an imperfect world. The chimera of ultimate progress offered no hope whatsoever—"Even though the world is getting older, it is not changing," he wrote in the midst of his long struggle to publish the seditious *Encyclopedia;* "individual man may be improving, but the mass of mankind is getting neither better nor worse"[27] —and for the present he could neither till his plot with the equanimity of Voltaire nor seek refuge in pathless wilds with the temerity of Rousseau. His "Conversation of a Father with His Children," although subtitled "The Danger of Placing Oneself above the Law," gives at least equal prominence to the opposite danger of submitting to laws that bear no relation to any discernible human justice. "Isn't man anterior to legal man?" Diderot here demands of his father, whose disclosure of a discarded will known only to himself had once resulted in the disinheritance of an old priest's impoverished relations. "Isn't the reason of the human species altogether more sacred than some legislator's reason? We call ourselves civilized, and we are worse than savages"[28] — and never more savage than when strictly adhering to law.

This paradox of savagery in civilization Diderot provocatively elaborates in his "Supplement to Bougainville's Voyage," in which the frank speech and plain dealing of Tahitian natives lay bare the moral hypocrisy of their uninvited European guests. "So what shall we do," one interlocutor inquires at the end of the dialogue, "go back to nature or submit to the laws?" To which the second rejoins: "We shall speak out against senseless laws until they are reformed, and in the interim submit to them . . . There is less disadvantage in being mad among madmen than in being wise all alone."[29] By this enigmatic counsel Diderot refutes his own disturbing contention, in the "Conversation" with his father, that "there are no laws for a wise man."[30] In the world as it is persistence in solitary wisdom would be proof of singular folly. What sets the sage apart is not immunity from laws patently absurd but conscious participation in the general madness that they codify. The situation is fairly fraught with comic potential.

The paradox of rebellious conformity is the subject of *Rameau's Nephew,* in which Diderot portrays his unsettling encounter with an articulate ne'er-do-well who cheekily sets his most inviolate values at naught. The eminent philosopher is openly intrigued by Rameau's self-contradictory compounding "of haughtiness and baseness, of good sense and folly," and he confesses an irresistible attraction — moral principles notwithstanding — to nonconformists whose "character stands out from that of others and breaks that dull uniformity which our education, our social conventions, and our accustomed proprieties have introduced."[31] Such an eccentric acts as a grain of yeast in whatever circle he appears, and brings out the truth of those whom his incongruous presence disturbs. Rameau is far more than a catalyst or touchstone for others, however, for his outspoken effrontery deliberately menaces the fragile conventions and polite evasions that buttress the social order. What he confutes above all, by rudely reminding his civilized interlocutor of their shared animality, is the untenable pretext of essential distinctions between man and man. "The important point," he rapturously exclaims, "is to go to the toilet easily, freely, agreeably, copiously, every evening, *O stercus pretiosum!* There you have the great result of life in every condition. At the last moment all are equally rich: Samuel Bernard, who by dint of theft, pillage, and bankruptcy leaves twenty-seven millions in gold, and Rameau, who will leave nothing . . . "[32] Compared to the urgent demands of ingestion and defecation the values extolled by moralists and divines pale into insignificance, for "the voice of conscience and honor," Rameau informs the encyclopedist whose hungry youth was now long behind him, "is very feeble when the guts cry out."[33]

Like Falstaff before him Rameau is conscious both of the role he is playing and of the challenge he poses; his sedition is open-eyed and unblinking. "There is no better role among the great than that of fool," he declares with keen appreciation of his own worth. ". . . A wise man would not need a fool; so he who has a fool is no wise man; if he's not a wise man, he's a fool."[34] A conscious fool in a world of fools (or madman in a world of madmen; the French *fou* has both meanings) is perhaps the true sage, since only he who knows his own ignorance can be declared wise: Rameau, in any event, will always have the last laugh on those who are foolish enough to deride him. Unlike the contented proponents of virtue and order he knows that nothing (unless self-interest) "is absolutely, essentially, without exception true or false," and draws the disturbing conclusion that "if we really explained ourselves we might find that you would call vice what I call virtue, and virtue what I call vice."[35] Rameau prides himself not without reason as an indispensable man, for without this brash parasite to undermine the semantic bedrock of its cherished morality society could never become aware how tenuous are the values it holds immutably sacred.

Yet despite his articulate irreverence and Falstaffian virtuosity Rameau is more cynical than comic and less heroic than servile; he neither envisages nor aspires to invent an alternative to the values he deftly subverts. "Here, in truth, was the most remarkable difference between my man and most of our acquaintances," Diderot reflects. "He confessed the vices that he had, and that others have; but he was not a hypocrite."[36] In every other respect there is indeed small distinction between Rameau and his putative betters. He is an outsider who only wants in, and would gladly act like the others if given the chance. To swindle employers fat with ill-gotten gains gives him no qualms, Rameau nonchalantly explains, since "In nature all species devour one another; all classes devour one another in society. We settle with one another without letting the law interfere."[37] He perceives the process with relentless clarity but never disputes it; like the sadly degenerate Falstaff he finds no reason in nature why the old pike should not snap up the young dace. Those on top of the heap he regards with resentful envy, and secretly mocks them while openly coveting their good fortune. His desires are limited, like the Plautine slave's, to his masters' possessions: "a good bed, a good table, a warm garment in winter, a cool one in summer, some rest, some money, and many other things that I would rather owe to benevolence than acquire by work."[38] And in the true picaresque tradition he never contemplates doing otherwise than the others. For all his sardonic commentary Rameau dissents from the practices of his world far less radically than the good-natured, if not particularly quick-witted, Tom Jones. For his keen intelligence, like every true parasite's, remains without consequence for his actions. The disgruntled bohemian turns out, in the end, to be the conformist of Diderot's dialogue, since unlike the philosopher who responds to his ferment Rameau questions everything but himself.

Very few among Diderot's small manuscript audience would have been sufficiently self-critical to discern anything of themselves in Rameau's unflattering mirror. To most educated readers in this comfortable age his idle freaks and diverting gibes could have threatened their peace of mind no more than their beds or other belongings. With none of the comic hero's determined purpose to guide him, Rameau, for all his multifarious talents, remains a drifter and hanger-on. He ekes out a marginal livelihood by the indulgence of a society that no longer banishes its dissidents to the Fleet or carts them home in a cage, but entertains itself with their antics. Their fool may mimic their folly on condition that he continue to serve them; for if they are such fools, more fool he.

The stolidly submissive protagonist of *Jacques the Fatalist and His Master* would appear, at first sight, to be made of even less heroical stuff. Jacques' determined resignation, however, paradoxically proves itself a potent arm of sedition. Diderot's unconventional novel owes both its digressive form and several passages of pirated copy to Laurence Sterne's *Tristram Shandy*, of which it has sometimes been dismissed as an inferior imitation. But its most fundamental affinity—by contrast as much as resemblance—is with *Don Quixote*. A master and servant again encounter comic adventures as they amble across the countryside of their native land, but now no impelling mission endows their haphazard wanderings and intermittent discourses with perceptible purpose. "How had they met? By chance, like everyone else. What were their names? What does it matter to you? Whence had they come? From the nearest possible spot. Where were they going? Do we ever know where we're going?" (3). A book so relentlessly systematic, from its opening words, in the demolition of every possible certainty precludes even the desperate confidence of heroical madness.

Throughout his baffling novel the author obtrusively intervenes to anticipate or frustrate his readers' conventional expectations and cast them adrift by professions of ignorance or indifference concerning his story. Goethe, one of Diderot's earliest translators and most avid admirers, delighted in "following the intentions of this artificial cook and table-setter,"[39] but less tolerant (or intelligent) readers have found the author's encroachments offensively flippant. Diderot's insistent travesties of fictional convention are not, however, mere annoyances or titillations. "He who takes what I'm writing for the truth," he remarks, "will be, perhaps, less in error than he who takes it for a fable" (13). In a problematic world where nothing is absolute the apprehension of truth demands not the passive surrender but the energetic participation of the questioning intellect, and to this end Diderot's unpredictable provocations contribute by keeping the mind continually on the alert. He manipulates his

frustrated readers' responses no less cavalierly than those of his
fictional creatures, but his purpose is not gratuitous insult, as it
sometimes seems, it is rather—as he wrote about the *Encyclopedia* that engrossed so much of his lifetime—"to change men's
common way of thinking." "It is only the presence of men that
makes the existence of other beings significant," Diderot reflects in this article, since "... if one banishes from the face of
the earth the thinking and contemplating entity, man, then the
sublime and moving spectacle of nature will be but a sad and
silent scene; the universe will be hushed; darkness and silence
will regain their sway."[40] Truth is not a datum but the product
of strenuous thought, and the impertinent vagaries of *Jacques
the Fatalist* have as their real object to unsettle the reader's lax
presuppositions about his world and thereby stimulate the
activity of contemplation that bestows significance on existence.

As persistently as the author disorients his reader Jacques
thwarts his doctrinaire master's craving for certitude and finality. "Come now, Jacques, you're out of your mind," the
master hotly protests; "aren't you sure of yourself?" "No, sir, I
am not," Jacques placidly replies, "And who *is* sure of himself?"
(42). (The pompous rejoinder, "Every virtuous man," gives an
accurate measure of the master's concept of virtue, and is not
dignified by an answer.) Jacques is unperturbed by man's ignorance of what heaven intends, nor does he blanch at the far
more chaotic suggestion that "perhaps heaven itself knows
nothing about it" (89). This self-professed fatalist demonstrates
his autonomy by affirming a meaningless world with nonchalant disregard for society's fiercely defended dogmas concerning its meaning. And since his postulation of universal
incertitude inevitably challenges all those, like his master, who
must be certain, the argumentative lackey steps forth as a new
breed of comic hero. "There is very probably no one head
under heaven," Jacques' master not unjustly laments, "which
contains as many paradoxes as yours" (51). In contrast to his
rationalizing master Jacques understands that "each of us
judges of good and evil in his own manner; and perhaps not
two seconds in our whole life do we have the same judgment"
(53). The truth he advocates is by nature contingent, and para-

dox is its one apt expression. Finality does not pertain to human existence, and Jacques dismisses it without a regret. In the life to come, he declares, "I neither believe nor disbelieve. I don't think about it. I am enjoying as best I can the life that has been granted me in advance inheritance" (182). By his steadfast determination "to be just what I am" (77) irrespective of rational and religious coercions, he thus, like the comic heroes of every age, makes a conscious choice of life in its manifold and inexhaustible imperfection.

It is the central paradox of the novel that Jacques' "fatalism" —his reiterated insistence, on his former captain's authority, "that everything that happens to us down here, good or bad, was written up yonder" (3)—is in fact a doctrine of liberation. For the "fate" that he zealously avouches cannot be predestination, if heaven itself knows nothing about it, but can only be chance.[41] Of what is written up yonder *we* know only that it can never be known, and this certainty of our ignorance—the one true certainty accorded mankind—is the charter of manumission that restores our effective freedom of will. The master's rigidly conventional outlook unconsciously conditions his clock-like responses, despite all his protestations of freedom, but Jacques' determinism, by leaving causation to the inscrutable heavens, gives free rein to the most capricious behavior. "I am inconsistent and violent," he confesses, "and I forget my principles and my captain's lessons, and I laugh and I cry like a fool" (155).

It is Jacques the fatalist, not his libertarian master, who resolutely puts the brigands to flight in the early pages of the book. "Not knowing what is written up yonder," he explains with a fine discrimination of his pliable doctrine's loopholes and nuances, "we know neither what we want nor what we do; so we follow our fancy which we call reason, or our reason, which is very often but a dangerous fancy and which turns out sometimes well, sometimes badly" (11). Such a profession of fatalism amounts, in practice, to an emphatic vindication of impulse. The true nature of the fate to which Jacques does obeisance is eloquently suggested by the oracle whose authority he consults. "When destiny became mute in his head," we are told, "he took counsel by the gourd; it was a sort of portable Pythia, which was silenced the instant it was empty. At Delphi, the Pythia, with skirts pulled up, and seated barebottomed on her tripod, received her inspiration from the bottom up; Jacques, on his horse, his head turned up toward heaven, his gourd uncorked and the mouth of the vessel near his own, received his inspiration from the top down" (207). So rhapsodic a form of divination is hard to distinguish from the promptings of his own uninhibited nature.

As both his devotion to the oracular bottle and the bawdy story of his loves confirm, Jacques is not a comic hero of the intellect only, but partakes of the appetites and stratagems indigenous to the species. His seduction of neighboring wives by dissimulation of sexual innocence is no more than a variation on the time-honored motifs of fabliau already exploited in Diderot's scatological romance *The Indiscreet Jewels*.[42] But through gleeful mockery of the vicar who irately anathematizes his flagrant delights from the involuntary perch of a hayloft Jacques elevates instinctive concupiscence to a defiant celebration of animal freedom that occasions the author's most scathing indictment of his pharisaical readers. "Nasty hypocrites, leave me in peace," Diderot abjures, enlarging on a text from Montaigne:[43] "Go and f—— like mad donkeys, but at least permit me to say f——; I offer you the action, grant me the word. You pronounce quite brazenly: kill, steal, and betray, and yet the other, you only dare mutter between your teeth. Is it because the less you exhale these so-called impurities in words, the more there remains of them in your mind?" (206).[44] Here the lackey's reckless irreverence and the author's calculated abuse converge in a forthright challenge to the fallacious morality of a social order that persists in imposing immutable prohibitions on a world of intrinsic uncertainty and perpetual change.

Thus despite his apparently phlegmatic assent to whatever is written "up yonder" Jacques thoroughly confounds the ramshackle assurances personified in his hidebound master and effortlessly bests him in every encounter. His ostensible passivity is in fact the key to his triumph. By relinquishing the grandiose aspirations of Falstaff or Don Quixote and adopting the external demeanor of Sancho Panza he turns the inherited order of things on its head while leaving it, to all outward appearance, unchanged. His substantive if unheralded victory consists not in accommodating his values to a cleansed society's, as Tom Jones finally does, but in maintaining a precarious modus vivendi that permits him to exercise in fact the mastery that he gladly surrenders in name.

His master is a mere automaton utterly at a loss "without his watch, his snuffbox, and Jacques" (24). Unlike Rameau's envious nephew, however, Jacques is content to remain in his menial station and to leave this superfluous being in undisturbed possession of his empty perquisites so long as he himself can enjoy the freedom to be what he is: "a man like any other," as he proudly affirms, and "sometimes better" (157). Despite the chaotic flux of everything else in his world no comic hero ever laid more confident claim to absolute sovereignty than this lackey does in dictating the compact by which his relationship to his titular master is defined. "Let us stipulate, then," he brazenly begins, "that first, since it is written up yonder that I'm essential to you, and since I feel and know that you cannot get along without me, therefore I shall abuse these advantages at any and all times that the occasion permits" (161). His master must "submit to the law of necessity, from which it is not in your power to free yourself"; for in the very nature of things, Jacques coolly informs him, "It was decreed that you would have the title and I should have the stuff . . . All our quarrels up to now have come only from the fact that we had not yet clearly said to ourselves that you would be called my master and that it is I who would be yours" (161-62). From his superior understanding of the multiple contingencies of human life illegibly written in the Great Book up yonder Jacques has gained this one incontrovertible certitude; and although his master may balk at the hard conditions he has no alternative but to accede, and thereby to ratify Jacques' saturnalian dispensation as a permanent fait accompli. If the comic hero no longer boldly aspires to remake the world in his image he will at least deign to accept it on no other terms than his own.

VIII

Insouciant Lover and Insatiable Stumblebums

— ❧ —

A LAX AND tolerant age could lightly indulge or loftily dismiss the marginal triumphs of Fielding's seductive foundling and Diderot's paradoxical lackey, neither of whom discerns any need to alter the world as he knows it. Only on the threshold of revolution did a more intransigent comic spirit give clear notice of the cataclysm at hand. "What have you done to earn so many advantages?" Figaro demands of his absent master, and scornfully answers: "You took the trouble to be born, nothing more. Apart from that, you're a rather common type. Whereas I — by God! — lost in the nameless crowd, I had to exert more strategy and skill merely to survive than has been spent for a hundred years in governing the Spanish Empire . . . And you want to tangle with me!"[1] The rebellious overtones of Beaumarchais' comedy were lost neither on the king who vainly strove to prevent nor on the crowd that tumultuously hailed its premiere: "Why, if this play were performed," Louis XVI is supposed to have said, "the Bastille would have to be pulled down! This man mocks at everything that should be respected in government!"[2] Yet the spirited valet's pretensions extend no farther than to keep what is rightfully his, and the play's implausible vaudeville finale accommodates itself without strain to the sprightly airs of Mozart's *opera buffa*.

With the momentous upheavals that fulfilled the king's prophecy and hastened the century of light toward fiery extinction a few years later, however, the cordial entente between an indulgent social order and its good-humored dissidents was abruptly rescinded: the diverting Rameau had donned a red bonnet and the amicable spat between Jacques and his master had turned into a lethal jacquerie. A chastened society might succeed, after a quarter-century of throes and exertions, in re-establishing and extending its shaken supremacy. But in the era of militant respectability that patterned itself on Victoria, neither a sovereign nor her subjects would be amused, as Good Queen Bess and the groundlings of a merrier England had been, by the seditious impudence of upstarts like Falstaff. Laughter, like charity, would be frugally disbursed to those who proved themselves morally worthy and who limited their aberrations to acts of innocuous whimsy. Under such adverse conditions the bare survival of the comic hero's unconformable humanity will be his most remarkable, if not his only, approximation to triumph.

"Unheroic as bourgeois society is," Karl Marx acutely observed in looking back from the Third Napoleon to the First, "it nevertheless took heroism, sacrifice, terror, civil war and battles of peoples to bring it into being. And in the classically austere traditions of the Roman republic its gladiators found the ideals and the art forms, the self-deceptions that they needed in order to conceal from themselves the bourgeois limitations of the content of their struggles and to keep their enthusiasm on the high plane of the great historical tragedy."[3] Once the Corsican emperor's clothes had been finally stripped away, however, the void that remained where so many grand illusions had been was all the more oppressively empty by contrast. The self-consciously unheroic nineteenth century was equally—as Carlyle's fervid exhortations, Hugo's pompous odes, and Tennyson's stirring dirges attest—an age that keenly felt its absence of heroes. High over the capitals of Great Britain and France the towering figures of Nelson and Bonaparte looked down on the workaday shops and counting houses that lay in their shadow and sternly rebuked the pedestrian normalcy of the reactionary new era. And in the grey aftermath of Waterloo and Vienna the stormy romantic outcast of the waning eighteenth century achieved his extreme formulation and popular apotheosis as the Byronic hero.[4]

"I mark this day!" Byron wrote in his journal of April 9, 1814, at the age of twenty-six: "Napoleon Buonaparte has abdicated the throne of the world."[5] The heroic lay was now suddenly tuneless, and a sense of diminished magnitude and irretrievable loss would henceforth envelop his most swashbuckling rebels in gloom. Deprived of external dominions commensurate with his boundless spirit the post-Napoleonic hero could only be a creature of daydream striving inwardly to attain the fulfillment denied him by a philistine world. In Childe Harold and in Childe Harold's poetical children Byron supplied the type for a generation of readers eager to picture themselves, before humdrum duties reclaimed them, as spiritual rebels against the shrunken reality to which they had fallen heir. Withdrawn from a world incapable of comprehending his anguish, passionate yet disillusioned, gnawed by secret guilt yet pure and even childlike of heart, and driven by tempestuous yearnings which only uninhabited nature could soothe, the Byronic hero gave flamboyant embodiment to desires that could find no adequate object in an ignominiously commercial society. Not what he does (which is next to nothing) but what he feels (which is vast beyond words) made Childe Harold the prodigy of an age that methodically dissociated its dreams from its deeds. Because he invited his readers to thrill at his greatness of soul and identify with his inexpressible torments while not molesting the daily course of their lives he indulged their innermost fantasies with minimal effect on their outward behavior. The repudiation of everything in general affronted no one in particular, and Harold's piquantly scandalous creator found himself suddenly catapulted to European renown.

Having achieved precocious celebrity with *Childe Harold's Pilgrimage* and consolidated his youthful fame with successive sagas of pashas and pirates Byron awoke not many years later, however, to find himself infamous. *Don Juan,* whose opening cantos he issued over his publisher's strenuous protests, was "a

Work so atrocious," one reviewer inveighed, that it "must not be suffered to pass into oblivion without the infliction of that punishment on its guilty author due to such a wanton outrage on all most dear to human nature."[6] By its saucy refusal to treat its subject—the Byronic hero himself—with a veneration appropriate to his exalted pretensions Byron's distressing new poem offended precisely those who had been his most fervent adorers, and they viewed it as an act of betrayal. "*This* is the charge which we bring against Lord Byron," Francis Jeffrey wrote in the influential *Edinburgh Review*. "We say that, under some strange misapprehension as to the truth, and the duty of proclaiming it, he has exerted all the powers of his powerful mind to convince his readers, both directly and indirectly, that all ennobling pursuits, and disinterested virtues, are mere deceits or illusions."[7] Such a charge could not have been leveled at Don Juan's somber forerunners, who secretly personified the noble qualities crassly spurned by the world that wronged and traduced them. In "The Corsair" one virtue of the chivalrous Conrad—whose "heart was form'd for softness, warp'd to wrong"[8]—is sufficient to balance a thousand crimes, and Childe Harold magnanimously trusts that his martyred spirit will move "In hearts all rocky now the late remorse of love."[9] Sentiments so impeccable licensed the most moral reader to participate with voluptuous impunity in the cult of the dark outsider whom admirers and detractors alike persistently identified, in defiance of coy disclaimers, with Byron—until Byron, to everybody's dismay, turned out to have been someone else.

In fact this aristocratic adventurer, with his appetite for physical pleasure and his capacity to laugh at his own affectations, was from the beginning far more multiple and complex than his own theatrical self-projections gave cause to believe. Having tailored a legend from part of himself Byron disconcerted those who discovered how ill it fit him. "The impression of the first few minutes disappointed me," Lady Blessington candidly wrote of her meeting with Byron in Italy; ". . . I looked in vain for the hero-looking sort of person with whom I had so long identified him in imagination."[10] But the "flippancy" which this observant visitor found incongruous in the terrible Childe, and which scintillates throughout Byron's glorious letters, is much more than the cynical wit of a jaded roué. For Byron possessed in rare degree the ironic self-vision that enabled him to perceive — and the native high spirits that permitted him, on occasion at least, to enjoy — the multifarious inconsistencies of his nature. "God knows," he writes of his journal, "what contradictions it may contain"; for "If I am sincere with myself (but I fear one lies more to one's self than to anyone else), every page should confute, refute, and utterly abjure its predecessor."[11] And to Lady Blessington (who came to see him as "a perfect chameleon")[12] he declared, "Now, if I know myself, I should say, that I have no character at all . . . that I am so changeable, being every thing by turns and nothing long, — I am such a strange *mélange* of good and evil, that it would be difficult to describe me. There are but two sentiments to which I am constant," he added " — a strong love of liberty, and a detestation of cant, and neither is calculated to gain me friends."[13]

These cardinal sentiments were two facets of one need, since detestation of cant was in fact the condition of Byron's artistic liberty. The rhapsodist who apostrophized the eternal Ocean in grandiose stanzas at the close of *Childe Harold's Pilgrimage* could later remark to Lady Blessington, as they rode along the seashore at Nervi, "I suppose you expected me to explode into some enthusiastic exclamations on the sea, the scenery, &c., such as poets indulge in, or rather are supposed to indulge in; but the truth is, I hate cant of every kind, and the cant of the love of nature as much as any other."[14] In his youthful works, of which he remained justifiably proud, he had puffed out the most rhetorical propensities of his nature at the expense of others at least equally genuine, and this too (as Byron discerned long before his adulators turned sour) was a species of cant. For in order to be sincere with himself, in his poetry as in his journals, he would have to give full expression to the conflicts and contradictions of his "wayward, uncertain disposition,"[15] and this demanded not only a new style of poetry but a different kind of hero.

Amidst the outraged cacophony that greeted the early cantos of *Don Juan*, only one critic—John Gibson Lockhart, in the pseudonymous *Letter to the Right Hon. Lord Byron by John Bull*—perceived that Byron, far from going deplorably astray, had found his bearings at last. Upbraiding the self-styled slayer of cant for his own indulgence in "humbug" ("every boarding-school in the empire still contains many devout believers in the amazing misery of the black-haired, high-browed, blue-eyed, bare-throated Lord Byron"), Lockhart counseled the poet to "Stick to Don Juan: it is the only sincere thing you have ever written; and it will live many years after all your humbug Harolds have ceased to be, in your own words,

'A school-*girl's* tale—the wonder of an hour.' "[16]

Byron, who was fully aware that *Don Juan* would win no plaudits from schoolgirls—"all works which refer to the *comedy* of the passions, and laugh at sentimentalism," he wryly remarked, "of course are proscribed by the whole *sect*"[17]—was delighted by John Bull's Letter, which he found "diabolically *well* written, and full of fun and ferocity."[18] Without his ability to acknowledge, and then to expunge, the sometimes bombastic solemnities that he had made synonymous with his name, Byron could never have brought his masterpiece of heroical mockery to the light.

Against those who misguidedly saw in *Don Juan* the betrayal of his true poetic vocation—and these included his Italian mistress, his English publisher, and most of his friends with the striking exception of Shelley[19]—Byron was adamant in its defense. He stubbornly refused to allow apprehensive well-wishers in England to emasculate his manuscript for the sake of his public image. "Don Juan," he insisted, "shall be an entire horse, or none . . . I will not give way to all the cant of Christendom."[20] "It may be bawdy but is it not good English?" he demanded: "It may be profligate but is it not *life,* is it not *the thing*?"[21] To his skittish publisher, John Murray, who unctuously reminded him that "your portrait is engraved, and painted, and sold in every town throughout the Kingdom," and pleaded with him not to injure "this high estimation of your Countrymen,"[22] Byron firmly responded, "You sha'n't make *Canticles* of my Cantos. The poem will please, if it is lively; if it is stupid, it will fail; but I will have none of your damned cutting and slashing . . . You have so many '*divine*' poems, is it nothing to have written a *Human* one? . . . As to the Estimation of the English which you talk of," he emphatically added, "let them calculate what it is worth, before they insult me with their insolent condescension . . . They made me, without my search, a species of popular Idol; they, without reason or judgement, beyond the caprice of their good pleasure, threw down the Image from its pedestal; it was not broken with the fall, and they would, it seems, again replace it—but they shall not."[23] By his bold renunciation of the cant most dear to his readers, and most conducive to his own reputation, Byron achieved the spiritual and poetic freedom that he urgently required, and for this reason consented to let his high-spirited creation carry him whithersoever it would without regard to circumspection or any semblance of order. "You ask me for the plan of Donny Johnny: I *have* no plan," he gaily avowed, to Murray's consternation: ". . . Why, Man, the Soul of such writing is its licence; at least the *liberty* of that *licence,* if one likes."[24]

Liberty is the lodestar of Byron's vision, and his otherwise random satire takes deadly aim at the countless prohibitions by which society labors to stunt the human aspiration to freedom. "In every case," as Alvin B. Kernan comments in his incisive study, "what he holds up to ridicule is some attempt to restrain life, to bind and force it into some narrow, permanent form."[25] Byron thus remained faithful to the Romantic vision bequeathed by Rousseau. Born free but everywhere enchained by the constraints of an artificial civilization, man can only attain fulfillment by emancipation of his naturally beneficent instincts. It is this perspective that radically differentiates Byron's satire from that of Swift or Pope, whom he proudly claimed as his models. "Neoclassical satire presupposes that the City of Man owes allegiance to certain eternal laws that are known to human reason and conscience," W. H. Auden observes; "its purpose is to demonstrate that the individual or institution attacked violates these laws out of presumption, malice, or stupidity. Satire of the Byronic kind presupposes no such fixed laws. It is the weapon of the rebel who refuses to accept conventional laws and pieties as binding or worthy of respect. Instead of speaking in the name of all well-educated and sensible people, it speaks in the name of the individual whose innocence of vision has not been corrupted by education and social convention."[26] As soon as this individual is stripped of aggrandizing isolation, however, and juxtaposed with a corrupt reality that fails to correspond to his innocent vision, the comedy of his situation becomes apparent. Don Juan, unlike the privileged solitary, Childe Harold, is forever butting against the obstacles and limits of actual existence; he must herd with his fellow man, however unfit. The consequences can hardly fail to be ludicrous.

Although the poet takes mischievous delight in exposing the incongruity between his hero's lofty yearnings and the lowly demands (for example) of puberty or an empty stomach, his irony, even at its most flippant, is never cynical or reductive. He may ruthlessly deflate the pomposities of conventional romantic heroes, not excluding his own, but the frequently ridiculous figure whom he puts in their place is hardly less romantic and no less a hero. No irony in Byron's life and work was more central and deeply felt than the contradiction between his passionate longing for glory (as evoked in "The Isles of Greece") and his sober awareness that in the circumstances of his own world such exalted valor could find no occasion. To the despairing exhortation of the modern Hellenic bard—

> Must *we* but weep o'er days more blest?
>   Must *we* but blush?—Our fathers bled.
> Earth! render back from out thy breast
>   A remnant of our Spartan dead!
> Of the three hundred grant but three,
> To make a new Thermopylae!—

(III. 86. 7)

the voices of the dead might respond but the living were silent as the tomb. Disenchantment was the fruit of experience: "the sad truth," Byron laments, "which hovers o'er my desk Turns what was once romantic to burlesque" (IV. 3). Yet burlesque does not annul romance in *Don Juan* but throws it into relief through juxtaposition with the hard facts and sad truths that never cease to oppose it. By forcibly bringing romance into contact with a hostile reality burlesque becomes the vehicle of heroism in an ignominious world, and through assent to this paradox the poet is able, "in the dearth of Fame" (III. 86. 6), to create an authentic (if necessarily comic) hero tailored to the needs of his times. The alternative to weeping o'er days more blest was—to laugh.

In the derisive dedication of *Don Juan* to the renegade laureate Southey, however, laughter itself was scarcely less bitter than tears; for in the absence of heroism there could be satire but no comedy. The animus of these verses (which Byron chivalrously suppressed when he published his poem anonymously) is much more than personal, for Southey and his twittering fellow Lakers incarnate in miniature an age so little heroic as to cringe before the British sultan and his "intellectual eunuch Castlereagh" (Dedication. 11). In contrast to the incorruptible Milton, who bravely "closed the tyrant-hater he begun" (Dedication. 10), the once radical Southey proves himself, by his venal flattery, both cowardly and a fraud, "struggling convulsively," Byron writes in his preface, "to deceive others without the power of lying to himself."[27] In this he typifies the craven hypocrisy of an era.

After this prelude of unrelieved ignominy the opening words of Canto the First give vent to the poet's one imperative need: "I want a hero" (I. 1). Each of his numberless candidates fails to qualify, despite the encomiastic cant of the military gazettes, because he "is not the true one"—and whatever conventional attributes Byron's hero may lack he will be indisputably genuine. This thoroughly contemporary Don Juan owes little more than his mispronounced name and birthplace to the blasphemous libertine of the pantomime; his affinities are rather with the warm-hearted Tom Jones. In the early cantos he appears as a child of nature sheltered from a corrupting world by his own impregnable innocence and by the solicitude of those who respond to his highly infectious spontaneity. The education inflicted upon him by his prodigiously learned and fanatically virtuous mother, Donna Inez, is the first of the perils that Juan, who is blissfully ignorant of all danger, surmounts by dint of native impulse alone. His mother's pedantic erudition serves only to obfuscate — "Her thoughts were theorems, her words a problem, As if she deemed that mystery would ennoble 'em" (I. 13) — and her prim morality only to inhibit. Above all, the saintly perfection that she labors to cultivate and professes to practice is a deliberate act of aggression against "this naughty world of ours" (I. 18), at once contrary to nature and alien to fallen humanity. Juan's "strictly moral" education (I. 39) is equated with vigilant expurgation —

> not a page of anything that's loose
> Or hints continuation of the species
> Was ever suffered, lest he should grow vicious —
> (I. 40)

and because Donna Inez, whatever her own secret lapses, identifies vice with nature, the object of her son's education is quite properly "to destroy His natural spirit" (I. 50).

The social and moral constraints implanted by Juan's assiduous guardian instantly disintegrate, however, before the superior force of a passion that absorbs him as totally for the moment as it remains without lasting consequence in the sequel; and in this heedless obedience to the promptings of nature is an innocence of which his prudish parent knows nothing. His first love, Donna Julia, valiantly strives "For Honour's, Pride's, Religion's, Virtue's sake" (I. 75) to subdue a passion in conflict with her accustomed morality, and yields in the very act of refusing; but the ingenuous Juan surrenders without reserve to urges against which his education has left him unarmed. In the poem's most idyllic episode he momentarily shares with the island maiden who is "Nature's bride" and "Passion's child" a beatific immunity to all thoughts that are not of the present, since for Haidée, no less than for Juan,

                        what was said or done
    Elsewhere was nothing. She had nought to fear,
    Hope, care, nor love, beyond, — Her heart beat *here*.
                                        (II. 202)

But it is Haidée, like Julia before her, who must suffer for her
rash commitment, while the inconstant Juan meanders on to
new adventures with hardly more than a fleeting regret for a
past that vanishes as soon as he leaves it behind him. He is a
creature not of sentiment, and still less of intellect, but of impulse; and not even the most generous impulse is capable either
of retrospection or foresight.

    At first blush there could be no more implausible hero than
the aimless and infantile Juan of these early cantos. The tenacity that redeemed the most undignified escapades of wily Odysseus or mad Quixote is nowhere to be found, for Juan's responses to the stimuli of experience are largely fortuitous and
inconsequential. Yet in a world intent on the systematic obliter-
ation of natural spirit the very survival of spontaneous impulse,
however haphazard, is in itself a feat of heroic proportions.
Throughout the first four cantos, to be sure, Juan's mettle is
barely tested, since passion annihilates every obstacle in the
path of his thoughtless delights and makes him almost indifferent to the atrocities of education and shipwreck. Nor is there
any hint of conflict in Juan (as there was in the equally reckless
Tom Jones) between inclination and honor; never, despite his
strenuous moral indoctrination, does he conceive of any alternative to following his instincts wherever they happen to lead.
He lacks all conscious resolve to defy a world of which he remains, at best, incompletely aware. By this very neglect, however, he undermines the foundations of codes and restrictions
whose futility becomes manifest as neither bluestocking nor
buccaneer, moral suasion nor physical compulsion, impedes his
insouciant progress. Instinct itself entails an incipient challenge, then, but only Juan's increasingly conscious association
with a corrupt social order will bring the latent antagonism to a
head.

    The poet's caustic portrayal of this perverted world so dominates the latter part of his poem, especially after he resumed it with Canto the Sixth, that its evanescent protagonist often drops out of sight altogether. In consequence Don Juan has understandably seemed to many, including so sympathetic a reader as Auden, "the least interesting figure" in a work "the real hero" of which "is Byron himself." Yet to say that Juan's "most conspicuous trait is his gift for social conformity"[28] reduces pliancy to compliance and disregards the resistant properties of passivity. Between the lackadaisical yet impetuous hero and a poet simultaneously indignant and disillusioned the bond is surely more intimate and essential than Auden allows. The two complementary sentiments to which Byron declared himself constant, as we have observed, were "a strong love of liberty and a detestation of cant," and if the worldly poet grows ever more scathing in his expression of the second, his ingenuous alter ego never wholly ceases, in however desultory a fashion, to embody the first. Despite protracted exits into the wings Juan remains an indispensable counterweight to the depredations and depravities that repeatedly crowd him offstage. For it is only this wavering comic hero of frail flesh and hot blood — and not the "sylvan tribe of children of the chase" (VIII. 65) led by Daniel Boone, whom Byron extolled in one of his notable lapses — who persuasively incarnates the human freedom menaced on every side by an artificial and brutalizing civilization.

As Juan finds himself compelled by adversity to assert and defend his impulses they inevitably become less purely reflexive and more deliberate. Inarticulate biological drives have already prevailed against the restraints of coercive upbringing; now the still greater evils of slavery and war teach Juan his imperative need of the personal liberty and common humanity that his world likewise conspires to deny. Only after Nature's erstwhile bridegroom has been sold into bondage at Constantinople by Haidée's father, the Greek pirate Lambro, and decked out in woman's apparel to satisfy the caprice of the Turkish Sultana Gulbeyaz, does his perilous (and utterly ludicrous) extremity provoke his first words of defiance. "The prisoned eagle will not pair, nor I," he haughtily announces, "Serve a Sultana's sensual phantasy":

"Thou ask'st, if I can love? be this the proof
 How much I *have* loved—that I love not *thee*!
In this vile garb, the distaff, web, and woof,
 Were fitter for me: Love is for the free!
I am not dazzled by this splendid roof;
 Whate'er thy power, and great it seems to be,
Heads bow, knees bend, eyes watch around a throne,
And hands obey—our hearts are still our own."

           (V. 126-27)

The magniloquence of this valiant pronouncement is somewhat attenuated, no doubt, by the farcicality of Juan's position
and the unseemly abruptness with which "his great prepara-
tives for dying Dissolved like snow before a woman's crying"
(V. 141). But his resolve is no less heroic—and far more cred-
ible, under the circumstances—for being simultaneously comic.
For the first time his constitutional spontaneity is reinforced by
a conscious choice, since he has clearly seen the alternative and
willfully revolted against it. Under the implicit threat of Gulbeyaz' fury even Juan's unpremeditated possession of the drowsy
Dudù in the sultan's harem that night is a mutinous affirmation of impulse over compulsion. Only the lucky star that continues to guide him (or the charm that he exercises over the fellow slave commissioned to kill him) preserves him from the
consequences of his insurgent libido by removing him, in the
nick of time, from the caldron of Constantinople to the firing
line at Ismail.

Nowhere is Byron's satire more unsparing than in his brutal
account of the Russian siege of Turkish Ismail. He himself had
once commemorated the glamor and pathos of battle in stirring
verses on Waterloo in *Childe Harold's Pilgrimage*, but his passionate faith in heroism for the sake of freedom, as immortalized at Marathon and Salamis, only intensified his aversion to a
form of slaughter dedicated to no higher cause than riches and
power. Here Glory is only a euphemism for murder, and Fame
a perfunctory death notice in the official Gazette: "Thrice
happy he," the poet sardonically remarks, "whose name has
been well spelt" (VIII. 18). The official rhetoric that aspires to

ennoble massacres in which millions are "slain by soldiers for their ration" (VIII. 68), and even presumes (like Wordsworth at his dismal nadir) to lend divine sanction to human butchery by dubbing Carnage God's daughter,[29] epitomizes the self-serving cant of the age. For his own depiction of the sordid truth of contemporary warfare Byron employed instead the ironical realism already perfected in his shocking portrayal of shipwreck and cannibalism in Canto the Second. Each grisly detail and caustic aside is calculated to offend to the utmost "these ambrosial, Pharisaic times, With all their pretty milk-and-water ways" (VIII. 90) by confronting them with the horror of unadorned actuality. Yet in the very midst of "All that the Devil would do if run stark mad" (VIII. 123), Juan plunges into the fray "like an ass" blindly "following Honour and his nose" (VIII. 30, 32), swept along by the thirst for glory and pausing to question nothing.

Here if anywhere protagonist and poet would seem irreconcilably opposed, for Juan naïvely embraces the selfsame martial virtues that Byron exposes to withering scorn. Even in his puerile infatuation, however, Juan's conformity with the prevailing ethic of battle is more apparent than real, and when the need for decision abruptly presents itself his generous action speaks no less eloquently than the poet's indignant words. The plight of a Turkish child menaced by rampaging Cossacks forces him to choose — as his impatient companion Johnson demands — "Between your fame and feelings, pride and pity" (VIII. 101), and his choice is never in question. Amid the rubble of vanquished Ismail he affirms the bond of human compassion that unites him not with his rapacious fellow conquerors but with a defenseless victim of the savagery in which he himself has thoughtlessly taken part. By this stubborn adherence to common humanity in the teeth of pillage, as by his rash proclamation of personal liberty amid the Turkish seraglio, Juan heroically discards the conventional role in which he has been more or less complaisantly cast and proves true, in the moment of crisis, to his impulsive and still uncorrupted nature.

Juan's newly deliberate spontaneity will face its most severe trials, however, not in adversity but in the insidious favor lavished upon him by an artificial society avid to clasp the obliging *ingénu* in its languid embrace. The danger of fatal compromise lurks throughout the later episodes of the poem, and in the station of minion to Catherine the Great of Russia in Cantos the Ninth and Tenth Juan very nearly succumbs beyond reclamation. For once he does comply with demands wholly alien to his impetuous temper, and barely survives the unmanning ordeal. The fact that Juan falls prey to the cankerworm of Care at the apex of his worldly fortunes and sighs for Beauty in Royalty's vast arms is proof, indeed, that not even the blandishments of an empress whose "climacteric teased her like her teens" (X. 47) have entirely vitiated the drooping eagle's yearning for freedom. But the ignominy of his dissipated thralldom leaves him no alternative more heroic, after recuperating from his nearly fatal distemper, than flight from despotic Petersburg to the faraway Island of the Free.

Whether English liberty will succeed where Russian despotism has failed in destroying what remains of Juan's youthful vitality is left tantalizingly unresolved when the poem breaks off: "I leave the thing a problem," the poet writes in his fragmentary seventeenth canto, "like all things" (XVII. 13). Byron had suggested to Murray that he meant to display his hero "gradually *gâté* and *blasé* as he grew older, as is natural";[30] but in a work where the "liberty of license" overrides all prior design no statement of intention is binding, and the evidence of Juan's own conduct is fittingly inconclusive and contradictory. For all his ambiguity it is Juan alone, as outsider and touchstone, who embodies the potential authenticity by which the real and present falsity of a decadent high society *"fatal"*—as Byron knew from bitter experience—"to all great original undertakings of every kind"[31] is relentlessly exposed. Adaptable though he is, Juan nevertheless remains distinctly apart from those who threaten to engulf him, and his equivocal presence continually poses, if not a challenge to the existence of this society, a disturbing reminder of its human inadequacy. It is the belligerent poet who again articulates the deficiency accentuated by the contrasting example of his reticent hero. In an aristocracy "smoothed to that excess, That manners hardly differ more than dress" (XIII. 94) and reduced from the colorful multiplicity of heartier days to "one polished horde, Formed of two mighty tribes, the *Bores* and *Bored* " (XIII. 95), there is no longer a place, he laments, for bumptious Squire Westerns or "accomplished blackguards, like Tom Jones" (XIII. 110). It is above all the dispiriting *sameness* of this superficially glittering world that Byron lays bare in mordantly analytical verses:

> With much to excite, there's little to exalt;
>   Nothing that speaks to all men and all times;
> A sort of varnish over every fault,
>   A kind of common-place, even in their crimes;
> Factitious passions — Wit without much salt —
>   A want of that true nature which sublimes
> Whate'er it shows with Truth; a smooth monotony
> Of character, in those at least who have got any.
>
> (XIV. 16)

Into this artificial paradise Juan, by supplying its want of true nature and genuine passion, intrudes an alien individuality that imperils its delicate equilibrium. The ostensible diversity of the noble assemblage at Norman Abbey in the closing cantos of Byron's poem is nothing more than a "brilliant masquerade" (XIV. 17) of stereotypes without substance. Lord Henry Amundeville can be "all things to all men" (XVI. 71) because in himself he is nothing, and the mobility of temper displayed by his Lady in acting "all and every part By turns" (XVI. 97) occasions "Some doubt how much of Adeline was *real*" (XVI. 96). By contrast the "gift for social conformity" that Auden finds characteristic of Juan is altogether different in kind. "Juan — in this respect, at least, like saints — " the poet notes, "Was all things unto people of all sorts" (XIV. 31); with women in particular he can be whatever "They pleased to make or take him for" (XV. 16). But this capacity reflects not the practiced play-acting of the Amundevilles, nor simply the artless plasticity of his own more ingenuous youth, but the impassive wariness that experience has called to the aid of innocence. Juan, despite appearances, is no longer the thoughtlessly impetuous naïf of the early cantos. "He had the art," the poet observes, "of drawing people out, Without their seeing what he was about" (XV. 82). "Observant of the foibles of the crowd, Yet ne'er betraying this in conversation" (XV. 15), the impenetrable guest shrewdly sees through others whilst they see only themselves in him.

How the confrontation would have ended, had Byron lived to complete his poem, no one can know; but there are indications, at least, that Don Juan's "true nature" was destined to trouble the stagnant surface of English society rather than merely founder beneath it. Between himself and the beautiful Aurora Raby, Juan unexpectedly discovers an affinity of "two exceptions" (XVI. 105), for she is as much a stranger to the social masquerade as he.

> She gazed upon a World she scarcely knew,
>   As seeking not to know it; silent, lone,
> As grows a flower, thus quietly she grew,
>   And kept her heart serene within its zone.
>
> (XV. 47)

She renews in Juan feelings benumbed or forgotten since his forced separation from Haidée had brought a premature end to "The unbounded hope, and heavenly ignorance Of what is called the World, and the World's ways" (XVI. 108). Far from being corrupted, then, by the drab routine and factitious passions of aristocratic society Juan's dormant impulses are in fact revitalized by his instinctive attraction to a fellow outsider through whom he becomes aware, however tenuously, of his own estrangement. But innocence can now be recovered, if at all, only by *seeking* not to know the world, that is, by deliberate opposition to its ways. It demands a commitment and implies a defiance.

To others less self-sufficient than Aurora or Juan recrudescence of spontaneity would menace the tranquil apathy of their existence. So closely has Lady Adeline, for example, become identified with her worldly role that she easily blinds herself (in matchmaking schemes that always omit Aurora) to

Juan's disposition and to her own. It is this indispensable self-deception, the cornerstone of her social pre-eminence, that her attraction to Juan surreptitiously endangers. "She loved her lord, or thought so; but *that* love," the poet remarks, "Cost her an effort" (XIV. 86). Her hesitant inclination toward the charming foreigner, on the other hand—"She was, or thought she was, his friend" (XIV. 92)—is utterly without effort but therefore potentially out of control.

Thus Juan's innate spontaneity not only survives the blighting influence of a fraudulent "paradise of Pleasure and *Ennui*" (XIV. 17), and even begins to revive under the radiance of Aurora, but infects this static order with an element of unpredictability that threatens to sap its foundations. This convulsive element is his unattenuated ability to love; for love, as the poet observes, "bears within its breast the very germ Of Change; and how should this be otherwise?" (XIV. 94). What alterations this virus might have effected in the torpid society gathered in Norman Abbey must be left to surmise, since only the frolicsome Duchess of Fitz-Fulke (in the guise of the ghostly Black Friar) had overtly responded to its contagion when Byron interrupted his story forever. But once the germ of change has entered its bloodstream this world of laborious artifice and monotonous manners could never again be entirely the same. Through renewed fidelity to his still uncorrupted nature Juan's very existence has become a disruptive challenge to a social order that can neither absorb nor dismiss him.

To concur that Byron is the "real hero" of a poem in which Don Juan is "the least interesting figure" would thus be to sunder two facets of a composite persona. The evolving relationship of poet and hero is not one of rigorous dichotomy but of dialectical counterpoint and reciprocal interdependence. The lucid consciousness that allows the poet to "laugh at *all* things" as no more than "a *show*" (VII. 2), far from deprecating his more ingenuous hero, highlights the spontaneity of Juan's equally radical opposition to a denatured civilization. Without the poet's denunciations of ennui and hypocrisy, Juan's mute comedy would lack the heroic defiance vociferated by less retiring comic heroes of ages past. But without Juan's guileless impulsiveness to offset the deceits of a blasé society, Byron's poem would not be comedy at all, but unrelieved satire. Byron is the real hero only to the extent that Juan remains inseparable from him.

Like Diderot before him, Byron continually subverts his readers' presuppositions by the vagaries of his "nondescript and ever-varying rhyme" (VII. 2), and his systematic insolence has a militant purpose. In the war against cant his deadliest weapon was truth, and despite condemnation of his opening cantos "for having too much truth" (IV. 97), he persisted in his "immoral" determination to "show things really as they are, Not as they ought to be" (XII. 40). He knows the near impossibility of stating "A fact without some leaven of a lie" (XI. 37), yet only in unembellished fact does he find "the grand desideratum" (VII. 81) of poetry, which is truth. Therefore, he emphatically declares,

> 't is the part
> Of a true poet to escape from fiction
> Whene'er he can; for there is little art
> In leaving verse more free from the restriction
> Of Truth than prose, unless to suit the mart
> For what is sometimes called poetic diction,
> And that outrageous appetite for lies
> Which Satan angles with for souls, like flies.
>
> (VIII. 86)

By his impassioned conviction that his Muse, whatever her flaws, is "The most sincere that ever dealt in fiction" (XVI. 2), the sophisticated poet again reveals his temperamental affinity with the candid Juan; and from their shared commitment to authenticity stems the common challenge of the satirist and the comic hero to a false social order.

But the truth that Byron asserts and Juan exemplifies is far more complex than simple fidelity to "a repertory of facts" (XIV. 13) or to an immutable nature. No less than Diderot (or Cervantes) Byron knows that in a contingent world truth itself is paradoxical and uncertain. This awareness finds expression in the apparently aimless convolutions of the "desultory rhyme"

(XV. 20) that he "carelessly" sings (VIII. 138) in violation of every established rule and convention; for "if a writer should be quite consistent," he asks, "How could he possibly show things existent?"

> If people contradict themselves, can I
>   Help contradicting them, and everybody,
> Even my veracious self?
>
> (XV. 87-88)

Through his spirited refusal to submit the "versified Aurora Borealis" (VII. 2) of his poem to the distorting prisms of rigid consistency or predetermined design — "I rattle on," he jauntily affirms, "exactly as I'd talk" (XV. 19) — the artful *Improvvisatore* proclaims himself, after all, no less obedient to the capricious spontaneity of nature than his haphazard young hero. Truth lies, for both alike, in the unpredictable variability of human existence; and in their steadfast allegiance to this emancipating reality is the heroism that unites them, for all their differences of temper and outlook, in resistance to a civilization whose uniform and coercive cant is finally a denial of life itself.

Byron's poem resembles Diderot's novel in inconclusiveness as well as provocation. In neither do the terms of the comic hero's world permit him so much as the possibility of definitive triumph, much less of regeneration. Far from striving to make the world over, like his classical and Renaissance forebears, it is enough that he somehow manage to hold his own. But since the perimeters of Don Juan's world are far wider than those of Jacques' — not only geographically but in the scope of its dreams and aspirations — and his antagonists far more insidious than Jacques' simple master, the risk of disillusionment or corruption is correspondingly greater. If Byron's ironical vision allowed him to see the romantic hero in a comic light it also saw that this comic hero might imperceptibly lose the spontaneity that set him apart from his world; and as the prosaic nineteenth century doggedly advanced the danger grew still more acute. In the far from romantic light of common day no hero could dissent with impunity from an evangelical social order that looked on itself as the chosen vessel of inexorable progress and considered the benighted recusant (as Mr. Podsnap considered the unfortunate Frenchman) an object of solicitous condescension rather than laughter. The age took itself far too seriously to view the questioning of its fundamental values as either praiseworthy or amusing, and in its literature the frustrated alien, whether aesthete or miscreant, des Esseintes or Raskolnikov, was increasingly driven to far from comic extremes of futility or desperation.

In the early decades of the century, the prudent outsider could still be reconciled to a social order guardedly tolerant of dissidence within reason. Jane Austen's sharp-tongued Elizabeth Bennet is keenly aware of her willful nonconformity with the conventions of provincial English society. "The more I see of the world," she tells her complaisant sister, "the more am I dissatisfied with it."[32] Yet because she knows of no alternative world she must endeavor to find a place for herself in this one without surrendering the critical independence that sets her apart. What distinguishes her from others is no incompatible vision of life but the superior intelligence that enables her, despite the rueful comedy of reciprocal misunderstanding in which she becomes involved, to find fault not only with social prejudice (as embodied by her arrogant suitor) but with her own pride, and thus to moderate her temperamental aversion to the world while preserving her essential integrity. Her victory is over herself, and society is partly redeemed by her chastening triumph. Even in Jane Austen's eminently civilized world, however, the gulf separating the thinking and feeling individual from a polished and often cold-hearted society becomes—especially in her last novel, *Persuasion*—very nearly too wide to bridge. In its quiet isolation the heroism of nonconformity seems painfully remote from the comic.

The cruel dilemma of comic heroism in such a world is central to Byron's French contemporary and fellow ironist Stendhal, who regarded the novel as "the comedy of the nineteenth century,"[33] yet brought the protagonists of his two major novels to melancholy endings in a prison cell and a monastery. Far more than the nonchalant Don Juan, Stendhal's restless young heroes vex themselves with the impossible task of accommodating Napoleonic dreams to the realities of reaction and the *juste milieu*; they are, in Harry Levin's happy phrase, Don Quixotes in a Machiavellian world,[34] and both heroism and comedy succumb to the irresolvable contradiction. Julien Sorel, the consummate arriviste of *The Red and the Black,* fanatically dedicates his skills to a game that he finally knows is not worth the candle; his sole heroism lies in his reckless repudiation of social comedy for the annihilating truth of passion. In *The Charterhouse of Parma,* on the other hand, Fabrice del Dongo's heroic impetuosity on the field of Waterloo is rendered involuntarily comic by the incompatibility of his grandiose expectations with the confused realities of battle, or indeed of life. The morose anchorite is already implicit in the starry-eyed volunteer, for Fabrice can never live up to the impossible roles, whether as soldier or lover, in which he repeatedly casts himself in revulsion from the cynical court of Parma, where "the essential quality in a young man of the present day," as Count Mosca explains, "is not to be liable to enthusiasm and not to shew any spirit."[35] Only rebellious youth can momentarily sustain the high comedy of heroic illusions celebrated by Stendhal with the irony and regret of one who knows how quickly youth will become a reproachful memory.

If accommodation between the dissident and his world is precarious in Jane Austen and unattainable in Stendhal, in the novels of Dickens harmonious endings seem habitually willed more truly than won. Victorian society could tolerate and even encourage strenuous criticism of its failings but could scarcely imagine a frontal assault on its premises; hence its comic heroes were obliged by force of convention to keep within exceedingly narrow limits. Only the first of Dickens' many novels has an unequivocally comic protagonist, and the irrepressible gaiety of *The Posthumous Papers of the Pickwick Club*—finished in the year of the new Queen's accession—had its origin in a less earnest age. The good-natured benevolence and high-spirited spontaneity of Mr. Pickwick are qualities that he shares with Tom

Jones and Don Juan, but unlike those scandalous precursors
(whom he would surely have blushed to name) Pickwick is
scrupulously chaste even in a strange lady's bedchamber and
temperate in his very cups. He violates no taboo and gives no
offense either to his fellow characters or to the most delicate
reader. He inhabits a fairy-tale world of carefree frivolity from
which any real danger is rigorously excluded, and neither the
ubiquitous scoundrel Jingle nor the tenacious ogres Dodson and
Fogg nor the forbidding walls of the Fleet (which he enters at
his own high-minded insistence) can threaten his ineradicable
innocence. Instead of re-enacting the Fall, as Auden suggests,[36]
the incorruptible Pickwick puts Satan far behind him, if only
by sheer inadvertency, and carries Eden wherever he goes.
Having wrathfully driven the pettifogging Dodson and Fogg
from the Temple his countenance regains its smiling placidity
and he becomes "perfectly comfortable and happy"[37] as before.
He is less comic hero than comic Genius, and the aura that he
irradiates from serenely above the battle extends its protection
to all who enter his magical realm. It is his scrappy esquire,
Sam Weller, who does battle with the unregenerate adversary
in his saintly master's behalf, just as Sam's veteran father continues to tangle with drunken Methodists and disconsolate
widows. Not even *sub regno Pickwicki,* as the scars of the Well-
ers bear witness, can the Golden Age be perpetuated without
an occasional scuffle. But if nothing can finally challenge Pickwick, it follows that Pickwick finally challenges nothing. By
safeguarding the innocence of a childlike existence he may win
the hearts of his readers, but in harsh reality it is Dodson and
Fogg who win the lawsuit and pocket the proceeds, undeterred
by a portly old gentleman's spluttering imprecations.

In the subsequent novels of Dickens a massive infusion of
harsh reality drastically reduces the scope and obstructs the
efficacy of comic benevolence. Pickwick's jolly avatars, like the
brothers Cheeryble in *Nicholas Nickleby,* seem grotesquely
inadequate outside the enchanted confines of the merry Pick-
wickian kingdom. The virtuous but fallible protagonists of
these novels are too sober for comedy and too deferential for
heroism: hapless victims, more often than not, of a malice from

which they are providentially if improbably rescued. Determined innocence could get the best of a Jingle, but against a Fagin, a Quilp, or a Pecksniff it is sadly mismatched, and the confrontation therefore inclines to pathos rather than comedy. It is not only the imaginative preponderance of villainy, however, that militates against comic heroism in Dickens' novels but the timidity of those who deplore society's vices without venturing to question its virtues. The contest with the social order is never truly joined, since these stoical heroes incorporate no alternatives—beyond gentle remonstrances or saccharine daydreams—to its governing values. Not until *Great Expectations* does the corrupting potential of compliance become explicit when Pip discovers that his meticulous rise to respectability has involved more culpable delinquencies than any committed by the convict whom society has righteously banished from its midst. At the same time, this most self-critical of Dickens' narrators is perhaps the first who is able—however ruefully and however late—to look back on his own misguided actions and represent them as comic. Whatever heroism attaches to Pip's sad comedy of unconscious self-betrayal lies not in the acting but in the telling, for by retrospectively questioning his own fallacious assumptions and exposing his solemn foibles to laughter Pip deliberately challenges the moral complacency that he shared for so long with his age. For the first time a Dickensian hero proves adequate to the complexities of a fallen world through his difficult realization that he himself has taken part in its incriminating fall.

A deep-seated paradox lies at the heart of the comic hero's perplexity since the Renaissance. In a world where absolute truth is perceived to be inapprehensible society gives the impression of being more smugly confident of its values (perhaps because it half suspects their shaky foundations) than ever before. The comic hero, in consequence, can rely on no unquestioned certainties of his own in his battle with the false certainties that impede his impulse to liberty. Don Quixote, the most overtly heroic of modern comic heroes, sets out with demented confidence in his capacity to revive the truths of the Golden Age, but after Dulcinea's enchantment and the vision of Montesinos this confidence is eroded by his awareness that truth exists nowhere on earth unless in his own determined but flagging imagination. And in their evasion of all doctrinaire rigidities both Jacques the fatalist and Don Juan, in turn, forgo the demand for any truth more absolute than that of their own wayward natures. This tolerance of uncertainty could be a besetting danger, however, for a comic hero, like Juan, whom only impulse sustains in his negligent encounter with a self-assured adversary; for his lack of any compensating assurance might easily become a source of susceptibility to corruption.

In the late nineteenth century the comic dissenter is typically diffident to the point of apology in his affirmation of instincts ostracized by polite society. Mark Twain's Huckleberry Finn, for example, is never fully at ease about his aversion to the Widow Douglas' efforts to "sivilize" him; from beginning to end he looks admiringly up to Tom Sawyer for being "respectable" as Huck never quite can. By his spontaneous resistance to any constriction of personal freedom, his instinctive identification with fellow misfits like Miss Watson's runaway nigger Jim, and his quick-witted versatility in the face of danger, Huck deserves a prominent place among the comic heroes of his age. Whenever his socially implanted "conscience" is set in motion, however, he is tempted to scuttle his genuine feelings and capitulate to the enemy by abject repentance. In the end his brave resolution to risk hellfire for Jim's sake peters out in inconsequential burlesque as Tom Sawyer reasserts his old sway. Whether Huck's heroic nonconformity will survive his brief fellowship in freedom with a fugitive slave on the vast Mississippi or be submerged in sivilization with the passing of childhood remains unanswered. That he has "been there before," as he says at the end, provides scant assurance that he will not return.

The comic heroes of the diligent and industrious nineteenth century are by and large either children or childlike: ingenuous youths like Juan or Fabrice, eternal innocents like Pickwick and the Pickwickians, or impulsive truants like Huckleberry Finn. The risk they inevitably run, in the absence of any firmly articulated values to buttress their generous instincts, is that in putting aside childish things for adulthood they might become indistinguishable from the Others. In Ibsen's *Peer Gynt* the danger becomes stark reality. No comic hero since the Renaissance can surpass the youthful Peer in exuberant imagination. He is a known liar from the opening line, but as he evokes his breathtaking chase of a buck along the dizzying cliffs of Gendin his audacious fabrications take on a visionary force that sweeps even his skeptical mother away in the avalanche of his words. His aspirations are imperial, and neither the routine expectations of village society nor the desperate reprimands of his mother and neighbors can withstand the ebullient verve of his ego. Yet Peer's fantasies of empire, unlike the emancipating visions of his great comic precursors, envisage not the creation of an alternative world but his own self-aggrandizement in this one. Without the courageous faith that motivated Don Quixote's redemptive mission Peer's imaginings swiftly degenerate into idle daydreams and hollow boasts. Despite an inventive gusto worthy of the foremost comic heroes of yore he lacks the integral self-assurance that made them truly heroic, and easily falls prey to his own unsubstantial illusions, so that the multiple roles he enacts mask the absence of any directing self. Through his frenetic endeavors to fill this void at the center by maniacal acquisition of wealth or knowledge he squanders the bountiful vitality of his youth in futile compromises and is finally left with the gnawing consciousness of his own emptiness. In order to realize his goals the comic hero, like any hero, must resolutely repudiate values alien to himself, whether Calypso's languorous immortality or the grinning honor of Sir Walter Blunt. But Peer Gynt cannot discern what is alien to a self that he never discovers, and therefore repudiates nothing. The internal subversion of his vital impulses is the ineluctable consequence, and his redemption must come — if it comes at all — from beyond him.

In Peer Gynt the comic hero of the romantic ironists comes of age and reveals the vulnerability of thoughtless instinct to irreversible corrosion. And because Peer is manifestly a poet manqué the piecemeal disintegration of his glorious dreams contained a particular pertinence for the late nineteenth-century artist, who saw his own integrity continually imperiled by the crass expectations of a presumptuous new class. In the despondent outbursts of the self-styled *bourgeoisophobus* Gustave Flaubert, the caustic wit of Byron gives way to splenetic revulsion. "Nothing is left," he writes with characteristic morbidity, "except the vulgar and stupid mob. All of us are equally mired in mediocrity. Social equality has spread to the mind. Our books, our Art, our science, are designed for everybody, like railroads and public shelters. Mankind is frenziedly seeking moral abasement, and I resent being a part of it."[38]

If the defeat of the grand aspirations dubiously personified by the great Napoleon at Waterloo had resulted, for Byron and others of his generation, in a disillusioned awareness of the limitations of heroism, the ignominious dissolution of the dreams of '48 in the coup d'état of Napoleon the Little engendered a nihilistic despair in the possibility of meaningful action. On the stage of history tragedy was repeated (Marx wryly observed) as farce; in literature Julien Sorel and Fabrice del Dongo were superseded by Emma Bovary and Frédéric Moreau. Out of the wreckage of shattered ideals nothing survived to endow the human struggle with heroic significance: "Absolute doubt," Flaubert affirms, "now seems to me so completely substantiated that it would be almost silly to seek to formulate it."[39] The Romantic fantasies to which Flaubert himself gave extravagant expression in the hallucinatory visions of *Salammbô* and *The Temptation of Saint Anthony* had become nightmares of futile yearning and obstructed escape, while in the dreary world of the waking every reverie was cruelly exposed as a mocking phantom. Madame Bovary and Frédéric have not ceased to dream, any more than their author, but their dreams have ceased to have any authentic relation to their experience, leaving them nothing but bitter anguish or weary regret. The irony that gives such intensity to Flaubert's narratives of tedium and disenchantment stems not from dispassionate analysis, then, but from self-lacerating pain. Like Baudelaire's *heautontimoroumenos* Flaubert is consciously both the wound and the knife, the victim and the executioner.[40] "Haven't you realized," he writes to Louise Colet during the prolonged martyrdom of composing *Madame Bovary,* "that all the irony I let loose against emotion in my works is nothing but a cry of the vanquished—unless," he adds, "it was a paean of victory?"[41]

But if defeat may be regarded as victory a potential for triumph is implicit even in Flaubert's most scathing irony, which intermittently enables him to step back and observe himself with an amused detachment far more "objective" than his habitual disgust. "There are in me, literarily speaking, two distinct persons [*bonshommes*]," he writes: "one who is infatuated with bombast, lyricism, eagle flights, sonorities of phrase and the high points of ideas; and another who digs and burrows into the truth as deeply as he can, who likes to treat a humble fact as respectfully as a big one, who would like to make you feel almost *physically* the things he reproduces; this latter person likes to laugh, and enjoys the animal sides of man."[42] "What prevents me from taking myself seriously, although I am quite grave by nature," he further confesses, "is that I find myself very ridiculous; and my ridiculousness is not relative, as in stage comedy, but the intrinsic ridiculousness of human life, which manifests itself in the simplest action or the most commonplace gesture. Never, for instance, do I shave without laughing—the process seems to stupid."[43] In the comic sense and in laughter, where comprehension mingled with contempt, he found "the highest manner of seeing life."[44]

High-spirited merriment and unashamed animality were facets of himself that Flaubert largely banished from the completed novels, in which physical appetite is seldom free of nausea and laughter is nearly always sardonic. In their all-absorbing banality the pharmacist Homais and the priest Bournisien in *Madame Bovary*, for example, occasion none of the conflict between aversion and sympathy that the heroine continually elicits by her pathetic endeavor to overcome the platitudes of existence. They are pictured, in the classic tradition of satirical comedy, exclusively from without and above. But in a world bemired by the commonplace the impregnable "satisfaction de soi-même"[45] of Homais and his ilk takes on an aspect of terror, because it precludes the very desire for that elusive transcendence toward which Emma and Frédéric, like Saint Anthony and Saint Julian the Hospitaler, never cease to aspire so long as a glimmer of hope remains. It is their redemptive *dis*satisfaction with self that gives these misfits, for all the apparent futility of their efforts, a tincture of heroism in an age whose mortal sin was complacency. And since each of these characters was in some sense himself—as he said of Mme Bovary—Flaubert's propensity to glimpse in his own pursuits "the intrinsic ridiculousness of human life" raised the possibility that even so despondent a heroism as theirs might be seen in a comic light. In *Bouvard and Pécuchet,* the unfinished labor of his disillusioned last years, this latent comic potential in Flaubert's work, adumbrated in some of his earliest sketches, comes at last to fulfillment. Under cover of a philistinism apparently no less stolid than that of M. Homais the incompetent heroes of this ponderous comedy gradually evince a restless spirit that allies them not merely with the aimlessly daydreaming Emma Bovary but with the great standard-bearer of dauntless illusion, Don Quixote himself. Unlike Don Juan, Fabrice, or Huck Finn, the aging Bouvard and Pécuchet can no longer rely on the thoughtless impulses of youth to set them apart from the ways of a treacherous world, but through toilsome perseverance and skeptical observation must doggedly *accomplish* their alienation from a society whose imbecilities they were once content to epitomize. By so doing, infantile though their antics appear and childlike as their spirit remains, they are very nearly the first *adult* comic heroes of the waning nineteenth century.

Just as Don Quixote began his illustrious career as a farcical crackpot, Bouvard and Pécuchet make their debut as fatuous caricatures of the bourgeois stupidity, or *bêtise,* that Flaubert fanatically loathed. One after another these hapless mannequins take up their ill-assorted and disconnected pursuits, agricultural, geological, medicinal, literary, historiographical, spiritualistic, religious, and so on, and one after another, with clocklike dependability, their misguided efforts culminate in fiasco. "The great danger," Flaubert confided to Turgenev as he began his "long voyage toward unknown shores," "is monotony and boredom,"[46] and on those shoals many readers have concurred that the author foundered. "If I heard that anyone I knew was trying to write a book to such specifications," Flaubert himself remarked three weeks before death brought his long project to a premature end, "I'd urge that he be sent to an insane asylum. I can only put my trust in God."[47]

Yet even in the opening pages his characters are far from being mere automatons predestined to cyclical frustration. The fortuitous meeting of Bouvard and Pécuchet one sultry day on the empty Boulevard Bourdon takes on mythic significance when the observation that both have written their names in their hats initiates for these middle-aged copyists a veritable *vita nuova* of unsuspected affinities. "Their meeting," the author portentously affirms, "had assumed the importance of an adventure" (I, 24). Both, like every self-respecting bourgeois, are creatures of settled habits — "Bouvard smoked a pipe, liked cheese, never missed his small black coffee. Pécuchet took snuff, ate only preserves at dessert, and with his coffee sucked a lump of sugar" (I, 25) — but their chance encounter produces the truly epochal result that "their habits changed." They discover "forgotten corners" of themselves (I, 20) and "bewildering and wonderful" possibilities (I, 26) outside their customary routine, in consequence of which their unquestioning placidity gives way to a radical dissatisfaction with their existence. "At one time they had been almost happy; but now they had a higher opinion of themselves, their work humiliated them, and they made common cause in this disgust" (I, 27). Thus a momentous change in their humdrum lives has already taken place, relegating every prior event to oblivion. The outward transformation of circumstances produced soon afterwards by Bouvard's unexpected inheritance merely reinforces the change of outlook that has already bound the two men together in a cause that sets them apart from the rest of their world.

What most obviously marks them off from the solid citizens of Chavignolles, the village to which they migrate to begin their new lives, is the folly of the projects that they repeatedly initiate with unbounded enthusiasm and infinitesimal understanding. Like "their prototype, Monsieur Jourdain," as Lionel Trilling remarks, Bouvard and Pécuchet "want to learn too quickly,"[48] and derision unavoidably crowns their abortive endeavors. But Flaubert's social order, in contrast to Molière's, betokens not reason and good sense but swinishness and stupidity, so that the foolish intruders become (in Trilling's phrase again)[49] catalysts of the far more vicious foolishness of others; for their foibles arouse not amused condescension but blind suspicion and panic fear. Flaubert well knew the fierce hatred of the respectable bourgeois for unassimilable outsiders, like the gypsies whom he observed at Rouen. "This hatred stems from a deep and complex source," he writes to George Sand; "it's to be found in all champions of order. It's the hatred felt for the bedouin, the heretic, the philosopher, the recluse, the poet; and it contains an element of fear. I, who am always on the side of minorities, am driven wild by it."[50] By virtue of recalcitrant idiosyncracy Bouvard and Pécuchet, who at first desire only to please, soon find themselves the bedouins and heretics of Chavignolles. "Their way of life, which was not other people's, caused displeasure. They became suspect, and even inspired a vague terror" (VIII, 237).

In contrast again to Monsieur Jourdain, who ineffectually strives to make himself identical with his mockers, Bouvard and Pécuchet are not only different from the respectable Chavignollais but consciously, deliberately, even heroically different. Their gradual recognition of fundamental incompatibility with their world transforms involuntary alienation into a purposeful choice and a stubborn commitment. Their politics may fluctuate with the tide of events in Paris but their indignation at hypocrisy and repression in Chavignolles becomes steadily more irate and outspoken. "The rights of the individual," Pécuchet bluntly tells the notary during the turmoil of '48, "are as respectworthy as those of the community, and you've nothing to oppose him with, except force" (VI, 187). Although Pécuchet is predictably denounced as a communist for challenging hereditary prerogatives, the two friends embrace no partisan creed like that of the Jacobin schoolmaster Petit, but neither do they ingloriously capitulate, like the same Petit, to the forces of triumphant reaction. At the luncheon held to honor the Count for his preordained electoral victory only Pécuchet rashly dares to interpose a word in defense of liberty, and "as they walked over the dead leaves" after departing from this celebration of obedience to authority the two friends "breathed like men who have been set free" (VI, 196). Their hearts and minds, Trilling rightly observes, "instinctively take the side of the insulted and injured,"[51] and their compassion for outcasts like the beggar Gorju and the harelip Marcel survives even the disillusionments of melancholy experience. What first attracts them to Christianity is "the tenderness toward the humble, the defence of the poor, the exaltation of the oppressed" (IX, 265) which they discover in the New Testament, and what finally repels them is the sad realization that this religion of the downtrodden has become "the tool of government" (IX, 296). By the time the novel breaks off these harmless eccentrics are being hauled into court for provocatively taking the part of a captured poacher and Pécuchet is seditiously fulminating against the sacrosanct Penal Code. By persevering in their willful devotion to liberty and their outspoken advocacy of the unfortunate the farcical interlopers have become an appreciable menace to the self-contented equilibrium of the social order.

Resistance to oppression and sympathy with misfortune are not their only titles to glory, however, for Bouvard and Pécuchet are pre-eminently the comic heroes of intellect. Even the most absurd of their blunders is motivated by a "burning thirst" for truth (VIII, 250) that cannot be slaked by evasions or lies, and in comparison with the smug certitudes of the village notables their very penchant for error appears enlightened. "By wishing to understand everything," the priest direly admonishes, "you run down a dangerous slope" (IX, 281). But neither the buffets of experience nor the warnings of authority can deter these intrepid investigators from pursuing their quest. Ludicrous the results often are, yet as their multifarious inquiries turn from horticulture and chemistry to the studies of man their observations increasingly manifest a mordant critical faculty not dissimilar to that of Gustave Flaubert.[52] (Apropos of Balzac, Pécuchet demurs, for example, "We shall have novels on every trade and every province, then on every town and the floors of every house and every individual, which will be no longer literature but statistics or ethnography" [V, 154].) Their reluctance to espouse partial or inadequate solutions is both the cause of their failure and the sign of their intellectual integrity. If they ascertain no answers they are all the more insistent in asking questions, and this subversive proclivity, more than anything else, isolates them from their community by laying bare the contradictions and falsehoods that underlie its complacent assumptions. That they give free utterance to "abominable paradoxes" that "undermined all foundations" is sufficient to classify Bouvard and Pécuchet as revolutionaries and to call down anathema on their heads, for their "pitiable faculty . . . of perceiving stupidity and no longer tolerating it" (VIII, 258) is the one challenge that Chavignolles can least affort to condone.

"Oh, doubt! doubt!" Pécuchet laments: "I should like extinction better!" (VIII, 250). Even so, neither he nor his comrade shrinks from confronting the doubts that necessarily result from persistence in failure. And if the uncertainty in which their clownish efforts repeatedly culminate is a paramount source of their comedy, their willingness to acknowledge uncertainty and renew the interminable search is the crowning proof of their heroism. No goal can satisfy the restless desires of these Faustian fumblers; but perhaps, as Pécuchet comes to understand, "The object of one's thought has less value than the manner of thinking . . . The important thing is to believe at all" (IX, 305). With this provisional awareness Bouvard and Pécuchet are left at the end of Flaubert's unconcluded novel. Their refusal to remain content with any object unworthy of their belief is in itself the true measure of their boundless capacity to believe; their skepticism has preserved the ardor of faith, and in the Socratic cognition of ignorance is their authentic—if Pyrrhic—triumph. What they repudiate, with growing determination and insight, is the consolation of an illusive finality; and if ineptitude, as Flaubert once declared, "consists in wishing to conclude,"[53] Bouvard and Pécuchet prove to be paradoxically the least inept of men. By their joyful decision (as outlined in Flaubert's sketch for an ending) "to copy as in the old days" (348) they are deliberately electing not to conclude, and through this purposeful renunciation they at last attain—as Raymond Queneau remarks[54]—the wisdom that had hitherto eluded their most tenacious endeavors. No alternative to a world of ubiquitous stupidity is available to them; in that sure knowledge is their emancipation. Their copying will now be an act of discrimination, a critical compendium (such as those that Flaubert delighted to make and proposed to append to his novel)[55] of the most banal clichés and obtuse remarks of their age: the ripest fruit, in short, of their hard-earned and highly developed faculty of perceiving stupidity. "*Copier comme autrefois*" may indeed be a cry of defeat, since it means the sad relinquishment of every grandiose enterprise in which Bouvard and Pécuchet had placed their innocent hopes; but in the exhilarant certainty that here there will be no failure, since they have found their vocation at last, their gleeful resolution is simultaneously a paean of victory. They know the futility of concluding and wish instead to begin. In this high-hearted spirit, Flaubert's closing words tell us, "They set to work."

IX

ULYSSES AND HERMES

IN MODERN TIMES

———————— ❦ ————————

BETWEEN THE grand aspirations of the Renaissance visionaries who presumed to transubstantiate a world of iron into gold through audacious imagination and the desperate *pis aller* of Bouvard and Pécuchet, "to copy as in the old days," the comic hero's essential distinctness has grown ever more tenuous as the scope of his efforts diminished. The terminal disenchantment of Falstaff and Don Quixote has now become his point of departure, and in a world that he no longer hopes to alter he may even, like Kierkegaard's knight of faith, be difficult to distinguish from his adversaries. "When one looks at him one might suppose that he was a clerk who had lost his soul in an intricate system of book-keeping."[1] Yet through infinite resignation and by virtue of the absurd the comic hero, no less than the knight, abides by his faith and celebrates his quiet triumphs where others (if they notice at all) see only defeat.

Recognition of Joyce's *Ulysses* as "a great comic novel," and of its comedy as "an aspect of the heroic,"[2] was neither widespread nor immediate. In reaction to the intemperate calumnies of reviewers and customs officials—privately seconded by many prominent writers[3]—Joyce's early apologists, with Valery Larbaud and T. S. Eliot in the vanguard, strove to solemnize his book as a modern classic by emphasizing its mythical sub-structure and allusive technique.[4] Thenceforward its canoniza-tion as holy writ (with all the obscurity appropriate to the genre) was portentously rapid. Even Judge Woolsey's celebrated decision in the case of *United States of America* v. *One Book Called "Ulysses"* condoningly found the accused "somewhat tragic,"[5] thus raising the question of whether a comic novel would have been so readily exculpated. Joyce himself, to be sure, had decreed in his Paris notebook of 1903 that "tragedy is the imperfect manner and comedy the perfect manner in art,"[6] and Joyce was above all things a perfectionist. But the laughter that his friend Frank Budgen clearly heard reverberating throughout a book whose "prevailing mood" he found to be humor[7] awakened little response in readers gravely intent on ferreting out the recondite and symbolic. The unassuming Mr Leopold Bloom was soon submerged by the commentators in a hydra-headed avatar of Ulysses, Moses, Elijah, Ahasuerus, Hamlet *père,* and Jesus Christ, among others; he cannot take a bath without his tub (one eminent exegete apprises his readers) becoming "a chalice or ciborium and he, Jesus Himself or the wine and bread of the Eucharist."[8] And the wife of this prodigy is even more awesome: "regarded under her prototypal and symbolic aspects," Stuart Gilbert affirms on the implied au-thority of her creator, she is "a trinity of personages: Penelope, Calypso and the Earth herself, Gaea-Tellus," with Cybele tacked on for good measure — "the Great Mother of gods, giants and mankind, a personification of the infinite variety of Nature as she has developed by gradual differentiation from the form-less plasma of her beginning."[9]

By giving license to folderol of this nature Joyce, who took delight in arcane correspondences long before plunging into the bottomless wordpool of *Finnegans Wake,* permitted the richly comic and deeply human core of his book to be entangled and very nearly engulfed by an overgrowth of symbolic accre-tions. But the flesh and blood of the corpulent Leopold Bloom happily resist reduction to wafer and wine (or any such hocus-pocus penny a lump), and not all the mumbo-jumbo of Gaea-Tellus and formless plasma can wholly obscure the reassuringly firm outlines of Molly. "O, rocks!" she perpetually defies her heedless expositors: "Tell us in plain words" (64).

The words in which *Ulysses* is told are of course notoriously not plain, for the narrative is complex in proportion to the hidden depths of its subject. The meek and ostensibly unexceptional Bloom gradually emerges, when seen in the multiplicity of his inner life and latent affinities, as a hero no less versatile and resilient, mutatis mutandis, than the resourceful Odysseus of Homeric legend. Only from without is Bloom's existence drab and insignificant; to follow the peregrinations of his mind is to be struck by its vividness and diversity. As his thoughts zigzag from the movement of bowels to the transmigration of souls he too, like his eminent prototype, is a man of numberless twists and turns. In contrast to the brooding Stephen Dedalus, who single-mindedly strives to discern an ineluctable modality in the signatures of all things, Bloom is content to allow his untethered reflections to drift more or less at random on the stream of life, spurning nothing as too trivial or too exalted for his inquisitive scrutiny. Whatever crosses his consciousness, however fleetingly, strikes a sympathetic chord. By his capacity to assimilate the experience and know the mind of many men he ranges no less widely than the first Ulysses, and through the extraordinary catholicity of his responses an unremarkable June day in a minor European capital takes on the dimensions of an adventure illimitable by place or time.

Mr Bloom is not, to be sure, a prodigy of learning, and his many detractors have scorned both the plebeian vulgarity of his preoccupations (although the obsession with things cloacal is not his) and the embarrassing superficiality of his intellect in comparison with their own. But in Bloom's case, at least, the lack is distinctly an asset, since his mind, if not by any measure profound, has a flexibility and inventiveness that formal education never bestows and seldom enhances. His culture is sufficiently ecumenical to extend from *Hamlet* to *Sweets of Sin* and from "Là ci darem la mano" to "Love's Old Sweet Song"; every *objet trouvé,* whether diamond or paste, contributes to the cinematic mosaic of a consciousness forever in progress. The concatenation of seemingly random thoughts and impressions to which we are rendered privy in the confessional of interior monologue exhibits not a lifeless collection of isolated banalities, as many early readers assumed, but an incessant mental activity striving with intense curiosity after the elusive connection and secret meaning of things apparently insignificant and unrelated. (Under the single rubric of "Scientific curiosity" Richard M. Kain catalogues such diverse phenomena as "feelings of mice," "electricity from cat," "taste of swan meat," "sensation of blind," "nature of perfume," sunspots, acoustics, ventriloquism, and Spinoza;[10] for Bloom they are somehow all of a piece in a world that comprises them all.)

His intelligence is not only speculative, however, but symbolic — indeed mythopoeic — as well. Like the potato in his pocket everything within his broad purview is potentially talismanic. An ad for Plumtree's potted meat evokes the corpse of Paddy Dignam, and the strains of Don Giovanni's amorous proposition intermingle with stealthy thoughts of the lecherous Boylan. Bloom overlooks nothing and inwardly transfigures all that he sees and remembers into something frequently rich and almost invariably strange. By virtue of this transformative mental power he is no mere travesty of bygone glory, despite the immeasurably altered circumstances and shrunken opportunities of his world, but a worthy counterpart and successor to the tirelessly inventive Ulysses of yore.

"Among other things," Joyce remarked to Budgen, "my book is the epic of the human body":[11] here too his well-rounded hero upholds an ancient tradition. The prevalent reference to the bodily functions in *Ulysses* — often by the "old Saxon words known," as Judge Woolsey sagely opined, "to almost all men and, I venture, to many women"[12] — seemed to early readers a bold if not a scandalous innovation in a "serious" work of fiction. In comedy, of course, it had long been the stock in trade. What Joyce revived was not simply the "obscenity" of Aristophanes or Rabelais but the immemorial comic celebration of man's sublimely defiant animality. From his breakfast of grilled mutton kidneys until he wearily sinks to rest at the end of his day Bloom steadfastly affirms the dignity of man in his humblest pursuits and least dignified postures. This mental man is equally a physical man, albeit modest of appetite and sparing of gratification. Like his prudent classical model he shuns dearth and surfeit alike and neither exalts nor mortifies his bodily needs. He may daydream of oriental languor and voluptuous torments but in humble fact he assuages his sexual cravings no less expeditiously than his stomach pangs: "Up like a rocket, down like a stick . . . For this relief much thanks" (364, 366). Yet the very sparsity of Bloom's sensual pleasures is the index of their supreme importance, since despite recurrent nostalgia and sporadic fantasies he is fundamentally content with what life provides, and demands no more. He is a man for whom the physical world not only exists but suffices; he affirms it not with Molly's somnolent ecstasy but with a wide-awake recognition of its imperfections and limits.

In the end, after all, there is no other; for Bloom is serenely free of the lingering transcendental beliefs and doubts that torment the apostate Stephen. In All Hallows Church he observes the communicants with a detached yet sympathetic amusement wholly devoid of regret or envy. "Now I bet it makes them feel happy," he muses. "Lollipop. It does. Yes, bread of angels it's called. There's a big idea behind it, kind of kingdom of God is within you feel. First communicants. Hokypoky penny a lump" (79-80). But his tolerance for the Christian communion does not extend to the Christian doctrine of afterlife. When Mr. Kernan solemnly intones "*I am the resurrection and the life*" at Paddy Dignam's graveside and observes, "That touches a man's inmost heart," Bloom politely assents, but thinks to himself:

Your heart perhaps but what price the fellow in the six feet by two with his toes to the daisies? No touching that. Seat of the affections. Broken heart. A pump after all, pumping thousands of gallons of blood every day. One fine day it gets bunged up and there you are. Lots of them lying around here: lungs, hearts, livers. Old rusty pumps: damn the thing else. The resurrection and the life. Once you are dead you are dead. That last day idea. Knocking them all up out of their graves. Come forth, Lazarus! And he came fifth and lost the job. Get up! Last day! Then every fellow

mousing around for his liver and his lights and the rest of his
traps. Find damn all of himself that morning. Pennyweight
of powder in a skull. Twelve grammes one pennyweight.
Troy measure.

(104)

On no other subject does the gentle Bloom's wit wax so sardonic or his patience wear so thin: "Plant him," he savagely
thinks, "and have done with him" (111). Death is no stranger to
his thoughts, which several times revert to his father's suicide
and the premature death of his only son; but he will not pal-
liate its grim horror ("Saltwhite crumbling mush of corpse"
[113]) or seek to gainsay its finality with comforting falsehoods.
The placebo of life after death is a derogation of life before
death, and Bloom will have none of it; his sole recompense for
the sorrow of dying is the joy of being alive. The poignant recol-
lection of little Rudy's death, aroused by a glimpse of young
Dedalus from the funeral carriage, immediately revives the
memory of his conception ("Must have been that morning in
Raymond terrace she was at the window, watching the two dogs
at it by the wall . . . Give us a touch, Poldy. God, I'm dying for
it. How life begins"), then brings to mind the living daughter
whose letter Bloom has just received: "Molly. Milly. Same thing
watered down . . . Yes, yes: a woman too. Life. Life" (88). For
Bloom, as for his regal precursor in the kingdom of shadows,
the overwhelming awareness of death serves to intensify his
commitment to life by making the terms of his choice unmistakably clear. "Back to the world again. Enough of this place
. . . There is another world after death named hell," he reflects,
and transforms a slip of the pen by his lovelorn correspondent
Martha Clifford into a fervent affirmation: "I do not like that
other world she wrote. No more do I. Plenty to see and hear
and feel yet. Feel live warm beings near you. Let them sleep in
their maggoty beds. They are not going to get me this innings.
Warm beds: warm fullblooded life" (113). Despite his intimate
acquaintance with the imperfections and frustrations of living
no hero has ever been more absolute than the mildmannered
Bloom in proclaiming this most fundamental of all comic val-

ues. "In the midst of death," he meditates, reversing the solemn memento of Christian homiletics, "we are in life" (106). In his steadfast allegiance to the world of the living this comic hero will be shaken by nothing.

Yet if he firmly renounces "that other world," in this one Mr Bloom finds himself, for all his deference, almost as much an alien as the self-conscious young poet whose destiny, on this notable sixteenth of June, inexorable chance repeatedly intertwines with his own. What sets him apart is less the external peculiarity of being a converted Jew in pugnaciously Catholic Ireland than the attendant emancipation of his feelings and thoughts. His skeptical bent and inquisitive temper derive in large part from his knowledge that he belongs to no sect and can rely on no unquestioned beliefs, and it is this openness to contingency that marks him off (both in their eyes and his own) from his smug fellow townsmen. In a world of facile clichés and overblown rhetoric — a world buffeted by the winds of "Aeolus" and steeped in the treacle of "Nausicaa" — Bloom exercises the hazardous freedom of thinking thoughts and expressing opinions unmistakably his own, and others obliquely acknowledge his heroism by finding the eccentricity comic.

Bloom is distinguished (and isolated), however, not only by independence of thought but by tolerant concern for the thoughts and feelings of others — by "that plenitude of sufferance which base minds jeer at, rash judgers scorn and all find tolerable and but tolerable" (401). He is above all, Joyce observed to Budgen, "a good man,"[13] and his goodness stems from his boundless capacity for sympathetic identification. No bedraggled cur or mangy nag can cross his path without arousing commiseration, and his vegetarian impulse is reinforced by the thought of "wretched brutes there at the cattlemarket waiting for the poleaxe to split their skulls open. Moo. Poor trembling calves. Meh" (168). Among his own species his compassion extends not only to the dead, from poor Dignam to his own heartbroken old father, but to the bereft and helpless, like Dignam's orphaned son, and to all who suffer derision or pain. Joyce himself "preferred people whom the world rated as failures,"[14] according to his brother Stanislaus, and Bloom continually evinces the comic hero's ancient affinity with outcasts and underdogs. His compassion arises not from abstract principles of charity but from his vivid ability to project himself into the situation of others, like Mina Purefoy whom he plans to visit during the travails of a difficult labor: "Three days imagine groaning on a bed with a vinegared handkerchief round her forehead, her belly swollen out! Phew! Dreadful simply! Child's head too big: forceps. Doubled up inside her trying to butt its way out blindly, groping for the way out. Kill me that would" (159). Circumscribed though his opportunity for beneficence may be, Bloom's unheralded efforts on behalf of the unfortunate, whether Dignam's family, Mina Purefoy, or Stephen Dedalus, entirely justify his protestation, amid the mocking shadows of Nighttown, that he is "doing good to others" (445), and validate the mild satisfaction he takes, at the end of his day, "To have sustained no positive loss. To have brought a positive gain to others. Light to the gentiles" (660).

It is fittingly Bloom's humanity that brings him into collision with the imperfectly humanized denizens of the Cyclops' cave known to Dubliners as Barney Kiernan's tavern. The Homeric parallel—often little more than a private joke—here plays a key role in contrasting the brute and the human, but between the *Odyssey* and *Ulysses* the terms of the contrast have significantly changed. The Cyclops of Homer's epic was a savage, dwelling in rude seclusion from his lawless fellow-creatures, "a man clothed in great strength," as Odysseus described him to Alcinous, "a wild man, ignorant of laws and customs."[15] Against his invincible might the Greek hero opposed the agile intelligence that constituted the new-found glory of civilization. The Dublin Cyclops, in contrast, despite his kindred penchant for stupid force, is no primitive herdsman but a "citizen" and self-proclaimed spokesman for Irish national culture. Only in bellicose rodomontade is this patriot gigantic, but by its means he becomes "a broadshouldered deepchested stronglimbed frankeyed redhaired freely freckled shaggybearded widemouthed largenosed longheaded deepvoiced barekneed brawnyhanded hairylegged ruddyfaced sinewyarmed hero" adorned with "the tribal images of many Irish heroes and heroines of antiquity"

(291), from Cuchulin and Dante Alighieri to the Bride of Lammermoor and Patrick W. Shakespeare.

To this doughty Hibernian's magniloquent braggadocio, which is barely distinguishable from the bloated parodies that envelop it, his reluctant antagonist, "O'Bloom, the son of Rory . . . he of the prudent soul" (292), returns soft words that signally fail to turn away wrath. Indeed, the sweet reasonableness of the professorial Bloom, "with his jawbreakers" (the abusive narrator scoffs) "about phenomenon and science and this phenomenon and the other phenomenon" (299), is in itself a red flag to the bigoted citizen, who brusquely dismisses the quibbling irrelevancies of mere reason.

> —The memory of the dead, says the citizen taking up his pintglass and glaring at Bloom . . .
> —You don't grasp my point, says Bloom. What I mean is . . .
> —*Sinn Fein!* says the citizen. *Sinn fein amhain!* The friends we love are by our side and the foes we hate before us.
>
> (301)

Not the citizen's insults alone, but his rabid xenophobia—"We want no more strangers in our house" (318)—and above all his mindless exaltation of force finally provoke the softspoken Bloom to denounce persecution and proclaim his passionate solidarity with the archetypal nation of outcasts from which he is sprung: "a race," he declares, ". . . that is hated and persecuted. Also now. This very moment. This very instant" (326).

> —Are you talking about the new Jerusalem? says the citizen.
> —I'm talking about injustice, says Bloom.
>
> (327)

And if this momentary defiance seemingly "collapses all of a sudden . . . as limp as a wet rag," it is not for lack of courage but because Bloom sadly perceives the futility of any resistance

that employs the instruments of the oppressor even for justified
defense or retaliation.

>   —But it's no use, says he. Force, hatred, history, all that.
> That's not life for men and women, insult and hatred. And
> everybody knows that it's the very opposite of that that is
> really life.
>   —What? says Alf.
>   —Love, says Bloom. I mean the opposite of hatred.
>
> (327)

His insistent adherence to life has now become, by definition, a
commitment to love, and by promulgating his heretical gospel
in the very lair of the beast this comic Messiah for Ireland does
indeed bring light to the gentiles, even though the gentiles (in
true Cyclopean fashion) be too nearly blind to discern it from
darkness.

Charity for his fellow man—the most distinctly Christian of
virtues—has drawn Bloom to this alien habitat in an effort to
secure Dignam's widow her due. Yet the false rumor that he is
hoarding the earnings made on a racehorse at odds of twenty to
one is sufficient, in his enemy's clouded eye, to convict him as a
defrauder of widows and orphans, a wolf in sheep's clothing, an
Ahasuerus cursed by God. "There's a jew for you!" the narrator
sneers: "All for number one. Cute as a shithouse rat. Hundred
to five" (335). Persecution ceases to be a foreign affair when
Bloom returns to the tavern after a brief departure and unexpectedly encounters a pint-sized pogrom. In the face of a
chorus of defamation the apostle of peace—like Jesus among
the moneychangers—flings his customary forbearance aside
and surpasses the grandiose Gael himself in asserting the claims
of his own maligned race. "Mendelssohn was a jew," he proudly
affirms, "and Karl Marx and Mercadante and Spinoza. And
the Saviour was a jew and his father was a jew . . . Your God
was a jew. Christ was a jew like me" (336). To this outrageous
affirmation the citizen can only retort by seizing a biscuitbox
and threatening apt retribution: "—By Jesus, says he, I'll brain
that bloody jewman for using the holy name. By Jesus, I'll cru-

cify him so I will." But as "old sheepface" gesticulates from a
vanishing taxi pursued by the blinded citizen's clattering tin
and snarling mongrel his colossal encounter with the Polyphemus of Dublin culminates instead in a dazzling apotheosis
that annihilates the separation of styles in this episode by infus-
ing the biblical sublime of high parody with the narrator's irrepressibly colloquial verve.

> And they beheld Him in the chariot, clothed upon in the
> glory of the brightness, having raiment as of the sun, fair as
> the moon and terrible that for awe they durst not look upon
> Him. And there came a voice out of heaven, calling: *Elijah!*
> *Elijah!* And he answered with a main cry: *Abba! Adonai!*
> And they beheld Him even Him, ben Bloom Elijah, amid
> clouds of angels ascend to the glory of the brightness at an
> angle of fortyfive degrees over Donohoe's in Little Green
> Street like a shot off a shovel.
>
> (339)

In Joyce no less than in Aristophanes or Rabelais the grand
solemnity of burlesque transcends mere derision, and not even
the jaundiced "I" through whom we have witnessed these events
in their everyday light can wholly restrain his wonder. (The
narrator, Joyce remarked to Budgen, turns out to be "really a
great admirer of Bloom who, besides being a better man, is also
more cunning, a better talker, and more fertile in expedients"[16]
than his brutish opponent.) Nowhere else does Bloom so explicitly articulate the humane dedication to justice and love
that sets him apart—far more essentially than his foreign origins or eccentric notions—from his meaner compatriots, and
nowhere else does he so overtly dispute the communal codes
that foment injustice and hatred. Nor is he unaware of the
secret strength of those who meekly hunger and thirst after
righteousness. "People could put up with being bitten by a
wolf," he later reflects as he chuckles over his devastating
riposte to the citizen, "but what properly riled them was a bite
from a sheep" (642). Pacifist though he be, his goodness by no
means lacks teeth, for like the deprecated comic heroes of every

age this milquetoast of a man commands the determination and skill to defy an implacably hostile world, if need be, in defense of his paramount values. "Justice!" will be his cry in the swirling vortex of Circe, when humanity itself is at stake: "All Ireland versus one!" (531). The odds are nothing short of heroic.

Yet from his sense of being apart arise his deepest affinities. No one could be further removed from Bloom's sensuous immediacy and sympathetic responsiveness than the remorseful and inward-looking Stephen Dedalus, yet "Though they didn't see eye to eye in everything," Bloom ruminates toward the end of their day, "a certain analogy there somehow was, as if both their minds were travelling, so to speak, in the one train of thought" (640). Each has abandoned his ancestral faith with no certainty of finding another, and their common "disbelief in many orthodox religious, national, social and ethical doctrines" unites them in "an inherited tenacity of heterodox resistance" (650). In contrast to their respective antagonists and bêtes noires, Malachi Mulligan and Blazes Boylan — the joking Jesus and the jaunty Giovanni — both Stephen and Bloom endure the loneliness of autonomy, although Bloom has attained a degree of objective (and therefore comic) detachment from his private cares that permits him a solicitude for others lacking in the self-centered and humorless Stephen. Both are exiles more or less consciously searching for a communion that neither church nor country can offer, and in this shared awareness of want their true affinity lies. Bloom's beneficent impulse at last finds an outlet in action when he magnanimously rescues Stephen from the Circean sty into which his false companions have lured him, and the latent kinship between them is symbolized by the haunting visions of a lost parent and child in which this nightmare episode reaches its emotional climax. What long-range consequences, if any, their encounter may have lie outside the drama; but the compassionate humanity of the comic Ulysses provides, at least for the moment, a sorely needed corrective to the brooding introspection of the mordant Telemachus, and suggests a possible future escape from the solipsistic labyrinth in which the young artificer has imprisoned himself.

Bloom's tenuous relation with Stephen rests on an essentially intellectual attraction; his union with Molly is of a more instinctive and durable nature. Despite a "deficient mental development" (670) thoroughly impervious to amelioration and a literary taste more inclined to Paul de Kock than to Shakespeare, Molly turns out, in her highly unorthodox fashion, to be the faithful Penelope with whom a vagrant Ulysses is (somewhat imperfectly) reunited in the somnolent epithalamium that brings the comedy to its jubilant close. Her wayward reflections concerning her cuckolded husband are by no means uniformly flattering, yet she alone is genuinely responsive to the qualities that make him heroic as well as comic. To others Bloom's attractions (unlike his wife's well-distributed charms) remain an enigma: "In God's name," the solicitor John Henry Menton marvels, "what did she marry a coon like that for?" (105). But though John Henrys come and go till one resembles another, Poldy abides. In independence of judgment and warmth of emotion, frank corporeality and instinctive hunger for life he is Molly's unique counterpart; and again their shared unlikeness is what binds them together. "Why me?" he remembers asking in the days of their courtship: "Because you were so foreign from the others" (373).

In the end, contrary to all appearances, faith triumphs over infidelity. Throughout the day thoughts of Boylan's assignation with Molly oppress Bloom's spirit, reaching a frenzied crescendo as he pictures the insolent usurper's arrival at 7 Eccles Street: "One rapped on a door, one tapped with a knock, did he knock Paul de Kock, with a loud proud knocker, with a cock carracarracarra cock. Cockcock" (278). But when he himself returns to his desecrated bedchamber in the small hours of the morning he has already passed through envy and jealousy to abnegation and the equanimity of his weary reflection "that each one who enters imagines himself to be the first to enter whereas he is always the last term of a preceding series even if the first term of a succeeding one, each imagining himself to be first, last, only and alone, whereas he is neither first nor last nor only nor alone in a series originating in and repeated to infinity" (716). The usurping suitors have been reduced to uniform ciphers: resignation can go no farther.

Bloom's triumph is not confined, however, to acquiescence in his serial lot, for in the inner sanctum of dream and memory he attains the devoutly wished consummation that persistently eludes him in his waking existence. In "The Dead," the last and longest story of *Dubliners*, Gabriel Conroy's fragile self-possession is shattered by the chance discovery that his outwardly faithful wife has remained attached in her heart to a boy who had died — "for me," she quietly tells him — many years before. "While he had been full of memories of their secret life together, full of tenderness and joy and desire, she had been comparing him in her mind with another."[17] With this obliterating realization he feels himself irresistibly drawn toward the vast impalpable region of the dead. In contrast to the highly respected Gabriel Conroy Leopold Bloom is a cuckold notorious to all Dublin, yet to him his adulterous wife devotes her most ardent thoughts in a region emphatically of the living. Even though Hugh Boylan has performed yeoman service "with that tremendous big red brute of a thing he has" (727), he is an "ignoramus that doesnt know poetry from a cabbage" (761), and poetry is at least as essential to Molly as copulation; her rhapsody, unlike her coitus, is uninterrupted. Bloom, on the other hand, for all his "plabbery" manner and vexatious foibles, not only touches his wife's warm heart with his gallantries and kindness but "has more spunk in him" too (727). If he is not first, last, nor alone in partaking of Molly's generous favors neither is he no more than one of a series, since it is into Bloom that all the others finally dissolve in a rapturous celebration not of brute sexuality but of passionate love.

Several times during his day Bloom reverts to the memory of his ecstatic first union with Molly on Howth Hill. "Wildly I lay on her, kissed her; eyes, her lips, her stretched neck, beating, woman's breasts full in her blouse of nun's veiling, fat nipples upright" (173), he recalls, until the buzzing of a stuck fly awakens the inescapable knowledge of subsequent infidelity. "I am a fool perhaps," he reflects in the aftermath of his barren tryst with the lame Nausicaa of Sandymount, Gerty McDowell: "He gets the plums and I the plumstones . . . Names change: that's all" (370). Only in the inviolate intimacy of nocturnal reflection does the long-suffering hero vanquish his numberless rivals by the invisible arrows of love, for in the rapturous memory that they share with none other husband and wife, for all their divisions, are secretly one. The swelling magnificat of Molly's climactic affirmation — "and I thought well as well him as another and then I asked him with my eyes to ask again yes and then he asked me would I yes to say yes my mountain flower and first I put my arms around him yes and drew him down to me so he could feel my breasts all perfume yes and his heart was going like mad and yes I said yes I will Yes" (768) — pays unforgettable tribute to the invincible prowess of the self-effacing and faintly ridiculous conqueror who lies with his head at her toes, "the childman weary, the manchild in the womb" (722), serenely at rest and sublimely oblivious of his moment of triumph.

The subject of Ulysses was for Joyce "the most human in world literature,"[18] and while composing his book, as Budgen recalls, he talked "first of the principal character . . . and only later of the manifold devices through which he presented him."[19] By his paramount humanity the modern Ulysses elevates the common man's tenacious passivity to the status of heroism in the service of life, which is really love; and his unassuming preeminence endows Joyce's tour de force of avantgarde technique with the indelibly "popular character"[20] that Budgen was initially among the few to discern. Despite sporadic daydreams of oriental luxury or nirvana and fleeting hallucinations of a "new Bloomusalem in the Nova Hibernia of the future" (475), Bloom knows, with the tempered resignation of a man in the middle of life, that his world is subject neither to radical mutation nor to lasting transcendence. He can draw no strength from madness or youth, like Don Quixote or Don Juan, but must patiently make do with the here and now; for immutable and inescapable though it be, this workaday world is not without glory. But his modest heroism, if far less venturous than that of his bold precursors, is all the more essential because his century knows no other. No Achilles or Lancelot, Hotspur or Amadis, nor even so much as a Pamela or Childe Harold inspires him by the example of high heroical contrast. It is now paradoxically by the comic dissenter himself, in default of more honored defenders, that "the much despised 'bourgeois' virtues of honesty, kindliness, prudent generosity and the rest," as Budgen observes with regard to Bloom, "are reaffirmed and even exalted."[21] Once a society has lost its self-confident sense of purpose it makes a mockery precisely of those who most truly embody its deepest values, and its legitimate heroes, in consequence, must be comic.

There is, at the same time, an inherent pathos—and potential danger—in this diffident outsider's attempts to abide by the rules (and even win the esteem) of a social order whose human deficiencies he challenges almost by inadvertence. Because he envisages no viable alternative to the world as it is he cannot exempt himself from its characteristic lack of direction; what he stands for, and against, will often be far from apparent even in his own eyes. Joyce's hero largely avoids this pitfall by the unimpaired vitality of his instincts (most forcefully articulated in "Hades" and "Cyclops"); but for others the prevalence of incertitude frustrates or precludes heroic response.

Franz Kafka's hapless protagonists, for example, fully share the benevolent impulse of comic heroes since Don Quixote but are powerless to battle an adversary whom they can never define nor even clearly distinguish from themselves. They are aliens perpetually compromised by their desire to belong. ("Men are afraid of freedom and responsibility," Kafka purportedly remarked to Gustav Janouch. "So they prefer to hide behind the prison bars which they build around themselves.")[22] Gregor Samsa in "The Metamorphosis" and Joseph K. in *The Trial* are beyond the point of questioning or protesting the absurdity of their circumstances; but the youthful Karl Rossmann of Kafka's fragmentary first novel, *Amerika*, rushes no less ardently than the comic heroes of Fielding or Byron to the defense of his downtrodden fellow man. When the stoker whom he encounters by chance amid the ship's numberless cabins

bemoans his ill-treatment by his superior, Schubal, Karl unhesitatingly urges him to protest and proclaims to the ship's assembled officers that his friend has been the victim of an injustice.
Despite his unquestioning belief in the stoker's cause, however,
Karl finds himself bereft of trustworthy guidelines either in his
comrade's incoherent plea or in his own uncorroborated con-
victions. Spontaneous sympathy, he discovers, is no grounds on
which to rest a persuasive defense. Karl's impassioned advocacy
is undermined, moreover, by his obtrusive preoccupation with
the verdict that others might be passing on *him*. "If only his
father and mother could see him now, fighting for justice in a
strange land before men of authority, and, though not yet triumphant, dauntlessly resolved to win the final victory! Would
they revise their opinion of him?" he wonders. "Set him between them and praise him? Look into his eyes at last, at last,
these eyes so filled with devotion to them? Ambiguous questions, and this the most unsuitable moment to ask them!"[23]
Karl's exacerbated self-consciousness saps his impetuous faith
by reducing it to nothing more than a subjective and troub-
lingly self-indulgent emotion. He in fact knows nothing about
the rights and wrongs of the cause he has so warmly espoused,
since the culpability of the plausible Schubal is no more demonstrable than the innocence of the pitiful stoker. Karl's comforting assumption that a confrontation between the two
"would achieve, even before a human tribunal, the result which
would have been awarded by divine justice"[24] merely begs the
question by injecting still another unknown. There is simply no
way for Karl to confirm the validity of his faltering instincts,
and this impossibility corrodes his initial predisposition to action and leaves him as much a victim of irresolution as the
tongue-tied stoker whom he at last abandons. His eerily disconnected adventures in the comic wonderland of a new world will
only exacerbate his bewilderment, and the Theatre of Oklahoma toward which he is hopefully journeying when the book
breaks off will be no more certain of access, in this America of
receding mirages, than the enigmatic castle that will beckon
the land surveyor K. in the last and most tantalizing of Kafka's
unfinished parables.

Those who do persevere in the sisyphean labor of upholding
the values of life in the twentieth century are not impetuous
adolescents like Rossmann, on the whole, but seasoned veterans
like Schweik, Chaplin, and Bloom, who can summon stamina
to their aid when spontaneity fails. In his native land Saul Bellow's middle-aged Henderson, to take a further example, is a
"regular bargain basement of deformities"[25] beaten down and
bewildered by a society whose lunacy he can cope with only by
flight. But "When you come right down to it," he recognizes in
the wilds of tribal Africa, "there aren't many guys who have
stuck with real life through thick and thin, like me. It's my
most basic loyalty."[26] The rediscovery of this fundamental but
long dormant allegiance stirs his deadened spirit to unaccustomed exultation, and by redeeming the senseless suffering of a
wasted lifetime transmutes the pathetic victim of a disordered
civilization into a comic hero striving manfully to achieve his
rejuvenation: "no Milquetoast," as he proudly asserts, "but a
person of strength and courage. Plenty of moxie."[27]

Among the most courageous standard-bearers of human
autonomy in our age have been the dissident old, who have
stubbornly refused to be cast aside as outworn remnants of a
utilitarian social order. The feisty heroine of Elio Vittorini's
short novel *La Garibaldina* remembers her youthful glory with
a zest reminiscent of the Wife of Bath: "You should have seen
me, even at the beginning of the century," she boasts to the
puzzled soldier whom she has befriended on their train ride
through Sicily, "what a fine strapping whore I was!"[28] But when
this rebel aristocrat makes her last apparition, on horseback at
dawn, to the fellow maverick who has joined her in a gleeful
communion overriding all distinctions of sex, class, or age, she
is marvelous "exactly in this," the author declares, "that she
accepted being, and made no effort not to be, old—beyond
everything one can have when young and yet not beyond everything in life."[29] She is no less capriciously winsome—and no less
resolutely combative—in the pride of old age than in the impulsiveness of youth, and from her infectious vitality arises the
jubilation that irrepressibly wells into song in the young soldier's heart. In this flabby-cheeked, preposterous old lady the

spirit of Garibaldi's high-hearted Red Shirts survives the extinction of their incandescent ideals.

Nor have sixty-seven years of continuous poverty and intermittent imprisonment deterred Gulley Jimson, the scandalous artist-hero of Joyce Cary's *The Horse's Mouth*, in his guerrilla warfare in behalf of passion and imagination. Those who denounced modern art as a public menace "were all quite right," Gulley confides to his unwanted disciple, young Nosy: "They knew what modern art can do. Creeping about everywhere, undermining the Church and the State and the Academy and the Law and Marriage and the Government—smashing up civilization, degenerating the Empire."[30] "If it wasn't for imagination," he explains, "we shouldn't need any police or government. The world would be as nice and peaceful and uninteresting as a dead dog full of dead fleas."[31] So long as Gulley Jimson survives to shatter its hallowed taboos and bedaub its colorless walls with the fauna of his refractory fancy, however, such drab tranquility will remain hypothetical and police be in constant demand. Even when his most magnificent wall, "the crowning joy of my life,"[32] is condemned to the wrecker's ball and his magnum opus crumbles away from his brush, toppling Gulley to the ground amid the debris of a smiling whale, he finds no time for recrimination or lament. "Get rid of that sense of justice," he enjoins the sniveling Nosy as an ambulance bears him away half-paralyzed by a stroke, ". . . or you'll feel sorry for yourself, and then you'll soon be dead—blind and deaf and rotten."[33] The Fall of man is for Gulley a "Fall into freedom,"[34] and it is man's freedom to scoff at misfortune that he courageously reaffirms after his own last fall. The inattentive world may be too young to learn but Gulley will not therefore cease to instruct it, and his concluding words in the novel are a solemnization of truly heroic joy. When the ambulance nurse sternly warns him not to talk because "you're very seriously ill," Gulley irreverently replies, "Not so seriously as you're well. How don't you enjoy life, mother," he adds. "I should laugh all round my neck at this minute if my shirt wasn't a bit on the tight side." And to her pious admonishment, "It would be better for you to pray," he answers with eloquent finality, "Same thing, mother."[35] For Gulley laughter in the face of adversity is the ultimate act of imagination and therefore of worship, and every temporal defeat is the stuff of spiritual triumph: "Because," as his tutelary poet proclaimed, "the soul of sweet delight can never be defiled."[36]

Gulley Jimson exalts the dissident but aimless impulsiveness of the Romantic comic hero to a consciously disruptive fine art. With the heedless abandon of an old man who knows his own mind and has nothing to lose he throws the indecision of Rossmann and the prudence of Bloom to the winds and flaunts an outspoken defiance of governing mores almost unparalleled since Falstaff bearded the Lord Chief Justice. When Cary's novel was published in 1944 the prestige of civilization was at a low ebb, and a reckless disregard of its lethal exactions was perhaps the one heroic alternative to existential despair. ("It's the Nazis, is it?" Gulley asks on learning that war has erupted. "Yes, I know all about them. They're against modern art."[37] It is, if not all, enough.) A further consequence of civilized society's collapse as the arbiter of religious and moral values has been the re-emergence of the trickster or charlatan as a figure commanding esteem and even applause. In satirical comedy on the pattern of *Tartuffe* or *Volpone* both the unscrupulous swindler and his willing dupes were subjected to ridicule for violating accepted norms of conduct to which a sagacious observer sometimes gave voice. Once these traditional standards have ceased to compel conviction, however, society, instead of providing a normative paradigm, becomes the main target of a satire that no longer views its perversities as aberrations. In the resulting absence of any higher tribunal that might justly condemn him, the cunning deceiver achieves vindication—like Odysseus or Reynard in more primitive days—by the ingenuity and sheer success of his machinations, for amid universal delusion he alone is in command of himself.

In Alexander Ostrovsky's late nineteenth-century comedy *Enough Stupidity in Every Wise Man* (or *The Scoundrel*)[38] the dissembler Glumov proves no less adept than the knaves of Jonson or Molière in exploiting society's foibles for his own profit by the ancient arts of flattery and deception. But the originality

of Ostrovsky's play lies in its dénouement, for Glumov's unmasking (through the theft of his scathingly forthright diary)
results not in his downfall and exemplary punishment but in
the collective incrimination of his infatuated victims. This
ingratiating master of falsehood betters his smug antagonists in
the end by the truths that he articulates and forces them to confront. "I have far more brains than you," he apprises one of
his outraged accusers, "and you know it." His cajolery has not
so much pandered to accidental weaknesses, it becomes apparent, as ministered to permanent needs — "You can't get on in the
world," he coolly announces, "without a person like me" — and
this knowledge enables him to dismiss them all with sovereign
disdain. "You think that I'll forgive you," he says by way of
farewell. "No, ladies and gentlemen, there'll be plenty to pay
for this."[39] Both his indictment and his threat go unchallenged,
for in a world permeated by self-deception he speaks with the
incontrovertible sincerity that only the deliberate charlatan can
convey. The moral victory of the ending is his by default.

Not until the mid-twentieth century, however, in Thomas
Mann's uncompleted *Confessions of Felix Krull, Confidence
Man*, does an impostor again intertwine dissimulation and
truth with the bold artistry of the consummate comic heroes of
old. *Felix Krull* — an early sketch deftly expanded into a novel
after a forty-year intermission[40] — has been called a picaresque
novel, by Mann himself among others; but in his aptitude for
high fantasy its hero far more nearly resembles the protean
Odysseus and thespian Falstaff, or the inveterate dreamer Don
Quixote, than the cagey offspring of Lazarillo.[41] In contrast to
the hard-boiled pícaro of Spanish tradition, who learns dissimulation through disenchantment and employs it as a calculated technique of brute survival, Felix exults from earliest
childhood in "the independent and self-sufficient exercise of
my imagination" (I. 2) and remains, through all the vicissitudes
of maturity, "a child and dreamer indeed," as he confides to his
reader, "my whole life long" (I. 8). The impersonations in
which he delights, beginning with the masquerades of his
youth, are not stratagems shaped by external need so much as
autonomous creations of an instinctive mimetic urge: an urge

whose utility, it is true, he very quickly perceives. Felix knows that any deception not grounded in a higher truth is incomplete and easily discernible as a mere lie (I. 6). Thus art, as he understands and exemplifies it, is not a denial of nature but its realization, since only by perfecting the make-believe that constitutes his congenital calling does the artist attain authentic fulfillment.

The "perpetual responsiveness" (III. 6) to the physical world and its manifold pleasures that justifies the fortunate name of this Sunday child, Felix, is not a passive but a "concentrated and sustained receptivity" (III. 5). Enjoyment of the infinitely enticing phenomenon of the world demands unremitting solicitude, for all nature — including the artist's own — is no more than the raw material on which the disciplined imagination incessantly strives to improve. "He who really loves the world," Felix declares, "shapes himself to please it" (II. 2) — and the world to please himself. For all its gratifications, then, life is "a heavy and exacting task"; yet from the unstinting performance of this labor of love come the freedom and "joy of life" (I. 5) that Felix first descries as a child in the physically repugnant actor Müller-Rosé. The artist's discipline, unlike the soldier's (which it superficially resembles), must, however, be self-imposed; the essence of his freedom, Felix observes, is "to live like a soldier but not as a soldier, figuratively but not literally, to be allowed in short to live symbolically" (II. 6). The arduously nurtured illusion in which the artist discovers his truth is at the same time the source of his emancipation from the tyranny of unregenerate fact.[42]

The artist can be heroic in solitude — like Gustav von Aschenbach or Adrian Leverkühn in Mann's somberer fictions Felix knows that "privacy and separateness" (III. 1) are his destiny — but he can be a *comic* hero only in relation to others. To the confidence man, by virtue of his profession, society is an indispensable if unwitting accessory, since his art, even more than the actor's, demands an audience that will not begrudge him its credence. The mesmerized spectators who surrendered themselves en masse to the theatrical tricks of Müller-Rosé in Felix' youth remind him of moths or gnats rushing into a flame:

"What unanimity," he retrospectively marvels, "in agreeing to let oneself be deceived! Here quite clearly there is in operation a general human need, implanted by God Himself in human nature, which Müller-Rosé's abilities are created to satisfy" (I. 5). Society stands in need of deceivers (as Ostrovsky's scoundrel had shrewdly discerned) to corroborate its cherished delusions, and by his adeptness in meeting this need the pliable Felix, unlike the intransigent Gulley, becomes as much an accomplice as an antagonist, a pander as a pariah, in his intercourse with a world that he can only defraud by shaping himself to its pleasure.

In the delectable ambiguities of this risky relationship lies the comedy of Felix' situation. Yet to the extent that his impersonations achieve their immediate object of deceiving others, as they almost invariably do, he alone is aware of the contradictions and hence of the comedy. He is fully cognizant, in raptly admiring the skill of Stoudebecker's circus performers, of "a certain distrust . . . in my penetrating observation of the tricks and arts and their effects" (III. 1), and he brings the same detachment to bear in observing his own machinations. This authentic impostor is in fact far too intimately involved in his world to exempt himself from the laughter to which his critical intellect subjects it. Because of his privileged consciousness of his own dissimulation he is uniquely able to see himself as others fail to see him and to take delight in a spectacle so extraordinarily amusing.

Nowhere is Felix' talent for collaborating in the delusions of others—or his adroitness in portraying the comedy of his own equivocal posture—more apparent than in his brief but intense liaison, as a liftboy in Paris, with Diane Philibert Houpflé, the authoress whose jewels he had pocketed when crossing the French frontier. What this bluestocking *d'une intelligence extrême* extorts from her baffled lover is not only physical gratification but the more intense ecstasy of spiritual degradation. "The intellect," she exclaims, "longs for the delights of the non-intellect, that which is alive and beautiful *dans sa stupidité,* in love with it, oh, in love with it to the point of idiocy, to the ultimate self-betrayal and self-denial" (II. 9). Stupidity is not

Felix' forte, yet he fills the lady's unexpected demand with unfailing (if somewhat reluctant) dexterity and even hits on the inspiration of heightening her delicious humiliation by confessing the theft of her jewels. But Diane Philibert will not be outdone and caps his brainstorm by urging him to rifle her remaining valuables while she luxuriates in his stealth. "Fool!" she cries when he momentarily demurs, "It would be the most enchanting fulfilment of our love!" And it is she who rapturously informs her mystified pupil that in perpetrating this theft he is re-enacting the role of Hermes, the primordial trickster and "suave god of thieves" who will henceforth haunt Felix' imagination no less than that of his civilized and respected creator. Only through a self-deluded scribbler of psychological novels and passionate verses who asks, in her ecstasy of abasement, "Tu ne connais pas donc le vers alexandrin — ni le dieu voleur, toi-même si divin?" does Felix "make the acquaintance," as Mann later remarked, "of his mythical archetype,"[43] and thereby of the godlike potential within himself. The comic hero's most momentous encounters, as we have seen, are not infrequently deficient in dignity.

Felix plays the felon in this episode much as Byron's Don Juan played the libertine, by responding almost without volition to the overpowering needs of another; his deceptions are ancillary to his partner's insistent delusions. It is less by deliberate artistry than spontaneous charm that Felix advances himself in the artificial world of Parisian society, and what skill he displays is mainly in extricating himself from unwanted attachments. His native pliability is counterbalanced, however, by a firm awareness that he can never encompass his genuine goals by surrendering to the demands of this world. When the crisis comes he chooses to go his own way. "The main thing," he writes concerning his crucial rejection of Lord Strathbogie's (alias Lord Kilmarnock's) alluring offer to make him his heir in return for his services, "was that a confident instinct within me rebelled against a form of reality that was simply handed to me and was in addition sloppy — rebelled in favour of free play and dreams, self-created and self-sufficient, dependent, that is, only on imagination" (III. 2). The comic hero, like any true hero, may prize worldly fortune but never to the detriment of his autonomy; even at his most complaisant he remains independent and apart. By his unwavering decision to repudiate what is merely given for what he himself can create Felix reaffirms the fundamental intuition of his childhood, that he can be true to his nature only by faithful adherence to the rigors of art.

Felix is a virtuoso and the world is his instrument; he perceives its imperfections with amusement, not outrage, and sees no reason to change it. Even so, his inherently contradictory relationship to society implies a tacit but none the less radical critique of its institutions. Ever since Odysseus slept on the floor of the swineherd Eumaeus' hut the comic hero has tended to disregard or transcend the distinctions of social class, and in our age such figures as Chaplin and Bloom have revealed the heroic potentialities of the allegedly common man. But Felix Krull's aristocratic leanings remind us that the comic hero has long been allied to Athena as well as to Eumaeus, since by virtue of his dissident values and superior talents he is necessarily an *un*common man. "I should have to be a fool or a hypocrite to pretend that I am of common stuff," Felix openly if immodestly professes, "and it is therefore in obedience to truth that I repeat that I am of the finest clay" (I. 2). Before long, however, young Krull's patrician inclinations run afoul of a social order whose assessments rudely fail to coincide with his own. After his father's bankruptcy and suicide he finds himself an object of condescension to the reputable folk of his native town, and only in the lowly stations of liftboy and waiter is he permitted to mingle with an international high society in which a proclivity to his attractions constitutes — as Diane Philibert ecstatically avouches and Lord Strathbogie discreetly confirms — a perversion. "It is simply an aberration," Felix compassionately assures the lovesick Eleanor Twentyman, "and even if it corresponded to your nature and temperament, you would nevertheless have to triumph over it out of respect for propriety and the natural laws of society" (III. 2).

Despite such apologies for things as they are, however, Felix becomes increasingly critical of a society so arbitrarily — and hence inartistically—structured that it neglects to take notice of the natural aristocrat in its midst. Watching his fellow waiters fawn on their wealthy guests he is bemused by what he calls "The idea of *interchangeability*," and reflects that "With a change of clothes and make-up, the servitors might often just as well have been the masters, and many of those who lounged in the deep wicker chairs . . . might have played the waiter. It was pure accident," he concludes, "that the reverse was the fact, an accident of wealth; for an aristocracy of money is an accidental and interchangeable aristocracy" (III. 3). Only to the extent that its superior actors are infrequently cast in its leading parts does an aristocracy of wealth approximate to an aristocracy of merit: a conjunction which Felix, by his own social ascent, does his best to promote.

For so inveterate a performer there is no essential distinction between masquerade and self, whether he be cast as servant or noble: "the undisguised reality behind the two appearances, the real I, could not be identified," he observes, "because it actually did not exist" (III. 3). His illicit bank account removes even his dreary job as a liftboy at the Hotel Saint James and Albany from the sphere of necessity and transforms it into a freely enacted role. "Although later on I achieved dazzling success in passing myself off for more than I was," he avows, "for the time being I passed myself off for less, and it is an open question which deception gave me the greater inner amusement, the greater delight in this fairy-tale magic" (III. 1). By venturing to impersonate the young marquis de Venosta when the opportunity unpredictably materializes, however, he does acknowledge a more than coincidental affinity between the part and the player. The true aristocrat of a world "of free play and dreams" such as Felix labors to fabricate for himself will be the master pretender, and none is more masterful in pretending—hence more the aristocrat—than he. As a nobleman's double, then, he at last attains the "equality of seeming and being" (III. 4) that his humble station had always before denied,[44] and thereby initiates an important new stage in his career of artistic and human fulfillment.

En route from Paris to Lisbon disguised as the voyaging marquis Felix undergoes nothing less than "the change and renewal of my worn-out self" (III. 5). Since this confidence man's mature artistry had its roots in infantile make-believe it is fitting that his most accomplished imposture should bring back memories of tales heard in childhood and restore the ardent receptiveness compromised in the interim by his position as reluctant gigolo to the rich. His hypnotic encounter with the eccentric Professor Kuckuck in the dining car of the Nord-Sud Express opens new or forgotten vistas to an imagination hitherto captivated by the absorbing exigencies of survival. The starry-eyed director of the Lisbon Natural History Museum holds his responsive auditor spellbound by his fervid discourses "of Being, of Life, of Man—and of the Nothingness from which all this had been generated and into which it would all return." The "vast expansiveness" that Felix experiences "was closely related to, or rather was identical with, what as a child or half a child I had described in the dreamlike phrase 'The Great Joy' ": a resurrection of childlike wonder at the boundless possibilities of the world. Knowledge of his minuscule and momentary place in a universe encompassed by nothingness does not, as Felix discovers with mounting exhilaration, obliterate man but endows him with intense delight in the cognition of being alive: "Transitoriness . . . was exactly what lent all existence its worth, dignity, and charm." Kuckuck's proclamation of a "universal sympathy" implicit in human consciousness itself is a grand theoretical formulation of the indissoluble unity with the physical world and his fellow beings which the comic hero, by the tenacity of his animal spirits, has instinctively affirmed through the ages; and through rapt attention to his mesmerizing evocation the self-centered Felix becomes aware of his fundamental affinity with a larger creation in which Being itself, like the art that reflects it, is "joy and labour."

Therefore, now that semblance is essence and fantasy one with the real, the reawakening of Felix' imagination occasions a simultaneous recrudescence of sensual delight. "What would become of life and what would become of joy—without which there can be no life—" he demands of Kuckuck's intriguing daughter, the fastidious Zouzou, "if appearance and the surface world of the senses no longer counted for anything?" (III. 10). Love between man and woman, Hermes and Aphrodite, is the particular force by which universal sympathy strives to overcome the singleness of each through the hermaphroditic union in which two become momentarily one:[45] the resurrection of wonder is at the same time a resurrection of love.

It will not, however, be Zouzou, with her tantalizing resemblance to Venosta's Parisian mistress Zaza, but rather her more austere and more passionate mother who will bring the erotic propensity revived by the disquisitions of her professorial husband to an unexpectedly rhapsodic fulfillment. The final pages of Krull's fragmentary confessions, broken off in Thomas Mann's eightieth year, comprise a kômos of almost Aristophanic abandon, a "tumultuous festival" (III. 5) not of sexuality only but of elemental Kuckuckian Being. Returning from the primitive rites of a bullfight at once procreative and murderous (like the ritual blood baths of Mithra), where she "had, as it were, been truly and completely herself for the first time" (III. 11), the stern materfamilias icily dismisses the daughter whom she surprises in the young foreigner's arms and then, in an astonishing peripeteia, flings herself with a jubilant *Holé! Heho! Ahé!* into his welcoming arms. "A whirlwind of primordial forces seized and bore me into the realm of ecstasy," Felix concludes this first (and only surviving) part of his memoirs: "And high and stormy, under my ardent caresses, stormier than at the Iberian game of blood, I saw the surging of that queenly bosom." Their spontaneous ecstasy is the ripe fruit of a disciplined art of living that elevates the irruption of chaos in which the primeval trickster-god exulted to the willed intensity of symbol or dream; and precisely this is the freedom that Felix has sought to recover ever since the exhilarant games of his earliest childhood.

The novel's abrupt termination is no doubt "rather slack and offhanded,"[46] as Mann lamented in one of many disgruntled moments; but comic endings are tentative and inconclusive by nature since comedy, like life, cannot come to an end without contradicting its essence. Despite the misgivings that he experienced, however, in returning to this sprightly fragment of his earlier years after coming to grips with the tragic disintegration of European civilization in *Doctor Faustus*, Mann signally fulfilled his own heroic determination "to find a plethora of gaiety despite the gloomiest of world situations" in the comedy, laughter, and humor which "seem to me," the distinguished laureate wrote, "more and more the soul's salvation."[47]

By engaging with soldierly diligence and aristocratic finesse in a contest of wits with an inexhaustibly fascinating world Felix Krull transcends the pathos and uncertainty that intermittently afflict his less presumptuous comic brethren like Leopold Bloom. Yet for all their temperamental dissimilarities Mann's hero has much in common with Joyce's. Ever since Don Quixote's disillusioning failure to refashion the world in accord with his vision of liberty, the option of overt opposition to an immovable order of things has been perceived as tragic or suicidal, not comic, and the achievement of a modus vivendi permitting the preservation of his own beleaguered humanity has been the comic hero's most nearly glorious victory. He has been content, by and large, to let the world take its course unmolested so long as it reciprocated the favor. Both Bloom and Krull, by different paths, come to satisfactory terms with a world that they no longer hope to alter, and find recompense for its constitutional shortcomings in the self-sufficiency of imagination. For both the one heroic task is to safeguard this precious autonomy, whether by diffident anonymity or ingenious impersonation.

But in extreme circumstances that preclude even such marginal exercise of autonomy the comic hero may be compelled, against his basic instinct for survival, to take the offensive in existential desperation: an act of defiance "comic" only by virtue of its absurdity. Hašek's imperturbable good soldier Schweik could evade the worst horrors of World War I by outward deference and a genius for personal safety; but for Yossarian, the frenzied bombardier of Joseph Heller's savagely comic *Catch-22*, there is no escape from the homicidal madness of a second World War. Insanity itself can offer no refuge to Yossarian, as it did to Schweik, since by the provision of Catch-22, as Doc Daneeka blandly explains, "Anyone who wants to get out of combat duty isn't really crazy."[48] Yossarian's openly professed mission is to remain alive against all odds in a war where the real enemy, as he tells the scandalized Clevinger, "is anybody who's going to get you killed, no matter *which* side he's on."[49] Yet, despite the "morbid aversion to dying"[50] acutely diagnosed by the staff psychiatrist as his ailment, when the opportunity to escape finally does present itself Yossarian makes an unpredictably heroic decision. By rejecting the ticket to easy street dangled before him by Colonel Korn as a reward for relinquishing his seditious refusal to continue flying, Yossarian implicitly affirms that his overriding goal has been not merely preservation of life but resistance to death and to those who inflict it on others. To save himself by becoming one of the boys, thus betraying his own mutinous example, would be no less a defeat for Yossarian than to die; and if he cannot end the war he will at least not collaborate in its prolongation. His utterly mad resolution—madness being, of course, the sole evidence of sanity in this world—to make his way to Sweden as Orr had improbably done requires a newly heroic determination to persevere in his hitherto largely instinctive testimony of opposition even at the risk of the death that he frantically seeks to avoid. "I'm not running *away* from my responsibilities," he rightly insists, "I'm running *to* them";[51] and the undetermined outcome of his attempt is secondary to his buoyant realization that survival would be without value if bought by abandonment of the struggle that has given it meaning.

No less dangerous than the madness of war to the comic hero's imperiled freedom has been the procrustean sanity ordained by a rigid social order determined to assure domestic tranquility by eliminating the virus of potential dissent. Leopold Bloom's eccentricities and Felix Krull's masquerades presupposed a willingness on society's part to tolerate, if only by oversight, a less than monolithic compliance with its certified norms of thought and behavior. Such indulgence has not, however, been universal. In totalitarian countries the comic hero could only be viewed as a public menace and dealt with accordingly, since nothing, as tyrants have always known, is more subversive of order than laughter. The only heroes permitted under Fascist or Communist regimes are those who pattern their actions on the ideology proclaimed by the State; he who recklessly values his skin must remain a hero unsung and indeed unnoticed. Democracy too has its instruments of coercion, and under its more illiberal manifestations tolerance of peculiarities has relentlessly given way to suppression of aberrations. The mental hospital of Ken Kesey's *One Flew Over the Cuckoo's Nest* is an institution established with the unimpeachably benign object of reconstituting the psychologically disabled outsider as a functioning component of the social order. To this end it demands, however (unlike the anarchic asylum where Schweik experienced the bliss of doing just as he pleased), that "*everyone*," as Nurse Ratched firmly enjoins, ". . . must follow the rules."[52] It is a microcosm that magnifies the repressive tendencies of the social order it serves—the efficient mechanism which the narrator, Chief Bromden, knows as the Combine— and it can only view dissidence as a pathological infection which it exists for the purpose of extirpating. "The Big Nurse tends to get real put out," Chief Bromden observes, "if something keeps her outfit from running like a smooth, accurate, precision-made machine."[53]

When a boisterously unruly newcomer, Randle Patrick McMurphy, enters the hospital seeking shelter from the rigors of a work farm, confrontation is unavoidable, although only gradually do its dimensions and implications become apparent. McMurphy, whose only purported ailment is a psychopathic tendency to overzealousness in sexual (as indeed in all other) relations, is not only intractably dissident in his own behalf but provocatively seditious as well. "Even the best-behaved Admission is bound to need some work to swing into routine," Bromden comments, "and, also, you never can tell when just that *certain* one might come in who's free enough to foul things up right and left, really make a hell of a mess and constitute a threat to the whole smoothness of the outfit."[54] In his ebullience McMurphy tauntingly invites a showdown with the Big Nurse's authority while prodding his cowed fellow inmates to join in his challenge. And bit by bit—despite the inertia of followers long accustomed to the security of unthinking submission — the contagion of his refractory example begins to spread. "That's what McMurphy can't understand," the Chief complains, "us wanting to be safe. He keeps trying to drag us out of the fog, out in the open where we'd be easy to get at."[55] Only by rashly exposing himself to the dangers which he urges the others to share can McMurphy hope to entice them out of their self-defensive subservience, but since coercive power remains firmly in the Big Nurse's hands every victory at her expense intensifies the risk of retaliation.

If Nurse Ratched finds herself impotent to re-establish her jurisdiction by overbearing her wards when they persist, at McMurphy's instigation, in watching the television that she has turned off to squelch their inchoate rebellion, she can quietly bide her time, confident in her prophecy "that our redheaded hero will cut himself down to something patients will all recognize and lose respect for: a braggart and a blowhard."[56] Only slowly, indeed, does McMurphy grasp the full extent of her powers and the risk of opposing her, and when he learns that his own release is contingent on her consent, his appetite for resistance suddenly slackens. His dilemma is not unlike Yossarian's: liberation demands a servility that would render it worthless, yet by continued opposition he runs the risk of sacrificing for himself the autonomy that he seeks to inspire in others. The possibility of defeat is inherent in any true heroism, of course, but the choice of the comic hero in extremis, as personified by McMurphy, is not less than tragic. Once he has comprehended the full dimensions of the struggle he has undertaken, a struggle not only against the Big Nurse but against the Combine she serves, his defiant freedom becomes a fatality which he cannot renounce even when its exercise threatens his own extinction. Every victory that he wins in his escalating contest with repression is purchased at a higher price than the last, until his final triumph destroys him.

McMurphy himself becomes fully aware of this contradiction, which only Chief Bromden, among the inmates roused by his example, appears to observe; and the immense value of his perilous freedom is commensurate with the cost of its increasingly desperate affirmation. He laughs, the Chief perceives,

"Because he knows you have to laugh at the things that hurt you just to keep yourself in balance, just to keep the world from running you plumb crazy."[57] The laughter with which he infects his previously cheerless companions on their fishing expedition is a testimonial to their resurrected self-confidence; yet in the dim reflection of a windshield during their return to the hospital Bromden glimpses on McMurphy's haggard face an expression "dreadfully tired and strained and *frantic*, like there wasn't enough time left for something he had to do."[58] There is a "helpless, cornered despair"[59] in his voice when he fatalistically intervenes to defend a terrorized patient against harassment by his attendants, and his jaunty disdain for the electric shock therapy inflicted on him in consequence of his outburst deliberately masks his own fear. McMurphy has made himself into a legend by a prodigious effort of will, and at the revels secretly celebrated within the hospital walls as the climax of his incitement to independence he presides like a mock-king who knows that his own fall must promptly ensue. He consents to the role of victim as the alternative to capitulation and authenticates the possibility of freedom — and of life — for others by voluntarily resigning his own. "It was like he'd signed on for the whole game," Chief Bromden remarks as the end approaches, "and there wasn't any way of him breaking his contract."[60] It is in response to the imperative need of others for the autonomy which he supremely embodies in his capacity to forgo it that McMurphy smashes through a glass door and rips the uniform from the Big Nurse's suddenly vulnerable body before collapsing with a cry of "fear and hate and surrender and defiance"[61] like a cornered animal that now cares only for dying. Lobotomy is the tribute by which a thwarted society signalizes the irrevocability of his triumph, and none of the inmates mistakes the living corpse that remains — even before Chief Bromden snuffs out its superfluous breath and vaults into the moonlight — for McMurphy, who survives only inasmuch as they themselves reincarnate his spirit. The regenerative force of his liberating example certifies Randle Patrick McMurphy, by the ultimate paradox, a comic hero in death.

Never has comedy required greater heroism than in a world where exuberance verges on desperation and laughter is suspect as a form of sedition. The more the margin of human freedom contracts, the more urgent its affirmation becomes. In this hazardous task ours has not, after all, been an age without heroes.

Afterword:
In Lieu of
Conclusion

— ❧ —

C ONCLUSION, LIKE definition, is antithetical to the comic hero, whose fugitive nature will not abide formulation. Even so, we may reasonably reaffirm that his essence lies in being at once heroic and comic. Comic not primarily because he is laughed at but because—in the root sense of kômos —he celebrates life, of body and mind. He can never wholly relinquish the joy in living that is both his innate disposition and his final object, and he perpetually solemnizes existence by willfully refusing to see it as solemn.

But in a world that is neither Cloudcuckooland nor the Boar's Head—as no human world is for long—holidays, though ardently wished for, come seldom. From the immemorial beginnings of comedy every kômos presupposes an agôn, and the comic hero proves himself heroic inasmuch as he takes up the struggle mandated by the pursuit of a festive end in a workaday world. Between fact and wish, discipline and caprice, "Thou shalt not" and "I will," the antagonism is reciprocal and eternal, and toward the existing order the comic hero's posture will always be one of implicit dissidence inclining toward open rebellion. He is most completely a hero when most intentionally comic, and at the peak of his prowess is audaciously conscious both of the ridicule he provokes and of the challenge he poses. Although the odds are always against him he never shrinks from the contest, and by the countless contrivances of wit and imagination he most often emerges not as the victim of fate but as the virtuoso of fortune—wary or cunning, prudent or froward as befits the occasion, but forever adaptable and inventive. He assimilates each of his multiple roles to his own comprehensive and pliable nature and magnifies himself by the stratagems that belittle his baffled opponents. He spurns a world bridled by an alien law and substitutes in its stead, to the best of his ample powers, a realm of bodily and spiritual freedom fabricated by fantasy in the shape of desire. By exalting his stubbornly animal nature to the jubilance of the divine he testifies to the multifarious wholeness of his battered humanity, and thereby achieves his most indelible triumph.

The comic hero's indigenous versatility has enabled him, from the beginning, to tailor his coat to the times. In ancient Greece, where civilization was not yet divorced from its ritual origins, Homer's Odysseus elevated the beastly tricks and daemonic antics of the invincible trickster of folklore to heroic devices in behalf of determined mortality, and thus provided a regal paradigm, both in cunning and courage, for the most motley successors in subsequent ages. At his pinnacle of presumption the Aristophanic upstart could hurtle the omnimpotent gods from their heavens by force of consummate bravado. In graver cultures, such as the Roman, he circumspectly took his place on the sidelines, either tirelessly intriguing in the interest of others, after the manner of Plautus' wily slaves, or dumbly suffering penitential subjection while awaiting a higher vocation, like Apuleius' philosophical ass. Even during the hierarchical Middle Ages an insubordinate Reynard contested, albeit in fabulous form, the rigid stratification of feudal society. In the heady ebullience of the Renaissance the resurgent comic hero once again boldly ventured to erect an alternative to existing reality. But although Falstaff more than equals the gusto and Don Quixote the valor of the comic heroes of old, their opposition to a Christian order sanctioned by the authority both of Church and State is perforce oblique, and their grandiose visions of liberty can only eventuate in defeat when society proves impervious to their allure.

By setting out in audacious defense of virtues honored by a world that neglects them in practice Don Quixote and his faithful squire inaugurate a new comic heroism that combats falsity and delusion not by guileful calculation but by reckless impulse and ingenuous candor. Both the moral Tom Jones and the outspoken Jacques, despite Odyssean traits, are their heirs, but both achieve modest victories by tempering their aspirations and accommodating themselves to a passable world which they see no need (and have no capacity) to transform. In the militantly earnest nineteenth century, however, the temptation to compromise with a corrupt society threatens to undermine the innate spontaneity in which Byron's desultory Don Juan and his youthful contemporaries find their only grounds for resistance. Not romantic outsiders or hotblooded rebels but the aging and disenchanted Bouvard and Pécuchet confront the complacent philistinism of their age with its most intransigently comic opponents. And in the collectivist twentieth century the dissident comic hero, though necessarily low of profile and restricted in scope, assumes an intensified importance arising from the conspicuous failure of a discredited civilization to generate heroes of any other description. An age that has no authentic surrogates for Achilles is in desperate need even of a diminished Ulysses or a smalltime Hermes to corroborate its residual but priceless humanity.

If his shapes and tactics have continually changed with his circumstances, however, the comic hero's guiding purpose — the emancipation of the unconformable self — has been constant throughout the ages. Not in any definitive victory (since his task is coextensive with life and must likewise issue in death) but in the combative tenacity of his will to freedom is the vindication that defeat can never entirely annul. What particular shapes this durable champion of elemental humanity will take in the future none will foolishly dare to conjecture; but even though his demise be pronounced and a requiem sung his eventual resurrection in some unpredictable guise may be safely predicted. For comic heroism is no mere literary convention but the most articulate expression of a will to autonomy firmly rooted in the refractory nature of man, and until the millennium dawns or final darkness descends it will not be wholly suppressed. While life remains the comic hero will glory in its possession, knowing well that his revels will sooner or later be ended but determined to celebrate, to the utmost reach of his powers, their brief but momentous duration.

APPENDIX

Ancient Views of the *Odyssey* as Tragedy and as Comedy

> Is it possible that eminent Homeric scholars have found
> so much seriousness in the more humorous parts of the
> "Odyssey" because they brought it there? To the serious
> all things are serious.
>
> Samuel Butler, *The Authoress of the Odyssey*

If tragedy is distinguished from comedy, as by Aristotle, in that it represents persons of the nobler and better rather than the meaner sort, *spoudaioi* rather than *phauloi*, then the *Odyssey*, with its aristocratic and capable hero, could only be categorized, along with the *Iliad* and in contrast to the burlesque *Margites*, as a prototype of tragedy (*Poetics* IV.9).[1] Even so, it is apparent that Aristotle himself felt the need to qualify this initial classification. The brave and noble Odysseus, he knew, could also be portrayed as uniquely *phaulos*.[2] In *Poetics* XIII.7-8 he remarks that the pleasure derived from tragedies that have, like the *Odyssey*, a double plot and an opposite outcome for good and bad characters "is proper rather to Comedy," and must be considered inferior to the strictly tragic pleasure derived from a single plot that portrays a change from good fortune to bad. In this regard the *Odyssey* is clearly more akin to comedy than the *Iliad*, in which the tragic pleasure is unalloyed. And in *Poetics* XXIV.2 Aristotle significantly broadens his distinction between the two poems. "The Iliad is at once simple and 'pathetic' [*pathêtikon*]," he writes, "and the Odyssey complex (for Recognition scenes run through it), and at the same time 'ethical' [*êthikê*]."

For Aristotle the presentation of suffering (*pathos*) was an integral component of tragedy (*Poetics* XI.6). By contrast, we might infer that the study of character (*êthos*) could be considered an especial attribute of comedy. For although Aristotle recognizes an "ethical" kind of tragedy (*Poetics* XVIII.2), he strongly emphasizes the primacy of tragic action and even asserts that tragedy could exist "without character" (*Poetics* VI.11) — a statement that could hardly be made about comedy. The inference is in fact confirmed by Quintilian, who in the first century A.D. explicitly likens *pathos* to tragedy and *êthos* to comedy, associating the former with violent emotions inducing *ad perturbationem* and the latter with gentle emotions inducing *ad benivolentiam*.[3] An analogous distinction is applied to Homer's two epics by the Greek author of *On the Sublime*, who remarks that "with the decline of their emotional power [*pathos*] great writers and poets give way to character-study [*êthos*]. For instance, [Homer's] character-sketches of the daily life in Odysseus's household are in the style of some comedy of character."[4] Here, as in Aristotle, the comic is again regarded as the inferior mode.

Thus in several crucial respects — a "double" plot in which the protagonist moves from bad fortune to good; the complexity introduced by multiple recognitions; and the prominence of character-study — Aristotle himself might well have classified the *Odyssey*, in opposition to the *Iliad*, as a model of comedy rather than tragedy if the essentially social distinction between characters better and worse than ourselves had not remained his primary criterion. Despite such premonitions, however, the outright reversal of Aristotle's classification in the brief treatise "De Fabula" (now attributed to Evanthius), at the beginning of Donatus' commentary on Terence in the mid-fourth century A.D., is a bold innovation. Commenting on the originators of tragedy and comedy, such as Thespis and Eupolis, Evanthius writes: "Homerus tamen, qui fere omnis poeticae largissimus fons est, etiam his carminibus exempla praebuit et uelut quandam suorum operum legem praescripsit: *qui Iliadem ad instar tragoediae, Odyssiam ad imaginem comoediae fecisse monstratur.*"[5] ("But Homer, who is the most abundant source of almost every poetics, provided examples for these genres too, and prescribed the law of his own works, so to speak; *for he manifestly composed the Iliad as a likeness for tragedy, the Odyssey as an image for comedy.*") The grounds for this reversal of outlook are implicit in Evanthius' subsequent differentiation between tragedy and comedy, which goes far beyond Aristotle's:

> inter tragoediam autem et comoediam cum multa tum inprimis hoc distat, quod in comoedia mediocres fortunae hominum, parui impetus periculorum laetique sunt exitus actionum, at in tragoedia omnia contra, ingentes personae, magni timores, exitus funesti habentur; et illic prima turbulenta, tranquilla ultima, in tragoedia contrario ordine res aguntur; tum quod in tragoedia fugienda uita, in comoedia capessenda exprimitur; postremo quod omnis comoedia de fictis est argumentis, tragoedia saepe de historica fide petitur.[6]

> [Between tragedy and comedy, however, there are many differences, but this in particular: that in comedy men's fortunes are middling, the onslaughts of danger slight, and the outcomes of actions joyful, but in tragedy everything is the reverse, characters are immense, fears great, outcomes funereal; in the former, beginnings are turbulent, endings tranquil, in tragedy events happen in the opposite order; again, in tragedy life is represented as something to flee, in comedy, to seize hold of; finally, every comedy is made from fictional plots, tragedy is often sought from historical fidelity.]

Insofar as comedy is here defined by the humble condition of its characters, or by its relative freedom from the terrors associated with tragic *pathos*, or by its fictional, that is, nontraditional subject matter (cf. *Poetics* IX.5-8), the *Odyssey* ought to have remained for Evanthius, as for Aristotle, a model of tragedy; for its hero is not mediocre, its perils not small, and its argument not fabricated (in the manner of New Comic plots) by Homer. But in distinguishing comedy from tragedy by its joyful outcome and its movement from turbulence to tranquility Evanthius laid down a criterion that would largely predominate in the Middle Ages and later. In emphasizing the fundamental antithesis between the tragic renunciation and the comic affirmation of life (*in tragoedia fugienda uita, in comoedia capessenda*) he might justly be said to anticipate the most recent investigations of comedy as a celebration of vital impulse. It is in these essential respects that Evanthius can proclaim the *Odyssey* to be, as it surely remains, the very image of comedy.

After the rediscovery of the *Poetics* in the Renaissance, Aristotle's classification of the *Odyssey* as tragedy was seen to conflict with that contained in Donatus, whose *Commentary* had been widely known throughout the Middle Ages; and "sixteenth-century scholars puzzled

for some time," as Marvin J. Herrick remarks, "before they finally resolved the contradiction in favor of Aristotle. The decision in favor of
Aristotle was based on the types of characters in the drama, not on the
kind of ending."[7] Even so, the consensus was not quite universal, and
one of the great comic dramatists of the age, Lope de Vega, preferred
to echo Donatus rather than Aristotle, even if he seemingly misinter-
preted the phrase *ad imaginem comoediae* to imply anachronistic
imitation instead of precursory paradigm:

> Homero, a imitación de la comedia,
> la *Odisea* compuso, mas la *Iliada*
> de la tragedia fué famoso ejemplo.[8]

("Homer composed the *Odyssey* in imitation of comedy, but the *Iliad*
was a famous example of tragedy.")

In sum, the modern conception of the *Odyssey* as a comic poem can
lay title to a pedigree of considerable antiquity and distinction.

Notes

The brief bibliographies in the headnote to the notes for each chapter list only those works, whether few or many, which I have found directly pertinent to my concerns or which might otherwise be of especial interest to the reader. They are by no means intended to be exhaustive.

Introduction: Comic Butt and Comic Hero

For the origin of my conception of comic heroism I am most deeply indebted to Cedric H. Whitman, *Aristophanes and the Comic Hero* (Cambridge, Mass.: Harvard University Press, 1964); then to C. L. Barber, *Shakespeare's Festive Comedy* (1959; rpt. Cleveland and New York: World, 1963), and Susanne K. Langer, "The Great Dramatic Forms: The Comic Rhythm," in *Feeling and Form: A Theory of Art* (New York: Scribner's, 1953), pp. 326-350. Another work of primary importance for the "festive" conception of comedy is Mikhail Bakhtin, *Rabelais and His World,* trans. Hélène Iswolsky (Cambridge, Mass.: MIT Press, 1968).

Several collections of writings on comedy have been of great value to me, especially in this introductory chapter. *Theories of Comedy,* ed. Paul Lauter (Garden City, N.Y.: Doubleday Anchor, 1964), brings together important discussions of the subject from Plato and Aristotle to Langer. *Comedy,* ed. Wylie Sypher (Garden City, N.Y.: Doubleday Anchor, 1956), contains George Meredith's "An Essay on Comedy" and Henri Bergson's "Laughter," along with Sypher's long appendix, "The Meanings of Comedy." *Comedy: Meaning and Form,* ed. Robert W. Corrigan (Scranton,

Pa.: Chandler, 1965), comprises a broad diversity of contemporary viewpoints.

Among modern writers on comedy, besides those cited above, W. H. Auden is frequently illuminating throughout *The Dyer's Hand and Other Essays* (1962; rpt. New York: Vintage, 1968); see especially "Notes on the Comic," pp. 371-385. Northrop Frye's contributions to comic theory—notably "The Argument of Comedy," in *English Institute Essays, 1948,* ed. D. A. Robertson, Jr. (New York: Columbia University Press, 1949), pp. 58-73 (rpt. in *Theories of Comedy,* ed. Lauter, pp. 450-460), and "The Mythos of Spring: Comedy," in *The Anatomy of Criticism* (Princeton: Princeton University Press, 1957), pp. 163-186—are of interest even though his polarization of comedy between satire and romance gives little prominence to the heroic. Other pertinent books and essays include James K. Feibleman, *In Praise of Comedy* (New York: Horizon, 1970); Walter Kerr, *Tragedy and Comedy* (New York: Simon and Schuster, 1967); L. C. Knights, "Notes on Comedy," in *Determinations,* ed. F. R. Leavis (London: Chatto and Windus, 1934), pp. 109-131 (rpt. in Lauter, pp. 432-443); and Nathan A. Scott, Jr., "The Bias of Comedy and the Narrow Escape into Faith," *The Christian Scholar,* 44 (Spring 1961), 9-39 (rpt. in *Comedy,* ed. Corrigan, pp. 81-115). A work that parallels mine in several respects, although I discovered it only after completing my manuscript, is William B. Guthrie, *The Comic Celebrant of Life* (Diss., Vanderbilt University, 1968; Ann Arbor, Mich.: University Microfilms, 1975); see esp. the discussion of comedy as criticism and celebration in his introduction.

Theories of laughter and humor lie somewhat outside the province of my book except when they deal directly with literary comedy, like Bergson's. For an overall treatment of this much-discussed topic see D. H. Munro, *Argument of Laughter* (1951; rpt. Notre Dame, Ind.: University of Notre Dame Press, 1963). Special mention must be made, however, of Sigmund Freud, *Jokes and Their Relation to the Unconscious,* trans. James Strachey (New York: Norton, 1960; rpt. 1963), since Freud's study, first published in 1905, only five years after Bergson had given classic reformulation to the socially oriented conception of comedy, was among the first to see the elemental impulse to humor as an act of rebellion and liberation. Finally, Johan Huizinga's *Homo Ludens: A Study of the Play-Element in Culture* (Eng. trans. 1950; rpt. Boston: Beacon, 1955), even though it explicitly excludes comedy from its purview, is of seminal importance for an understanding of the role of festivity in civilization: and what else is the *kômos* from which comedy takes its origin and name?

1. For Aristotle's remarks on comedy in the *Poetics,* see esp. chaps. II, III.3, IV.7-12, and V.1-3; my citations are from these passages. Important editions of the *Poetics* in English include S. H. Butcher, *Aristotle's Theory of Poetry and Fine Art,* 4th ed. (London: Macmillan, 1907; rpt. New York: Dover, 1951), and Gerald F. Else, *Aristotle's Poetics: The Argument* (Cambridge, Mass.: Harvard University Press, 1967). Both contain a Greek text as well as translation and commentary; I have quoted Butcher's translation and followed his text. Lane Cooper, *An Aristotelian Theory of Comedy* (New York: Harcourt, Brace, 1922), provides further commentary and attempts a reconstruction of Aristotle's views.

2. It follows that for Aristotle, as Lionel Trilling remarks in *Sincerity and Authenticity* (Cambridge, Mass.: Harvard University Press, 1972), pp. 86-87, "it is only in the genre of tragedy that the hero exists. . . . There can be no comic hero." See Else, *Aristotle's Poetics,* p. 75: "The dichotomy [between those of high and low character, *spoudaioi* and *phauloi*] is absolute and exclusive for a simple reason: it began as the aristocrats' view of society and reflects their idea of the gulf between themselves and the 'others.' In the minds of a comparatively small and close-knit group like the Greek aristocracy there are only two kinds of people, 'we' and 'they'; and of course 'we' are the good people, the proper, decent, good-looking, right-thinking ones, while 'they' are the rascals, the poltroons, the good-for-nothings—in short, everyone else. It is inherent in the idea and the terminology of the division that there cannot be any third class." (Cf. Plato, *Euthydemus* 307a, where Socrates declares that in every discipline the *phauloi* are many and worthless, the *spoudaioi* few and worthy.) In one form or another this underlying prejudice will persist among writers on comedy almost until our own century. Given this "absolute" dichotomy, however, I think that Else subsequently (pp. 144-145) somewhat overstates Aristotle's distinction between invective (*psogos*) and the laughable (*to geloion*) by translating them, in his commentary, as "satire" and "humor." Aristotle sees the laughable, or ridiculous, which is proper to comedy, as a great refinement on the personal invective of iambic lampoons, and attempts to dissociate the former from the element of malice or *Schadenfreude* censured by Plato (*Philebus* 48a-50b); but his point is that one grew naturally out of the other and is not *essentially* different from it, since the lampoonists developed into comic writers (just as the epic poets became tragic writers) in accord with their "natural bent," *kata tên oikeian physin* (*Poetics* IV.10). Any

form of laughter directed by "us" at "them" — by the "better" sort at the "worse" — is surely more akin to satire, in our modern sense of the term, than to humor.

On the other hand, Aristotle apparently considered the "Old Comedy" of Aristophanes' day, with its large admixture of personal abuse, "a relatively minor episode, in fact a survival" (Else, p. 188). His remark in *Poetics* IX.5 that in comedy "the poet first constructs the plot on the lines of probability, and then inserts characteristic names; — unlike the lampooners who write about particular individuals" would presumably apply to the so-called "Middle Comedy" of Aristotle's own time rather than to Aristophanes, whom he would classify, in this regard, along with the more primitive writers of invective. See Else, pp. 309-313.

3. In *Poetics* III.3 Aristotle cites without comment, and with apparent approval, the Dorian claim "that Comedians were so named not from *kômazein,* 'to revel,' but because they wandered from village to village (*kata kômas*)"; the derivation was accepted by such later writers as Donatus (see Lauter, p. 27). Concerning this passage Sir A. W. Pickard-Cambridge writes, in *Dithyramb, Tragedy and Comedy,* 2nd ed. (Oxford: Clarendon, 1962), p. 132: "The linguistic argument adduced is worthless: there can be no doubt that *kômoidia* is connected with *kômos* (*kômazein*), not with *kômê.* " See also Else, pp. 118-120, to the same effect. As for phallic rites, the text of *Poetics* IV.12 is questionable, as Else points out (p. 163), but virtually all other editors have accepted the reading *ta phallika.* Pickard-Cambridge judiciously discusses the extant evidence on the subject of phallic festivities and concludes (p. 147), "It seems, therefore, at least possible that Aristotle, if he was deriving comedy from *ithyphalloi* or *phallophoroi,* was once more theorizing, not recording an ascertained historical development." (For *ithyphalloi* and *phallophoroi* see ibid., pp. 140-41.) This cautious and carefully hedged demurral, however, is at least as speculative as Aristotle's assertion, and Aristotle may of course have had evidence no longer accessible even to the diligent Pickard-Cambridge.

4. *Poetics* IV.8, 9. For the extant fragments of the *Margites,* see Hugh G. Evelyn-White, ed., *Hesiod, The Homeric Hymns and Homerica,* rev. ed. (Cambridge, Mass., and London: Harvard University Press, and Heinemann, 1936), pp. 536-539.

5. Giovanni Giorgio Trissino, *Poetics,* Division VI (c. 1543-1550), trans. Anita Grossvogel, as revised by Lauter in *Theories of Comedy,* p. 42. Lauter gives a generous and useful selection from the influential

Italian theorists of the sixteenth century. For a discussion of the subject, see Marvin T. Herrick, *Comic Theory in the Sixteenth Century* (Urbana: University of Illinois Press, 1950; rpt. 1964), which demonstrates the importance during this period of the ancient commentators on Terence as well as of Aristotle. Already in late antiquity, Herrick notes (p. 66), "Both Donatus and Servius stressed the didactic function of comedy, which mirrors everyday life and so teaches us what is useful and what must be avoided. The Renaissance followers of Donatus and Servius agreed." For Donatus, see Lauter, p. 27: "Comedy is a fable [*fabula*] involving diverse arrangements of civic and private concerns, in which one learns what is useful in life and what on the contrary is to be avoided." Needless to say, these late commentators, like Cicero and others before them, had themselves been at least indirectly influenced by Aristotle, in whom a strong ethical bent is already apparent.

Among their many Renaissance followers in this regard, besides the Italians, was Sir Philip Sidney, for whom the teaching of comedy has already become, moreover, an entirely negative one. In *An Apologie for Poetrie* (1595), ed. Evelyn S. Shuckburgh (Cambridge: Cambridge University Press, 1896), p. 30, Sidney writes: "Onely thus much now is to be said, that the Comedy is an imitation of the common errors of our life, which he ['the Comick'] representeth in the most ridiculous and scornefull sort that may be; so as it is impossible that any beholder can be content to be such a one . . . And little reason hath any man to say, that men learne evill by seeing it so set out: sith, as I sayd before, there is no man living but, by the force trueth hath in nature, no sooner seeth these men play their parts, but wisheth them in *Pistrinum:* although perchance the sack of his owne faults lye so behinde hys back, that he seeth not himselfe daunce the same measure: whereto yet nothing can more open his eyes, then to finde his own actions contemptibly set forth."

6. Lauter, p. 40, cites the following passage from Lucio Olimpio Giraldi's *Ragionamento in difesa di Terentio* (1566), as translated by Bernard Weinberg in *A History of Literary Criticism in the Italian Renaissance* (Chicago: University of Chicago Press, 1961), vol. I, p. 289: "Just as tragedy purges men's minds, through terror and pity, and induces men to abstain from acting wickedly, so comedy, by means of laughter and jokes, calls men to an honest private life." Unknown to the critics of the Renaissance, a theory of comic catharsis had been stated long before in the so-called "Tractatus Coislinianus," a brief treatise rediscovered in the nineteenth century and thought by some to be a digest of the purportedly lost second book of Aristotle's

Poetics. In terms that parallel Aristotle's celebrated definition of tragedy, the "Tractatus" defines comedy as "an imitation of an action that is ludicrous and imperfect . . . through pleasure and laughter effecting the purgation of the like emotions" (trans. Lane Cooper, in *An Aristotelian Theory of Comedy,* p. 224; rpt. in Lauter, p. 21).

7. The quotations from Jonson are conveniently reprinted in Lauter, pp. 118 and 125.

8. The phrase—"Le devoir de la comédie étant de corriger les hommes en les divertissant"—appears as an accepted commonplace in the opening words of Molière's "Premier Placet présenté au roi Sur la comédie du Tartuffe" (1664), in Molière, *Oeuvres complètes,* ed. Robert Jouanny (Paris: Garnier, 1962), vol. I, p. 632.

9. "Letter on *The Impostor,*" trans. Mrs. George Calingaert and Paul Lauter, in Lauter, p. 152. The French text of 1667, reproduced in *Lettre sur la comédie de l'Imposteur,* ed. Paul Lacroix (1870; rpt. Geneva: Slatkine Reprints, 1969), p. 71, reads: "Car la connoissance de defaut de Raison d'une chose que nous donne l'apparence du ridicule, qui est en elle, nous fait la mesestimer necessairement parce que nous croyons que la Raison doit regler tout." I have substituted "Reason" for Calingaert and Lauter's "good sense" as a translation of *Raison,* although "Reason" in this context clearly connotes "reasonable" behavior rather than "rational" thought. In an earlier passage (*Lettre,* pp. 61-62; see Lauter, p. 147), ridicule is assigned the function of policing derelictions from Reason, which is here explicitly associated with social decorum: "Le ridicule est donc la forme exterieure et sensible que la providence de la nature a attachée à tout ce qui est déraisonnable, pour nous en faire apercevoir, et nous obliger à le fuir. Pour connoistre ce ridicule il faut connoitre la Raison dont il signifie le defaut, et voir en quoy elle consiste. Son caractere n'est autre dans le fond, que la convenance, et sa marque sensible la bienseance, c'est-à-dire le fameux *quod decet* des anciens."

10. Henri Bergson, "Laughter," I.ii., in *Comedy,* ed. Wylie Sypher, p. 73. The quotation that follows is from III.i., pp. 147-48; the phrase "something mechanical encrusted on the living" first appears in I.v., p. 84. See also II.i., p. 117: "The comic is that side of a person which reveals his likeness to a thing, that aspect of human events which, through its peculiar inelasticity, conveys the impression of pure mechanism, of automatism, of movement without life. Consequently it expresses an individual or collective imperfection which calls for an immediate corrective. This corrective is laughter, a social gesture that singles out and represses a special kind of absentmindedness in men and events."

11. See Jean-Jacques Rousseau, *Politics and the Arts: Letter to M. d'Alembert on the Theatre,* trans. Allan Bloom (Glencoe, Ill.: Free Press, 1960; rpt. Ithaca, N.Y.: Cornell University Press, 1968), pp. 34-45. "You could not deny me two things," Rousseau writes (pp. 36-37), "one, that Alceste in this play is a righteous man, sincere, worthy, truly a good man; and, second, that the author makes him a ridiculous figure. This is already enough, it seems to me, to render Molière inexcusable." Most interpreters, in defending Molière, have avoided Rousseau's dilemma by seeing Alceste as either ridiculous or heroic, not both. Although it is certainly the case that "Molière made a point of highlighting everything in Alceste that could minimize the justice of his revolt by making him ridiculous," as Paul Bénichou stresses in *Man and Ethics: Studies in French Classicism,* trans. Elizabeth Hughes (Garden City, N.Y.: Doubleday Anchor, 1971), p. 236, and although Molière's contemporaries apparently perceived Alceste as a wholly ludicrous figure, within the play itself Eliante indicates that his sincerity has something heroic about it:

> Et la sincérité dont son âme se pique
> A quelque chose, en soi, de noble et d'héroïque.
> > (*Le Misanthrope,* IV. i)

That Alceste might be intrinsically both ridiculous and heroic, and not simply a hero exposed to unjust ridicule, lay outside Rousseau's moral categories; yet Molière's misanthrope can be understood only when the two aspects of his refractory conduct are seen as inseparable. Even so, Alceste lacks the true comic hero's conscious willingness to accept (and even welcome) derision as the consequence of his dissent. As Ramon Fernandez writes in his suggestive study, *Molière: The Man Seen through the Plays,* trans. Wilson Follett (New York: Hill and Wang, 1958; rpt. 1960), p. 155, "[Alceste] can no more laugh at himself than he can at others. He has an outlook on life that is precisely Molière's, but he cannot turn it into comedy." He is a comic hero, if at all, *malgré lui.*

12. The widespread interest in popular comedy in the twentieth century has given rise to many important works on the subject. Among psychologists and anthropologists Freud was the first to emphasize the insurrectionary character of popular humor directed, as he writes, against "institutions, people in their capacity as vehicles of institutions, dogmas of morality or religion, views of life which enjoy so much respect that objections to them can only be made under the mask of a joke and indeed of a joke concealed by its façade . . .

What these jokes whisper," he adds, "may be said aloud: that the wishes and desires of men have a right to make themselves acceptable alongside of exacting and ruthless morality" (*Jokes and Their Relation to the Unconscious,* pp. 108-110). Paul Radin's *The Trickster: A Study in American Indian Mythology,* with commentaries by Karl Kerényi and C. G. Jung (New York: Philosophical Library, 1956; rpt. New York: Schocken, 1972), portrays one version of the primordial trickster of myth whom Kerényi describes (p. 185) as "the spirit of disorder, the enemy of boundaries" — a function that his comic successors have robustly continued. On the subject of early trickster-figures see also Joseph Campbell, *The Masks of God: Primitive Mythology* (New York: Viking, 1959), pp. 267-281, and Norman O. Brown, *Hermes the Thief* (1947; rpt. New York: Vintage, 1969).

Studies of the knaves, rogues, fools, and clowns of popular (and sometimes royal) entertainment include Enid Welsford, *The Fool: His Social and Literary History* (London: Faber and Faber, 1935); M. Willson Disher, *Clowns and Pantomimes* (1925; rpt. New York: Benjamin Blom, 1968); Allardyce Nicoll, *Masks, Mimes and Miracles: Studies in the Popular Theatre* (1931; rpt. New York: Cooper Square Publishers, 1963), and *The World of Harlequin: A Critical Study of the Commedia dell'Arte* (Cambridge: Cambridge University Press, 1963); Giacomo Oreglia, *The Commedia dell'Arte,* trans. Lovett F. Edwards (New York: Hill and Wang, 1968); and George Speaight, *The History of the English Puppet Theatre* (London: Harrap, 1955), which gives extensive treatment to Punch and Judy. See also Richard Boston's chapter "Fools and Tricksters" in his *An Anatomy of Laughter* (London: Collins, 1974). On Eulenspiegel, see the Introduction and Critical Appendix to *A Pleasant Vintage of Till Eulenspiegel,* trans. Paul Oppenheimer (Middletown, Conn.: Wesleyan University Press, 1972).

On popular celebrations as antecedents of literary comedy see Francis M. Cornford, *The Origin of Attic Comedy,* ed. Theodor H. Gaster (1914; rpt. Garden City, N.Y.: Doubleday Anchor, 1961), as modified in some of its speculations by A. W. Pickard-Cambridge, *Dithyramb, Tragedy and Comedy;* George E. Duckworth's chapter "Early Italian Popular Comedy" in his *The Nature of Roman Comedy* (Princeton: Princeton University Press, 1952); Mikhail Bakhtin's chapter "Popular Festive Forms" in *Rabelais and His World;* and C. L. Barber's chapters "Holiday Custom and Entertainment" and "Misrule as Comedy; Comedy as Misrule" in *Shakespeare's Festive Comedy.*

13. Few professors have shown a more discerning awareness of the heroic dimension in popular comedy than the Punch-and-Judy showman Professor John Stafford (whose title is a perquisite of his calling) in his discourse "In Defence of Punch," recorded by Michael Byrom in *Punch and Judy: Its Origin and Evolution* (Aberdeen: Shiva Publications, 1972), p. xi: "A lady told me once that she never engaged a Punch and Judy show at her parties because he was so cruel and wicked. Cruel and wicked, Punch? If I believed that, I would never have been a Punch showman . . . It was the knocking about that used to worry people. And it's true that in the old days Punch and Judy was a very rude show indeed . . . People in those days laughed at Punch because he was deformed — because of his hump, his nose, and his spindley legs. They laughed at him because he was a cripple. So what did Punch do? He said to himself, 'All right. If they're going to laugh at me, then I'll be a proper comedian.' And he pads out his hump, and he dresses up in his tomfool colours, and he did things to make people laugh on purpose . . . So you see, Punch isn't a criminal at all; he's a clown. But he isn't just a clown, he's a hero. Because if you can laugh at your own deformities and misfortunes as Punch does, you're a hero. This is what I base my own show on — this belief that Punch is a hero."

14. Jaroslav Hašek, *The Good Soldier: Schweik,* trans. Paul Selver (New York: C. Boni, 1930; rpt. New York: New American Library, 1963), p. 45. The quotation that follows is from p. xv.

15. The theory that Greek drama originated in fertility rites did not begin with the speculations of Gilbert Murray and Francis Cornford in the aftermath of *The Golden Bough.* In addition to Aristotle's mention of phallic songs (n. 3 above), the treatise "De Fabula" now attributed to Evanthius and included by Donatus in his commentary on Terence in the fourth century A.D. opens with the assertion that tragedy and comedy had their beginning in rituals of prayer for a fruitful harvest: "Initium tragoediae et comoediae a rebus diuinis est incohatum, quibus pro fructibus uota soluentes operabantur antiqui." Aelius Donatus, *Commentum Terenti,* ed. Paul Wessner (Leipzig: Teubner, 1902; rpt. Stuttgart, 1962), vol. I, p. 13.

16. Susanne Langer, "The Great Dramatic Forms: The Comic Rhythm," in *Feeling and Form,* pp. 331, 348-49.

1. Beggar Man, King

Although Homer's Odysseus has served comic writers from Aristophanes to Joyce as a kingly paradigm for their heroes, scholars and critics, with few exceptions, have largely ignored the comic aspects of the *Odyssey*. By far the most valuable treatment, for my purposes, is that of W. B. Stanford in *The Ulysses Theme: A Study in the Adaptability of a Traditional Hero,* 2nd ed. (Oxford: Basil Blackwell, 1963; rpt. Ann Arbor: University of Michigan Press, 1968), especially chaps. II ("The Grandson of Autolycus"), III ("The Favourite of Athene"), and V ("The Untypical Hero"), to which I am indebted at many points in the present chapter. Other pertinent discussions include Walter Morris Hart, "High Comedy in the *Odyssey*," *University of California Publications in Classical Philology,* 12 (1943), 263-278, and E. D. Phillips, "The Comic Odysseus," *Greece and Rome,* 2nd series, 6 (1959), 58-67.

Among many treatments of folklore motifs in the *Odyssey* see, e.g., Andrew Lang, *Homer and the Epic* (1893; rpt. New York: AMS Press, 1970), pp. 226-231; Sir James George Frazer, "Ulysses and Polyphemus," Appendix XIII to Apollodorus, *The Library* (Cambridge, Mass., and London: Harvard University Press, and Heinemann, 1921), vol. II, pp. 404-455; Rhys Carpenter, *Folk Tale, Fiction and Saga in the Homeric Epics* (Berkeley and Los Angeles: University of California Press, 1956); and Denys Page, *The Homeric Odyssey* (Oxford: Clarendon, 1955) and *Folktales in Homer's Odyssey* (Cambridge, Mass.: Harvard University Press, 1972). By and large, the folklorists are not inclined to view their material in a comic light.

Modern translations of the *Odyssey* include those of Robert Fitzgerald (Garden City, N.Y.: Doubleday Anchor, 1963) and Richmond Lattimore (New York: Harper and Row, 1975). In this chapter I have supplied my own translations from the *Odyssey* and the *Iliad*. For the Greek text of the *Odyssey* I have used W. B. Stanford's second edition, 2 vols. (London and New York: Macmillan, and St. Martin's, 1958-59); for that of the *Iliad,* vols. I and II of *Homeri Opera,* ed. David B. Monro and Thomas W. Allen, 3rd ed. (Oxford: Clarendon, 1920). Parenthetical references in my text are to book and line numbers of the *Odyssey* (Od.) and *Iliad* (Il.).

1. See Appendix, "Ancient Views of the *Odyssey* as Tragedy and as Comedy." Among many discussions of Achilles as tragic hero, see especially that of Cedric H. Whitman, *Homer and the Heroic Tradition* (Cambridge, Mass.: Harvard University Press, 1958), pp. 181-220.

2. On the post-Homeric denigration of Odysseus, see Stanford, *The Ulysses Theme,* esp. chaps. VII-VIII.

3. For several interpretations of *polytropos* see Stanford, pp. 98-99 and 260-61 (n. 28); and cf. Plato, *Hippias Minor* 365b, where *polytropos* is taken to mean "mendacious" or "false," in contrast to the truth and simplicity characteristic of Achilles.

4. "To Hermes" 13, in *Hesiod, the Homeric Hymns and Homerica,* trans. H. G. Evelyn-White, rev. ed. (Cambridge, Mass., and London: Harvard University Press, and Heinemann, 1936), p. 364.

5. See George E. Dimock, Jr., "The Name of Odysseus," *The Hudson Review,* 9 (1956), 52-70, rpt. in *Homer: A Collection of Critical Essays,* ed. George Steiner and Robert Fagles (Englewood Cliffs, N.J.: Prentice-Hall, 1962), pp. 106-121.

6. Quoted by Frank Budgen in *James Joyce and the Making of Ulysses* (London: Grayson, 1934; rpt. Bloomington, Ind.: Indiana University Press, 1960), p. 15.

7. See Stanford's chapter "The Favourite of Athene," and Hart, pp. 137-142.

8. The meaning of *epêtês* remains in dispute. Stanford, pp. 31 and 250 (n. 11), interprets it to mean "civilized" (from *hepo,* "attend to"); but the ancient scholiasts connect it with *epos,* "word" or "speech." My translation, "voluble," corresponds to Fitzgerald's "well-spoken" and Lattimore's "fluent."

2. Jackanapes in the Highest

I am indebted in this chapter, above all, to Cedric H. Whitman, *Aristophanes and the Comic Hero* (Cambridge, Mass.: Harvard University Press, 1964), especially to the chapters "Comic Heroism" and "The Anatomy of Nothingness." Among other works of primary importance for an understanding of early Greek comedy are Francis M. Cornford, *The Origin of Attic Comedy,* ed. Theodor H. Gaster (London: Arnold, 1914; rpt. Garden City, N.Y.: Doubleday Anchor, 1961), and A. W. Pickard-Cambridge, *Dithyramb, Tragedy and Comedy,* 2nd ed. (Oxford: Clarendon, 1962). The opening chapters of Allardyce Nicoll's *Masks, Mimes and Miracles: Studies in the Popular Theatre* (1931; rpt. New York: Cooper Square Publishers, 1963) provide an account of the early mime from which Old Comedy may in part have derived. Other valuable books include Victor Ehrenberg, *The People of Aristophanes: A Sociology of Old Attic Comedy,* rev. ed. (New York: Schocken, 1962), and K. J. Dover, *Aristophanic Comedy* (Berkeley and Los Angeles: University of California Press, 1972).

I have used the text of *Aristophanis Comoediae,* ed. F. W. Hall and W. M. Geldart, 2nd ed., 2 vols. (Oxford: Clarendon, 1906-07).

1. See Quintilian, *Inst.* X.i. 65-66; Horace, *Ars poetica* 281-284.

2. "Summary of a Comparison Between Aristophanes and Menander," in *Plutarch's Moralia,* vol. X, ed. Harold North Fowler (Cambridge, Mass., and London: Harvard University Press, and Heine-

mann, 1936), p. 469. This summary of Plutarch's views by an unknown compiler concludes (pp. 471-473): "Certainly even whatever he [Aristophanes] imitates he makes worse; for with him roguishness is not urbane but malicious, rusticity not simple but silly, facetiousness not playful but ridiculous, and love not joyous but licentious. For the fellow seems to have written his poetry, not for any decent person, but the indecent and wanton lines for the licentious, the slanderous and bitter passages for the envious and malicious."

3. Ben Jonson, *Timber, or Discoveries,* in *Critical Essays of the Seventeenth Century,* ed. J. E. Spingarn (Oxford: Clarendon, 1907; rpt. Bloomington, Ind.: Indiana University Press, 1957), vol. I, p. 59.

4. Voltaire, "Athée, Athéisme," in *Dictionnaire philosophique* (Paris: Garnier-Flammarion, 1964), p. 51. This article appeared in the first edition of the *Dictionnaire* in 1764.

5. August Wilhelm Schlegel, *Lectures on Dramatic Art and Literature* (Lecture XI), trans. John Black, rev. A. J. W. Morrison (London: George Bell, 1883), pp. 148, 149-50. The preceding phrases are found on pp. 145 and 147; those that follow, on p. 157 (Lecture XII). Schlegel's *Vorlesungen* were originally delivered in 1808.

6. Werner Jaeger, *Paideia: The Ideals of Greek Culture,* trans. Gilbert Highet, 2nd ed. (New York: Oxford University Press, 1945), vol. I, pp. 364, 365. The moral interpretation of Aristophanic comedy did not of course originate in the twentieth century. It is implicit in Horace, *Satires* I. iv. 1-5, for example, and fully developed in Antonio Sebastiano Minturno's *The Art of Poetry* (1563). For the latter see Paul Lauter, ed., *Theories of Comedy* (Garden City, N.Y.: Doubleday Anchor, 1964), pp. 77-78.

7. Bruno Snell, *The Discovery of the Mind,* trans. T. G. Rosenmeyer (Oxford: Basil Blackwell, 1953), pp. 132, 115.

8. But see Introduction, n. 3.

9. Cornford, *The Origin of Attic Comedy,* p. 76.

10. Ibid., p. 178.

11. Whitman, *Aristophanes and the Comic Hero,* pp. 22-23. The preceding phrases are from pp. 7 and 10.

12. Ibid., p. 30.

13. Ibid., pp. 52, 57.

14. Aristophanes, *Knights* 836-840 (with omissions), trans. R. H. Webb, in *The Complete Plays of Aristophanes,* ed. Moses Hadas (New York: Bantam Books, 1962), pp. 82-83.

15. *Clouds* 444-451.

16. "Introduction" to Aristophanes, *The Wasps,* trans. Douglass

Parker (Ann Arbor: University of Michigan Press, 1962; rpt. New York and Toronto: New American Library, 1970), p. 9.

17. *Peace* 93.

18. This is essentially the view adopted, to cite one recent example, by William Arrowsmith in the brief introduction to his translation of Aristophanes, *The Birds* (Ann Arbor: University of Michigan Press, 1961; rpt. New York and Toronto: New American Library, 1970). Of Peisthetaerus' audacious undertaking Arrowsmith writes (p. 9): "This is the *hybris* of enterprise and daring, the trait from which no Athenian can ever escape. Aristophanes' irony is, I think, loving."

19. A. W. Schlegel, *Lectures on Dramatic Art and Literature* (Lecture XII), p. 166.

20. Gilbert Murray, *Aristophanes: A Study* (New York: Oxford University Press, 1933), p. 156.

21. I have adopted the manuscript spelling "Peisthetairos" (in slightly Latinized form), although most editors "correct" the impossible Greek by reading either "Peithetairos" (*peithô,* "persuade," plus *hetairos,* "companion") or "Pisthetairos" (*pistos,* "trusty," plus *hetairos*). It seems to me not impossible that Aristophanes might have been playing on both meanings through a hybrid prefix, since the manuscripts are consistently "in error" and the copyists, even when Byzantine, were after all Greeks who may have recognized a play on words when they saw one. Future scholars of English will no doubt someday likewise correct the first Folio's untenable spelling of Shakespeare's Abhorson.

22. *Birds* 252.

23. Ibid. 848.

24. Ibid. 1259.

25. Ibid. 1447-48.

26. Whitman, *Aristophanes and the Comic Hero,* p. 198.

3. Bondservant and Beast of Burden

The books on Plautus and Roman comedy which I have found useful are George E. Duckworth, *The Nature of Roman Comedy: A Study in Popular Entertainment* (Princeton: Princeton University Press, 1952), and Erich Segal, *Roman Laughter: The Comedy of Plautus* (Cambridge, Mass: Harvard University Press, 1968; rpt. New York: Harper and Row, 1971). The text to which I refer is that of Alfred Ernout, ed., *Plaute,* 7 vols. (Paris: Société d'Edition "Les Belles Lettres," 1957-1963); I have also made use of Paul Nixon, ed., *Plautus,* 5 vols. (Cambridge, Mass., and London: Harvard University Press, and Heinemann, 1916-1938).

On Apuleius, see above all the valuable critique in P. G. Walsh, *The Roman Novel* (Cambridge: Cambridge University Press, 1970), esp. chaps. 6 and 7. Other books include Elizabeth Hazelton Haight, *Apuleius and His Influence* (New York: Longmans, 1927), and *Essays on Ancient Fiction* (New York: Longmans, 1936), esp. chaps. 5 and 8; Ben Edwin Perry, *The Ancient Romances* (Berkeley and Los Angeles: University of California Press, 1967), esp. chap. 7; and Alexander Scobie, *Aspects of the Ancient Romance and Its Heritage* (Meisenheim am Glan: Anton Hain, 1969). On Isis and the conversion of Lucius, see also André-Jean Festugière, *Personal Religion Among the Greeks* (Berkeley and Los Angeles: University of California Press, 1954), chap. 5; A. D. Nock, *Conversion* (Oxford: Clarendon, 1933), chap. 9; and J. D. Orders, II, *Isiac Elements in the* Metamorphoses *of Apuleius* (Diss., Vanderbilt University, 1971; Ann Arbor, Mich.: University Microfilms, 1973). I have used S. Gaselee's text of Apuleius, *The Golden Ass* (Cambridge, Mass., and London: Harvard University Press, and Heinemann, 1915), in consultation with *Apulei Metamorphoseon Libri XI*, ed. Caesar Giarratano, rev. Paulus Frassinetti (Turin: Paravia, 1961).

1. For the Greek text, see *The Dyskolos of Menander,* ed. E. W. Handley (Cambridge, Mass.: Harvard University Press, 1965); for an English prose translation, see *The Plays of Menander,* trans. Lionel Casson (New York: New York University Press, 1971). For the fragments of Menander's other plays, in both Greek and English, see *Menander: The Principal Fragments,* trans. Francis G. Allinson, rev. ed. (Cambridge, Mass., and London: Harvard University Press, and Heinemann, 1930). A brief introductory account of New Comedy is given by Albin Lesky in *A History of Greek Literature,* trans. James Willis and Cornelis de Heer (New York: Crowell, 1966), pp. 642-665.

2. From "Unidentified Minor Fragments" in *Menander,* ed. Allinson, p. 491.

3. Terence, *Phormio* 841.

4. For an exhaustive study of Plautus' innovations, see Eduard Fraenkel, *Elementi Plautini in Plauto,* trans. Franco Munari (Florence: La Nuova Italia, 1960), a revised Italian edition of the author's *Plautinisches im Plautus* (Berlin: Weidmannsche Buchhandlung, 1922), esp. chap. VIII, "Il predominio della parte dello schiavo."

5. See Horace, *Ars poetica* 270-274, and *Epistles* II.i.170-176; Michel de Montaigne, *Essais* II.x ("Des Livres"), ed. Albert Thibaudet (Paris: Bibliothèque de la Pléiade, 1946), p. 392; Ben Jonson, *Timber, or Discoveries,* in *Critical Essays of the Seventeenth Century,* ed.

J. E. Spingarn (1907; rpt. Bloomington: Indiana University Press, 1957), pp. 57-59. Perhaps the most extreme modern deprecation of Plautus is that of Gilbert Norwood in *Plautus and Terence* (New York: Cooper Square Publishers, 1963). Plautus, Norwood asserts (p. 4), is "on the whole and in regard to the most fundamental aspects of a playwright's work, the worst of all writers who have ever won permanent repute . . . the offence that puts Plautus outside the pale of art, almost of civilization, is his practice of tying together—not only in the same play, sometimes in the same scene—modes of feeling and treatment utterly incongruous." By some, it might be added, incongruity has been considered the essence of laughter.

6. Erich Segal, *Roman Laughter,* pp. 101, 31. Segal's well-written book is full of interesting insights from which I have profited, but its central thesis seems to me an excessively simplistic application of C. L. Barber's "saturnalian" view of comedy to a playwright whom it only partially and imperfectly fits. The Saturnalia was indeed a Roman holiday, but its spirit is by no means pervasive in Plautus' comedies.

7. *Miles gloriosus* 1435.

8. Ibid. 189a-192.

9. *Pseudolus* 96.

10. Ibid. 401-404.

11. Ibid. 679-80.

12. The apparent discrepancy between Pseudolus' claim (508-510) that he will defraud Simo himself of the money, and the actual outcome, has been more bothersome to scholars than to viewers. Plautus' wording may be the result of careless workmanship, yet in an oblique way Pseudolus does fulfill his pledge, since by his success in defrauding Ballio he persuades Simo (1241-2) that he deserves the payment that he has vowed to extort. Thus he is able to obtain his master's money, as he promised, while remaining on the up-and-up—a most comfortable solution.

13. *Pseudolus* 1037, 1051 (reading *triumphi*).

14. Ibid. 1317.

15. Ibid. 1244. For Socrates and Agathocles, see ibid. 465, 532. Such comparisons are by no means unique to *Pseudolus;* in *Mostellaria* 775-777, e.g., the slave Tranio likens himself to Alexander the Great and Agathocles, and in *Bacchides* 925-972 another slave, Chrysalus, compares his exploits with those of the Atridae and Ulysses. But in the case of Pseudolus the comparison gains credit by the fact that his vanquished master makes it.

16. *Pseudolus* 1258.

17. "Fortibus est fortuna viris data." Ennius, *Annals,* Fragment

254, in *Remains of Old Latin,* trans. E. H. Warmington, rev. ed. (Cambridge, Mass., and London: Harvard University Press, and Heinemann, 1956), vol. I, p. 92.

18. See Cicero, *De oratore* II.lviii.236.

19. *Apologia* 55, in *The Apologia and Florida of Apuleius of Madaura,* trans. H. E. Butler (Oxford: Clarendon, 1909; rpt. Westport, Conn.: Greenwood Press, 1970), p. 96.

20. *Florida* 20, ibid. p. 209.

21. *Golden Ass* IX.13.

22. Ibid. I.1: "Reader, pay attention; you will be delighted."

23. Ibid. I.20 ("lepidae fabulae festivitate nos avocavit").

24. Plutarch, "Isis and Osiris," in *Plutarch's Moralia,* vol. V, ed. Frank Cole Babbitt (Cambridge, Mass., and London: Harvard University Press, and Heinemann, 1936), pp. 183-185. On the subject of Lucius' conversion to Isis consult the works by Festugière, Nock, and Orders cited in the headnote above.

4. Renegade Vassal

The most authoritative study of the Old French Reynard poems remains Lucien Foulet, *Le Roman de Renard* (Paris: Champion, 1914). Among important earlier works are Jacob Grimm's pioneering study of the legend, *Reinhart Fuchs* (Berlin: Reimer, 1834); Léopold Sudre, *Les Sources du Roman de Renart* (Paris: E. Bouillon, 1892); and Gaston Paris, "Le Roman de Renard," in *Mélanges de littérature française du moyen âge* (Paris: Champion, 1912), pp. 337-423. More recent books include the exhaustive study of John Flinn, *Le Roman de Renart dans la littérature française et dans les littératures étrangères au Moyen Age* (Toronto: University of Toronto Press, 1963), and the succinct account of Robert Bossuat, *Le Roman de Renard,* rev. ed. (Paris: Hatier, 1967), which provides the most convenient general introduction to the poem and its background.

The text that I have followed is that of Ernest Martin, ed., *Le Roman de Renart,* vols. I and II (Strasbourg, and Paris: Trübner, and Leroux, 1882 and 1885). Martin's text of Branches I-V, VIII, X, and XV is conveniently reprinted (with minor modifications and helpful notes and glossary) in *Le Roman de Renart,* ed. Jean Dufournet (Paris: Garnier-Flammarion, 1970), and I have used this easily accessible edition wherever possible. The excellent text of Mario Roques, ed., *Le Roman de Renart,* 6 vols. (Paris: Champion, 1948-1963), follows another manuscript and numbers the branches differently, but includes parenthetical line references to the corresponding branches in Martin's edition. There is at present no accurate English version, but a German prose translation of Branches II, Va, III, IV, and I is included along with the Old French text in *Le Roman de Renart,* ed. Helga Jauss-Meyer (Munich: Wilhelm Fink, 1965).

1. Pindar, *Nemean* VIII.35-36. On the post-Homeric discrediting of Odysseus in Greek poetry and drama, see W. B. Stanford, *The Ulysses Theme,* 2nd ed. (1963; rpt. Ann Arbor, Mich.: University of Michigan Press, 1968), chaps. VII-VIII, esp. pp. 92-94, on Pindar.

2. Plato, *Republic* III. 389b, 388e-389a, in *The Dialogues of Plato,* trans. Benjamin Jowett (New York: Random House, 1937), vol. I, p. 651.

3. On Virgil's Ulysses, see Stanford, *The Ulysses Theme,* chap. X. For denunciations of Jacob by the Prophets, see Hosea 12:2-8 and Jer. 9:4-5 (where Jeremiah puns on the name of Jacob, "He [who] supplants").

4. *The Confessions of St. Augustine* II. i., trans. F. J. Sheed (New York: Sheed and Ward, 1943), p. 27.

5. 2 Corinthians 4:2, Revised Standard Version.

6. *La Chanson de Roland* LXXXIX (1128-29, 1134), ed. Joseph Bédier, rev. ed. (Paris: Piazza, 1937), p. 96.

7. See the poems of Guillem comte de Peitau (William IX of Aquitaine) beginning "Companho, faray un vers . . . covinen" and "Farai un vers, pos mi sonelh" in *Anthology of the Provençal Troubadours,* ed. Raymond Thompson Hill and Thomas Goddard Bergin (New Haven and London: Yale University Press, 1941), pp. 1-2 and 4-6. For translations, see *Songs of the Troubadours,* ed. Anthony Bonner (New York: Schocken, 1972), pp. 33-37.

8. Erich Auerbach, *Mimesis: The Representation of Reality in Western Literature,* trans. Willard R. Trask (Princeton: Princeton University Press, 1953; rpt. 1968), p. 110.

9. Andreas Capellanus, *The Art of Courtly Love,* trans. John Jay Parry (New York: Columbia University Press, 1941; rpt. New York: Norton, 1969), p. 187.

10. Chrétien de Troyes, *Le Chevalier au Lion* (*Yvain*) 31-32, ed. Mario Roques (Paris: Champion, 1970), p. 2.

11. Marc Bloch, *Feudal Society,* trans. L. A. Manyon (London: Routledge & Kegan Paul, 1961; rpt. Chicago: University of Chicago Press, 1964), vol. I, p. 106.

12. From the poem beginning "Cum in orbem universum," rpt. in *The Goliard Poets,* trans. George F. Whicher (New York: New Directions, 1949), p. 274.

13. Rpt. in *The Oxford Book of Medieval Latin Verse,* ed. F. J. E. Raby (Oxford: Clarendon, 1959), p. 172.

14. From the poem beginning "Aestuans intrinsecus," ibid., p. 264.

15. From the poem beginning "Advertite, omnes populi," ibid., p. 170 ("sic fraus fraudem vicerat").

16. Joseph Bédier, *Les Fabliaux,* 4th ed. (Paris: Champion, 1925), p. 371. Bédier's view, that the fabliaux are "the *fabellae ignobilium . . .* the poetry of the little people," has been modified, though hardly refuted, by Per Nykrog in *Les Fabliaux: Etude d'histoire littéraire et de stylistique médiévale* (Copenhagen: Munksgaard, 1957). Nykrog contends, e.g. (p. 229), that "satire in the fabliaux is directed against those who are not courtiers"; but his conclusion from this, that it is therefore courtly in essence ("elle doit donc partir de l'interiéur même de la courtoisie, et de la courtoisie authentique"), seems to me a curious non sequitur, even if the premise were true, since the external deference of the bourgeoisie to their social betters prevailed more or less until the French Revolution. Nykrog successfully documents what Bédier had already conceded, that fabliaux were performed for lords as well as burghers, and tempers some of Bédier's more categorical statements; he does not, I think, establish that these were poems composed principally for aristocratic audiences.

For an excellent selection of Old French *fabliaux* with English verse translations, see Robert Harrison, trans., *Gallic Salt: Eighteen Fabliaux Translated from the Old French* (Berkeley and Los Angeles: University of California Press, 1974). The fabliau "The Silly Chevalier," by Gautier le Leu (pp. 322-341), sufficiently demonstrates that the upper classes were not immune from the general derision of the genre.

17. Bédier, *Les Fabliaux,* p. 385.

18. Béroul, *The Romance of Tristan* 2165-194 (with omissions), trans. Alan S. Fredrick (Baltimore: Penguin, 1970), pp. 96-97.

19. Bédier, *Les Fabliaux,* p. 333.

20. Quoted in G. G. Coulton, *Medieval Panorama* (New York, and Cambridge: Macmillan, and Cambridge University Press, 1938; rpt. Cleveland and New York: World, 1955), p. 582. See Brunetto Latini, *Li Livres dou Tresor* II. i. 34, ed. P. Chabaille (Paris, Imprimerie impériale, 1863), p. 302: "Jugleor est cil qui converse entre la gent à ris et à geu, et moque soi et sa feme et ses enfans, et touz autres."

21. For collections of medieval fables in Latin and French, see *Les Fabulistes latins depuis le siècle d'Auguste jusqu'à la fin du moyen âge,* ed. Léopold Hervieux, 5 vols. (Paris: Firmin-Didot, 1893-1899);

Der Lateinische Äsop des Romulus, ed. Georg Thiele (Heidelberg: C. Winter, 1910); *Die Fabeln der Marie de France,* ed. Karl Warnke (Halle: M. Niemeyer, 1898); and *Recueil général des Isopets,* ed. Julia Bastin, 2 vols. (Paris: Champion, 1929-30).

22. See *Ecbasis Cuiusdam Captivi per Tropologiam: Escape of a Certain Captive Told in a Figurative Manner,* ed. Edwin H. Zeydel (Chapel Hill, N.C.: University of North Carolina Press, 1964); the appendix to this volume contains the earlier poem ascribed to Paul the Deacon. For a Greek prose version of this influential fable, see *Aesopica,* ed. Ben Edwin Perry (Urbana: University of Illinois Press, 1952), p. 421. The story reappears in Book III of *Ysengrimus* and Branch X of the *Roman de Renart,* as well as in Fable LXVIII of Marie de France (ed. Warnke).

23. See *Ysengrimus,* ed. Ernst Voigt (Halle: Buchhandlung des Waisenhauses, 1884); my line references are to this edition. For a German prose translation, see *Isengrimus,* trans. Albert Schönfelder (Münster and Cologne: Böhlau, 1955). Among later medieval renditions of these and similar tales, besides the *Roman de Renart,* see Adriaan J. Barnouw's translation of Willem's Flemish poem in *Reynard the Fox and Other Mediaeval Netherlands Secular Literature,* ed. E. Colledge (Leyden: Sijthoff, 1967); William Caxton's translation (1481) of the Flemish prose version, *The History of Reynard the Fox,* ed. Donald B. Sands (Cambridge, Mass.: Harvard University Press, 1960); and (in modern German verse) *Reineke Fuchs: Das Niederdeutsche Epos "Reynke de Vos" von 1498,* trans. Karl Langosch (Stuttgart: Reclam, 1967). Both Chaucer's "Nun's Priest's Tale" in *The Canterbury Tales* and the anonymous Middle English "The Fox and Wolf in the Well" narrate analogous episodes; for the latter poem, see *Middle English Humorous Tales in Verse,* ed. George Harley McKnight (Boston and London: Heath, 1913), and the translation by Brian Stone in *Medieval English Verse* (Baltimore: Penguin, 1964), pp. 244-251.

24. Concerning the Old French poems, e.g., which he considers Germanic in origin ("eine wahrhaft *fränkische* sage, und darum schon deutschartig, nicht romanisch"), Grimm surmises that the poets merely versified beast-tales told by the people: "Wahrscheinlich giengen die meisten dieser thierfabeln, und ausser ihnen manche ähnliche, im munde der leute herum; sie brauchten nur von den dichtern aufgefasst und in reime gebracht zu werden." *Reinhart Fuchs,* pp. cxvi, cxxxviii.

25. Léopold Sudre, *Les Sources du Roman de Renart,* p. vii.

26. Lucien Foulet, *Le Roman de Renard,* p. 570.

27. Ibid., p. 11. The conclusion of Gaston Paris (*Mélanges de littérature française du moyen âge,* p. 398), that both monastic studies and popular lore played their part, is surely more balanced: "C'est, en effet, dans le monde des clercs que se sont propagées les fables antiques qui ont pénétré dans le *Roman de Renard.* Mais il ne faut pas croire à une transmission purement littéraire et scolastique."

28. See Roger Sherman Loomis, *The Grail: From Celtic Myth to Christian Symbol* (New York: Columbia University Press, 1963), chaps. II-III.

29. *Ysengrimus* I. 495, 499: "Peius agit, qui plura potest, luit omnia pauper . . . Quod locuples, quod pauper habet, locupletis utrumque est." Other sallies in this vein include V. 73 ("Nobilis est locuples, ignobilis omnis egenus") and V. 87-88 ("Lucrum iustitiae, lucrum praefertur honori, Nil nisi diuitias non habuisse pudet").

30. See ibid. I. 843 ("Venit honor nimio, quem leto comparat emptor") and V. 81 ("Quid michi nobilitas, quae non ieiunia tollit?").

31. Ibid. I. 217: "Saepe ebetes magni, subtiles saepe pusilli."

32. *Self and Society in Medieval France: The Memoirs of Abbot Guibert of Nogent* III. 8, trans. C. C. Swinton Bland, rev. John F. Benton (New York and Evanston: Harper and Row, 1970), p. 176. For the Latin text, see Guibert de Nogent, *Histoire de sa vie,* ed. Georges Bourgin (Paris: A. Picard, 1907). p. 167.

33. This evaluation of Gaudry, by an anonymous canon of Laon, as "vir insolens, in litteratura nil valens omnino, litteratos despectui habens," is quoted by Bourgin (after Dachery) in his edition of Guibert, pp. 137-38, n. 4; "litteratura" means not so much "literature" as "literacy" in the Latin language. According to Guibert himself (*Self and Society,* III. 11, p. 188), Gaudry inclined in his speech not to learned allusions but to earthy epithets like "shitty peasant." Guibert elsewhere notes (III. 4, p. 154) that his was an age when priests "scarcely knew the rudiments of Latin" and the Pope himself "was less learned than he should have been in his office." All this makes it seem extremely far-fetched that this worldly Bishop, as Foulet would have us believe, should have wittily dubbed an upstart serf with a nickname culled from an obscure (and purely hypothetical) Latin poem. Far more probable is the inference of Gaston Paris (*Mélanges,* p. 361), "que l'épopée animale était connue au coeur de la France, avec les noms de ses principaux héros, dès les premières années du XIIe siècle," i.e., that both the tales and the names Renart and Isengrin were widely known well before Nivardus combined them with monastic versions of Aesopian fables in his learned satire.

34. *Le Roman de Renart* II. 1-13, in Jean Dufournet's edition of the text of Ernest Martin (see headnote). On the text of these opening lines, see Gunnar Tilander, *Remarques sur le Roman de Renart* (Göteborg: Wettergren & Kerbers, 1923), p. 41, and "Notes sur le texte du Roman de Renart," *Zeitschrift für romanische Philologie,* 44 (1924), 664-65. Dufournet follows Tilander in accepting Wilmotte's conjecture *d'Yvain* in line 8 (where Martin's text reads *de lui*); for other possibilities, see Foulet, pp. 141-42.

35. See *Ysengrimus* V. 795-820, and Marie de France, Fable LXIX.

36. *Le Roman de Renart* I. 1-7.

37. Ibid. 23.

38. Ibid. IV. 238-39.

39. *Fables of Aesop,* trans. S. A. Handford (Baltimore: Penguin, 1954), p. 9. Compare Phaedrus IV. 9, in *Babrius and Phaedrus,* ed. Ben Edwin Perry (Cambridge, Mass., and London: Harvard University Press, and Heinemann, 1965), pp. 314-317.

40. *Aesopica,* ed. Perry, p. 628. Cf. p. 633, where the deceitful Reinardus becomes a prototype of the damned.

41. C. G. Jung, "On the Psychology of the Trickster Figure," in Paul Radin, *The Trickster: A Study in American Indian Mythology* (New York: Philosophical Library, 1956; rpt. New York: Schocken, 1972), p. 203.

42. See John of Salisbury, *Policraticus* VI. xx, in *The Statesman's Book,* trans. John Dickinson (New York: Knopf, 1927; rpt. New York: Russell and Russell, 1963), pp. 243-44.

43. Henri Pirenne, *Economic and Social History of Medieval Europe,* trans. I. E. Clegg (London: K. Paul, Trench, Trubner, 1936; rpt. New York: Harcourt, Brace, n.d.), p. 44.

44. Pirenne, *Medieval Cities,* trans. Frank D. Halsey (Princeton: Princeton University Press, 1925; rpt. Garden City, N.Y.: Doubleday, 1956), pp. 86-87.

45. Guibert of Nogent, *Self and Society in Medieval France* III.7, p. 166.

46. Marc Bloch, *Feudal Society,* vol. II, p. 355.

47. Henri Pirenne, *Early Democracies in the Low Countries,* trans. J. V. Saunders (Manchester: The University Press, 1915; rpt. New York: Norton, 1971), p. 52.

48. *Le Roman de Renart* I. 1231.

49. Ibid. 1342. The principal meaning of *loi* in Old French is "religion."

50. Ibid. II. 1111: "Acolez moi, si me baisiez!" The meaning of the second verb was already (or rather, still) ambiguous in Old French. On *aventure* (line 1032), cf. Auerbach, *Mimesis,* pp. 134-136.

51. *Le Roman de Renart* VII. 437-38 (in Martin, vol. I, p. 253): "For the noblest name that exists in this world is *cunt.*"

52. For the text of an "Ass's mass" ("Orientis partibus/adventavit Asinus") and a song for the Feast of Fools ("Gregis pastor Tityrus,/ asinorum dominus"), see *The Oxford Book of Medieval Latin Verse,* pp. 307-309. See also C. G. Jung's remarks on these festivals in Paul Radin, *The Trickster,* pp. 196-199.

53. *Le Roman de Renart* I. 1377-78.

54. Ibid. 1511-24.

55. Ibid. XVII. 873-876, 911-12 (in Martin, vol. II, pp. 220-21):

> Fucking seems suitable to me.
> Therefore fucking shall never be
> Forbidden, I say to all of you.
> For fucking the cunt was split in two . . .
> And those who follow my advice
> Will find true bliss in paradise.

56. "He is what the rest of the world would be, if their powers were equal to their desires," James Anthony Froude wrote in a fascinating attempt to explain the appeal of Reynard (whom he knew in Goethe's version) to a mid-Victorian generation appalled by his morals. See his essay "Reynard the Fox" in *Short Studies on Great Subjects* (New York and London: Everyman's Library, 1906), p. 280.

5. Monarch of Make-Believe

Among countless writings on Falstaff those which I have found most valuable are Maurice Morgann, "An Essay on the Dramatic Character of Sir John Falstaff" (1777), in *Shakespearian Criticism,* ed. Daniel A. Fineman (Oxford: Clarendon, 1972), pp. 143-215; William Hazlitt, "Henry IV, in Two Parts," in *Characters of Shakespeare's Plays* (London: R. Hunter, 1817; rpt. London: Oxford University Press, 1916), pp. 148-158; A. C. Bradley, "The Rejection of Falstaff," in *Oxford Lectures on Poetry,* 2nd ed. (London: Macmillan, 1909), pp. 247-275; C. L. Barber, "Rule and Misrule in *Henry IV,*" in *Shakespeare's Festive Comedy* (Princeton: Princeton University Press, 1959; rpt. Cleveland and New York: World, 1963), pp. 192-221; and W. H. Auden, "The Prince's Dog," in *The Dyer's Hand and Other Essays* (New York: Random House, 1962; rpt. Vintage, 1968), pp. 182-208. For other predominantly "positive" interpretations see, e.g., J. B. Priestley, *The English Comic Characters* (1925; rpt. New York: Dutton, 1966); Harold C. Goddard, *The Meaning of Shakespeare* (Chicago: University of Chicago Press, 1951), vol. I; Derek Traversi, *Shakespeare from Richard II to Henry V* (Stanford, Cal.: Stanford University Press, 1957); and Jonas Barish, "The Turning Away of Prince Hal," in *Shakespeare Studies,* 1 (1965), ed. J. Leeds Barroll, 3rd (Cincinnati: The University of Cincinnati, 1965), pp. 9-17. Walter Kaiser, in *Praisers of Folly: Erasmus, Rabelais, Shakespeare* (Cambridge, Mass.: Harvard University Press, 1963), studies Falstaff within the context of the Renaissance fool. Among harsher estimates of Falstaff as a "braggart soldier" or figure of Vice might be mentioned Elmer Edgar Stoll, *Shakespeare Studies* (1927; rpt. New York: G. E. Stechert, 1942), pp. 403-490; and J. Dover Wilson, *The Fortunes of Falstaff* (Cambridge: Cambridge University Press, 1943). Useful collections of modern essays include *Twentieth Century Interpretations of Henry IV, Part One,* ed. R. J. Dorius, and of *Part Two,* ed. David P. Young (Englewood Cliffs, N.J.: Prentice-Hall, 1970 and 1968).

My citations are from *The Riverside Shakespeare,* ed. G. Blakemore Evans (Boston: Houghton Mifflin, 1974). I have also consulted the Arden editions of the two parts of *Henry IV,* ed. A. R. Humphreys (Cambridge, Mass.: Harvard University Press, 1960 and 1966), and the Signet Classic editions of *Part One,* ed. Maynard Mack, and *Part Two,* ed. Norman N. Holland (New York: New American Library, 1965); in a few instances I have substituted a reading from Humphreys' text in preference to Evans', as in the spelling "Bolingbroke" for "Bullingbrook," and in one or two matters of punctuation. Parenthetical references in my text are to the two parts of *Henry IV;* the annotation (2.II.iv.), e.g., refers to *Part Two,* Act II, scene iv. Where consecutive quotations from the same scene appear in a single paragraph, only the first is identified.

1. Maurice Morgann, "An Essay on the Dramatic Character of Sir John Falstaff," in *Shakespearian Criticism,* ed. Fineman, p. 200. Morgann is illustrating the point that Falstaff "is a character made up by *Shakespeare* wholly of incongruities," and if it were the case (as Fineman suggests, p. 92) that he would "no doubt . . . have disposed of" these particular phrases in his projected revision of the "Essay" for the sake of greater consistency, the increase in his own congruity might not have been wholly our gain. As a "liar" Falstaff surely comes under Sir Philip Sidney's defense of the poet, who, "though he recount things not true, yet, because hee telleth them not for true, he lyeth not." *An Apologie for Poetrie,* ed. Evelyn S. Shuckburgh (Cambridge: Cambridge University Press, 1896), p. 39.

2. *The Tempest* V.i.208-213. On this subject see Bernard Knox's excellent essay " 'The Tempest' and the Ancient Comic Tradition," in *English Stage Comedy: English Institute Essays, 1954,* ed. W. K. Wimsatt, Jr. (New York: Columbia University Press, 1955), pp. 52-73, rpt. in Shakespeare, *The Tempest,* ed. Robert Langbaum (New York: New American Library, 1964), pp. 163-181.

3. *As You Like It* V.iv.109-10.

4. Ibid. III.ii.400-404.

5. *Henry V* II.Chorus.6.

6. Raphael Holinshed, *Chronicles of England, Scotland, and Ireland* (1587 edition), as excerpted in Maynard Mack's Signet Classic edition of *Henry IV, Part One,* p. 170.

7. *The Famous Victories of Henry the Fifth,* scene vi, ibid., p. 201.

8. *3 Henry VI* III.ii.188-193.

9. W. H. Auden, "Brothers and Others," in *The Dyer's Hand,* p. 221. The long tradition of moral condemnation of Falstaff overlooks Morgann's paradox that a knave and liar might — in his own comic world — be neither malicious nor deceitful; the most perceptive critics, from Morgann to Auden, have known better. Falstaff "is represented as a liar, a braggart, a coward, a glutton, &c.," Hazlitt writes (*Characters of Shakespeare's Plays,* p. 150), "and yet we are not offended but delighted with him; for he is all these as much to amuse others as to gratify himself. He openly assumes all these characters to show the humorous part of them. The unrestrained indulgence of his own ease, appetites, and convenience, has neither malice nor hypocrisy in it. In a word, he is an actor in himself almost as much as upon the stage, and we no more object to the character of Falstaff in a moral point of view than we should think of bringing an excellent comedian, who should represent him to the life, before one of the police offices." Cf. Bradley, *Oxford Lectures,* pp. 264, 270: "Falstaff is neither a liar nor a coward in the usual sense, like the typical cowardly boaster of comedy. He tells his lies either for their own humour, or on purpose to get himself into a difficulty. He rarely expects to be believed, perhaps never . . . You no more regard Falstaff's misdeeds morally than you do the much more atrocious misdeeds of Punch or Reynard the Fox. You do not exactly ignore them, but you attend only to their comic aspect." Auden has taken these insights one step further by discerning Falstaff's "effect of calling in question" the incompatible values of a world that cannot see (or cannot condone) his comic aspect.

10. Auden, "The Prince's Dog," in *The Dyer's Hand,* p. 186.

11. Lewis Carroll, *Through the Looking-Glass,* chap. VI, in *Alice in Wonderland,* ed. Donald J. Gray (New York: Norton, 1971), p. 163.

12. C. L. Barber, *Shakespeare's Festive Comedy,* p. 198.

13. On the rejection of Falstaff by King Henry V see, in addition to the authors cited in the headnote above (especially Bradley and Barish), the remarks of Northrop Frye in "The Argument of Comedy," cited in the headnote to my Introduction above, as rpt. in *Theories of Comedy,* ed. Lauter, pp. 458-59: "Clearly, if the Prince is ever to conquer France he must reassert the moral norm. The moral norm is duly reasserted, but the rejection of Falstaff is not a comic resolution. In comedy the moral norm is not morality but deliverance, and we certainly do not feel delivered from Falstaff as we feel delivered from Shylock with his absurd and vicious bond. The moral norm does not carry with it the vision of a free society: Falstaff will always keep a bit of that in his tavern. . . . Falstaff's world is not a golden world, but as long as we remember it we cannot forget that the world of *Henry V* is an iron one." A kingdom that has lost first Hotspur, then Falstaff, along with all that they embodied, has been irreparably diminished, even though the excision be a condition for its survival.

14. *Henry V* IV.i.176-180.

6. Aberrant Hidalgo

Works on Cervantes that I have found of especial value include Américo Castro, *El Pensamiento de Cervantes* (1925; rev. ed. Barcelona and Madrid: Noguer, 1972), *Hacia Cervantes,* 3rd ed. (Madrid: Taurus, 1967), and *Cervantes y los casticismos españoles* (Madrid and Barcelona: Alfaguara, 1966); José Ortega y Gasset, *Meditations on Quixote,* trans. Evelyn Rugg and Diego Marín (New York: Norton, 1961); Salvador de Madariaga, *Don Quixote: An Introductory Essay in Psychology,* rev. ed. (London: Oxford University Press, 1961); Georg Lukács, *The Theory of the Novel,* trans. Anna Bostock (Cambridge, Mass.: MIT Press, 1971); and Harry Levin, "The Example of Cervantes," in *Contexts of Criticism* (Cambridge, Mass.: Harvard University Press, 1957; rpt. New York: Atheneum, 1963), pp. 79-96. Among other works that I have consulted are Aubrey F. G. Bell, *Cervantes* (Norman: University of Oklahoma Press, 1947); Joaquín Casalduero, *Sentido y forma del Quijote* (Madrid: Insula, 1966); E. C. Riley, *Cervantes's Theory of the Novel* (Oxford: Clarendon, 1962); and Richard L. Predmore, *The World of Don Quixote* (Cambridge, Mass.: Harvard University Press, 1967). Useful collections of essays include *Cervantes Across the Centuries,* ed. Angel Flores and M. J. Bernadete (1947; rpt. New York: Gordian Press, 1969), and *Cervantes: A Collection of Critical Essays,* ed. Lowry Nelson, Jr. (Englewood Cliffs, N.J.: Prentice-Hall, 1969); the latter volume notably includes, besides Levin's essay, generous excerpts from Thomas Mann's "Voyage with Don Quixote," printed in full in *Essays of Three Decades,* trans. H. T. Lowe-Porter (New York: Knopf, 1947), pp. 429-464.

I have referred to the Spanish text of Cervantes' *Obras completas,* ed. Angel Valbuena Prat (Madrid: Aguilar, 1962), in consultation with the critical edition of *Don Quijote de la Mancha,* ed. Martín de Riquer (Barcelona: Juventud, 1958). Modern English translations of *Don Quixote* include those of Samuel Putnam (New York: Viking, 1949), J. M. Cohen (Baltimore: Penguin, 1950), and Walter Starkie (London and New York: Macmillan, and St. Martin's, 1954; rpt. New York: New American Library, 1957). The translations in this chapter are my own. Parenthetical references are to chapters of *Don Quixote;* the annotation (I.5), e.g., refers to Part One, chapter 5. Where consecutive quotations from the same chapter appear in a single paragraph, only the first is identified.

1. See Cervantes, *Obras completas,* ed. Valbuena Prat, pp. 497-538. For a translation (*Pedro, the Artful Dodger*), see *Eight Spanish Plays of the Golden Age,* trans. Walter Starkie (New York: Modern Library, 1964), pp. 99-164.

2. Ben Jonson, *Volpone* I.i.25-27, ed. Alvin B. Kernan (New Haven and London: Yale University Press, 1962), p. 39.

3. Geoffrey Chaucer, "The Pardoner's Prologue" (Fragment VI, Group C, 421-22), in *The Works of Geoffrey Chaucer,* ed. F.N. Robinson, 2nd ed. (Boston: Houghton Mifflin, 1957), p. 149.

4. Chaucer, "The Wife of Bath's Prologue" (Fragment III, Group D, 622-23), ibid., p. 82.

5. Ibid. (190-192), p. 78.

6. Shakespeare, *Henry IV, Part Two* V.v.100-101.

7. Rabelais, *Gargantua,* chap. 57, in *Oeuvres complètes,* ed. Jacques Boulenger (Paris: Bibliothèque de la Pléiade, 1934), p. 181. Cf. chap. 54, p. 173.

8. Mikhail Bakhtin, *Rabelais and His World,* trans. Hélène Iswolsky (Cambridge, Mass.: MIT Press, 1968), pp. 90-91.

9. Ibid., p. 275.

10. Rabelais, *Pantagruel,* title page, *Oeuvres complètes,* p. 187.

11. Quoted by Jacques Le Clercq in the Introduction to his translation of *Gargantua and Pantagruel* (New York: The Limited Editions Club, 1936; rpt. New York: Modern Library, n.d.), p. xxii. See the

treatise "De Scandalis" (1550) in *Joannis Calvini Opera Selecta,* ed. Petrus Barth and Dora Scheuner (Munich: Chr. Kaiser, 1952), vol. II, pp. 201-02. Calvin condemns Rabelais, among others, for profaning the sacrament "sacrilega ludendi aut ridendi audacia," and writes: "Solennis mos est impuris istis canibus, quo plus ad ructandas blasphemias licentiae habeant, scurrilem personam agere. Ita in conviviis et sermonibus suaviter iocando, omnia religionis principia convellunt."

12. Jean de La Bruyère, *Les Caractères* ("Des ouvrages de l'esprit," 43), quoted by Bakhtin, *Rabelais and His World,* pp. 107-08.

13. Voltaire, *Lettres philosophiques* 22, quoted by Bakhtin, ibid., p. 117.

14. Rabelais, *Le Quart Livre,* chap. 39, *Oeuvres complètes,* p. 666: "Ce sera icy une belle bataille de foin."

15. Rabelais, *Le Tiers Livre,* title page, *Oeuvres complètes,* p. 337.

16. Cervantes, "Author's Prologue" to *The Exemplary Novels,* in *The Deceitful Marriage and Other Exemplary Novels,* trans. Walter Starkie (New York: New American Library, 1963), p. xxxiv.

17. See Américo Castro, *El Pensamiento de Cervantes,* pp. 27-30. Although Castro in later writings has modified the positions set forth in this early book, and although the distinction between the so-called courtly and bourgeois literatures of the Middle Ages is no longer understood by medievalists as a rigid class division (see Chap. Four, n. 16 above), the dichotomy in sixteenth-century Spanish literature remains profound.

18. Cervantes, "The Dogs' Colloquy," in *The Deceitful Marriage,* trans. Starkie, pp. 255-56.

19. Bernal Díaz del Castillo, *The Discovery and Conquest of Mexico,* trans. A. P. Maudslay (New York: Farrar, Straus, 1956), chap. lxi, pp. 190-91. Another Renaissance soldier, Sir Philip Sidney, remarks: "Truely I have knowen men, that even with reading *Amadis de Gaule,* (which God knoweth wanteth much of a perfect Poesie) have found their harts mooved to the exercise of courtesie, liberalitie, and especially courage" (*Apologie for Poetrie,* ed. Shuckburgh [Cambridge: Cambridge University Press, 1896], p. 26).

20. José Ortega y Gasset, *Meditations on Quixote,* p. 130.

21. *Lazarillo de Tormes,* chap. 1, in *Two Spanish Picaresque Novels,* trans. Michael Alpert (Baltimore: Penguin, 1969), p. 27. I have substituted "be sharper than the devil" (Spanish *saber más que el diablo*) for Alpert's "be sharper than a needle."

22. Ibid., chap. 2, p. 44.

23. Mateo Alemán, *Guzmán de Alfarache* II.v., ed. Samuel Gili

Gaya (Madrid: Espasa-Calpe, 1927), vol. II, p. 78. For an elaboration of the same sentiment, see Francisco de Quevedo, *Historia de la Vida del Buscón* I.6: " 'Haz como vieres,' dice un refrán, y dice bien. De puro considerar en él, vine a resolverme de ser bellaco con los bellacos, y más, si pudiese, que todos." (Alpert translates, in *Two Spanish Picaresque Novels,* p. 112: " 'When in Rome, do as the Romans do,' says the proverb, and how right it is. After thinking about it I decided to be as much a tearaway as the others and worse than them if I could.")

24. *Lazarillo de Tormes,* chap. 7, in *Two Spanish Picaresque Novels,* p. 78.

25. *The Defence of Cony-Catching,* by "Cuthbert Cony-Catcher," in *Cony-Catchers and Bawdy Baskets: An Anthology of Elizabethan Low Life,* ed. Gāmini Salgādo (Baltimore: Penguin, 1972), p. 346.

26. Cervantes, "The Dogs' Colloquy," in *The Deceitful Marriage,* p. 247.

27. "Rinconete and Cortadillo," ibid., p. 145.

28. "The Illustrious Kitchen Maid," ibid., p. 175. I have substituted "carried away by a picaresque inclination" (Spanish *llevado de una inclinación picaresca*) for Starkie's "prompted solely by his spirit of adventure." The phrase "virtuous rogue" (Spanish *pícaro virtuoso*) occurs on p. 176: the oxymoron is extreme.

29. "The Dogs' Colloquy," ibid., p. 298.

30. "The Little Gypsy," ibid., pp. 71-72.

31. Cervantes, *El Trato de Argel,* Act II, in *Obras completas,* ed. Valbuena Prat, p. 128.

32. St. Teresa, *The Life of Teresa of Jesus,* trans. E. Allison Peers (Garden City, N.Y.: Doubleday Image, 1960), chap. I, p. 66.

33. *The Autobiography of St. Ignatius Loyola,* ed. John C. Olin, trans. Joseph F. O'Callaghan (New York: Harper and Row, 1974), chap. 2, pp. 31-32.

34. Harry Levin, "The Example of Cervantes," in *Contexts of Criticism,* p. 87.

35. Georg Lukács, *The Theory of the Novel,* p. 56.

36. Ibid., p. 78. Lukács further writes (pp. 103-04), concerning *Don Quixote:* "Thus the first great novel of world literature stands at the beginning of the time when the Christian God began to forsake the world; when man became lonely and could find meaning and substance only in his own soul, whose home was nowhere; when the world, released from its paradoxical anchorage in a beyond that is truly pres-

ent, was abandoned to its immanent meaninglessness . . . *Don Quixote* is the first great battle of interiority against the prosaic vulgarity of outward life, and the only battle in which interiority succeeded, not only to emerge unblemished from the fray, but even to transmit some of the radiance of its triumphant, though admittedly self-ironising, poetry to its victorious opponent." Contrast the assessment of Erich Auerbach in *Mimesis,* trans. Willard R. Trask (1953; rpt. Princeton: Princeton University Press, 1968), p. 347: "There is, then, very little of problem and tragedy in Cervantes' book—and yet it belongs among the literary masterpieces of an epoch during which the modern problematic and tragic conception of things arose in the European mind. Don Quijote's madness reveals nothing of the sort. The whole book is a comedy in which well-founded reality holds madness up to ridicule." If Lukács passes over the comedy of *Don Quixote* in his dialectical discourse, Auerbach refuses throughout his great work to acknowledge that comedy might involve problematic dimensions. He therefore takes no more notice of the heroic than Lukács of the comic.

37. See Ramón Menéndez-Pidal, "The Genesis of 'Don Quixote'," trans. George I. Dale, in *Cervantes Across the Centuries,* ed. Angel Flores and M. J. Bernadete, pp. 32-55.

38. *Lazarillo de Tormes,* chap. 1, in *Two Spanish Picaresque Novels,* trans. Alpert, p. 25.

39. See the ballad "Muerte de Durandarte" in *Flor nueva de romances viejos,* ed. Ramón Menéndez-Pidal (Buenos Aires: Espasa-Calpe Argentina, 1938), pp. 74-75.

40. Coleridge considered Don Quixote's account of his adventures in the Cave of Montesinos "the only impeachment of the knight's moral character" and declared that "Cervantes just gives one instance of the veracity failing before the strong cravings of the imagination for something real and external; the picture would not have been complete without this; and yet it is so well managed, that the reader has no unpleasant sense of Don Quixote having told a lie." "A Course of Lectures," Lecture XII, in *The Literary Remains of Samuel Taylor Coleridge,* ed. Henry Nelson Coleridge (London: Pickering, 1836), vol. I, p. 130.

41. Salvador de Madariaga, *Don Quixote,* p. 145. Madariaga designates this process "La Quijotización de Sancho" and "La Sanchificación de Don Quijote" in his titles to chaps. VII and VIII of the Spanish edition of his book, *Guía del lector del Quijote* (Buenos Aires: Editorial Sudamericana, 1961).

7. Moral Rake and Masterful Lackey

Books that I have found especially useful on Fielding and the English eighteenth century are Stuart M. Tave, *The Amiable Humorist: A Study in the Comic Theory and Criticism of the Eighteenth and Early Nineteenth Centuries* (Chicago: University of Chicago Press, 1960) and Martin C. Battestin, *The Moral Basis of Fielding's Art: A Study of Joseph Andrews* (Middletown, Conn.: Wesleyan University Press, 1959). Other works that I have consulted include Ian Watt, *The Rise of the Novel* (Berkeley and Los Angeles: University of California Press, 1957); Robert Alter, *Fielding and the Nature of the Novel* (Cambridge, Mass.: Harvard University Press, 1968); Aurélien Digeon, *The Novels of Fielding* (London: Routledge, 1925); and Andrew Wright, *Henry Fielding: Mask and Feast* (Berkeley and Los Angeles: University of California Press, 1965). Early responses to Fielding are collected in *Henry Fielding: The Critical Heritage,* ed. Ronald Paulson and Thomas Lockwood (London and New York: Routledge & Kegan Paul, and Barnes & Noble, 1969); more recent essays in *Fielding: A Collection of Critical Essays,* ed. Ronald Paulson (Englewood Cliffs, N.J.: Prentice-Hall, 1962). I have quoted from Martin C. Battestin's edition of *Joseph Andrews* (Middletown, Conn.: Wesleyan University Press, 1967) and Sheridan Baker's of *Tom Jones* (New York: Norton, 1973); the latter includes a generous selection of early and modern criticism. My parenthetical references are to book and chapter of *Tom Jones;* the annotation (IV. 6), e.g., refers to Book IV, chapter 6.

Among works on Diderot that I have found most pertinent are Lester G. Crocker, *The Embattled Philosopher: A Biography of Denis Diderot* (East Lansing, Mich.: Michigan State College Press, 1954), and *Diderot's Chaotic Order: Approach to Synthesis* (Princeton: Princeton University Press, 1974); J. Robert Loy, *Diderot's Determined Fatalist* (New York: King's Crown Press, 1950); Alice Green Fredman, *Diderot and Sterne* (New York: Columbia University Press, 1955); Lionel Trilling, *Sincerity and Authenticity* (Cambridge, Mass.: Harvard University Press, 1972), pp. 26-47; and J.-J. Mayoux, "Diderot and the Technique of Modern Literature," *The Modern Language Review,* 31 (1936), 518-531. Other works that I have consulted include Arthur M. Wilson, *Diderot* (New York: Oxford University Press, 1972); Carol Blum, *Diderot: The Virtue of a Philosopher* (New York: Viking, 1974); Daniel Mornet, *Diderot* (Paris: Hatier, 1966); Henri Lefèbvre, *Diderot* (Paris: Hier et aujourd'hui, 1949); and Roger Kempf, *Diderot et le roman* (Paris: Seuil, 1964). I have quoted from *Jacques the Fatalist and His Master,* trans. J. Robert Loy (New York: New York

University Press, 1959), in consultation with the French text of Diderot's *Oeuvres romanesques,* ed. Henri Bénac (Paris: Garnier, 1962). Parenthetical references are to page numbers in Loy's translation of *Jacques the Fatalist.*

1. Ben Jonson, Epistle dedicatory to *Volpone,* ed. Alvin B. Kernan (New Haven and London: Yale University Press, 1962), pp. 29, 32.

2. William Hazlitt, *Lectures on the English Comic Writers,* Lecture II (London: Taylor and Hessey, 1819; rpt. Garden City, N.Y.: Doubleday Dolphin, n.d.), p. 55.

3. Paul Bénichou, *Man and Ethics: Studies in French Classicism,* trans. Elizabeth Hughes (Garden City, N.Y.: Doubleday Anchor, 1971), p. 116.

4. Ibid., p. 232.

5. Jean-Jacques Rousseau, *Politics and the Arts: Letter to M. d'Alembert on the Theatre,* trans. Allan Bloom (Glencoe, Ill.: Free Press, 1960; rpt. Ithaca, N.Y.: Cornell University Press, 1968), p. 34.

6. Molière, *L'Ecole des femmes* V. iv. (l. 1507): "Je n'entends point de mal dans tout ce que j'ai fait."

7. William Congreve, *The Way of the World* I. ii. and II. ii., in *Complete Plays,* ed. Alexander Charles Ewald (New York: Hill and Wang, 1956), pp. 304, 321.

8. Ibid., IV. i., p. 348.

9. Congreve, *Love for Love* IV. iii., ibid., pp. 267, 269.

10. Pierre de Marivaux, *The False Confessions* III. xii., trans. W. S. Merwin, in *The Classic Theatre,* vol. IV, ed. Eric Bentley (Garden City, N.Y.: Doubleday Anchor, 1961), p. 350.

11. Hans Jakob Christoffel von Grimmelshausen, *Abenteuerlicher Simplicius Simplicissimus* II. x. (Munich: Goldmann, n.d.), p. 100.

12. Daniel Defoe, *Moll Flanders,* ed. Paul J. Hunter (New York: Crowell, 1970), p. 266.

13. Samuel Richardson, *Pamela* (London and New York: Everyman's Library, 1914), vol. I, p. 4.

14. John Cleland, *Memoirs of a Woman of Pleasure* (New York: Putnam's, 1963), p. 213.

15. Henry Fielding, *An Apology for the Life of Mrs. Shamela Andrews,* ed. Sheridan W. Baker (Berkeley and Los Angeles: University of California Press, 1953), original title page. The phrase "young Politician" also appears on this title page. I have corrected the apparent misprint "MISREPRSENTATIONS."

16. Anthony, Earl of Shaftesbury, "An Inquiry Concerning Virtue or Merit," Book I, Part III, Section iii, in *Characteristics of Men, Manners, Opinions, Times,* ed. John M. Robertson (Indianapolis and New York: Bobbs-Merrill, 1964), vol. I, p. 268. In *The Moral Basis of Fielding's Art,* chaps. I and II, Martin C. Battestin demonstrates, however, that Fielding's conception of virtue or goodness was directly influenced less by Shaftesbury, a Deist, than by the latitudinarian Anglican divines of the seventeenth and early eighteenth centuries.

17. Fielding, *Joseph Andrews,* Preface, ed. Battestin, p. 7.

18. See Stuart Tave, *The Amiable Humorist,* esp. p. 155: "So far as Fielding found any inspiration for the creation of honest Abraham Adams in the character of Don Quixote, he was creating a new concept of Don Quixote."

19. *Joseph Andrews* IV. ii., ed. Battestin, p. 283.

20. Samuel Richardson, letter to Astraea and Minerva Hill, August 4, 1749, in *Henry Fielding: The Critical Heritage,* ed. Paulson and Lockwood, p. 174. This volume is hereafter cited as Paulson and Lockwood.

21. Quoted by James Boswell, *The Life of Samuel Johnson* (April 6, 1772), in Paulson and Lockwood, p. 439; the quotation in the next sentence is from the same passage. Boswell, who had earlier defended Fielding against Johnson's "unreasonable prejudice" (*Life,* A.D. 1768, in Paulson and Lockwood, p. 438), here again expresses his "wonder at Johnson's excessive and unaccountable depreciation of one of the best writers that England has produced." But Johnson was not assuaged. Hannah More, in a letter of 1780 (Paulson and Lockwood, p. 443), recounts: "I never saw Johnson really angry with me but once; and his displeasure did him so much honour that I loved him the better for it. I alluded rather flippantly, I fear, to some witty passage in Tom Jones: he replied, 'I am shocked to hear you quote from so vicious a book. I am sorry to hear you have read it: a confession which no modest lady should ever make. I scarcely know a more corrupt work.' "

22. Horace Walpole, letter to Madame du Deffand, August 3, 1773, in Paulson and Lockwood, p. 442. In a letter to John Pinkerton, June 26, 1785 (ibid., p. 445), Walpole writes: "Fielding had as much humour perhaps as Addison, but having no idea of grace, is perpetually disgusting."

23. Sir John Hawkins, from *The Works of Samuel Johnson,* in Paulson and Lockwood, p. 446. Fielding did of course have eminent defenders in the eighteenth century, too. These included, in addition

to Boswell, Edward Gibbon, who grandly announced that "the romance of *Tom Jones,* that exquisite picture of human manners, will outlive the palace of the Escorial and the imperial eagle of the House of Austria." The nineteenth century mainly concurred with Coleridge in admiring Fielding's art and his warm humanity, but retained (unlike Coleridge) a Victorian reserve concerning his morals. "If it is right to have a hero whom we may admire," Thackeray wrote, "let us at least take care that he is admirable . . . But a hero with a flawed reputation; a hero spunging for a guinea; a hero who can't pay his landlady, and is obliged to let his honour out to hire, is absurd, and his claim to heroic rank untenable." See *The Autobiography of Edward Gibbon,* ed. Dero A. Saunders (New York: Meridian, 1961), chap. 1, p. 30; Samuel Taylor Coleridge, *Specimens of the Table Talk* (London: John Murray, 1836), July 5, 1834, p. 310, and "Notes on Tom Jones" in *The Literary Remains,* ed. Henry Nelson Coleridge (London: William Pickering, 1836), pp. 373-376; and William Makepeace Thackeray, *The English Humourists,* etc. (London and New York: Everyman's Library, 1912), p. 215.

24. Fielding, *The Covent Garden Journal,* No. 10 (February 4, 1752), in *The Criticism of Henry Fielding,* ed. Ioan Williams (New York: Barnes and Noble, 1970), p. 160. In No. 52 (June 30, 1752), ibid., pp. 195-96, Fielding calls Aristophanes "a Writer, whose Humour is often extravagant, his Wit coarse, and his Satire unjust and immoral." Ten years earlier, however, in his "Preface to *Plutus*" (ibid., pp. 153-158), his estimation had been far higher.

25. Shaftesbury, "An Inquiry Concerning Virtue or Merit," Book I, Part II, Section ii, in *Characteristics,* ed. Robertson, vol. I, p. 250.

26. Voltaire, "The World as It Is," in *Candide, Zadig and Selected Stories,* trans. Donald M. Frame (New York: New American Library, 1961), p. 207. The words are spoken by the genie Ithuriel, who takes the hint of his emissary Babouc and resolves "not even to think of correcting Persepolis, and to leave *the world as it is.*"

27. Diderot, Foreword to vol. VIII of the *Encyclopedia,* in Diderot, d'Alembert, et al., *Encyclopedia: Selections,* trans. Nelly S. Hoyt and Thomas Cassirer (Indianapolis and New York: Bobbs-Merrill, 1965), p. 114.

28. Diderot, "Entretien d'un père avec ses enfants," in *Ouevres philosophiques,* ed. Paul Vernière (Paris: Garnier, 1964), p. 436. A translation of this dialogue (and of the "Supplement to Bougainville's Voyage" and several others) by Ralph H. Bowen is included, along with Jacques Barzun's translation of "Rameau's Nephew," in

Rameau's Nephew and Other Works (Garden City, N.Y.: Doubleday Anchor, 1956), but I have here supplied my own translation.

29. "Supplément au Voyage de Bougainville," in *Oeuvres philosophiques,* p. 515.

30. "Entretien d'un père avec ses enfants," ibid., p. 443.

31. "Le Neveu de Rameau," in *Oeuvres romanesques,* ed. Henri Bénac, pp. 396, 397.

32. Ibid., p. 414.

33. Ibid., p. 427.

34. Ibid., pp. 448-49.

35. Ibid., p. 449.

36. Ibid., p. 477.

37. Ibid., p. 427.

38. Ibid., p. 490.

39. Letter from Goethe to Merck, quoted by J. Robert Loy in *Diderot's Determined Fatalist,* p. 6.

40. Article "Encyclopedia," in *Rameau's Nephew and Other Works,* trans. Barzun and Bowen, pp. 311, 307.

41. See Mayoux, "Diderot and the Technique of Modern Literature," p. 524: "Unpredictable chance [is] Jacques' true master"; Crocker, *The Embattled Philosopher,* p. 402: "Jacques . . . discovers that his real master is chance."

42. For *Les Bijoux indiscrets,* see *Oeuvres romanesques,* ed. Bénac, pp. 1-233. For its original source, see the fabliau "The Chevalier Who Made Cunts Talk" in *Gallic Salt,* trans. Robert Harrison (Berkeley and Los Angeles: University of California Press, 1974), pp. 218-255.

43. See Michel de Montaigne, *Essais* III. v. ("Sur des vers de Virgile"), ed. Albert Thibaudet (Paris: Bibliothèque de la Pléiade, 1946), p. 820: "Qu'a faict l'action genitale aux hommes, si naturelle, si necessaire et si juste, pour n'en oser parler sans vergongne et pour l'exclurre des propos serieux et reglez? Nous prononçons hardiment: tuer, desrober, trahir; et cela, nous n'oserions qu'entre les dents? Est-ce à dire que moins nous en exhalons en parole, d'autant nous avons loy d'en grossir la pensée?"

44. I have altered Loy's "you do not permit" to "you only dare mutter." The French text reads as follows (*Oeuvres romanesques,* ed. Bénac, pp. 714-15): "Vilains hypocrites, laissez-moi en repos. F..tez comme des ânes débatés; mais permettez-moi que je dise f..tre; je vous passe l'action, passez-moi le mot. Vous prononcez hardiment, tuer, voler, trahir, et l'autre vous ne l'oseriez qu'entre les dents! Est-ce que moins vous exhalez de ces prétendues impuretés en paroles, plus il vous en reste dans la pensée?"

8. Insouciant Lover and Insatiable Stumblebums

The most pertinent works on Byron for my purposes have been
Alvin B. Kernan, *The Plot of Satire* (New Haven and London:
Yale University Press, 1965), chap. 11; W. H. Auden, "Don Juan,"
in *The Dyer's Hand and Other Essays* (New York: Random House,
1962; rpt. Vintage, 1968), pp. 386-406; Leslie A. Marchand,
Byron's Poetry: A Critical Introduction (Boston: Houghton Mif-
flin, 1965); and Peter L. Thorslev, Jr., *The Byronic Hero: Types
and Prototypes* (Minneapolis: University of Minnesota Press, 1962).
Other works that I have consulted include Leslie A. Marchand,
Byron: A Biography, 3 vols. (New York: Knopf, 1957); Andrew
Rutherford, *Byron: A Critical Study* (Stanford, Cal.: Stanford
University Press, 1961); M. K. Joseph, *Byron the Poet* (London:
Gollancz, 1964); G. Wilson Knight, *Byron and Shakespeare* (New
York: Barnes and Noble, 1966); and Truman Guy Steffan, *Byron's
Don Juan,* vol. I: *The Making of a Masterpiece* (Austin: University
of Texas Press, 1957). Valuable essays are collected in *Byron: The
Critical Heritage,* ed. Andrew Rutherford (New York: Barnes and
Noble, 1970); *Byron: A Collection of Critical Essays,* ed. Paul West
(Englewood Cliffs, N.J.: Prentice-Hall, 1963); and *Twentieth
Century Interpretations of Don Juan,* ed. Edward E. Bostetter
(Englewood Cliffs, N.J.: Prentice-Hall, 1969). For *Don Juan* I have
quoted the text edited by Leslie A. Marchand (Boston: Houghton
Mifflin, 1958); for Byron's other poems I have used the one-volume
Cambridge edition of *The Complete Poetical Works of Lord
Byron,* ed. Paul Elmer More (Boston and New York: Houghton
Mifflin, 1905). The new edition of Byron's *Letters and Journals,*
ed. Leslie A. Marchand (Cambridge, Mass.: Harvard University
Press, 1973-), is incomplete at the time of this writing, and I have
therefore cited *The Works of Lord Byron: Letters and Journals,*
ed. Rowland E. Prothero, 6 vols. (London: John Murray, 1898-
1901), as supplemented by *Byron: A Self-Portrait,* ed. Peter Quennell, 2 vols. (London: John Murray, 1950). Parenthetical references are to Canto and stanza of *Don Juan;* the annotation (VIII.
86), for example, refers to Canto the Eighth, stanza lxxxvi. (The
third number in citations from "The Isles of Greece" refers to the
numbered stanzas of this inserted lyric.)

Works that I have found of especial value on Flaubert include
Lionel Trilling's Introduction to *Bouvard and Pécuchet* (New
York: New Directions, 1954), rpt. as "Flaubert's Last Testament"
in *The Opposing Self: Nine Essays in Criticism* (New York: Viking,
1955); Raymond Queneau, "Bouvard et Pécuchet, de Gustave
Flaubert," in *Bâtons, chiffres et lettres,* rev. ed. (Paris: Gallimard,
1965), pp. 97-124; René Dumesnil, "Bouvard et Pécuchet: sont-ils
des imbéciles," in *En marge de Flaubert* (Paris: Librairie de

France, 1928), pp. 31-57; and Claude Digeon, *Le dernier visage de Flaubert* (Paris: Aubier, 1946) and *Flaubert* (Paris: Hatiér, 1970). Among other works that I have consulted are Guy de Maupassant, "Gustave Flaubert," in *Lettres de Gustave Flaubert à George Sand* (Paris: Charpentier, 1884); René Descharmes and René Dumesnil, *Autour de Flaubert*, 2 vols. (Paris: Mercure de France, 1912); René Descharmes, *Autour de Bouvard et Pécuchet* (Paris: Librairie de France, 1921); René Dumesnil, *Gustave Flaubert: l'homme et l'oeuvre*, 3rd ed. (Paris: Desclée, De Brouwer, 1947); Victor Brombert, *The Novels of Flaubert* (Princeton: Princeton University Press, 1966); Harry Levin, *The Gates of Horn* (New York: Oxford University Press, 1963); and Hugh Kenner, *Flaubert, Joyce and Beckett: The Stoic Comedians* (Boston: Beacon, 1962). My quotations from *Bouvard and Pécuchet* are from the translation by T. W. Earp and G. W. Stonier (New York: New Directions, 1954), with reference to the French text in Flaubert, *Oeuvres,* ed. Albert Thibaudet and René Dumesnil (Paris: Bibliothèque de la Pléiade, 1952), vol. II. Since the new edition of Flaubert's *Correspondance,* ed. Jean Bruneau (Paris: Bibliothèque de la Pléiade, 1973-), is still in progress, I have made use of the *Correspondance,* 9 vols. (Paris: Conard, 1926-1933), to which the parenthetical references in my notes refer, and have quoted wherever possible from *The Selected Letters of Gustave Flaubert,* trans. Francis Steegmuller (New York: Farrar, Straus, 1953; rpt. New York: Vintage, 1957). Parenthetical references in my text are to chapter and page of *Bouvard and Pécuchet* in the New Directions edition; the annotation (VIII, 258), e.g., refers to chapter VIII, p. 258.

1. Pierre-Augustin Caron de Beaumarchais, *Figaro's Marriage* V.iii., trans. Jacques Barzun, in *The Classic Theatre,* vol. IV, ed. Eric Bentley (Garden City, N.Y.: Doubleday Anchor, 1961), p. 446.

2. Quoted in the introduction to *The Marriage of Figaro,* trans. Brobury Pearce Ellis (New York: Appleton-Century-Crofts, 1966), p. x. Cf. Félix Gaiffe, *Le Mariage de Figaro* (Paris: Editions Littéraires et Techniques, 1942), pp. 52-53.

3. Karl Marx, *The Eighteenth Brumaire of Louis Bonaparte* (New York: International Publishers, 1963), p. 16.

4. On this subject, see the excellent discussion in Thorslev, *The Byronic Hero.* In contrast to their eighteenth-century prototypes (the Child of Nature, the Hero of Sensibility, and the Gothic Villain), Thorslev writes (p. 22), "The Romantic Heroes . . . from the Noble Outlaw through Satan-Prometheus, stand firmly as individuals outside of society. Thoroughgoing rebels, they invariably appeal to the

reader's sympathies against the unjust restrictions of the social, moral, or even religious codes of the worlds in which they find themselves."

5. Journal for April 9, 1814, in *The Works of Lord Byron: Letters and Journals,* ed. Rowland E. Prothero, vol. II, p. 409.

6. From *Blackwood's Magazine,* July 1819, in *Byron: The Critical Heritage,* ed. Andrew Rutherford, p. 166. The "Remarks on Don Juan" in the August issue of *Blackwood's* declare that "The moral strain of the whole poem is pitched in the lowest key—and if the genius of the author lifts him now and then out of his pollution, it seems as if he regretted the elevation, and made all haste to descend again" (ibid., p. 167).

7. From the *Edinburgh Review,* February 1822, ibid., p. 202.

8. Byron, "The Corsair," stanza xxiii (l. 662), in *Complete Poetical Works,* ed. More, p. 365.

9. "Childe Harold's Pilgrimage," Canto IV, stanza cxxxvii (l. 1233), ibid., p. 75.

10. *Lady Blessington's Conversations of Lord Byron,* ed. Ernest J. Lovell, Jr. (Princeton: Princeton University Press, 1969), p. 5.

11. Journal for December 6, 1813, in *Letters and Journals,* vol. II, p. 366.

12. *Lady Blessington's Conversations,* p. 71.

13. Ibid., p. 220. Compare Keats's well-known description of the poetical character in his letter to Richard Woodhouse of October 27, 1818, in *The Letters of John Keats,* ed. Hyder Edward Rollins (Cambridge, Mass.: Harvard University Press, 1958), vol. I, pp. 386-87: "As to the poetical Character itself . . . it is not itself—it has no self—it is every thing and nothing—It has no character—it enjoys light and shade; it lives in gusto, be it foul or fair, high or low, rich or poor, mean or elevated—It has as much delight in conceiving an Iago as an Imogen. What shocks the virtuous philosop[h]er, delights the camelion Poet . . . A Poet is the most unpoetical of any thing in existence; because he has no Identity." Although Woodhouse comments, with regard to this passage, "Ld Byron does not come up to this Character" (ibid., p. 390), and although Keats was thinking mainly of Shakespeare, in contrast to "the wordsworthian or egotistical sublime" (p. 387), the appropriateness of his description to the chameleonic Byron is striking.

14. Lady Blessington, *The Idler in Italy,* II, 17; quoted in Leslie A. Marchand, *Byron: A Biography,* vol. III, p. 1063.

15. *Lady Blessington's Conversations,* p. 220.

16. *John Bull's Letter to Lord Byron,* ed. Alan Lang Strout (Nor-

man, Okla.: University of Oklahoma Press, 1947), pp. 80, 82. The allusion, as Strout notes, is to "Childe Harold's Pilgrimage," Canto II, stanza ii, line 6: "A schoolboy's tale," etc.

17. Letter to John Cam Hobhouse, July 6, 1821, in *Byron: A Self-Portrait,* ed. Peter Quennell, vol. II, p. 656. Byron suspected Hobhouse, as he wrote in the letter cited in the following note, as the possible author of "John Bull's Letter."

18. Letter to John Murray, June 29, 1821, in *Letters and Journals,* vol. V, p. 316.

19. "He has read to me one of the unpublished cantos [Canto the Fifth] of Don Juan, which is astonishingly fine," Shelley wrote to Mary Shelley on August 10, 1821, with rare appreciation of a genius in many respects antithetical to his own. " — It sets him not above but far above all the poets of the day: every word has the stamp of immortality. — I despair of rivalling Lord Byron, as well I may: and there is no other with whom it is worth contending. This canto is in style, but totally, & sustained with incredible ease & power, like the end of the second canto: there is not a word which the most rigid assertor of the dignity of human nature could desire to be cancelled: it fulfills in a certain degree what I have long preached of producing something wholly new & relative to the age — and yet surpassingly beautiful." *The Letters of Percy Bysshe Shelley,* ed. Frederick L. Jones (Oxford: Clarendon, 1964), vol. II, p. 323. See also Shelley's letter to Byron, October 21, 1821, ibid., pp. 357-58.

20. Letter to Hobhouse and Douglas Kinnaird, January 19, 1819, in *Byron: A Self-Portrait,* vol. II, p. 439.

21. Letter to Kinnaird, October 26, 1819, ibid., p. 491.

22. Letter from Murray to Byron, March 19, 1819, in *Letters and Journals,* vol. IV, p. 283n.

23. Letter to Murray, April 6, 1819, ibid., pp. 283-285.

24. Letter to Murray, August 12, 1819, ibid., p. 342.

25. Alvin B. Kernan, *The Plot of Satire,* p. 205.

26. W. H. Auden, "A That-There Poet," rpt. from *The New Yorker* (April 26, 1958), in *Twentieth Century Interpretations of Don Juan,* ed. Edward E. Bostetter, p. 16.

27. Byron, Preface to *Don Juan,* ed. Marchand, p. 4.

28. W. H. Auden, "Don Juan," in *The Dyer's Hand and Other Essays,* pp. 392-394.

29. " 'Carnage' (so Wordsworth tells you) 'is God's daughter' " (*Don Juan* VIII.9). In a note to this line, quoted in *Byron's Don Juan,* vol. IV: *Notes on the Variorum Edition,* ed. Willis W. Pratt (Austin: Uni-

versity of Texas Press, 1957), p. 169, Byron quotes Wordsworth's execrable stanza (which was prudently expunged from later editions of the poem) and adds his own acerbic comment as follows:

> But *Thy** most dreaded instrument
> In working out a pure intent,
> Is man arrayed for mutual slaughter;
> Yea, *Carnage is thy daughter!*
> Wordsworth's *Thanksgiving Ode*

*To wit, the Deity's: this is perhaps as pretty a pedigree for Murder as ever was found out by Garter King at Arms. — What would have been said, had any free-spoken people discovered such a lineage?

30. Letter to Murray, February 16, 1821, in *Letters and Journals,* vol. V, p. 242.

31. Letter to Thomas Moore, March 4, 1822, ibid., vol. VI, p. 33.

32. Jane Austen, *Pride and Prejudice,* ed. Donald J. Gray (New York: Norton, 1966), vol. II, chap. 1, p. 94.

33. Quoted in Harry Levin, *The Gates of Horn,* p. 108.

34. Harry Levin, ibid., p. 119.

35. Stendhal, *The Charterhouse of Parma,* trans. C. K. Scott Moncrieff (Garden City, N.Y.: Doubleday Anchor, 1956), chap. 6, p. 125.

36. W. H. Auden, "Dingley Dell and the Fleet," in *The Dyer's Hand and Other Essays,* pp. 408-409.

37. Charles Dickens, *The Posthumous Papers of the Pickwick Club* (New York: The Modern Library, n.d.), chap. 53, p. 767.

38. Letter to Louise Colet, September 1853, in *The Selected Letters of Gustave Flaubert,* trans. Francis Steegmuller, p. 162. (*Correspondance,* vol. III, pp. 349-50.)

39. Letter to Louise Colet, April 26-27, 1853, ibid., p. 148. (III, 183.)

40. See Charles Baudelaire, "L'héautontimorouménos," in *Les Fleurs du mal* ("Spleen et idéal" lxxxiii): "Je suis la plaie et le couteau . . ."

41. Letter to Louise Colet, February 25, 1854, in *Selected Letters,* p. 168. (IV, 29-30.)

42. Letter to Louise Colet, January 16, 1852, ibid., pp. 125-26. (II, 343-44.)

43. Letter to Louise Colet, August 21-22, 1846, ibid., p. 72. (I,

262.) I have altered Steegmuller's "comedy" to "stage comedy" (French *le comique théâtral*).

44. Letter to Louise Colet, March 2-3, 1854. (IV, 33.)

45. *Madame Bovary* II. i., in *Oeuvres*, ed. Thibaudet and Dumesnil, vol. I, p. 392.

46. Letter to Ivan Turgenev, July 25, 1874, in *Selected Letters*, pp. 244-45. (VII, 178.)

47. Letter to Mme Roger des Genettes, April 18, 1880, ibid., p. 270. (IX, 22.)

48. Lionel Trilling, Introduction to *Bouvard and Pécuchet*, p. xviii.

49. Ibid., p. xix.

50. Letter to George Sand, about June 15, 1867, in *Selected Letters*, p. 211. (V, 309.)

51. Trilling, Introduction to *Bouvard and Pécuchet*, p. xx.

52. Concerning Flaubert's affinity with his characters, Descharmes and Dumesnil write, in their early book *Autour de Flaubert*, vol. II, p. 43: "If he comes at last to hint, through his pitiless raillery, a kind of unavowed and restrained sympathy for the disillusionments of these two creatures, symbols of all the weaknesses and of all the deviations of human reason, the fact is that he too, even though he was essentially different, had to suffer the same sorts of doubt and anguish." To later critics the resemblances have seemed still more fundamental. Thus Claude Digeon writes of Bouvard and Pécuchet in *Flaubert*, pp. 237-38: "Their reflections and their behavior testify to a meritorious zeal to make themselves ridiculous . . . The fact is that they are truly serious and possessed by an authentic desire of the true, of the beautiful, of the good. Flaubert, who made them pass from the state of '*cloportes*' ['vermin'] to that of '*bonshommes*' ['good fellows'], can elevate them to the dignity of his spokesmen. For these two caricatured silhouettes are the beings in which his 'buffoonishly bitter' nature and his intelligence smitten with folly were able to rediscover themselves: 'Their stupidity is mine and I'm bursting with it' (VII, 237)."

53. Letter to Louis Bouilhet, September 4, 1850 (II, 239): *"L'ineptie consiste a vouloir conclure."*

54. See Raymond Queneau, "Bouvard et Pécuchet," in *Bâtons, chiffres et lettres*, p. 123: "ils ne deviennent sages (et ne s'identifient complètement à leur créateur) que lorsqu'ils compilent leur *Album* et leur *Dictionnaire* et cessent de vouloir conclure."

55. Flaubert, in a letter of August 18, 1872, to Mme Roger des Genettes, described his work in progress as "the story of these two good

fellows who copy a sort of critical encyclopedia as farce" (VI, 402). This collection would apparently have included the "Album de la marquise" (a sampler of various styles), the "Dictionnaire des ideés recues," the "Catalogue des idées chic," and some of the other items brought together by Geneviève Bollème in *Le second volume de Bouvard et Pécuchet* (Paris: Denoël, 1966). On this subject, see also D. L. Demorest, *A travers les plans, manuscrits et dossiers de Bouvard et Pécuchet* (Paris: Conard, 1931), and Marie-Jeanne Durry, *Flaubert et ses projets inédits* (Paris: Librairie Nizet, 1950). Flaubert's multiple scenarios, printed in Bollème and in Alberto Cento's critical edition of *Bouvard et Pécuchet* (Naples and Paris: Istituto universitario orientale, and Librairie Nizet, 1964), indicate that the two companions begin to copy at random but soon feel the need for a classification; at this point their enterprise becomes a critical encyclopedia and their joy becomes final. Their ultimate act of heroism is to copy, along with other stupidities, a confidential report by the village doctor diagnosing them as "two inoffensive imbeciles" (Bollème, p. 53, e.g.). The scenarios end "with the view of these two good fellows bending over their desk, and copying" (ibid.).

9. Ulysses and Hermes in Modern Times

Of the many books on Joyce I have found one of the earliest of particular value, Frank Budgen's *James Joyce and the Making of Ulysses* (London: Grayson, 1934; rpt. Bloomington: Indiana University Press, 1960). Among other works that I have consulted with profit are Anthony Burgess, *Re Joyce* (New York: Norton, 1965; rpt. New York: Ballantine, 1966); Richard Ellmann, *James Joyce* (New York: Oxford University Press, 1959) and *Ulysses on the Liffey* (New York: Oxford University Press, 1972); Edmund Wilson, *Axel's Castle* (New York: Scribner's, 1931); Harry Levin, *James Joyce: A Critical Introduction*, rev. ed. (Norfolk, Conn.: New Directions, 1960); Richard M. Kain, *Fabulous Voyager: A Study of James Joyce's Ulysses* (Chicago: University of Chicago Press, 1947; rpt. New York: Viking, 1959); S. L. Goldberg, *The Classical Temper: A Study of James Joyce's Ulysses* (New York: Barnes & Noble, 1961); Stuart Gilbert, *James Joyce's Ulysses: A Study*, 2nd ed. (New York: Knopf, 1952; rpt. New York: Vintage, 1955); A. Walton Litz, *James Joyce* (New York: Twayne, 1966); Marilyn French, *The Book as World: James Joyce's Ulysses* (Cambridge, Mass.: Harvard University Press, 1976); and Stanislaus Joyce, *My Brother's Keeper: James Joyce's Early Years* (New York: Viking, 1958; rpt. 1969). For further treatments of Joyce as a comic writer see also Vivian Mercier, *The Irish Comic Tradition* (Oxford: Clarendon, 1962); and Thelma Balagot Kintanar, *The Significance of the Comic in James Joyce's Ulysses* (Diss., Stanford University, 1968; Ann Arbor, Mich.: University Microfilms, 1975). A valuable collection of early critical responses to Joyce is contained in *James Joyce: The Critical Heritage,* ed. Robert H. Deming, 2 vols. (New York: Barnes & Noble, 1970); other essays and collections of essays are legion. I have quoted the text of the Vintage edition of *Ulysses* (New York: Vintage, 1961), with parenthetical reference to the pagination of the original Random House edition of 1934, as indicated in the margins of the Vintage edition.

Especially pertinent among works on Thomas Mann is Klaus Hermsdorf, *Thomas Manns Schelme: Figuren und Strukturen des Komischen* (Berlin: Rütten und Loening, 1968), a perceptive Marxist critique of the antagonism between the rogue and society, with especial reference to Mann's Felix and Joseph. Other valuable books and articles include Erich Heller, *Thomas Mann: The Ironic German* (Cleveland and New York: World, 1961); Georg Lukács, "The Playful Style," in *Essays on Thomas Mann,* trans. Stanley Mitchell (London: Merlin, 1964), pp. 98-134; Oskar Seidlin, "Picaresque Elements in Thomas Mann's Work," *Modern Language Quarterly,* 12 (1951), 183-200; Robert B. Heilman, "Variations on Picaresque *(Felix Krull),*" *The Sewanee Review,* 66 (1958), 547-577, rpt. in *Thomas Mann: A Collection of Critical Essays,* ed. Henry Hatfield (Englewood Cliffs, N.J.: Prentice-Hall, 1964), pp. 133-154; and George Steiner, "Thomas Mann's *Felix Krull,*" in *Language and Silence* (1967; rpt. New York: Atheneum, 1970), pp. 269-279. I have quoted from Denver Lindley's translation of *Confessions of Felix Krull, Confidence Man: The Early Years* (New York: Knopf, 1955; rpt. New York: Vintage, 1969), with reference to *Bekenntnisse des Hochstaplers Felix Krull: Der Memoiren Erster Teil* (Frankfurt: Fischer, 1954). For Mann's correspondence I have used *Briefe,* ed. Erika Mann, 3 vols. (Frankfurt: Fischer, 1961-1965), and have quoted where possible the selected *Letters of Thomas Mann,* trans. Richard and Clara Winston (New York: Knopf, 1971); these editions are cited in my notes as *Briefe* and *Letters.* The important correspondence with Karl Kerényi is separately published as Thomas Mann-Karl Kerényi, *Gespräch in Briefen,* ed. Karl Kerényi (Zurich: Rhein-Verlag, 1960), and translated by Alexander Gelley as *Mythology and Humanism: The Correspondence of Thomas Mann and Karl Kerényi* (Ithaca and London: Cornell University Press, 1975). Pertinent essays by Mann include "Humor und Ironie," in *Nachlese: Prosa 1951-1955* (Frankfurt: Fischer, 1956), pp. 166-169, trans. Henry Hatfield in *Thomas Mann: A Collection of Critical Essays,* pp. 170-172; "Rückkehr," in

Nachlese, pp. 190-195; "Einführung in ein Kapitel der 'Bekentnisse des Hochstaplers Felix Krull'," in *Reden und Aufsätze* (Frankfurt: Fischer, 1965), vol. I, pp. 780-782; and "Kleist's *Amphitryon,*" in *Essays of Three Decades,* trans. H. T. Lowe-Porter (New York: Knopf, 1947), pp. 202-240. My parenthetical page references are to book and chapter of *Felix Krull;* the annotation (I. 5), e.g., refers to Book I, chapter 5. Where consecutive quotations from the same chapter appear in a single paragraph, only the first is identified.

1. Søren Kierkegaard, *Fear and Trembling* ("Problemata: Preliminary Expectoration"), in *Fear and Trembling* and *The Sickness Unto Death,* trans. Walter Lowrie (Princeton: Princeton University Press, 1941; rpt. Garden City, N.Y.: Doubleday Anchor, 1954), p. 50.

2. Anthony Burgess, *Re Joyce,* p. 25: " 'Comic' is the key-word, for *Ulysses* is a great comic novel . . . The comedy of Joyce is an aspect of the heroic: it shows man in relation to the whole cosmos, and the whole cosmos appears in his work symbolised in the whole of language." See also A. Walton Litz, *James Joyce,* p. 95: "It was part of Joyce's purpose to present Bloom as simultaneously ridiculous and magnificent, comic and heroic. Bloom is comic in that his actions are often cramped and mean when compared with the wide-ranging experience of Ulysses. But Bloom is also magnificent; his inner fortitude and equanimity of mind reveal a kinship with the Classical hero that can never be completely obscured." Other writers who have remarked on the heroic aspect of Bloom include S. L. Goldberg in *The Classical Temper,* p. 137 ("His heroism . . . lies in openness to life, self-knowledge, and the sober acceptance of what cannot be changed") and Richard Ellmann in *Ulysses on the Liffey,* p. 30 ("The task was to exhibit heroism of a new kind, undistinguished by any acts, distinguished maybe by the absence of act"); and Lionel Trilling in *Sincerity and Authenticity* (Cambridge, Mass.: Harvard University Press, 1972), p. 90 ("both Bloom and Don Quixote transcend the imposed actuality to become what we, by some new definition of the word, are willing to call heroes"). In contrast, Harry Levin makes a sharp dichotomy that virtually precludes heroism when he writes, "Heroic deeds are one thing, and daily chores are another, and [Joyce] is careful to keep them in different spheres . . . Bloom . . . is a hero in disguise, 'Everyman or Noman,' though he lacks all the qualifications except the disguise" (*James Joyce,* pp. 71, 114).

3. Early reviewers, as quoted, e.g., in Marvin Magalaner and Richard M. Kain, *Joyce: The Man, the Work, the Reputation* (New

York: New York University Press, 1956), p. 171, not untypically described _Ulysses_ as "the foulest book that has ever found its way into print" (Alfred Noyes) and "the most infamously obscene book in ancient or modern literature" (James Douglas). Some eminent writers were hardly more laudatory in private. Virginia Woolf considered it the work of "a queasy undergraduate scratching his pimples"; Edmund Gosse denounced it as "a perfectly cynical appeal to sheer indecency" by "a literary charlatan of the extremest order"; and D. H. Lawrence declared, "The last part of it is the dirtiest, most indecent, obscene thing ever written." (Quoted in Richard Ellmann, _James Joyce,_ pp. 542, 628.)

4. Valery Larbaud's important article in the _Nouvelle Revue Française_ of June 1922 is reprinted in his _Oeuvres complètes,_ vol. III (Paris: Gallimard, 1951), pp. 316-346; excerpts are translated in _James Joyce: The Critical Heritage,_ ed. Deming, vol. I, pp. 252-262. Although Larbaud, in a letter to Sylvia Beach of February 22, 1921, had enthusiastically called Joyce "as great as Rabelais" and Bloom "an immortal like Falstaff" (trans. Marcelle Sibon, in Deming, vol. I, p. 185), in his article he emphasizes the Homeric parallels without which the reader of Joyce's "livre à clé" (p. 338) would find himself at a loss. T. S. Eliot's article "_Ulysses,_ Order and Myth," published in the _Dial_ of November 1923 (rpt. in Deming, vol. I, pp. 268-271), proclaims that "Mr Joyce's parallel use of the _Odyssey_ . . . has the importance of a scientific discovery . . . Instead of narrative method, we may now use the mythical method." This solemn emphasis on mythic technique, soon elaborated and codified in Stuart Gilbert's humorless commentary, largely dominated Joycean scholarship for a generation or more and established _Ulysses_ as a highly respectable if nearly inaccessible classic. Another influential early essay, Ezra Pound's "James Joyce et Pécuchet," published in the _Mercure de France,_ 156 (June 1, 1922), 307-320, helped establish the view of _Ulysses_ as a scathing satire on modern man by interpreting both Flaubert's novel and Joyce's as compilations of idiotic banalities: "Joyce a complété le grand sottisier" (p. 313). Pound was never distinguished for his sense of humor.

5. Hon. John M. Woolsey, Opinion A. 110-59, Southern District of New York, December 6, 1933, rpt. in James Joyce, _Ulysses,_ p. xi.

6. Joyce, "Paris Notebook," 13 February 1903, in _The Critical Writings of James Joyce,_ ed. Ellsworth Mason and Richard Ellmann (New York: Viking, 1959; rpt. 1964), p. 144.

7. Frank Budgen, _James Joyce and the Making of Ulysses,_ pp. 71-72: "There are moods of pity and grief in it, but the prevailing

mood is humour. Laughter in all tones and keys, now with the world and now at it, is heard continually."

8. William York Tindall, *A Reader's Guide to James Joyce* (New York: Noonday, 1959), p. 156.

9. Stuart Gilbert, *James Joyce's Ulysses,* pp. 395, 403.

10. Richard M. Kain, *Fabulous Voyager,* p. 246.

11. Budgen, *James Joyce and the Making of Ulysses,* p. 21.

12. Woolsey, in *Ulysses,* p. x.

13. Budgen, *James Joyce and the Making of Ulysses,* p. 17.

14. Stanislaus Joyce, *My Brother's Keeper,* p. 217.

15. Homer, *The Odyssey* IX.214-215.

16. Budgen, *James Joyce and the Making of Ulysses,* p. 165.

17. Joyce, "The Dead," in *Dubliners,* ed. Robert Scholes and A. Walton Litz (New York: Viking, 1969), pp. 220, 219.

18. From a conversation of 1917 recorded by Joyce's language pupil Georges Borach, quoted in Ellmann, *James Joyce,* p. 430.

19. Budgen, *James Joyce and the Making of Ulysses,* p. 17.

20. Ibid., p. 132.

21. Ibid., p. 279.

22. Gustav Janouch, *Conversations with Kafka,* trans. Goronwy Rees, 2nd ed. (New York: New Directions, 1971), p. 23.

23. Franz Kafka, *Amerika,* chap. 1 ("The Stoker"), trans. Willa and Edwin Muir (Norfolk, Conn.: New Directions, 1946; rpt. New York: Schocken, 1962), p. 22.

24. Ibid., p. 21.

25. Saul Bellow, *Henderson the Rain King,* chap. VII (New York: Viking, 1959; rpt. New York: Fawcett, 1965), p. 73.

26. Ibid., chap. XVI, p. 196.

27. Ibid., chap. XII, p. 145.

28. Elio Vittorini, *La Garibaldina,* chap. xviii, with *Erica e i suoi fratelli* (Milan: Bompiani, 1956), p. 173. An English translation of this novel, by Frances Keene, is included in *A Vittorini Omnibus* (New York: New Directions, 1973).

29. *La Garibaldina,* chap. xliii, p. 277.

30. Joyce Cary, *The Horse's Mouth* (New York: Harper, 1944; rpt. Perennial Library, 1965), chap. 6, p. 21.

31. Ibid., chap. 33, p. 259.

32. Ibid., chap. 44, p. 344.

33. Ibid., p. 343.

34. Ibid., chap. 26, p. 197.

35. Ibid., chap. 44, p. 345.

36. Quoted ibid., chap. 10, p. 38, from William Blake, *America* (Plate 8).

37. Ibid., chap. 42, p. 327.

38. The Russian title of Alexander Ostrovsky's comedy of 1868 (*Na vsyakovo mudretsa dovol'no prostoty*) was literally rendered by its first English translator, Polya Kasherman, as *Enough Stupidity in Every Wise Man*. Other translators have rechristened the play *Even a Wise Man Stumbles* (David Magarshack), *The Diary of a Scoundrel* (Rodney Ackland), and *The Scoundrel* (Eugene K. Bristow). I have quoted from the last of these.

39. *The Scoundrel*, Act V, in *Five Plays of Alexander Ostrovsky*, trans. Eugene K. Bristow (New York: Pegasus, 1969), pp. 354-55.

40. "I have taken up the ancient *Felix Krull* once again," Mann wrote to Erich Kahler on February 1, 1951, from California, "and am continuing it, letting him saunter on into the unknown without any real faith that I shall ever finish it. I suspended work on it in 1911 to write *Death in Venice,* and it is truly curious to take up the old fragment again after four decades and all I have done in between. I have actually resumed on the selfsame page of Munich manuscript paper (from Prantl on Odeonsplatz) where I stopped at that time, unable to go on" (*Letters* 607; *Briefe* III. 188). The comic *Felix Krull,* broken off before *Death in Venice* and resumed after *Doctor Faustus* an eventful generation later, thus accompanied Thomas Mann throughout his career and remained only partly told when he died.

41. In a letter to Agnes E. Meyer of October 10, 1947, e.g. (*Letters* 535; *Briefe* II. 557), Mann wrote that he was considering "working up the Felix Krull fragment into a modern picaresque novel [*Schelmen-Roman*] set in the hansom-cab era," and in an address of 1954, "Rückkehr," in *Nachlese,* p. 194, he declared that his book "belongs . . . to the type and to the tradition of the picaresque, of the adventurer novel, whose German archetype is 'Simplicius Simplicissimus'." While still at work on the novel he had high praise (*Briefe* III, 223, 228) for Oskar Seidlin's article, "Picaresque Elements in Thomas Mann's Work," in the *Modern Language Quarterly* of June 1951. In this article Seidlin argues, e.g. (p. 187), that both the Spanish pícaro and Mann's artist-hero "have one objective: *corriger la fortune;* and it makes little difference that, for Lazarillo, the highest satisfaction consists in getting his belly full, while Felix Krull aims at a complete victory of the creative ingenuity of mind over dead and sluggish matter." (The similarity indeed exists; the difference is surely not little.) On this subject see also Robert B. Heilman's article cited in the headnote above.

42. The best brief description of Felix Krull's natural and artistic vocation, apart from his own, is given by Mann in his "Einführung in ein Kapitel der 'Bekentnisse des Hochstaplers Felix Krull'," in *Reden und Aufsätze,* vol. I., pp. 780-81: "The boy, very amicably equipped by nature, very pretty, very engaging, is a sort of artist-nature, a dreamer, fantast, and bourgeois good-for-nothing, who deeply feels the illusoriness of the world and life and from the beginning is out to make himself into illusion, into a vital attraction. In love with the world, without being able to serve it in a bourgeois way, he endeavors to make it fall in love with him in return, in which, by virtue of his gifts, he easily succeeds. He is a human being who, however favored his individuality is by nature, is never satisfied with this individuality but strives, like an actor, toward something else—especially toward the sphere of nobility; for he feels himself privileged and noble by nature, but is not so by his social rank, and corrects this unjust accident through a deception that readily falls in with his charm, through illusion.

"But his particular concern, his deepest dissatisfaction with his own individuality, goes farther. It is a longing to get out of himself, into the whole, a universal yearning which, to put it in the briefest formula, might be called *pan-erotic.*" Cf. Erich Heller's comment, in *Thomas Mann: The Ironic German,* pp. 280-81, that Felix "is the comic version of what Keats . . . called 'the chameleon Poet'—comic because his 'creative imagination' expresses itself not in art but in life . . . He does not enact his changing identities, but creates them with the supreme imagination of the poet. Thus he closes with comic virtuosity the time-honored gulf between Art and Life."

43. "Einführung in ein Kapitel . . . ," in *Reden und Aufsätze,* vol. I, p. 781 ("So macht er die Bekanntschaft seines mythischen Urbildes"). The paradigm of Hermes plays a significant part both in the *Joseph* novels and in *Felix.* In a letter of February 18, 1941, to Karl Kerényi, who had sent him his monograph *Das göttliche Kind,* Mann wrote: "The mythological figure who of necessity attracts me more and more these days is the moon-oriented Hermes, about whom I have read excellent things in this book. He has already been a haunting presence here and there in the Joseph books; but in the last volume, where the hero is shown as a statesman and businessman of sovereign cunning, this figure changes more and more from the original Tammus-Adonis role to that of a Hermes. His actions and transactions cannot be well rendered in moral and aesthetic terms except in the spirit of a divine rogue's tale [*im Sinne des göttlichen Schelmenromans*]" (*Mythology and Humanism,* p. 101; *Gespräch in Briefen,* p.

98). And more than thirteen years later, when Kerényi sent him a copy of Paul Radin's *Der göttliche Schelm* (later published in English as *The Trickster*) just when *Felix Krull* was being published, Mann wrote, on October 17, 1954: "What a remarkable coincidence that the appearance of this book comes at the same time as that of the book I was in any case about to send you, but which I now hasten to link (though it is quite naturally linked already) to the volume on the primal and essential thief [*zu dem Ur- und Erzschelmenbuch*], and especially to your mythological contribution [Kerényi's appended essay on "The Trickster in Relation to Greek Mythology"]. I was not aware, God knows, of undertaking a Hermetic novel when I began with this forty years ago. I had no other intention than yet another impersonation and parody of art and the artist. It was only in the course of the subsequent continuation that certain associations, undoubtedly induced by the proximity of the *Joseph,* found their way in, and the name of the god arose" (*Mythology and Humanism,* p. 210; *Gespräch in Briefe,* pp. 193-195).

Among Kerényi's most significant comments concerning Hermes in *Das göttliche Kind,* as revised and included in C. G. Jung and Karl Kerényi, *Essays on a Science of Mythology,* trans. R. F. C. Hull (New York: Pantheon, 1949; rpt. New York and Evanston: Harper and Row, 1963), are his association of Hermes with Eros and Aphrodite (pp. 53-54) and his remark that "insofar as chance and accident are an intrinsic part of primeval chaos . . . Hermes carries over this peculiarity of primeval chaos — accident — into the Olympian order" (p. 57). In these respects, and not only in his trifling burglaries, Felix the *Panerotiker* and pupil of Kuckuck is indeed a contemporary reincarnation of the primordial rogue, even if his equivalent of "chaos" is an artistic order at odds with the social. On Hermes in Thomas Mann's works, see also Manfred Diecks's appendix "Untersuchungen zum Hermes-Motiv," in *Studien zu Mythos und Psychologie bei Thomas Mann* (Bonn and Munich: Francke, 1972), pp. 215-226.

44. "Krull must exert all his powers," Georg Lukács remarks, "to appear convincing where Venosta does it simply by birth and upbringing. As a result he becomes much more interesting and 'genuine' than Venosta himself, simply because, while everyone takes him for the real Venosta, he must prove himself such at every instant . . . Everywhere Krull is more 'genuine' than his original." ("The Playful Style," in *Essays on Thomas Mann,* pp. 130-31.)

45. It is not the exact double that fascinates Felix but "the double but dissimilar" (III. 6, Vintage ed. p. 281); and his fascination reveals

important aspects of his own multiple nature. The double-but-dissimilar suggests above all the object of erotic attachment, in which divisive individuality seems to be momentarily transcended. "It is true: a man lives separate and divided from others inside his own skin," Felix tells Zouzou, "not only because he must, but because he does not wish it otherwise." But love, he argues, "wipes out the division between one person and another, between the me and the you" and "does everything, exerts itself to the utmost, to make this closeness complete, perfect, to raise it to the actual oneness of two lives, but in this, comically and sadly, it is never successful despite all its efforts" (III. 10, pp. 355, 356, 358). With reference to this passage Mann wrote to his daughter Monika, on December 13, 1954, that Felix's "propensity for the double image is certainly not in contradiction with his precocious utterance about love's tragicomic exertion to make one out of two—which first succeeds in a baby" (*Briefe* III. 365). There is also an important temporal dimension to the double, namely the sensation, which Felix repeatedly experiences, not so much of déjà vu as of recurrence-with-difference. "Early experiences in life always recur in heightened form," he reflects (III. 7, p. 298) as he gazes at the lifelike replicas of primitive men in Kuckuck's museum and remembers his earlier search for ancestors; and it is the generational difference that especially intrigues him in the conjunction of Zouzou and her mother. In the dissimilar double of myth these dimensions are joined, for Felix both is and is not a modern Hermes forever seeking the other half of a once-united Hermaphrodite. (The myth of the androgyne was told, of course, by Aristophanes in Plato's *Symposium,* and its truth is appropriately comic.) Such was Thomas Mann's way—as he wrote of Kleist, whose *Amphitryon* is the classic German comedy of the double—"of deifying or demonizing the preposterous" (*Essays of Three Decades,* p. 204).

46. Letter to Erika Mann, June 7, 1954 (*Letters* 667; *Briefe* III. 345). "My view of the whole is distinctly disgruntled," Mann continued, "and I am steeling myself for its publication with some embarrassment. Certainly it's not a very dignified production. Is it right for a man to celebrate his eightieth birthday with such compromising jokes? . . . I have no impulse to go on spinning out the *Krull,* at least for the present." In his address "Rückkehr" (*Nachlese,* p. 194), Mann commented on the inherently inconclusive character of his book: "A fragment still, but a fragment the wonderful book will surely remain, even if time and disposition should be given to me to extend it by another 440 pages. The aim is not at all ever to be finished with it, one can

write further and further in it, spin it out further, it is a framework on which one can hang everything possible, an epic space for the disposal of everything that comes to one's mind and that life brings to one. This is probably the most characteristic thing I can say about it, that it may indeed break off and stop one day, but will never be finished." Concerning his never-resumed continuation, see Hans Wysling, "Thomas Manns Pläne zur Fortsetzung des 'Krull'," in *Dokumente und Untersuchungen: Beiträge zur Thomas-Mann-Forschung* (Bern and Munich: Francke, 1974), pp. 149-166.

47. Letter to Agnes E. Meyer, October 10, 1947 (*Letters* 535; *Briefe* II. 557). Mann was concerned, as he stated in "Rückkehr" (*Nachlese,* p. 194), that the humor of *Felix* not be confused with a frivolous escapism, and in a letter to Fritz Martini of October 17, 1954, he remarked: "Schiller thought that even the frivolous has a justification in art when form comes to its aid—and this modern Hermes is fundamentally not at all frivolous, but has a certain comically conciliating reverence for the world—so it seems to me" (*Briefe* III. 360). In his study *Thomas Manns Schelme* Klaus Hermsdorf objects that this very quality of reconciliation through humor undercuts the comic antagonism to society implicit in the earlier fragment: "The drastic consequence of superimposing the motif of universal sympathy on that of the rogue lies in the distortion of potentially comic collisions into humoristic ones—and in these there is neither deceiver nor deceived" (p. 322). Yet a capacity for humor that can generate a plethora of gaiety in the grimmest of situations is surely a heroic achievement in itself. "One who wrote the *Joseph* at the time of Hitler's victories," Mann's letter to Agnes Meyer continues, "will not let whatever is coming get him down, insofar as he lives to experience it." Felix Krull, who most fully shares his author's courageous predilection for humor, is to that extent Thomas Mann's truest "artist-hero."

48. Joseph Heller, *Catch-22* (New York: Simon and Schuster, 1961; rpt. New York: Dell, 1962), chap. 5, p. 47.

49. Ibid., chap. 12, p. 127.

50. Ibid., chap. 27, p. 312.

51. Ibid., chap. 42, p. 461.

52. Ken Kesey, *One Flew Over the Cuckoo's Nest* (New York: Viking, 1962; rpt. New York: New American Library, 1962), p. 28.

53. Ibid., p. 30.

54. Ibid., p. 41.

55. Ibid., p. 114.

56. Ibid., p. 136.

57. Ibid., p. 212.
58. Ibid., p. 218.
59. Ibid., p. 230.
60. Ibid., p. 260.
61. Ibid., p. 267.

Appendix

1. I have cited the text and followed the translation of Aristotle's *Poetics* contained in S. H. Butcher, *Aristotle's Theory of Poetry and Fine Art*, 4th ed. (London: Macmillan, 1907; rpt. New York: Dover, 1951). On the *Margites*, see Introduction, n. 4 above.

2. See *Rhetoric* III.xv.10, in Aristotle, *The "Art" of Rhetoric*, trans. John Henry Freese (Cambridge, Mass., and London: Harvard University Press, and Heinemann, 1926), p. 442.

3. Quintilian VI.ii.20 and VI.ii.9, in *The Institutio Oratoria of Quintilian*, ed. H. E. Fowler (Cambridge, Mass., and London: Harvard University Press, and Heinemann, 1921), pp. 428, 422.

4. "Longinus," *On the Sublime* IX.15, trans. W. Hamilton Fyfe, with Aristotle, *The Poetics*, rev. ed. (Cambridge, Mass., and London: Harvard University Press, and Heinemann, 1932), p. 155.

5. "Evanthius De Fabula" I.5, in Aelius Donatus, *Commentum Terenti*, ed. Paul Wessner (Leipzig: Teubner, 1902; rpt. Stuttgart, 1962), vol. I., pp. 14-15. My italics. The attribution of this treatise to Evanthius is based on a citation in the grammarian Rufinus.

6. Ibid. IV.2, p. 21. Wessner misprints *historia* for *historica;* I have substituted the correct reading from Georg Kaibel, ed., *Comicorum Graecorum Fragmenta* (1899; rpt. Berlin: Weidmann, 1958), vol. I, p. 66. My thanks to Professor David Traill of the University of California, Davis, for his help in resolving this textual difficulty.

7. Marvin J. Herrick, *Comic Theory in the Sixteenth Century* (Urbana: University of Illinois Press, 1950; rpt. 1964), p. 61.

8. Lope Félix de Vega Carpio, "Arte nuevo de hacer comedias," in *Obras escogidas,* ed. Federico Carlos Sainz de Robles (Madrid: Aguilar, 1961), vol. 2, p. 893. For a recent parallel, see Northrop Frye, *The Secular Scripture* (Cambridge, Mass., and London: Harvard University Press, 1976), p. 68: "The comic story is . . . the story of craft and guile, the triumph of *froda*. Its themes often feature disguise and concealment of identity . . . Its literary model is the *Odyssey*." With this, we have come full circle.

INDEX